Spring Cloud Data Flow

Native Cloud Orchestration Services for Microservice Applications on Modern Runtimes

Felipe Gutierrez

Apress®

Spring Cloud Data Flow: Native Cloud Orchestration Services for Microservice Applications on Modern Runtimes

Felipe Gutierrez
Albuquerque, NM, USA

ISBN-13 (pbk): 978-1-4842-1240-0 ISBN-13 (electronic): 978-1-4842-1239-4
https://doi.org/10.1007/978-1-4842-1239-4

Managing Director, Apress Media LLC: Welmoed Spahr
Acquisitions Editor: Steve Anglin
Development Editor: Matthew Moodie
Coordinating Editor: Mark Powers

Cover designed by eStudioCalamar

Cover image designed by Freepik (www.freepik.com)

Distributed to the book trade worldwide by Apress Media, LLC, 1 New York Plaza, New York, NY 10004, U.S.A. Phone 1-800-SPRINGER, fax (201) 348-4505, e-mail orders-ny@springer-sbm.com, or visit www.springeronline.com. Apress Media, LLC is a California LLC and the sole member (owner) is Springer Science + Business Media Finance Inc (SSBM Finance Inc). SSBM Finance Inc is a **Delaware** corporation.

For information on translations, please e-mail booktranslations@springernature.com; for reprint, paperback, or audio rights, please e-mail bookpermissions@springernature.com.

Apress titles may be purchased in bulk for academic, corporate, or promotional use. eBook versions and licenses are also available for most titles. For more information, reference our Print and eBook Bulk Sales web page at http://www.apress.com/bulk-sales.

Any source code or other supplementary material referenced by the author in this book is available to readers on GitHub via the book's product page, located at www.apress.com/9781484212400. For more detailed information, please visit http://www.apress.com/source-code.

Printed on acid-free paper

In memory of my grandparents: Juan Gutierrez and Baciliza Rivero and Simon Cruz and Elvira Galindo.
I love you and miss you guys!

Table of Contents

About the Author

Felipe Gutierrez is a cloud solutions software architect, with a bachelor's degree and a master's degree in computer science from Instituto Tecnólogico y de Estudios Superiores de Monterrey, Ciudad de Mexico. With more than 25 years of IT experience, he has developed programs for companies in multiple vertical industries, including government, retail, health care, education, and banking. Currently, he works as a senior cloud application architect for IBM, specializing in Red Hat OpenShift, IBM Cloud, app modernization, Cloud Foundry, Spring Framework, Spring Cloud Native applications, Groovy, and RabbitMQ, among other technologies. He has worked as a solutions architect for companies like VMware, Nokia, Apple, Redbox, and Qualcomm. Felipe is the author of *Introducing Spring Framework* (Apress, 2014), *Pro Spring Boot* (Apress, 2016), and *Spring Boot Messaging* (Apress, 2017).

About the Technical Reviewer

Manuel Jordan Elera is an autodidactic developer and researcher who enjoys learning new technologies for his own experiments and creating new integrations. Manuel won the Springy Award—Community Champion and Spring Champion 2013. In his little free time, he reads the Bible and composes music on his guitar. Manuel is known as dr_pompeii. He has tech-reviewed numerous books for Apress, including *Pro Spring, 4th Edition* (2014), *Practical Spring LDAP* (2013), *Pro JPA 2, Second Edition* (2013), and *Pro Spring Security* (2013). You can read his 13 detailed tutorials about many Spring technologies and contact him through his blog at `www.manueljordanelera.blogspot.com`, and follow him on his Twitter account, `@dr_pompeii`.

Acknowledgments

I would like to express all my gratitude to the Apress team: Steve Anglin for accepting my proposal, Mark Powers for keeping me on track and for his patience, and the rest of the Apress team involved in this project. Thanks to everybody for making this possible.

Thanks to my technical reviewer, Manuel Jordan, for all the details and effort in his reviews, and the entire Spring team for creating this amazing technology.

I want to dedicate this book to my grandparents: Juan Gutierrez and Baciliza Rivero on my dad's side, and Simon Cruz and Elvira Galindo on my mom's side. Thanks for being part of my life. I miss you so much.

—Felipe Gutierrez

PART I

Introductions

CHAPTER 1

Cloud and Big Data

The digital universe consists of an estimated 44 zettabytes of data. A zettabyte is 1 million petabytes, or 1 billion terabytes, or 1 trillion gigabytes. In 2019, Google processed approximately 3.7 million queries, YouTube recorded 4.5 million viewed videos, and Facebook registered 1 million logins every 60 seconds. Imagine the computer power to process all these requests, data ingestion, and data manipulation. Common sense tells us that the big IT companies use a lot of hardware to preserve data. A lot of storage needs to be incorporated to prevent limits of capacity.

How does an IT company deal with challenges like data overload, rising costs, or skill gaps? In recent years, big IT companies have heavily invested in developing strategies that use enterprise data warehouses (EDW) to serve as central data systems that report, extract, transform, and load (ETL) processes from different sources. Today, both users and devices (thermostats, light bulbs, security cameras, coffee machines, doorbells, seat sensors, etc.) ingest data.

Companies such as Dell, Intel, and Cloudera—to name a few—work together to create hardware and storage solutions that help other companies grow and become faster and more scalable.

A Little Data Science

When we talk about *data science*, a team of scientists with PhD degrees comes to mind. They probably earn big bucks, and they don't rest because companies depend on them. What is a data scientist's actual educational experience?

A few years ago, computing journals revealed that Spark and Scala skyrocketed in companies that wanted to apply data science with the addition of tools such as Hadoop, Kafka, Hive, Pig, Cassandra, D3, and Tableau.

Python has become one of the main programming languages for machine learning techniques, alongside R, Scala, and Java.

Machine learning normally works in business, math, computer science, and communication. Data scientists use data for predictions, classification, recommendations, pattern detection and grouping, anomaly detection, recognition, actionable insights, automated processes, decision-making, scoring and ranking, segmentation, optimization, and forecasts. That's a lot!

F. Gutierrez, *Spring Cloud Data Flow*, https://doi.org/10.1007/978-1-4842-1239-4_1

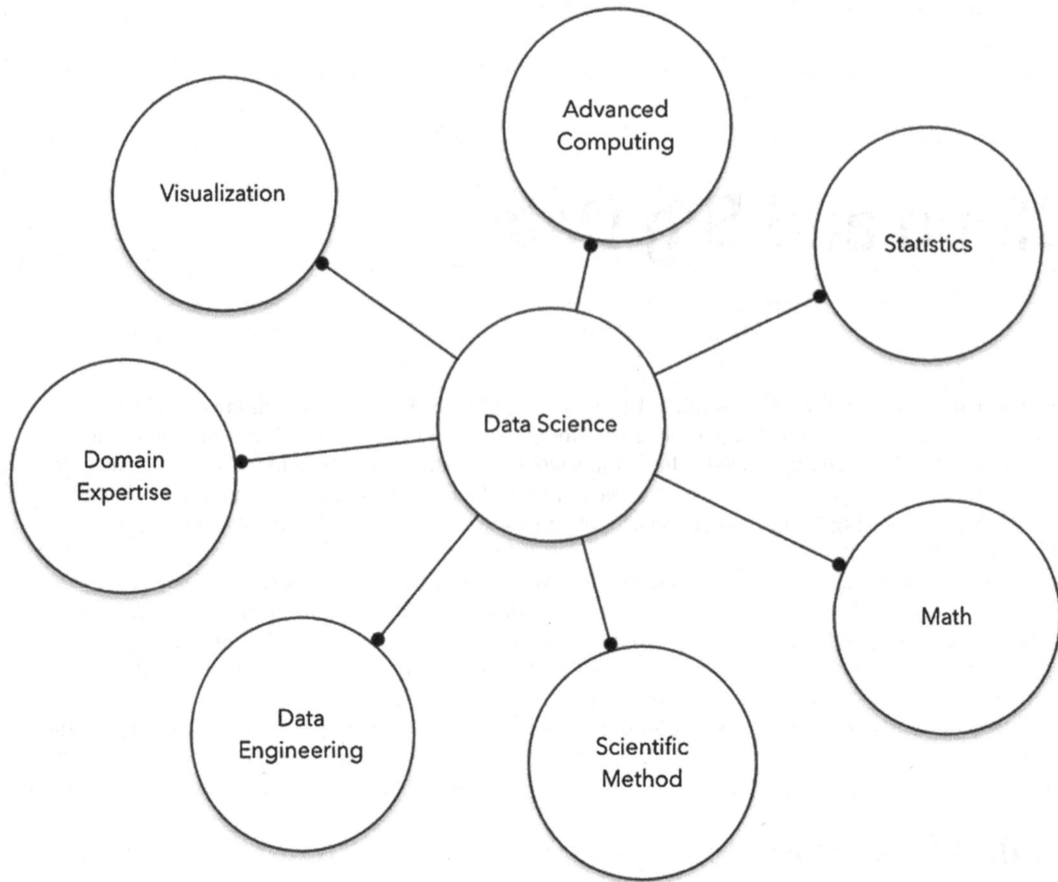

Figure 1-1. *Data science*

We need to have the right tools, platform, infrastructure, and software engineering knowledge to innovate and create. Machine learning should rely on a programming language that feels comfortable and easy to learn (like Python). The platform should have the right engines for processing the data. The infrastructure should be reliable, secure, and redundant. The development techniques should create awesome enterprise solutions that benefit not only the company but all its users around the world.

The Cloud

Over the past decade, many companies have gone into the so-called *cloud*, or they are *cloud native*, or they are in the *cloud computing* era; but what does that even mean? Several companies have said that they were always in the cloud because all their services live outside the company, managed by a third party, and they have faster responses if there is an outage. But is that accurate? Or does *cloud* mean architectural computing in which servers, networks, storage, development tools, and applications are enabled through the Internet?

In my opinion, we have *Internet* access through a public cloud environment, where users can "plug into" data and applications at any given time and place through an *Internet* connection. I see the cloud as a new *measure service* with a pay-as-you-go model, where you only pay for what you are using, from any server, network, storage, bandwidth, application, or more—very similar to an electric or water company that charges based on consumption.

I also see the cloud as an *on-demand self-service*. You can request any of those services, and they are provisioned very quickly with a few clicks.

I can see the cloud as a multitenancy model where a single instance of an application, network, or server is shared across multiple users. This is referred to as *shared resource pooling*. Once you finish using it, it returns to the pool to wait for another user to request it.

I can see the cloud as an elastic platform where the resources quickly scale up or down as needed (see Figure 1-2).

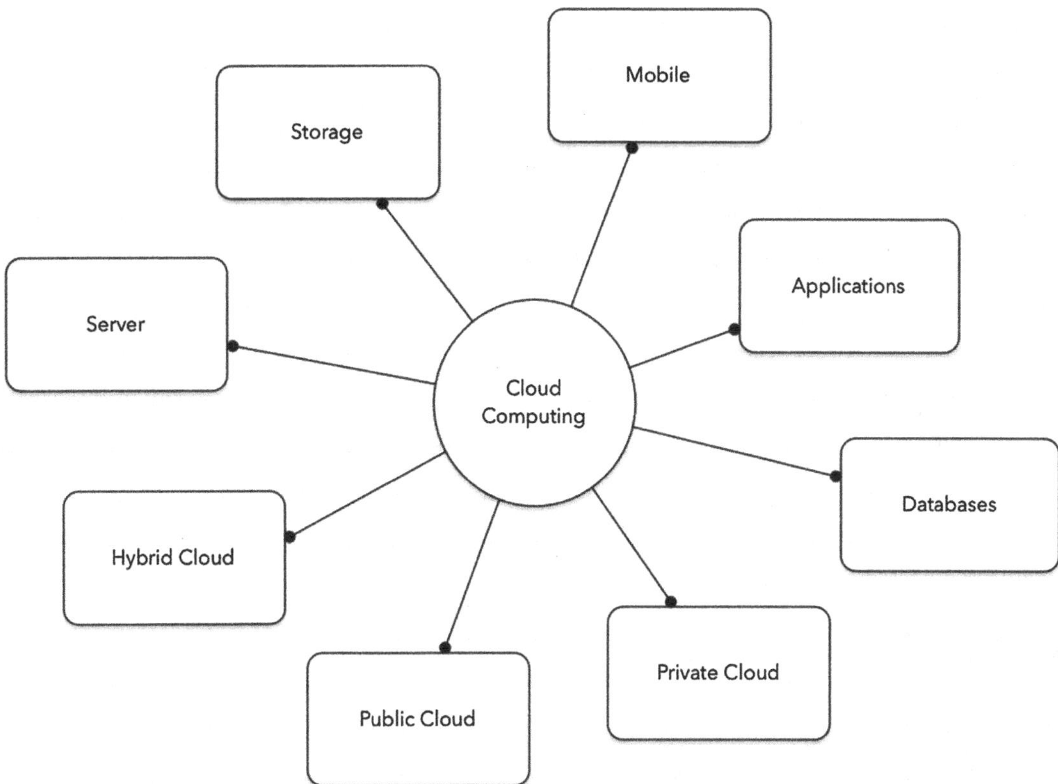

Figure 1-2. *Cloud computing*

Cloud Technology and Infrastructure

I think that today *cloud technology* means that companies can be scalable and adapt at speed. They can accelerate innovation, drive business agility more efficiently, streamline operations with confidence, and reduce costs to better compete with other companies. This leads companies to increased sustainable growth. Today, companies that are more strategic in their approach to technology are doing better financially, but how do these companies view new cloud technology?

Big IT companies like Amazon (the pioneer of on-demand computing), Google, and Microsoft offer cloud technology. These companies are well paid to provide companies a cloud infrastructure that delivers elasticity, managed services, on-demand computing and storage, networking, and more.

Storage, servers, or VMs are needed to implement cloud infrastructure. Managed services, hybrid operations, and data security and management are also required. Services that allow the companies to use their data against all these new machine learning tools and apply new artificial intelligence algorithms for system analytics to help with fraud detection help with decision making, to name a few growing features of data processing (see Figure 1-3).

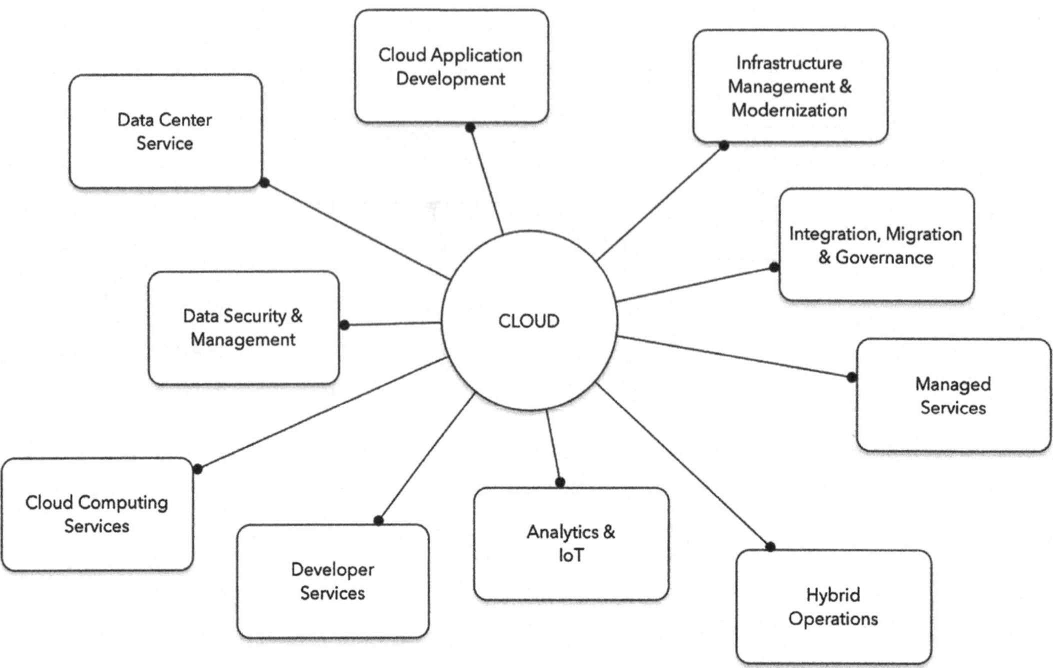

Figure 1-3. *Cloud infrastructure*

The Right Tools

In my 20 years of experience, I've seen big companies use tools and technologies that help them use collected data in the right way and to follow best practices and standards for data manipulation. Due to all new requirements and the way the demand for services increase, companies hire people who know how to use tools such as JMS, RabbitMQ, Kinesis, Kafka, NATs, ZeroMQ, ActiveMQ, Google PubSub, and others. We see more message patterns emerge with these technologies, such as event-driven or data-driven patterns (see Figure 1-4). These patterns aren't new, but they haven't received much attention until now.

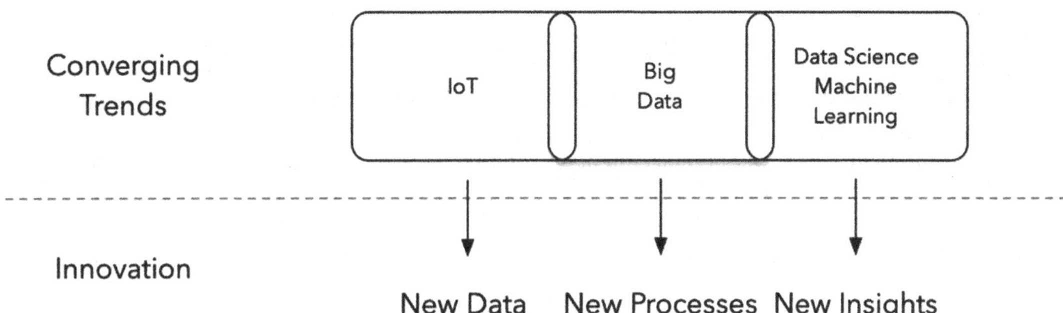

Figure 1-4. *Data-driven enterprise*

Technologies like Apache Hadoop distribute large data sets across clusters. Apache Flume is a simple and flexible architecture for streaming dataflows and a service for collecting, aggregating, and moving large amounts of log data. Apache Sqoop is a batch tool for transferring bulk data between Apache Hadoop and structured datastores (such as relational databases); it solves some of the data wrangling that you need to do.

A new wave of programming languages can process a large amount of data. These include languages like R, Python, and Scala, and a set of libraries and frameworks, like MadLib, for machine learning and expert systems (see Figures 1-5 and 1-6).

Figure 1-5. *Data streaming*

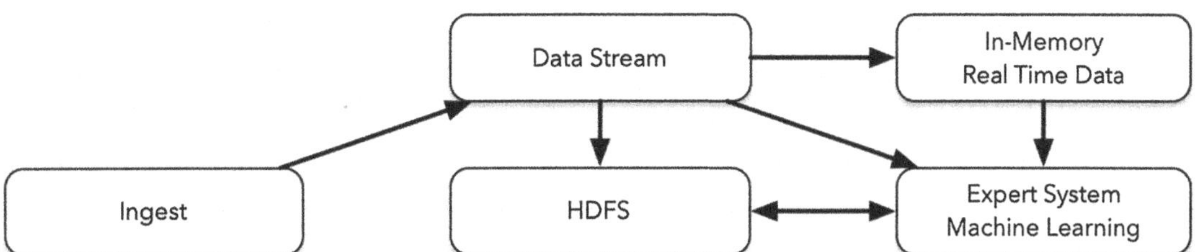

Figure 1-6. *Data stream*

New protocols for messaging brokers emerge every day. Should we learn all these new technologies? Or should we hire people with all these skill sets? I think we should at least have a technology that takes care of communication. Well, we do: Spring Cloud Stream and the orchestrator, Spring Cloud Data Flow (see Figure 1-7).

I'll discuss these two technologies. If you are a Spring developer, you don't need to learn any new APIs for messaging; you can work with what you already know—Java and Spring. If you are new to Spring, in the next two chapters, I give a quick tour of Spring Boot, Spring Integration, and Spring Batch and show you how to use them. These three technologies are the core of Spring Cloud Stream and Spring Cloud Data Streams (see Figure 1-7).

Next, you create your first Stream applications, which can connect regardless of the messaging broker. That's right; it doesn't matter which broker you set up between multiple Streams apps. Spring Cloud Stream has that capability. You will develop custom streams and create a custom binder that allows you to hide any API from a messaging broker.

Finally, I talk about Spring Cloud Data Flow and its components and how to create apps, streams, and tasks and monitor them (see Figure 1-7).

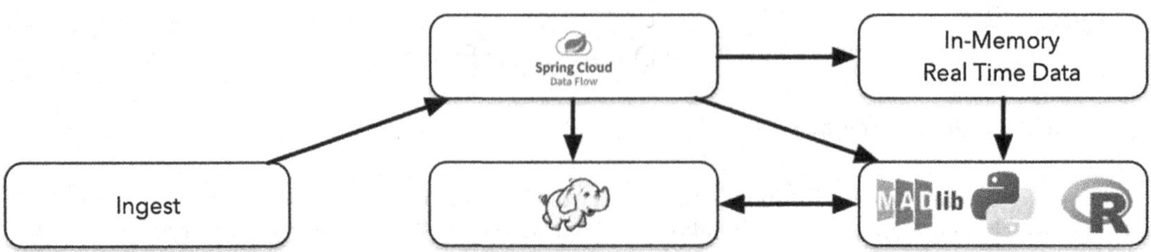

Figure 1-7. *Data stream: Spring Cloud Data Flow*

Summary

In this chapter, I talked about big data and new ways to improve services using cloud infrastructures that offer out-of-the-box solutions. Every company needs to have visibility, speed, the ability to enter the market quickly, and time to react.

In this short chapter, I wanted to set the context for this book. In the next chapters, I talk about technologies that help you use big data to create enterprise-ready solutions.

CHAPTER 2

Spring Boot

One way to build cloud-native applications is to follow the Twelve-Factor App guidelines (`https://12factor.net`) that facilitate running applications in any cloud environment. Some of these principles, like dependencies declaration (factor II), configuration (factor III), and port binding (factor VII), among others, are supported by Spring Boot! Spring Boot is a microservice and cloud-ready framework.

Why Spring Boot and not just Spring? Or maybe another technology, like NodeJS or the Go language? Spring Boot is a technology that has no comparison because is backed by the most-used framework in the Java community and lets you create an enterprise-ready application with ease. Other languages require you to do a lot of manual setup and coding. Spring Boot provides it for you. Even though technologies like NodeJS have hundreds of libraries, it is no match at the enterprise level like Spring, in my opinion. Don't get me wrong. I'm not saying that other technologies are bad or not useful, but if you want to build a fast, fine-grained, enterprise application, only Spring Boot offers minimal configuration and code. Let's look at why Spring Boot is important and how it helps you create cloud-native applications.

What Is Spring Framework and What Is Spring Boot?

Spring Boot is the next generation of Spring applications. It is an opinionated runtime technology that exposes the best practices for creating enterprise-ready Spring applications.

Spring Framework

Let's back up a little bit and talk about the Spring Framework. With the Spring Framework, you can create fine-grained enterprise apps, but you need to know how it works, and most importantly, how to configure it. Configuration is one of the key elements of the Spring Framework. You can decouple custom implementations, DB connections, and calls to external services, making Spring Framework more extensible, easy to maintain, and run. At some point, you need to know all the best practices to apply to a Spring app. Let's start with a simple Spring app that demonstrates how the Spring Framework works.

A Directory Application

Let's suppose that you need to create a Spring application that saves people's contact information, such as names, emails, and phone numbers. It is a basic directory app that exposes a REST API with persistence in any DB engine, and it can be deployed in any compliant J2EE server. The following are the steps to create such an application.

F. Gutierrez, *Spring Cloud Data Flow*, https://doi.org/10.1007/978-1-4842-1239-4_2

1. Install a building tool like Maven or Gradle to compile and build the source code's directory structure. If you come from a Java background, you know that you need a WEB-INF directory structure for this app.
2. Create `web.xml` and `application-context.xml` files. The `web.xml` file has the `org.springframework.web.servlet.DispatcherServlet` class, which acts as a front controller for Spring-based web applications.
3. Add a listener class that points to the `application-context.xml` file, where you declare all the Spring beans or any other configuration needed for your app. If you omit the listener section, you need to name your Spring beans declaration file the same as the `DispatcherServlet`.
4. In the `application-context.xml` file, add several Spring beans sections to cover every detail. If you are using JDBC, you need to add a datasource, init SQL scripts, and a transaction manager. If you are using JPA, you need to add a JPA declaration (a `persistence.xml` file where you configure your classes and your primary unit) and an entity manager to handle sessions and communicate with the transaction manager.
5. Because this is a web app, it is necessary to add some Spring beans sections in the `application-context.xml` file about HTTP converters that expose JSON views and MVC-driven annotations to use the `@RestController` and `@RequestMapping` (or @GetMapping, @PostMapping, @DeleteMapping, etc.) among other Spring MVC annotations.
6. If you are using JPA (the easiest way to do persistence with minimal effort), specify the repositories and the classes' location with the `@EnableJpaRepositories` annotation.
7. To run the app, package your application in a WAR format. You need to install an application server that is compliant with J2EE standards and then test it.

If you are an experienced Spring developer, you know what I'm talking about. If you are a newbie, then you need to learn all the syntax. It's not too difficult, but you need to spend some time on it. Or perhaps there is another way. Of course, there is. You can use annotation-based configuration or a JavaConfig class to set up the Spring beans, or you can use a mix of both. In the end, you need to learn some of the Spring annotations that help you configure this app. You can review the source code (`ch02/directory-jpa`) on this book's web site.

Let's review some of this application's code. Remember, you need to create a Java web structure (see Figure 2-1).

Figure 2-1. *A Java web-based directory structure*

Figure 2-1 shows a Java web-based directory structure. You can delete the `index.jsp` file, open the `web.xml` file, and replace it all with the content shown in Listing 2-1.

Listing 2-1. web.xml

```
<!DOCTYPE web-app PUBLIC
 "-//Sun Microsystems, Inc.//DTD Web Application 2.3//EN"
 "http://java.sun.com/dtd/web-app_2_3.dtd" >

<web-app>
  <display-name>Archetype Created Web Application</display-name>

  <listener>
    <listener-class>org.springframework.web.context.ContextLoaderListener</listener-class>
  </listener>

  <context-param>
    <param-name>contextConfigLocation</param-name>
    <param-value>/WEB-INF/application-context.xml</param-value>
  </context-param>

  <servlet>
    <servlet-name>app</servlet-name>
    <servlet-class>org.springframework.web.servlet.DispatcherServlet</servlet-class>
    <init-param>
      <param-name>contextConfigLocation</param-name>
      <param-value></param-value>
    </init-param>
    <load-on-startup>1</load-on-startup>
  </servlet>

  <servlet-mapping>
    <servlet-name>app</servlet-name>
    <url-pattern>/</url-pattern>
  </servlet-mapping>

</web-app>
```

Listing 2-1 shows you how to add a Spring servlet (`DispatcherServlet`, a front controller pattern) that is the main servlet to attend any request from the user.

Next, let's create the `application-context.xml` file by adding the content in Listing 2-2.

Listing 2-2. application-context.xml

```
<?xml version="1.0" encoding="UTF-8"?>

<beans xmlns="http://www.springframework.org/schema/beans" xmlns:xsi="http://www.
w3.org/2001/XMLSchema-instance"
       xmlns:mvc="http://www.springframework.org/schema/mvc"
       xmlns:context="http://www.springframework.org/schema/context"
       xmlns:jpa="http://www.springframework.org/schema/data/jpa"
       xmlns:tx="http://www.springframework.org/schema/tx"
```

```
       xmlns:jdbc="http://www.springframework.org/schema/jdbc"
       xsi:schemaLocation="
        http://www.springframework.org/schema/mvc http://www.springframework.org/schema/mvc/
        spring-mvc.xsd
        http://www.springframework.org/schema/tx http://www.springframework.org/schema/tx/
        spring-tx.xsd
        http://www.springframework.org/schema/jdbc https://www.springframework.org/schema/
        jdbc/spring-jdbc.xsd
        http://www.springframework.org/schema/data/jpa https://www.springframework.org/
        schema/data/jpa/spring-jpa.xsd
                http://www.springframework.org/schema/beans http://www.springframework.org/
                schema/beans/spring-beans.xsd
                http://www.springframework.org/schema/context http://www.springframework.
                org/schema/context/spring-context.xsd">

    <mvc:annotation-driven />
    <tx:annotation-driven />
    <jpa:repositories base-package="com.apress.spring.directory.repository" entity-manager-
    factory-ref="localContainerEntityManagerFactoryBean" />
    <context:component-scan base-package="com.apress.spring.directory" />

    <mvc:annotation-driven content-negotiation-manager="contentNegotiationManager">
        <mvc:message-converters>
            <bean class="org.springframework.http.converter.json.
            MappingJackson2HttpMessageConverter">
                <property name="objectMapper" ref="objectMapper"/>
            </bean>
            <bean class="org.springframework.http.converter.xml.
            MappingJackson2XmlHttpMessageConverter">
                <property name="objectMapper" ref="xmlMapper"/>
            </bean>
        </mvc:message-converters>
    </mvc:annotation-driven>

    <bean id="objectMapper" class="org.springframework.http.converter.json.
    Jackson2ObjectMapperFactoryBean">
        <property name="indentOutput"  value="true"/>
        <property name="modulesToInstall" value="com.fasterxml.jackson.module.paramnames.
        ParameterNamesModule"/>
    </bean>

    <bean id="xmlMapper" parent="objectMapper">
        <property name="createXmlMapper" value="yes"/>
    </bean>

    <bean id="contentNegotiationManager" class="org.springframework.web.accept.
    ContentNegotiationManagerFactoryBean">
        <property name="mediaTypes">
            <value>
                json=application/json
                xml=application/xml
```

```
            </value>
        </property>
    </bean>

    <bean id="localContainerEntityManagerFactoryBean"
         class="org.springframework.orm.jpa.LocalContainerEntityManagerFactoryBean">
        <property name="dataSource" ref="dataSource" />
        <property name="jpaVendorAdapter">
            <bean class="org.springframework.orm.jpa.vendor.HibernateJpaVendorAdapter" />
        </property>
        <property name="jpaProperties">
            <props>
                <prop key="hibernate.hbm2ddl.auto">create-drop</prop>
                <prop key="hibernate.dialect">org.hibernate.dialect.H2Dialect</prop>
            </props>
        </property>
    </bean>

    <bean id="dataSource"
         class="org.springframework.jdbc.datasource.DriverManagerDataSource">
        <property name="driverClassName" value="org.h2.Driver" />
        <property name="url" value="jdbc:h2:mem:testdb" />
        <property name="username" value="sa" />
        <property name="password" value="" />
    </bean>

    <bean id="transactionManager" class="org.springframework.orm.jpa.
    JpaTransactionManager">
        <property name="entityManagerFactory" ref="localContainerEntityManagerFactoryBean" />
    </bean>

    <bean id="persistenceExceptionTranslationPostProcessor" class=
            "org.springframework.dao.annotation.
            PersistenceExceptionTranslationPostProcessor" />

    <jdbc:embedded-database type="H2" >
        <jdbc:script location="classpath:META-INF/sql/schema.sql"/>
        <jdbc:script location="classpath:META-INF/sql/data.sql"/>
    </jdbc:embedded-database>
</beans>
```

Listing 2-2 shows the `application-context.xml` file, in which you add all the necessary configuration for the Spring container, which is where all your classes are initialized and wired up.

Before reviewing each tag and the way it is declared, see if you can guess what each does and why it is configured the way it is. Look at the naming and references between declarations.

If you are new to Spring, I recommend you look at the *Pro Spring* series published by Apress. These books explain every aspect of this declarative form of configuring Spring.

Next, add the following classes: `Person`, `PersonRepository`, and `PersonController`, respectively (see Listings 2-3, 2-4, and 2-5).

Listing 2-3. com.apress.spring.directory.domain.Person.java

```
package com.apress.spring.directory.domain;

import javax.persistence.Entity;
import javax.persistence.Id;

@Entity
public class Person {

    @Id
    private String email;
    private String name;
    private String phone;

    public Person() {
    }

    public Person(String email, String name, String phone) {
        this.email = email;
        this.name = name;
        this.phone = phone;
    }

    public String getEmail() {
        return email;
    }

    public void setEmail(String email) {
        this.email = email;
    }

    public String getName() {
        return name;
    }

    public void setName(String name) {
        this.name = name;
    }

    public String getPhone() {
        return phone;
    }

    public void setPhone(String phone) {
        this.phone = phone;
    }
}
```

Listing 2-3 shows the Person class that uses all the JPA (Java Persistence API) annotations, so it's easy to use, and no more direct JDBC.

Listing 2-4. com.apress.spring.directory.repository.PersonRepository.java

```
package com.apress.spring.directory.repository;

import com.apress.spring.directory.domain.Person;
import org.springframework.data.repository.CrudRepository;

public interface PersonRepository extends CrudRepository<Person,String> {
}
```

Listing 2-4 shows the `PersonRepository` interface that extends from another `CrudRepository` interface. Here it uses all the power of Spring Data and Spring Data JPA to create a repository pattern based on the entity class and its primary key (in this case, a `String` type). In other words, there is no need to create any CRUD implementations—let Spring Data and Spring Data JPA take care of that.

Listing 2-5. com.apress.spring.directory.controller.PersonController.java

```
package com.apress.spring.directory.controller;

import com.apress.spring.directory.domain.Person;
import com.apress.spring.directory.repository.PersonRepository;
import org.slf4j.Logger;
import org.slf4j.LoggerFactory;
import org.springframework.http.HttpHeaders;
import org.springframework.http.HttpStatus;
import org.springframework.http.MediaType;
import org.springframework.http.ResponseEntity;
import org.springframework.stereotype.Controller;
import org.springframework.web.bind.annotation.*;
import org.springframework.web.util.UriComponents;
import org.springframework.web.util.UriComponentsBuilder;

@Controller
public class PersonController {

    private Logger log = LoggerFactory.getLogger(PersonController.class);
    private PersonRepository personRepository;

    public PersonController(PersonRepository personRepository) {
        this.personRepository = personRepository;
    }

    @RequestMapping(value = "/people",
            method = RequestMethod.GET,
            produces = {MediaType.APPLICATION_JSON_VALUE, MediaType.APPLICATION_XML_VALUE})
    @ResponseBody
    public Iterable<Person> getPeople() {
        log.info("Accessing all Directory people...");
        return personRepository.findAll();
    }
```

```
    @RequestMapping(value = "/people",
            method = RequestMethod.POST,
            consumes = MediaType.APPLICATION_JSON_VALUE,
            produces = {MediaType.APPLICATION_JSON_VALUE})
    @ResponseBody
    public ResponseEntity<?> create(UriComponentsBuilder uriComponentsBuilder,
    @RequestBody Person person) {
        personRepository.save(person);

        UriComponents uriComponents =
                uriComponentsBuilder.path("/people/{id}").buildAndExpand(person.getEmail());

        return ResponseEntity.created(uriComponents.toUri()).build();
    }

    @RequestMapping(value = "/people/search",
            method = RequestMethod.GET,
            consumes = MediaType.APPLICATION_JSON_VALUE,
            produces = {MediaType.APPLICATION_JSON_VALUE})
    @ResponseBody
    public ResponseEntity<?> findByEmail(@RequestParam String email) {
        log.info("Looking for {}", email);
        return ResponseEntity.ok(personRepository.findById(email).orElse(null));
    }

    @RequestMapping(value = "/people/{email:.+}",
            method = RequestMethod.DELETE)
    @ResponseBody
    public ResponseEntity<?> deleteByEmail(@PathVariable String email) {
        log.info("About to delete {}", email);
        personRepository.deleteById(email);
        return ResponseEntity.accepted().build();
    }
}
```

Listing 2-5 shows the implementation of the `PersonController` class for any user request/response. There are many ways to implement a web controller in Spring, such as using `@RestController`. Avoid writing `@ResponseBody` in each method, or use dedicated annotations like `@GetMapping`, `@PostMapping`, and `@DeleteMapping` instead of `@RequestMapping`.

Next, create the SQL files that initialize the database (see Listings 2-6 and 2-7).

Listing 2-6. META-INF/sql/schema.sql

```
CREATE TABLE person (
   email VARCHAR(100) NOT NULL PRIMARY KEY,
   name VARCHAR(100) NOT NULL,
   phone VARCHAR(20) NOT NULL,
);
```

Listing 2-6 is a simple schema that consists of only one table.

Listing 2-7. META-INF/sql/data.sql

```
INSERT INTO person (email,name,phone) VALUES('mark@email.com','Mark','1-800-APRESS');
INSERT INTO person (email,name,phone) VALUES('steve@email.com','Steve','1-800-APRESS');
INSERT INTO person (email,name,phone) VALUES('dan@email.com','Dan','1-800-APRESS');
```

Listing 2-7 shows a few records to insert when the app starts up. Next, because this app is using JPA, it is necessary to provide a `persistence.xml` file. There is another option—you can add a bean declaration to `application-context.xml` and declare the persistence unit required for the JPA engine to work (see Listing 2-8).

Listing 2-8. META-INF/persistence.xml

```
<persistence xmlns="http://xmlns.jcp.org/xml/ns/persistence"
             xmlns:xsi="http://www.w3.org/2001/XMLSchema-instance" version="2.2"
             xsi:schemaLocation="http://xmlns.jcp.org/xml/ns/persistence http://xmlns.jcp.
             org/xml/ns/persistence/persistence_2_2.xsd">
    <!-- Define persistence unit -->
    <persistence-unit name="directory">
    </persistence-unit>
</persistence>
```

Listing 2-8 shows the required JPA file to declare the persistence unit. You can declare this as a property in the `localContainerEntityManagerFactoryBean` bean declaration (`persistenceUnitName` property).

Next is one of the most important files. This app was created using Maven as a building tool. Let's create a `pom.xml` file at the root of the project (see Listing 2-9).

Listing 2-9. pom.xml

```
<project xmlns="http://maven.apache.org/POM/4.0.0" xmlns:xsi="http://www.w3.org/2001/
XMLSchema-instance"
  xsi:schemaLocation="http://maven.apache.org/POM/4.0.0 http://maven.apache.org/
  maven-v4_0_0.xsd">
  <modelVersion>4.0.0</modelVersion>
  <groupId>com.apress.spring</groupId>
  <artifactId>directory-jpa</artifactId>
  <packaging>war</packaging>
  <version>1.0-SNAPSHOT</version>
  <name>directory-web-project Maven Webapp</name>
  <url>http://maven.apache.org</url>

  <properties>

    <java.version>1.8</java.version>
    <servlet.version>3.1.0</servlet.version>
    <spring-framework.version>5.2.2.RELEASE</spring-framework.version>
    <spring-data.jpa>2.2.3.RELEASE</spring-data.jpa>
    <slf4j.version>1.7.25</slf4j.version>
    <logback.version>1.2.3</logback.version>
    <h2>1.4.199</h2>
    <jackson>2.10.1</jackson>
  </properties>

  <dependencies>
```

```
<!-- Spring Core/MVC/Web -->
<dependency>
  <groupId>org.springframework</groupId>
  <artifactId>spring-context</artifactId>
  <version>${spring-framework.version}</version>
</dependency>
<dependency>
  <groupId>org.springframework</groupId>
  <artifactId>spring-aop</artifactId>
  <version>${spring-framework.version}</version>
</dependency>
<dependency>
  <groupId>org.springframework</groupId>
  <artifactId>spring-webmvc</artifactId>
  <version>${spring-framework.version}</version>
</dependency>
<dependency>
  <groupId>org.springframework</groupId>
  <artifactId>spring-web</artifactId>
  <version>${spring-framework.version}</version>
</dependency>

<dependency>
  <groupId>org.springframework.data</groupId>
  <artifactId>spring-data-jpa</artifactId>
  <version>${spring-data.jpa}</version>
</dependency>

<dependency>
  <groupId>org.slf4j</groupId>
  <artifactId>slf4j-api</artifactId>
  <version>${slf4j.version}</version>
</dependency>
<dependency>
  <groupId>ch.qos.logback</groupId>
  <artifactId>logback-classic</artifactId>
  <version>${logback.version}</version>
</dependency>

<!-- Other Web dependencies -->
<dependency>
  <groupId>javax.servlet</groupId>
  <artifactId>javax.servlet-api</artifactId>
  <version>${servlet.version}</version>
  <scope>provided</scope>
</dependency>

<!-- JPA -->
<dependency>
  <groupId>jakarta.activation</groupId>
  <artifactId>jakarta.activation-api</artifactId>
```

```
    <version>1.2.1</version>
    <scope>compile</scope>
  </dependency>
  <dependency>
    <groupId>jakarta.persistence</groupId>
    <artifactId>jakarta.persistence-api</artifactId>
    <version>2.2.3</version>
    <scope>compile</scope>
  </dependency>
  <dependency>
    <groupId>jakarta.transaction</groupId>
    <artifactId>jakarta.transaction-api</artifactId>
    <version>1.3.3</version>
    <scope>compile</scope>
  </dependency>
  <dependency>
    <groupId>org.hibernate</groupId>
    <artifactId>hibernate-core</artifactId>
    <version>5.4.9.Final</version>
    <scope>compile</scope>
    <exclusions>
      <exclusion>
        <artifactId>jboss-transaction-api_1.2_spec</artifactId>
        <groupId>org.jboss.spec.javax.transaction</groupId>
      </exclusion>
      <exclusion>
        <artifactId>javax.activation-api</artifactId>
        <groupId>javax.activation</groupId>
      </exclusion>
      <exclusion>
        <artifactId>javax.persistence-api</artifactId>
        <groupId>javax.persistence</groupId>
      </exclusion>
      <exclusion>
        <artifactId>jaxb-api</artifactId>
        <groupId>javax.xml.bind</groupId>
      </exclusion>
    </exclusions>
  </dependency>

  <!-- JSON/XML -->
  <dependency>
    <groupId>com.fasterxml.jackson.core</groupId>
    <artifactId>jackson-databind</artifactId>
    <version>${jackson}</version>
  </dependency>
  <dependency>
    <groupId>com.fasterxml.jackson.module</groupId>
    <artifactId>jackson-module-parameter-names</artifactId>
    <version>${jackson}</version>
  </dependency>
```

```
    <dependency>
      <groupId>com.fasterxml.jackson.dataformat</groupId>
      <artifactId>jackson-dataformat-xml</artifactId>
      <version>${jackson}</version>
    </dependency>

    <dependency>
      <groupId>com.h2database</groupId>
      <artifactId>h2</artifactId>
      <version>${h2}</version>
      <scope>runtime</scope>
    </dependency>
  </dependencies>

  <build>
    <finalName>directory-jpa</finalName>
    <plugins>
      <plugin>
        <groupId>org.apache.maven.plugins</groupId>
        <artifactId>maven-compiler-plugin</artifactId>
        <configuration>
          <source>8</source>
          <target>8</target>
        </configuration>
      </plugin>
    </plugins>
  </build>
</project>
```

Listing 2-9 shows the pom.xml file, where all the dependencies are declared. If you come from a J2EE background, you may find this difficult because you need to find a dependency that works well with the others. This can take a little while.

Next, you need to package your application. Install Maven (`https://maven.apache.org/download.cgi`) and make it reachable in your PATH variable so that you can simply run the following command.

```
mvn package
```

This command packages the application and generates the `target/directory-jpa.war` file. To run the application, you need an application server that can run J2EE apps; the most common is Tomcat. Download version 9 from `https://tomcat.apache.org/download-90.cgi`, and then unzip it and deploy/copy `directory-jpa.war` into the `webapps/` Tomcat folder. To start the Tomcat server, use the scripts in the `bin/` folder. Take a look at the scripts. To start Tomcat, you normally execute the script named `startup.sh` (for Unix users) or `startup.bat` (for Windows users).

You can test your application using the `cUrl` command line or any other GUI app, like Postman (`www.getpostman.com`), to execute all the requests. For example, to see all the people listed in the directory, execute the following command.

```
$ curl http://localhost:8080/directory-jpa/people -H "Content-Type: application/json"
```

You should get the following output.

```
[ {
  "email" : "mark@email.com",
  "name" : "Mark",
  "phone" : "1-800-APRESS"
}, {
  "email" : "steve@email.com",
  "name" : "Steve",
  "phone" : "1-800-APRESS"
}, {
  "email" : "dan@email.com",
  "name" : "Dan",
  "phone" : "1-800-APRESS"
} ]
```

As you can see, there are a lot of steps here, and I'm missing part of the business logic that you need to add to the app. A well-trained Spring developer spends probably up to three hours to deliver this app, and more than half of their time is spent configuring the app. How do you speed up this configuration process? Spending too much time in configuration can lead to errors and bad practices.

■ **Note** Remember that you have access to this book's companion source code. You can download it from Apress (`www.apress.com`). The folder for this example is in `ch02/directory-jpa`.

Spring Boot

Spring Boot to the rescue! The Spring engineers realized that Spring developers follow the same steps for every Spring app, so they came up with a better way to do configuration and add best practices. They created Spring Boot, an opinionated engine that sets the best practices for you so that you can focus on the code.

Spring Boot offers many features, which are discussed later. For now, let's return to the directory app.

A Directory App with Spring Boot

Let's start by creating the structure using Spring Initializr. Open your browser and point to `https://start.spring.io` (see Figures 2-2 and 2-3).

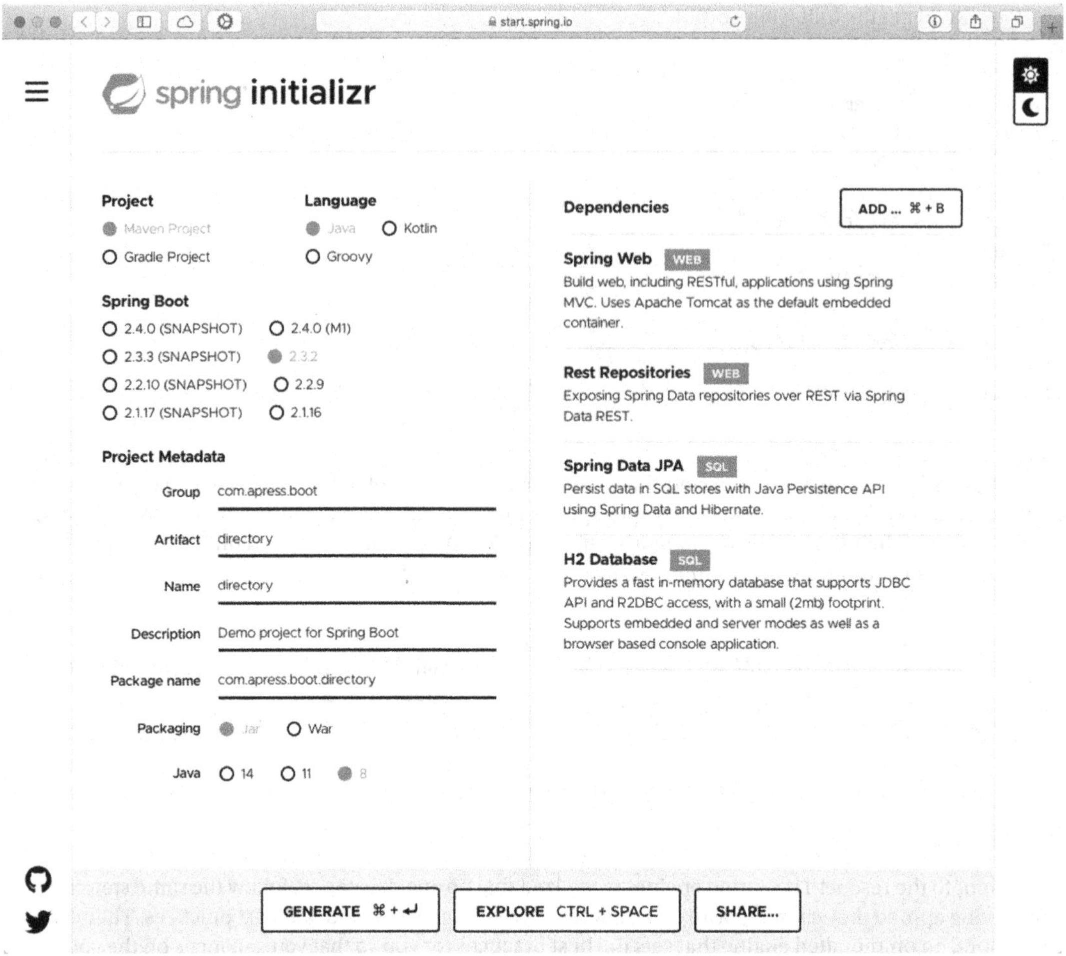

Figure 2-2. *`https://start.spring.io`*

Figure 2-2 is a screenshot of Spring Initializr. Add the following data into the fields.

- Group: `com.apress.boot`
- Artifact: `directory`
- Dependencies: Spring Web, Spring Data JPA, Rest Repositories, and H2 Database

You can leave the other options at their defaults. Click the Generate button. Open the ZIP file in any IDE that can run Java apps. I recommend IntelliJ Community Edition (`www.jetbrains.com/idea/download/`) or Microsoft Visual Code with the appropriate plugins to run Java and Spring apps (`https://code.visualstudio.com/download`).

Take a moment to analyze the structure. Recall the classes from Listing 2-3 (`Person.java`) and Listing 2-4 (`PersonRepository.java`) and the file from Listing 2-7 (`data.sql`). You can add the `Person` and `PersonRepository` classes to the `com.apress.boot.directory` folder/package and the `data.sql` file to the resources folder (see Figure 2-3).

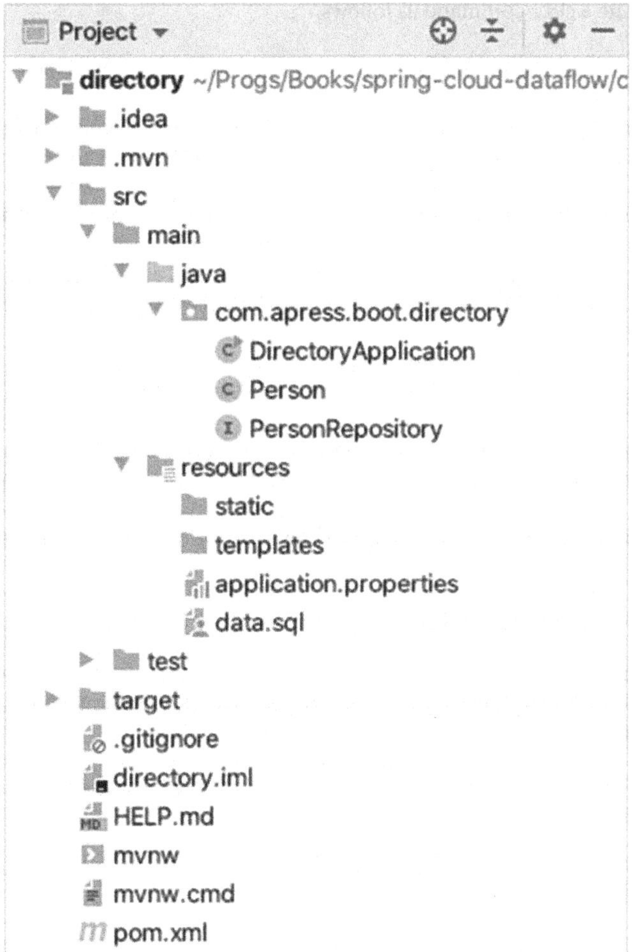

Figure 2-3. *IntelliJ CE: Spring Boot directory app structure*

Figure 2-3 shows the structure of the Spring Boot app and where the classes are. Note that there are extra files, including `mvnw*` scripts and a hidden `.mvn` folder. This is a thin wrapper for Maven, which means you don't need to have Maven installed. You can run it from the command line.

You are done! You don't need to do anything else. Run the application using either the IDE or the command line. Before you run the app, make sure to stop Tomcat. You can then run the app from the terminal by going to the `directory` folder and running the following command.

```
$ ./mvnw spring-boot:run
```

The preceding command runs only on Unix systems. If you use a Windows OS, then execute the following to run your app.

```
> mvnw.bat spring-boot:run
```

Then you can execute a cUrl command as follows.

```
$ curl http://localhost:8080/persons -H "Content-Type: application/json
```

You get the same result—a list of persons. An experienced Spring or Spring Boot developer can create this app in 5 minutes! A newbie to Spring Boot usually takes about 15 minutes to create it. (See, there was no configuration at all). Spring Boot is an opinionated runtime that discovers what's in your classpath, and based on that, it sets some defaults to avoid any other configurations, such as the DispatcherServlet setup, custom HttpMessageConverters, DB initializers, and the controllers. It uses the HATEOAS (Hypermedia as the Engine of Application State) protocol to generate the responses, and it adds all the HTTP method implementations. If you want to add a new person, execute the following command using cUrl.

```
$ curl -XPOST http://localhost:8080/persons -H "Content-Type: application/json" -d
'{"email":"mike@email.com","name":"Mike","phone":"1-800-APRESS"}'
```

How does Spring Boot do its magic? If you want to know more about Spring Boot and how this configuration is done without any extra effort, I recommend reading some of my other titles, like *Pro Spring Boot 2* (Apress, 2019).

You can easily create ready-to-run apps using the power of Spring and Spring Boot.

Beyond the Directory App Example

Often, books begin with a must-do HelloWorld example or a simple app like the directory app. Now let's witness the power of Spring Boot by creating a microservice that uses streaming processes from a Twitter feed. In this section, I give step-by-step instructions on building this app.

First, sign in to the Twitter developer program at https://developer.twitter.com. You need to get four keys: the consumer API key, the consumer API secret key, the access token key, and the access token secret key (see Figure 2-4).

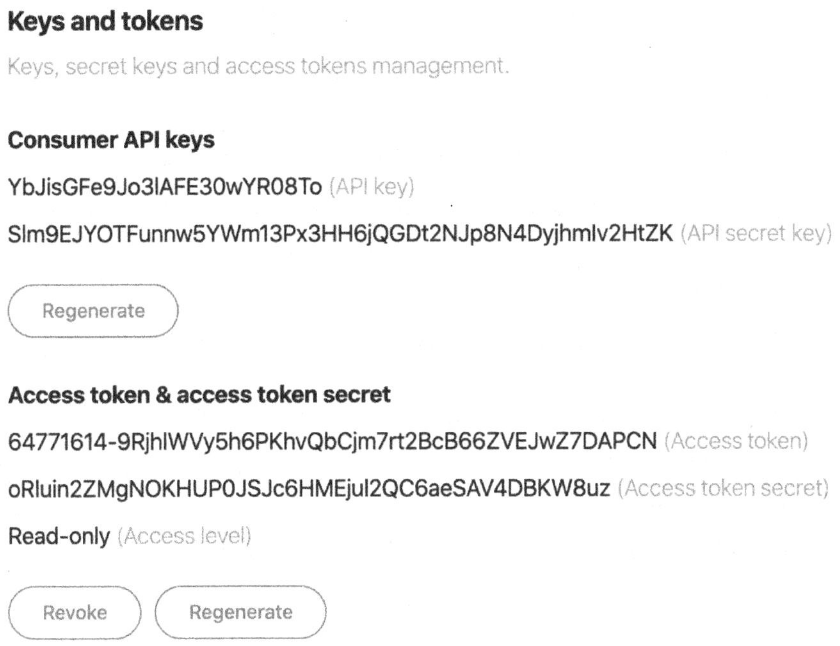

Keys and tokens

Keys, secret keys and access tokens management.

Consumer API keys

YbJisGFe9Jo3IAFE30wYR08To (API key)

SIm9EJYOTFunnw5YWm13Px3HH6jQGDt2NJp8N4DyjhmIv2HtZK (API secret key)

Regenerate

Access token & access token secret

64771614-9RjhlWVy5h6PKhvQbCjm7rt2BcB66ZVEJwZ7DAPCN (Access token)

oRIuin2ZMgNOKHUP0JSJc6HMEjul2QC6aeSAV4DBKW8uz (Access token secret)

Read-only (Access level)

Revoke Regenerate

Figure 2-4. *`https://developer.twitter.com/` keys and tokens*

Next, open a browser and point it to `https://start.spring.io` (see Figure 2-5). Use the following information.

- Group: `com.apress.boot`
- Artifact: `twitter`
- Dependencies: None

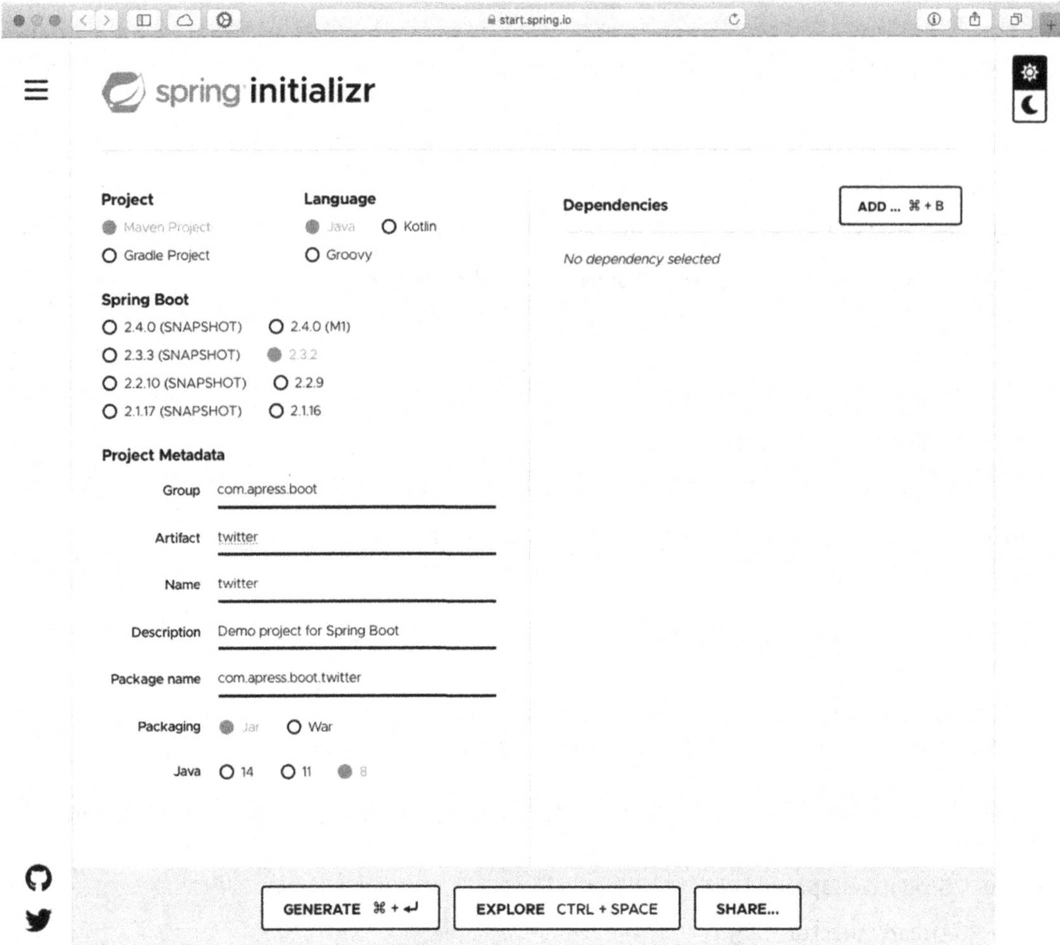

Figure 2-5. *`https://start.spring.io` Twitter app*

Click the *Generate* button to download a ZIP file. Unzip the file and open the project in any IDE. Create several classes, and you should have the final app, as seen in Figure 2-6.

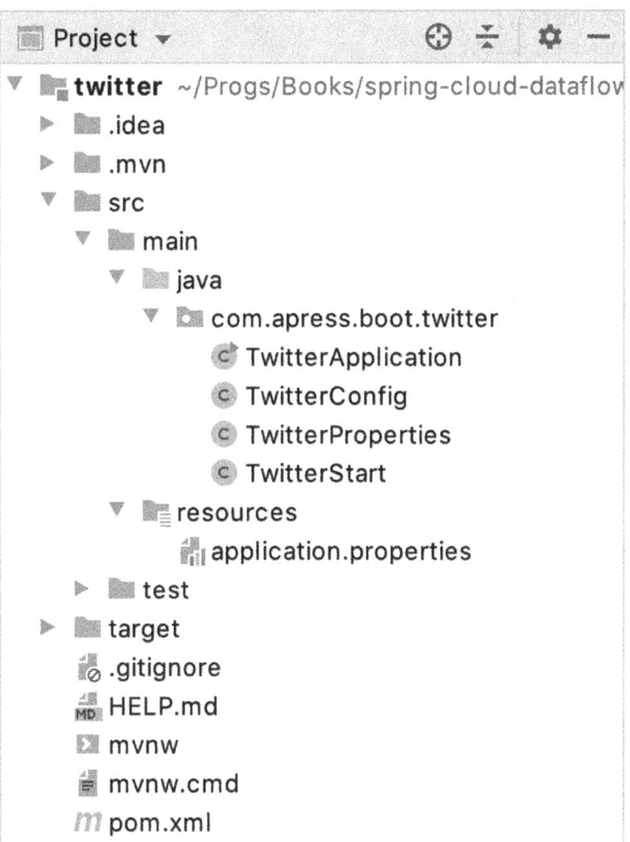

Figure 2-6. *Twitter app*

Next, open the `pom.xml` file and add the dependency shown in Listing 2-10.

Listing 2-10. pom.xml spring-social-twitter dependency

```
<dependency>
        <groupId>org.springframework.social</groupId>
        <artifactId>spring-social-twitter</artifactId>
        <version>1.1.0.RELEASE</version>
</dependency>
```

Next, create the `TwitterProperties` class (see Listing 2-11).

Listing 2-11. com.apress.boot.twitter.TwitterProperties.java

```
package com.apress.boot.twitter;

import org.springframework.boot.context.properties.ConfigurationProperties;

@ConfigurationProperties(prefix = "twitter")
public class TwitterProperties {
```

```
    private String consumerKey;
    private String consumerSecret;
    private String accessToken;
    private String accessTokenSecret;

    public String getConsumerKey() {
        return consumerKey;
    }

    public void setConsumerKey(String consumerKey) {
        this.consumerKey = consumerKey;
    }

    public String getConsumerSecret() {
        return consumerSecret;
    }

    public void setConsumerSecret(String consumerSecret) {
        this.consumerSecret = consumerSecret;
    }

    public String getAccessToken() {
        return accessToken;
    }

    public void setAccessToken(String accessToken) {
        this.accessToken = accessToken;
    }

    public String getAccessTokenSecret() {
        return accessTokenSecret;
    }

    public void setAccessTokenSecret(String accessTokenSecret) {
        this.accessTokenSecret = accessTokenSecret;
    }
}
```

Listing 2-11 shows the `TwitterProperties` class that holds the keys necessary for the Twitter API to work. All these properties are declared in the `application.properties` file, and it has the `twitter` prefix.

Next, create the `TwitterConfig` class (see Listing 2-12).

Listing 2-12. com.apress.boot.twitter.TwitterContig.java

```
package com.apress.boot.twitter;

import org.springframework.boot.context.properties.EnableConfigurationProperties;
import org.springframework.context.annotation.Bean;
import org.springframework.context.annotation.Configuration;
import org.springframework.social.twitter.api.impl.TwitterTemplate;
```

```
@Configuration
@EnableConfigurationProperties(TwitterProperties.class)
public class TwitterConfig {

    private TwitterProperties twitterProperties;

    public TwitterConfig(TwitterProperties twitterProperties){
        this.twitterProperties = twitterProperties;
    }

    @Bean
    TwitterTemplate twitterTemplate(){
        return new TwitterTemplate(twitterProperties.getConsumerKey(),
                twitterProperties.getConsumerSecret(), twitterProperties.getAccessToken(),
                twitterProperties.getAccessTokenSecret());
    }
}
```

Listing 2-12 shows the TwitterConfig class, which class has the initialization configuration that creates a TwitterTemplate instance. This instance handles the required connection and keys exchanges. It is a very simple way to sign in to Twitter and do several operations, like reading or creating tweets.

Next, create the TwitterStart class (see Listing 2-13).

Listing 2-13. com.apress.boot.twitter.TwitterStart.java

```
package com.apress.boot.twitter;

import org.springframework.boot.CommandLineRunner;
import org.springframework.context.annotation.Bean;
import org.springframework.context.annotation.Configuration;
import org.springframework.social.twitter.api.*;

import java.util.Collections;

@Configuration
public class TwitterStart {

    @Bean
    CommandLineRunner start(Twitter twitter){
        return args -> {
            twitter.streamingOperations().sample(Collections.singletonList(new
            StreamListener() {

                @Override
                public void onTweet(Tweet tweet) {
                    tweet.getEntities().getHashTags().forEach(hashTagEntity -> {
                        System.out.println(String.format("#%s",hashTagEntity.getText()));
                    });
                }
```

```
                @Override
                public void onDelete(StreamDeleteEvent streamDeleteEvent) { }

                @Override
                public void onLimit(int i) { }

                @Override
                public void onWarning(StreamWarningEvent streamWarningEvent) { }
            }));
        };
    }
}
```

Listing 2-13 shows the TwitterStart class. This class executes the start method once Spring Boot finishes the configuration and setup. One important detail here is the usage of StreamListener, which listens to every hashtag exposed on Twitter. The only thing the program does is print the hashtags.

Next, add the keys to the application.properties file (see Listing 2-14).

Listing 2-14. application.properties

```
# Twitter Properties
twitter.consumerKey=YbJisGFe9Jo3lAFE3OwYRO8To
twitter.consumerSecret=Slm9EJYOTFunnw5YWm13Px3HH6jQGDt2NJp8N4DyjhmIv2HtZK
twitter.accessToken=64771614-9RjhlWVy5h6PKhvQbCjm7rt2BcB66ZVEJwZ7DAPCN
twitter.accessTokenSecret=oRluin2ZMgNOKHUPOJSJc6HMEjul2QC6aeSAV4DBKW8uz
```

Remember, those keys are from your Twitter developer portal application. Now, you can run the app using the Maven wrapper.

```
$ ./mvnw spring-boot:run
```

You should see a bunch of hashtags that are sent to Twitter in real time!

As you can see, it is very easy to create a quick and fine-grained enterprise application. This is the beauty of Spring Boot.

Spring Boot Features

Spring Boot so many features, it requires an entire book to describe them all. However, I can describe some of them in this section.

- The SpringApplication class provides a convenient way to initiate a Spring application. It is in the main class.
- Spring Boot allows you to create applications without any XML configuration. It doesn't do code generation.
- Spring Boot provides a fluent builder API through the SpringApplicationBuilder singleton class, allowing you to create hierarchies with multiple application contexts. This feature is related to the Spring Framework. I explain this feature in the following chapters, but if you are new to Spring and Spring Boot, you just need to know that you can extend Spring Boot to get more control over your applications.

- Spring Boot offers more ways to configure Spring application events and listeners. This is explained in upcoming chapters.
- Spring Boot is an *opinionated* technology. This feature attempts to create the right type of application, either as a web application (by embedding a Tomcat, Netty, Undertow, or Jetty container) or as a single application.
- With the `org.springframework.boot.ApplicationArguments` interface, Spring Boot allows access to any application arguments. It is a useful feature when you run your application with parameters.
- Spring Boot allows you to execute code after the application has started. The only thing you need to do is implement the `CommandLineRunner` interface and implement the `run(String ...args)` method. A particular example is to initialize some records in a database during the start or to check some services to see if they are running before your application starts.
- Spring Boot allows you to externalize configurations by using `application.properties` or `application.yml` files. More about this in upcoming chapters.
- You can add administration-related features, normally through JMX, by enabling the `spring.application.admin.enabled` property in the `application.properties` or `application.yml` files.
- Spring Boot allows you to have *profiles* that help your application run in different environments.
- Spring Boot allows you to very simply configure and use logging.
- Spring Boot provides a simple way to configure and manage your dependencies by using starter poms. In other words, if you want to create a web application, you only need to include the `spring-boot-starter-web` dependency in your Maven `pom.xml` or `build.gradle` file.
- Spring Boot provides out-of-the-box non-functional requirements by using the Spring Boot Actuator with the new Micrometer platform-agnostic framework that allows you to instrument your apps.
- Spring Boot provides `@Enable<feature>` annotations that help you enable, include, configure, and use databases (e.g., SQL and NoSQL), Spring Integration, and the cloud, as well as cache, schedule, message, batch, and more.

I'll discuss other features in every chapter.

Summary

In this chapter, I showed you what Spring Boot is and what you can do with it. This is the primary technology that Spring Cloud Stream and Spring Cloud Data Flow uses for its components. I also showed you examples of some of the features that Spring Boot offers developers.

In the next chapter, I show you another technology base for creating Spring Cloud Data Flow streams. And don't worry about all the new terms; they will soon make sense to you.

CHAPTER 3

Spring Integration

If you search for the meaning of the word *communication*, you find that it comes from the Latin *commūnicāre,* which means "to share." Today, the word *communication* has become stronger, not only for people who want to share thoughts, ideas, and problems, but it's also used in technology. Enterprise applications need to share data between components or external systems by using messages as a regular communication protocol.

In this chapter, you learn about one of the best projects (in my opinion) of the Spring Framework—Spring Integration! It provides a simple, out-of-the-box way to use enterprise integration patterns.

By using lightweight messaging, Spring Integration supports integration with external systems through declarative adapters. In other words, you can connect JMS (IBM MQ and Tibco, among other brokers), AMQP, Socket, or UDP messages, and then process, transform, and deliver them into new systems like REST API endpoints, NoSQL persistence, or RabbitMQ messaging and only a few lines of code at most.

Integration Patterns

Spring Integration supports *enterprise integration patterns* (`www.eaipatterns.com`). This chapter covers only a few patterns to help you understand how they work and how Spring Integration facilitates their use because it is an essential piece of Spring Cloud Data Flow. Spoiler alert: Spring Cloud Data Flow is based on Spring Integration!

The enterprise integration patterns (EIP) conform to several patterns (see Figure 3-1); remember that a design pattern is a solution to a recurrent problem.

F. Gutierrez, *Spring Cloud Data Flow*, https://doi.org/10.1007/978-1-4842-1239-4_3

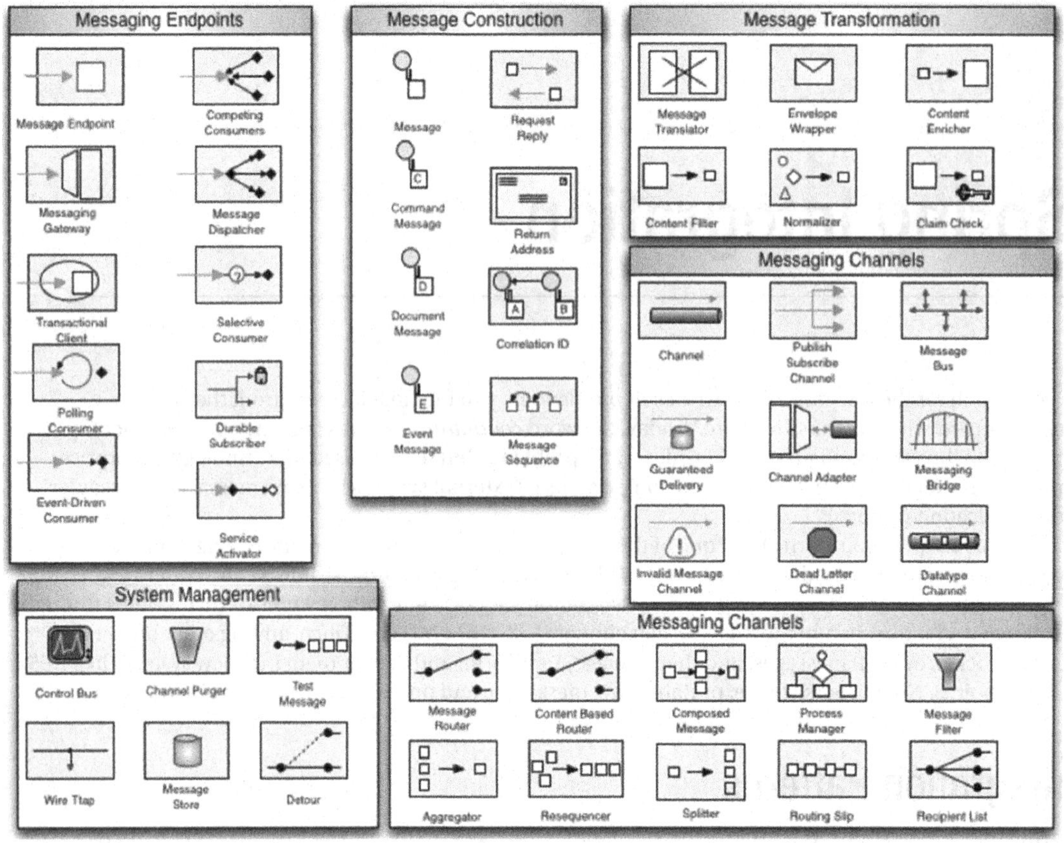

Figure 3-1. *Enterprise integration patterns*

You can see a clear division of each pattern by the role it plays in a specific business logic/rule. The most important part is message and messaging transport.

Messaging

Why is messaging so important? When you create a solution, you have an essential scenario in mind (see Figure 3-2). This is data that needs to be sent to an *input*, and then it is *processed,* and finally, it is *output* to a final stage (printed) or sent to another system.

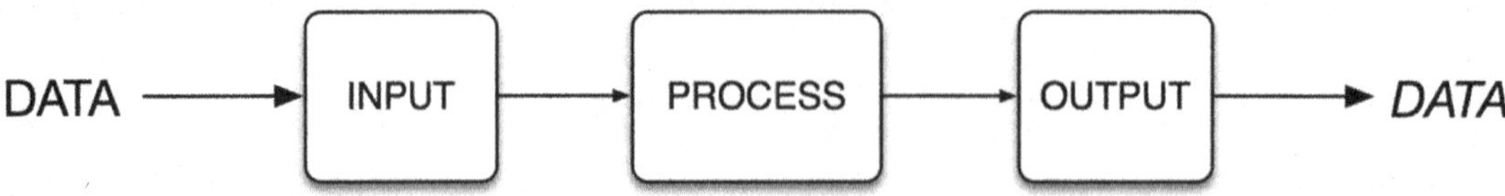

Figure 3-2. *Input-Process-Output*

If you think about it in terms of calling a particular logic within your solution, you are calling a method (INPUT), passing some parameters (DATA) based on data. You perform some logic (PROCESS) and then return (OUTPUT) a result (DATA).

Now think about it in terms of messaging. You send a message through a local process or to a remote server. Your message can be processed, enhanced, or trigger another event, and then you get a result, perhaps the same message you sent, or a message telling you that everything looks okay, or maybe there was an error. All this data passing across local or remote systems needs to be transported through *channels*. Channels play an important part in how messages are delivered.

As you can see, messaging plays an important role in communication.

Spring Integration

Messaging is applied by using channels that communicate between local or remote systems or other channels. It gives you a reference for integrating messaging components to create scalable solutions and exposes some of the existing messaging technologies (JMS, TIBCO, SOAP, MSMQ, NET, etc.) and how to integrate them. If you want to learn more about EIP, I recommend *Enterprise Integration Patterns: Designing, Building, and Deploying Messaging Solutions* by Gregor Hohpe and Bobby Woolf (Addison-Wesley Professional, 2003). This book offers a comprehensive explanation of each pattern.

In this section, I'll show you how Spring Integration works and how to use it. By showing you an example of a small integration app, you get a better picture of what Spring Integration is all about.

Movie App Specification Requirements

Let's create a movie application that consists of two parts.

Imagine that you get some information about new movies (title, actor, year) in a text file (CSV format), and you need to send this information to an external and remote system that only accepts a JSON format. This remote system has a REST API service that takes your collection (`/v1/movies`). After receiving the information, it saves it to a database (MySQL) and sends an email to the admin user (see Figure 3-3 for a general picture).

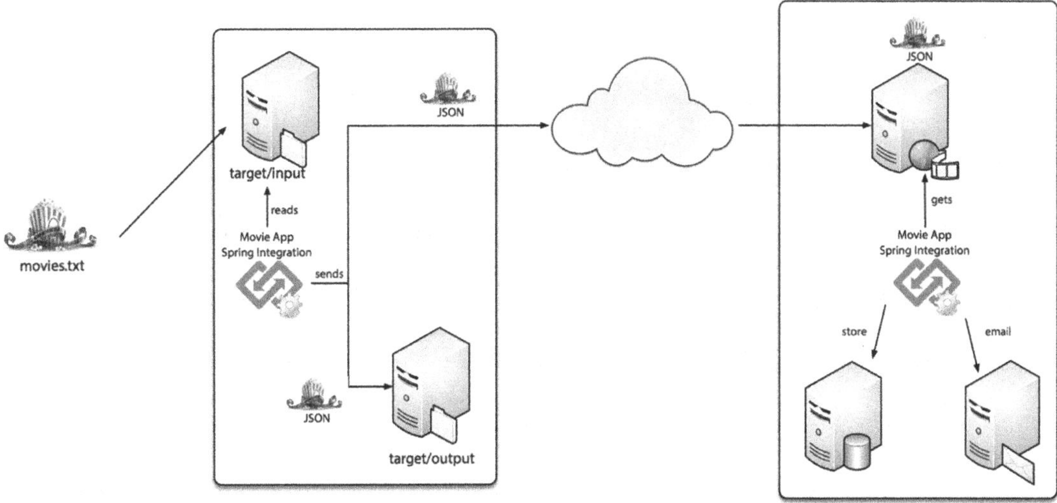

Figure 3-3. *Movie integration app*

Movie App Part I

The following are the specs/requirements for the Movie app.

- Gets new movie information in a CSV file format
- Converts the CSV content into a JSON format
- Needs to do the following in parallel
    - Save the movie information into a file system path (the filename needs to have a `.processed` suffix; e.g., `action-movies.txt > action-movies.txt.processed`)
    - Send the JSON-format movie information to an external server by calling a REST API

Movie App: Part II (External)

The following are the specs/requirements for the external system part of the app.

- Features a REST API service: `/v1/movies` for information for a collection of movies in JSON format
- Stores the new movie information into MySQL
- Sends an email after the movie information is stored

This example is very simple, but it is enough to show you how Spring Integration works.

Creating the Movie App: Part I

Let's start by creating the skeleton of the application. Go to `https://start.spring.io` and create a project. Export it into any IDE (see Figure 3-4). Or, use the STS IDE (`https://spring.io/tools`), click File ➤ New ➤ Spring Starter Project, and follow the wizard.

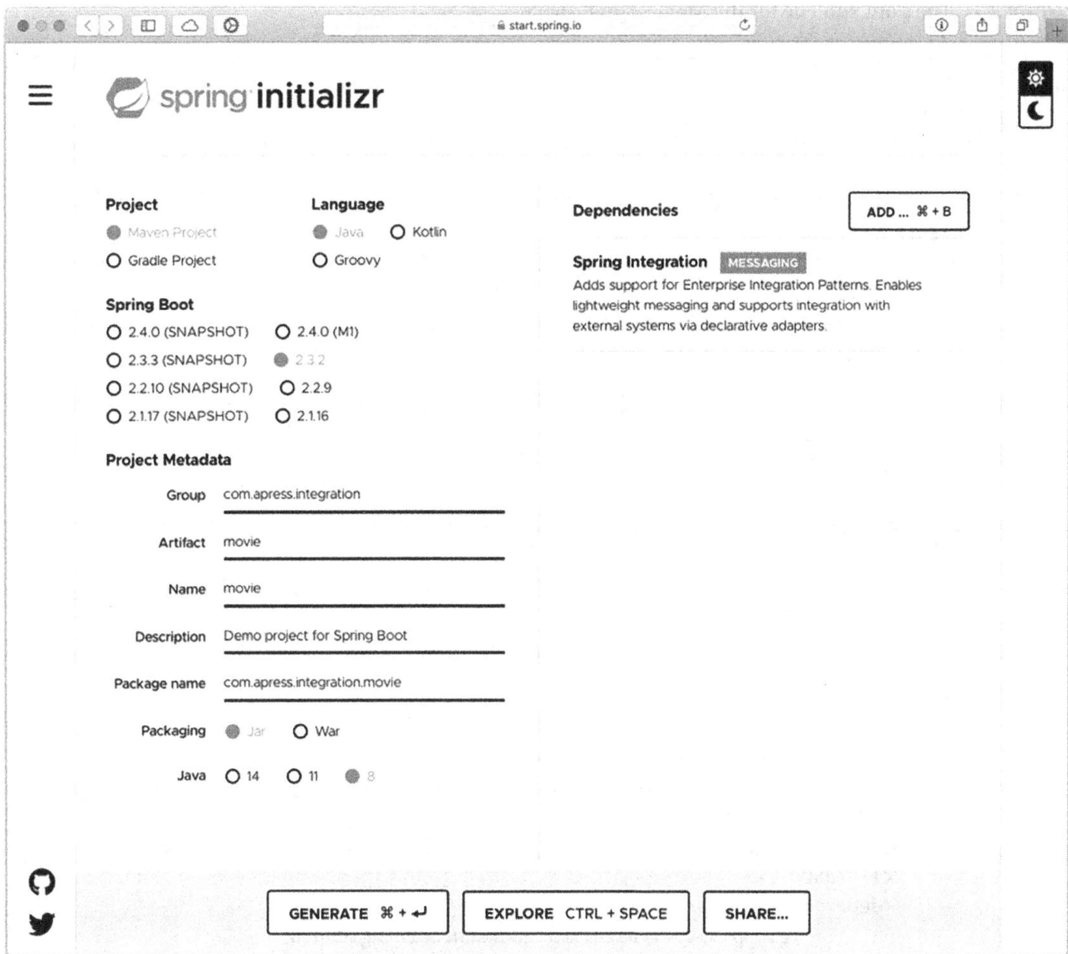

Figure 3-4. *Spring Initializr at* `https://start.spring.io`

Figure 3-4 shows the Spring Initializr homepage. You can add the following values.

- Group: `com.apress.integration`
- Artifact: `movie`
- Dependencies: Spring Integration

Click the Generate *Project* button. Unzip the project and use any IDE to import it.

Review your project structure and make sure you have the `pom.xml` file shown in Listing 3-1. I also added a dependency.

Listing 3-1. The pom.xml File for the Movie App Project

```
<?xml version="1.0" encoding="UTF-8"?>
<project xmlns="http://maven.apache.org/POM/4.0.0" xmlns:xsi="http://www.w3.org/2001/
XMLSchema-instance"
        xsi:schemaLocation="http://maven.apache.org/POM/4.0.0 https://maven.apache.org/xsd/
        maven-4.0.0.xsd">
        <modelVersion>4.0.0</modelVersion>
        <parent>
                <groupId>org.springframework.boot</groupId>
                <artifactId>spring-boot-starter-parent</artifactId>
                <version>2.2.2.RELEASE</version>
                <relativePath/> <!-- lookup parent from repository -->
        </parent>
        <groupId>com.apress.integration</groupId>
        <artifactId>movie</artifactId>
        <version>0.0.1-SNAPSHOT</version>
        <name>movie</name>
        <description>Demo project for Spring Boot</description>

        <properties>
                <java.version>1.8</java.version>
        </properties>

        <dependencies>
                <dependency>
                        <groupId>org.springframework.boot</groupId>
                        <artifactId>spring-boot-starter-integration</artifactId>
                </dependency>

                <!-- JSON -->
                <dependency>
                        <groupId>com.fasterxml.jackson.core</groupId>
                        <artifactId>jackson-databind</artifactId>
                </dependency>

                <!-- Spring Integration - File -->
                <dependency>
                        <groupId>org.springframework.integration</groupId>
                        <artifactId>spring-integration-file</artifactId>
                </dependency>

                <!-- Spring Integration - Http -->
                <dependency>
                        <groupId>org.springframework.integration</groupId>
                        <artifactId>spring-integration-http</artifactId>
                </dependency>

                <dependency>
                        <groupId>org.springframework.boot</groupId>
                        <artifactId>spring-boot-starter-test</artifactId>
                        <scope>test</scope>
```

```
                    <exclusions>
                        <exclusion>
                            <groupId>org.junit.vintage</groupId>
                            <artifactId>junit-vintage-engine</artifactId>
                        </exclusion>
                    </exclusions>
                </dependency>
                <dependency>
                    <groupId>org.springframework.integration</groupId>
                    <artifactId>spring-integration-test</artifactId>
                    <scope>test</scope>
                </dependency>
            </dependencies>

            <build>
                <plugins>
                    <plugin>
                        <groupId>org.springframework.boot</groupId>
                        <artifactId>spring-boot-maven-plugin</artifactId>
                    </plugin>
                </plugins>
            </build>

</project>
```

Listing 3-1 is the final `pom.xml that` you should have. You see the `spring-boot-starter-integration` JSON (*jackson-databind*) dependency needed to convert a CSV row into an object/JSON, the `spring-integration-file` dependency needed for processing files, and the `spring-integration-http` dependency needed for sending JSON to the external system.

One of the best features of making Spring Boot applications is the ability to configure your Spring context in different ways. You can use declarative programming through XML beans files, or you can use JavaConfig classes by annotating your class with `@Configuration` and declaring your beans with `@Bean` annotation. Depending on your app, you could avoid any configuration. Spring Boot has an opinionated runtime, so it tries to figure out the kind of application you are running, and by using its autoconfiguration and looking at the classpath, it does its best to create the correct application type.

In the following sections, I show you how to create Spring Integration applications using declarative XML. I think this is the best way to learn this particular technology because it is more readable than using JavaConfig classes (in my opinion); also, by using declarative XML, you can use the power of the IDE to generate an integration graph to visualize how enterprise integration patterns work.

Movie Application: Declarative XML

Let's start by using the JavaConfig classes. First, add a new class named `MovieConfiguration.java` with the content in Listing 3-2.

Listing 3-2. src/main/java/com/apress/integration/movie/MovieConfiguration.java

```
package com.apress.integration.movie;

import org.springframework.context.annotation.Configuration;
import org.springframework.context.annotation.ImportResource;
```

```
@Configuration
@ImportResource("META-INF/spring/movie-app-integration.xml")
public class MovieConfiguration {

}
```

The @ImportResource annotation imports the XML files. These files are part of the Spring configuration. When using declarative XML, I think Spring Integration is the best way to configure it. Don't worry. I'll explain how to creating the XML files in the next section.

Spring Integration Through Declarative XML

Next you need to create a file in src/main/resources/META-INF/spring/movie-app-integration.xml. You need to create the directory structure as well (see Listing 3-3).

Listing 3-3. src/main/resources/META-INF/spring/movie-app-integration.xml

```
<?xml version="1.0" encoding="UTF-8"?>
<beans xmlns="http://www.springframework.org/schema/beans"
    xmlns:xsi="http://www.w3.org/2001/XMLSchema-instance"
    xmlns:int-file="http://www.springframework.org/schema/integration/file"
    xmlns:int="http://www.springframework.org/schema/integration"
    xmlns:int-http="http://www.springframework.org/schema/integration/http"
    xsi:schemaLocation="http://www.springframework.org/schema/beans http://www.
    springframework.org/schema/beans/spring-beans.xsd
        http://www.springframework.org/schema/integration/file http://www.springframework.
        org/schema/integration/file/spring-integration-file.xsd
        http://www.springframework.org/schema/integration/http http://www.springframework.
        org/schema/integration/http/spring-integration-http.xsd
        http://www.springframework.org/schema/integration http://www.springframework.org/
        schema/integration/spring-integration.xsd">

    <!-- Spring Integration -->
    <int-file:inbound-channel-adapter channel="input" directory="target/input" filename-
    pattern="*.txt">
        <int:poller fixed-rate="500"/>
    </int-file:inbound-channel-adapter>

    <!-- Spring Integration: Direct Channel -->
    <int:channel id="input"/>

    <!-- Spring Integration: Service Activator -->
    <int:service-activator id="movieProcessor" input-channel="input" ref="movieEndpoint" />

</beans>
```

Listing 3-3 shows the Spring configuration file for this first part. To use the Spring configuration, you need to import several namespaces within the XML. The following are the important namespaces.

- xmlns:int
- xmlns:int-file
- xmlns:int-http

These namespaces contain several tag descriptions. One of the most used tags is `<int:channel />`. This tag creates a channel as a point of communication between the producer and the consumer, where the producer sends a message through this channel, and the consumer receives it. One of the benefits of using channels is that it makes sure the message arrives at its destination and decouples the producer from the consumer. The same process shown in Figure 3-2 is shown in Figure 3-5.

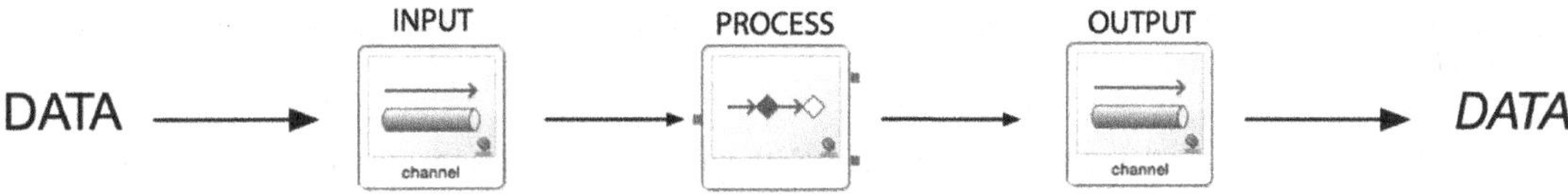

Figure 3-5. *Input-Process-Output with channels*

So, what does the new representation tell us?

- The symbol for input and output defines the channels that do the communication point-to-point or publish-subscribe patterns. The example uses a direct channel, which is a point-to-point pattern.
- The symbol for process defines a service activator, which is a processor of the received message. The message received is through an input channel, and if necessary, the service activator can return a message through an output channel.

Spring Integration handles an internal message format based on the `org.springframework.messaging.Message` class. This interface is defined as follows.

```
public interface Message<T> {

    /**
     * Return the message payload.
     */
    T getPayload();

    /**
     * Return message headers for the message (never {@code null} but may be empty).
     */
    MessageHeaders getHeaders();

}
```

Note that `Message` is an interface, and there is way to create it through the `MessageBuilder`-fluent API.

```
MessageBuilder.withPayload("Hello World").setHeader("myheader",
"Hi").setHeader("myotherheader","there").build();
```

This example uses two channels.

- One is a special channel named `inbound-channel-adapter` and represented by the symbol shown in Figure 3-6a.
- The second channel is named `outbound-channel-adapter` and represented by the symbol shown in Figure 3-6b.

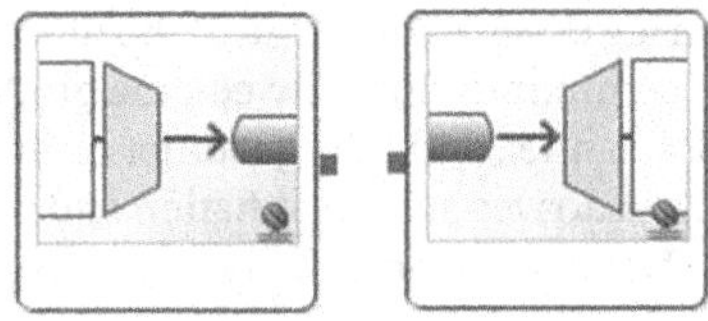

Figures 3-6a and 3-6b. *The `inbound-channel-adapter` channel is on the left, and the `outbound-channel-adapter` channel is on the right.*

Both channels are the same as the regular channel; the only difference is that these channels can poll for a source call.

Going back to the example, let's look at each part.

- `<int-file:inbound-channel-adapter />`. This channel is polling (watching) a file system path every few seconds. The following are its properties.
  - `directory="target/input"` indicates that the channel is watching the directory for any new file.
  - `filename-pattern="*.txt"` is only looking for files with .txt extensions.
  - `channel="input"` indicates that once a file is found (a .txt file), its contents are sent to the input channel.
  - `<int:poller fixed-rate="500"/>` is an inner tag that says it is watching every 500 milliseconds.
- `<int:channel id="input"/>`. This tag creates a channel that is ready to receive the content of a file. Normally, the id is the name of the channel that best matches, regardless of its usage (input or output).
- `<int:service-activator/>`. This tag is a processor of the file's contents. The following are its properties.
  - `input-channel="input"` listens to any message from the input channel.
  - `ref="movieEndpoint"` uses a bean named movieEndpoint to process the message that comes from the input channel.

If you are using the Spring Tool Suite, STS IDE for short (`https://spring.io/tools`), you can see the Spring Integration graph of this example (see Figure 3-7). You can do the same with IntelliJ, but you need to use the paid version and the Spring Integration Patterns plug-in.

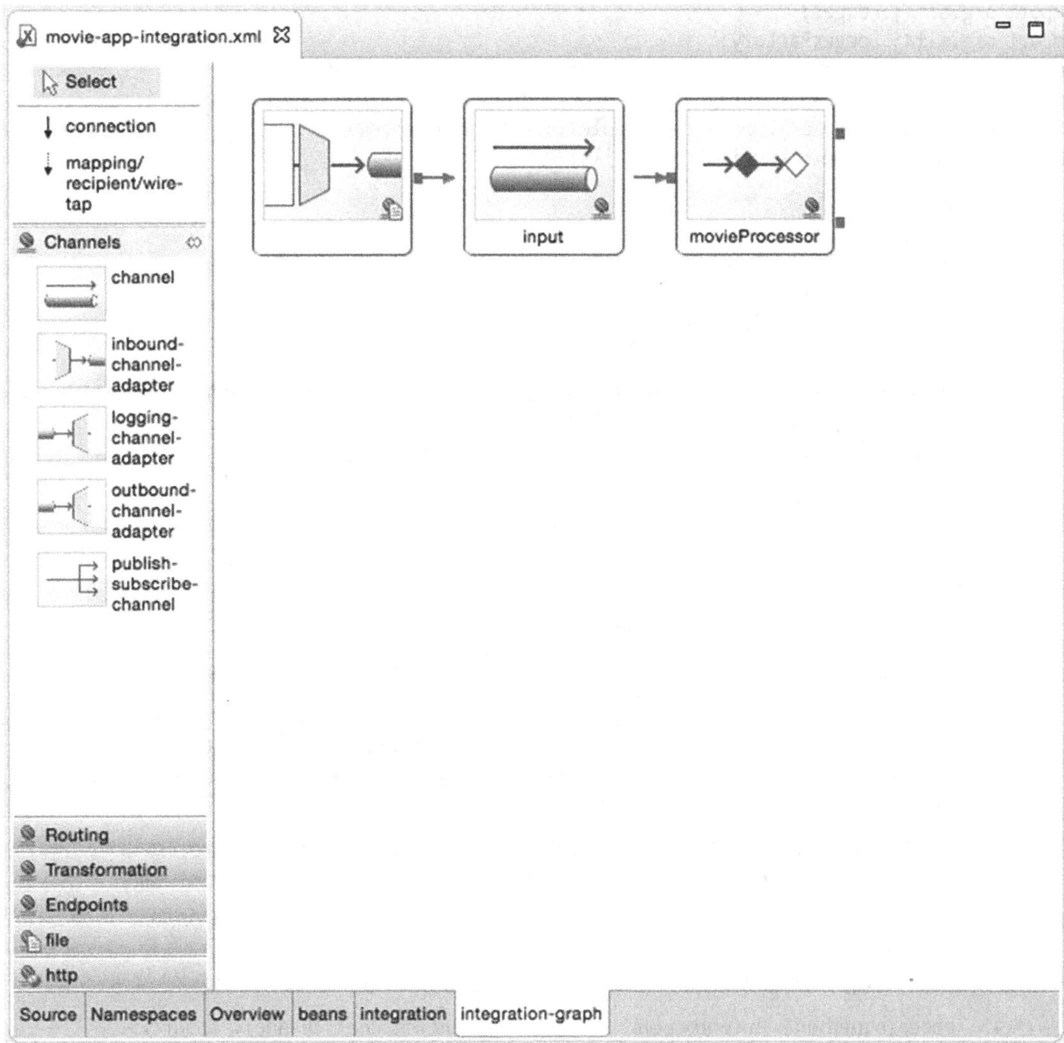

Figure 3-7. *Spring Integration graph from STS IDE*

Spring Integration Development

Next, let's create the `Service Activator` class, which receives the contents of the text file. Create the MovieEndpoint.java class with the content in Listing 3-4.

Listing 3-4. com.apress.integration.movie.MovieEndpoint.java

```
package com.apress.spring.integration.movie;

import java.io.File;
import java.io.FileInputStream;
import java.util.Map;
```

```
import org.slf4j.Logger;
import org.slf4j.LoggerFactory;
import org.springframework.integration.annotation.MessageEndpoint;
import org.springframework.integration.annotation.ServiceActivator;
import org.springframework.messaging.handler.annotation.Headers;
import org.springframework.util.StreamUtils;

@MessageEndpoint
public class MovieEndpoint {

    private static final Logger log = LoggerFactory.getLogger(MovieEndpoint.class);

    @ServiceActivator
    public void process(File input, @Headers Map<String,Object> headers) throws Exception {
        FileInputStream in = new FileInputStream(input);
        String movies = new String(StreamUtils.copyToByteArray(in));
        in.close();
        log.info("Received: \n" +  movies);
    }
}
```

Listing 3-4 shows the `MovieEndpoint.java` service activator. Let's look at each part.

- `@MessageEndpoint` is an annotation that tells Spring Integration that the class must be treated as an endpoint accessed by any other output channel.
- `@ServiceActivator` is an annotation over a method that tells Spring Integration that the method is the entry point where the message arrives and processes. The following are its parameters.
    - `File` is the `java.io.File` class. The `<int-file:inbound-channel-adapter />` tag sends java.io.`File` automatically, and it fills out all the headers in the `Message` interface.
    - `@Headers` is an annotation that has `org.springframework.messaging.MessageHeaders` class headers. Two of the headers are `id` and `timestamp`.
- `process` method is the entry point listening from `<int:channel channel="input"/>`.

Next, you need to create a small file with movies to test your first Spring Integration app—something like the following snippet (as simple as movie title, actor, year).

```
The Matrix, Keanu Reeves, 1999
Memento, Guy Pearce, 2000
The Silence of the Lambs, Jodie Foster, 1991
The Prestige, Christian Bale, 2006
Disturbia, Shia LaBeouf, 2007
```

Put the file in `target/input` (in the root of the project). When you use Maven, it automatically generates the `target` folder. You need to create the input folder and drop the file there.

Now it's time to run the app. Open a new terminal, and from the root's project, execute the following command line.

```
$ ./mvn spring-boot:run
```

You should see the following output.

```
INFO 5395 --- [ask-scheduler-1] o.s.i.file.FileReadingMessageSource      : Created message:
[GenericMessage [payload=target/input/movies-batch1.txt, headers={timestamp=1437355862115,
id=4fe905ee-8829-e3f2-df42-f5a7512635cd}]]
INFO 5395 --- [ask-scheduler-1] c.a.spring.integration.MovieEndpoint     : Movies Received:
The Matrix, Keanu Reeves, 1999
Memento, Guy Pearce, 2000
The Silence of the Lambs, Jodie Foster, 1991
The Prestige, Christian Bale, 2006
Disturbia, Shia LaBeouf, 2007
```

It worked! If you want to create a behavior to watch a file in a directory, you need to think about reusability and extensibility. This integration with a file system already exists with Spring Integration.

You need to convert the contents of the file (CSV) into a JSON format. Let's look at Listing 3-5.

Listing 3-5. com.apress.integration.movie.MovieService.java

```java
package com.apress.integration.movie;

import com.fasterxml.jackson.databind.ObjectMapper;
import org.slf4j.Logger;
import org.slf4j.LoggerFactory;
import org.springframework.stereotype.Component;

import java.io.IOException;
import java.util.ArrayList;
import java.util.Arrays;
import java.util.List;

@Component
public class MovieService {

    private static final Logger log = LoggerFactory.getLogger(MovieService.class);

    public String format(String contents){
        log.info("Formatting to Json...");

        String json = "{}";

        ObjectMapper mapper = new ObjectMapper();
        try {
            json = mapper.writeValueAsString(parse(contents));
            log.info("\n" + json);
        } catch (IOException e) {
            e.printStackTrace();
        }

        return json;
    }
```

```
    private List<Movie> parse(String contents){
        List<Movie> movies = new ArrayList<Movie>();
        String[] record = null;
        for(String line: contents.split(System.getProperty("line.separator"))){
            record = Arrays.asList(line.split(",")).stream().map( c -> c.trim()).toArray(
            size -> new String[size]);
            movies.add(new Movie(record[0],record[1],Integer.valueOf(record[2])));
        }
        return movies;
    }
}
```

Listing 3-5 shows that the `MovieService` class is annotated with `@Component`, making this class visible to the Spring container so that you can use it in your service activator. Let's look at each method.

- `format(String contents)` gets the file's content and uses the `ObjectMapper` class (from the Jackson library) to convert it (from the list of movies) into a JSON format by calling the private `parse` method.
- `parse(String contents)` is a method to get the file's content. It parses by stripping out every line and splitting (by comma) it into the actual values. It creates a `Movie` object that is added into an array list. This array list is the result. This method uses Java 8 streams notation to avoid any spaces in the values.
- Listing 3-5 introduced a `Movie` class, so let's look at this class (see Listing 3-6).

Listing 3-6. com.apress.integration.movie.Movie.java

```
package com.apress.integration.movie;

public class Movie {

    private String title;
    private String actor;
    private int year;

    public Movie(){}

    public Movie(String title, String actor, int year){
        this.title = title;
        this.actor = actor;
        this.year = year;
    }

    public String getTitle() {
        return title;
    }
    public void setTitle(String title) {
        this.title = title;
    }
    public String getActor() {
        return actor;
    }
```

```
    public void setActor(String actor) {
        this.actor = actor;
    }
    public int getYear() {
        return year;
    }
    public void setYear(int year) {
        this.year = year;
    }

    public String toString(){
        StringBuilder builder = new StringBuilder();
        builder.append("Movie(title: ");
        builder.append(title);
        builder.append(", actor: ");
        builder.append(actor);
        builder.append(", year: ");
        builder.append(year);
        builder.append(")");
        return builder.toString();
    }

}
```

Listing 3-6 is a basic Movie POJO that contains these basic fields: Title, Actor, and Year. Let's use this service in the service activator (see Listing 3-7).

Listing 3-7. com.apress.integration.movie.MovieEndpoint.java (version 2) Using MovieService

```
package com.apress.integration.movie;

import org.slf4j.Logger;
import org.slf4j.LoggerFactory;
import org.springframework.beans.factory.annotation.Autowired;
import org.springframework.integration.annotation.MessageEndpoint;
import org.springframework.integration.annotation.ServiceActivator;
import org.springframework.messaging.handler.annotation.Headers;
import org.springframework.util.StreamUtils;

import java.io.File;
import java.io.FileInputStream;
import java.util.Map;

@MessageEndpoint
public class MovieEndpoint {

    private static final Logger log = LoggerFactory.getLogger(MovieEndpoint.class);

    @Autowired
    private MovieService service;
```

```
    @ServiceActivator
    public void process(File input, @Headers Map<String,Object> headers) throws Exception {
        FileInputStream in = new FileInputStream(input);
        String movies = service.format(new String(StreamUtils.copyToByteArray(in)));
        in.close();
        log.info("Movies Received: \n" +  movies);
    }
}
```

Listing 3-7 is version 2 of the MovieEndpoint class, which uses MovieService. It uses the @Autowired annotation that allows MovieService to be injected and ready to use. If you run the app using Maven or the STS IDE, you should see the following output.

```
INFO 5677 --- [ask-scheduler-1] com.apress.integration.movie.MovieService    : Formatting to
Json...
INFO 5677 --- [ask-scheduler-1] com.apress.integration.movie.MovieService    :
[{"title":"The Matrix","actor":"Keanu Reeves","year":1999},{"title":"Memento","actor":"Guy
Pearce","year":2000},{"title":"The Silence of the Lambs","actor":"Jodie Foster","year":1991},
{"title":"The Prestige","actor":"Christian Bale","year":2006},{"title":"Disturbia","actor":"
Shia LaBeouf","year":2007}]
```

This output is the result of using MovieService; it is generated in JSON format, one of the requirements for this app.

The next requirement is to send the content to a file in target/output/<file>.txt.processed format. You can create all the logic in the service activator, and you are done with it. But what about with the requirement for sending the file to a remote service using a REST API? If you think about it, you can do both implementations in the Service Activator class in the same process method. But that would take time, right? Thanks to Spring Integration, this logic is already there as a tag! Let's start by sending the processed file to the output directory with the .processed extension.

You need to modify the movie-app-integration.xml file to look like Listing 3-8.

Listing 3-8. movie-app-integration.xml (version 2)

```
<?xml version="1.0" encoding="UTF-8"?>
<beans xmlns="http://www.springframework.org/schema/beans"
    xmlns:xsi="http://www.w3.org/2001/XMLSchema-instance"
    xmlns:int-file="http://www.springframework.org/schema/integration/file"
    xmlns:int="http://www.springframework.org/schema/integration"
    xmlns:int-http="http://www.springframework.org/schema/integration/http"
    xsi:schemaLocation="http://www.springframework.org/schema/beans http://www.
    springframework.org/schema/beans/spring-beans.xsd
        http://www.springframework.org/schema/integration/file http://www.springframework.
        org/schema/integration/file/spring-integration-file.xsd
        http://www.springframework.org/schema/integration/http http://www.springframework.
        org/schema/integration/http/spring-integration-http.xsd
        http://www.springframework.org/schema/integration http://www.springframework.org/
        schema/integration/spring-integration.xsd">

    <!-- Spring Integration -->
    <int-file:inbound-channel-adapter channel="input" directory="target/input" filename-
    pattern="*.txt">
        <int:poller fixed-rate="500"/>
    </int-file:inbound-channel-adapter>
```

```
    <!-- Spring Integration: Direct Channel -->
    <int:channel id="input"/>

    <!-- Spring Integration: Service Activator -->
    <int:service-activator id="movieProcessor" input-channel="input" ref="movieEndpoint"
    output-channel="output"/>

    <!-- Spring Integration: Direct Channel -->
    <int:channel id="output"/>

    <!--  Spring Integration: File -->
    <int-file:outbound-channel-adapter channel="output" directory="target/output"  filename-
    generator-expression="headers['name'] + '.processed'" />

</beans>
```

Listing 3-8 is version 2 of the movie-app-integration.xml file. Let's look at what is new.

- <int:service-activator /> has a new attribute: output-channel="output". This attribute identifies the channel where the message is sent out; in this case, the name of the channel is "output".
- <int:channel id="output"/> creates a new channel. This is the channel that sends the message from the service activator.
- <int-file:outbound-channel-adapter /> gets the content (in JSON format) and creates the file in a specified directory. The following attributes are used.
    - channel="output" sets the channel that listens to incoming content.
    - directory="target/output" specifies where the file is placed in the directory.
    - filename-generator-expression="headers['name'] + '.processed'" generates the filename by inspecting the message's header and adding the suffix.

You need to modify the service activator again because it now needs to return something. In this case, the <int-file:outbound-channel-adapter/> tag gives you a hint. You need to send back a Message instance with at least the header containing the new filename (see Listing 3-9).

Listing 3-9. com.apress.integration.movie.MovieEndpoint.java (version 3): Returning a Message Instance

```
package com.apress.integration.movie;

import org.slf4j.Logger;
import org.slf4j.LoggerFactory;
import org.springframework.beans.factory.annotation.Autowired;
import org.springframework.integration.annotation.MessageEndpoint;
import org.springframework.integration.annotation.ServiceActivator;
import org.springframework.messaging.Message;
import org.springframework.messaging.handler.annotation.Headers;
import org.springframework.messaging.support.MessageBuilder;
import org.springframework.util.StreamUtils;

import java.io.File;
import java.io.FileInputStream;
import java.util.Map;
```

```
@MessageEndpoint
public class MovieEndpoint {

    private static final Logger log = LoggerFactory.getLogger(MovieEndpoint.class);

    @Autowired
    private MovieService service;

    @ServiceActivator
    public Message<String> process(File input, @Headers Map<String,Object> headers) throws
    Exception {
        FileInputStream in = new FileInputStream(input);
        String movies = service.format(new String(StreamUtils.copyToByteArray(in)));
        in.close();
        log.info("Sending the JSON content to a file...");
        return MessageBuilder.withPayload(movies).setHeader("name",input.getName()).
        setHeader("Content-Type","application/json").build();
    }
}
```

Listing 3-9 is version 3 of `MovieService`, which returns a value from the service activator; in this case, an instance of the `org.springframework.messaging.Message<String>` interface. Also, it adds headers that contain the name and the `Content-Type`. This last header is useful for the HTTP request (coming later). The `org.springframework.messaging.support.MessageBuilder` utility class builds the message. This class provides a very nice fluent API.

If you have the STS IDE, you can see the graph results after modifying the configuration XML file, as shown in Figure 3-8.

Figure 3-8. *Spring Integration graph (version 2)*

After running the application, you should have the same output as before, but if you take a look at the `target/output` directory, you find a new file name, `movies.txt.processed` (if you named the file: `movies.txt`). The contents are in JSON format.

The next requirement is to send this file to an external REST API service. Listing 3-10 is version 3 of `movie-app-integration.xml`.

Listing 3-10. movie-app-integration.xml (version 3)

```
<?xml version="1.0" encoding="UTF-8"?>
<beans xmlns="http://www.springframework.org/schema/beans"
    xmlns:xsi="http://www.w3.org/2001/XMLSchema-instance"
    xmlns:int-file="http://www.springframework.org/schema/integration/file"
    xmlns:int="http://www.springframework.org/schema/integration"
    xmlns:int-http="http://www.springframework.org/schema/integration/http"
    xsi:schemaLocation="http://www.springframework.org/schema/beans http://www.
    springframework.org/schema/beans/spring-beans.xsd
```

```
        http://www.springframework.org/schema/integration/file http://www.springframework.
        org/schema/integration/file/spring-integration-file.xsd
        http://www.springframework.org/schema/integration/http http://www.springframework.
        org/schema/integration/http/spring-integration-http.xsd
        http://www.springframework.org/schema/integration http://www.springframework.org/
        schema/integration/spring-integration.xsd">

    <!-- Spring Integration -->
    <int-file:inbound-channel-adapter channel="input" directory="target/input" filename-
    pattern="*.txt">
        <int:poller fixed-rate="500"/>
    </int-file:inbound-channel-adapter>

    <!-- Spring Integration: Direct Channel -->
    <int:channel id="input"/>

    <!-- Spring Integration: Service Activator -->
    <int:service-activator input-channel="input" ref="movieEndpoint" output-
    channel="output"/>

    <!-- Spring Integration: Direct Channel -->
    <int:channel id="output"/>

    <!-- Spring Integration: Router -->
    <int:recipient-list-router input-channel="output">
        <int:recipient channel="toFile" />
        <int:recipient channel="toHttp"/>
    </int:recipient-list-router>

    <!-- Spring Integration: Direct Channels -->
    <int:channel id="toFile"/>
    <int:channel id="toHttp"/>

    <!-- Spring Integration: File and Http -->
    <int-file:outbound-channel-adapter channel="toFile" directory="target/output"  filename-
    generator-expression="headers['name'] + '.processed'" />
    <int-http:outbound-channel-adapter channel="toHttp" url="http://localhost:8080/v1/
    movies" http-method="POST"/>

</beans>
```

Listing 3-10 is version 3 of the movie-app-integration.xml file. Let's look at what is new.

- <int:recipient-list-router /> is a new tag that exposes a router. This example uses the output channel to send the content to the toFile and toHttp channels.
- <int:recipient/> declares the channel to be used by the router.
- <int:channel/> means there are two new direct channels (point-to-point): toFile and toHttp.
- <int-http:outbound-channel-adapter/> a new tag that makes a request to a remote service—the REST API that you need to point to (/v1/movies).

Based on Listing 3-10, your graph should be similar to Figure 3-9.

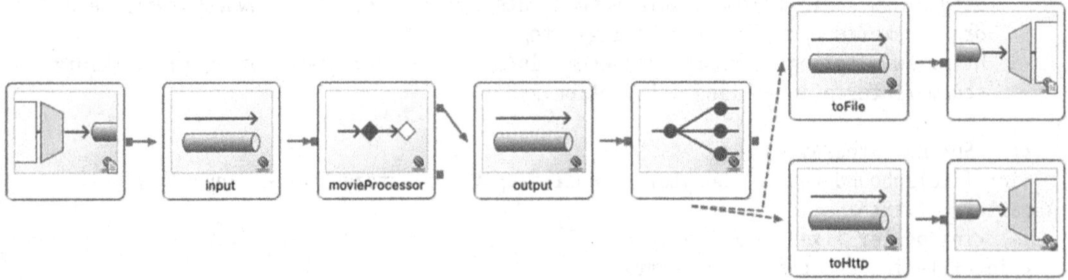

Figure 3-9. *Spring Integration graph*

Running the application results in some errors because it's looking for the `http://localhost:8080/v1/movies` endpoint, and it's not ready yet; it's in the next part of the integration. As you can see, trying to implement the last part of the requirements is time-consuming, but Spring Integration already has these reusable modules (EIP implementations).

Creating a Movie App: Part II (External)

This app is oriented to create a REST API, do database insertions, and send an email. You can use the same URL to generate the project (`http://start.spring.io`) or use the STS IDE to generate the same templates.

The following are the new field values for this project (see Figure 3-10).

- Group: `com.apress.integration`
- Artifact: `movie-web`
- Dependencies: Spring Web, Spring Integration, Java Mail Sender, JDBC API, H2 database

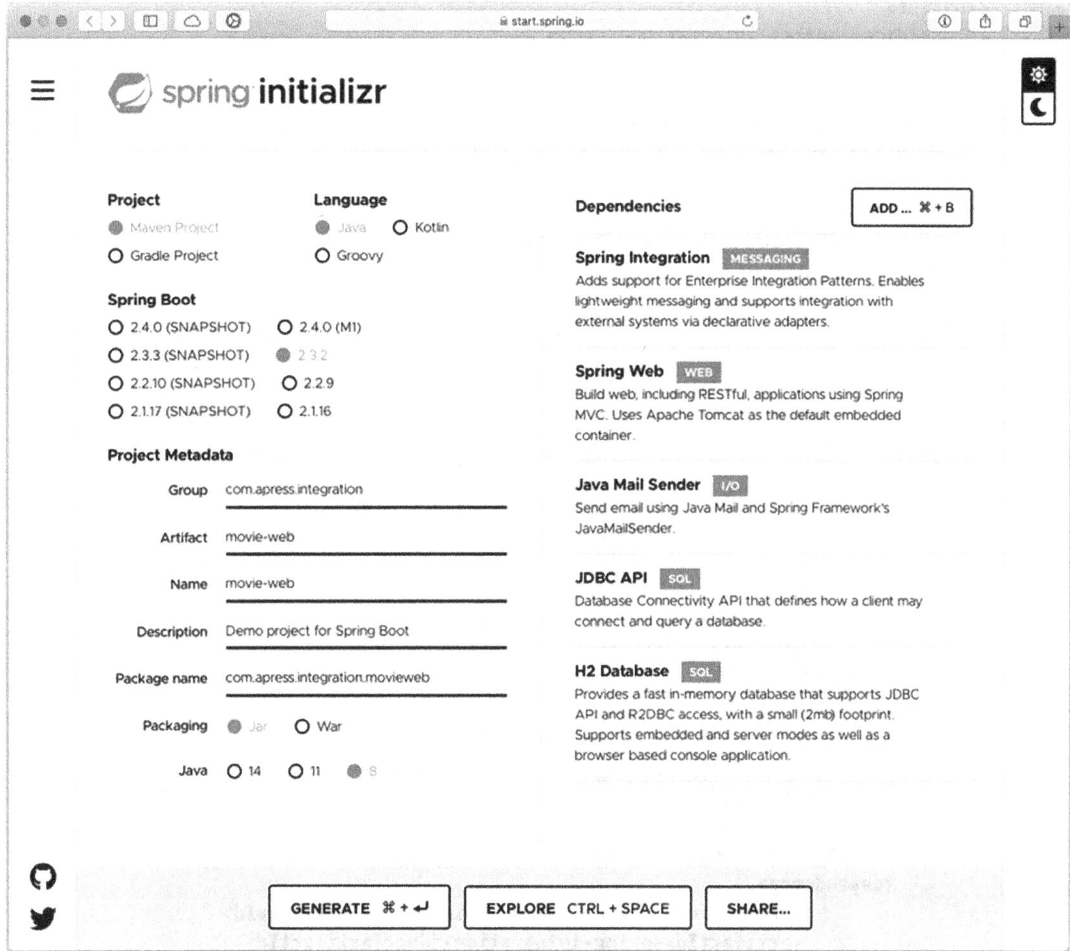

Figure 3-10. *Spring Initializr at* `https://start.spring.io`

Once you generate the project, unzip it and import it to your favorite IDE. You should have the `pom.xml` shown in Listing 3-11. (Please modify it to match Listing 3-11 if necessary.)

Listing 3-11. pom.xml

```
<?xml version="1.0" encoding="UTF-8"?>
<project xmlns="http://maven.apache.org/POM/4.0.0" xmlns:xsi="http://www.w3.org/2001/
XMLSchema-instance"
        xsi:schemaLocation="http://maven.apache.org/POM/4.0.0 https://maven.apache.org/xsd/
        maven-4.0.0.xsd">
        <modelVersion>4.0.0</modelVersion>
        <parent>
                <groupId>org.springframework.boot</groupId>
                <artifactId>spring-boot-starter-parent</artifactId>
                <version>2.2.2.RELEASE</version>
                <relativePath/> <!-- lookup parent from repository -->
```

```
</parent>
<groupId>com.apress.integration</groupId>
<artifactId>movie-web</artifactId>
<version>0.0.1-SNAPSHOT</version>
<name>movie-web</name>
<description>Demo project for Spring Boot</description>

<properties>
        <java.version>1.8</java.version>
</properties>

<dependencies>
        <dependency>
                <groupId>org.springframework.boot</groupId>
                <artifactId>spring-boot-starter-integration</artifactId>
        </dependency>
        <dependency>
                <groupId>org.springframework.boot</groupId>
                <artifactId>spring-boot-starter-jdbc</artifactId>
        </dependency>
        <dependency>
                <groupId>org.springframework.boot</groupId>
                <artifactId>spring-boot-starter-mail</artifactId>
        </dependency>
        <dependency>
                <groupId>org.springframework.boot</groupId>
                <artifactId>spring-boot-starter-web</artifactId>
        </dependency>

        <!-- Spring Integration -->
        <dependency>
                <groupId>org.springframework.integration</groupId>
                <artifactId>spring-integration-jdbc</artifactId>
        </dependency>
        <dependency>
                <groupId>org.springframework.integration</groupId>
                <artifactId>spring-integration-mail</artifactId>
        </dependency>

        <!-- JDBC -->
        <dependency>
                <groupId>mysql</groupId>
                <artifactId>mysql-connector-java</artifactId>
        </dependency>

        <!-- Http -->
        <dependency>
                <groupId>org.springframework.integration</groupId>
                <artifactId>spring-integration-http</artifactId>
        </dependency>
```

```
        <dependency>
            <groupId>com.h2database</groupId>
            <artifactId>h2</artifactId>
            <scope>runtime</scope>
        </dependency>
        <dependency>
            <groupId>org.springframework.boot</groupId>
            <artifactId>spring-boot-starter-test</artifactId>
            <scope>test</scope>
            <exclusions>
                <exclusion>
                    <groupId>org.junit.vintage</groupId>
                    <artifactId>junit-vintage-engine</artifactId>
                </exclusion>
            </exclusions>
        </dependency>
        <dependency>
            <groupId>org.springframework.integration</groupId>
            <artifactId>spring-integration-test</artifactId>
            <scope>test</scope>
        </dependency>
    </dependencies>

    <build>
        <plugins>
            <plugin>
                <groupId>org.springframework.boot</groupId>
                <artifactId>spring-boot-maven-plugin</artifactId>
            </plugin>
        </plugins>
    </build>

</project>
```

Listing 3-11 is the pom.xml that you are going to use. Take a look at the Spring Integration and JDBC section. You need to add spring-integration-jdbc, spring-integration-mail, spring-integration-http, and h2. The first two dependencies add the namespaces to use the special tag in this part of the solution.

Movie App Part II with Spring Boot MVC

Let's look at how easy it is to use Spring MVC components. In this section, you create the com.apress.integration.movieweb.MovieController.java class and reuse the Movie class (see Listing 3-6). The MovieController class must have the content shown in Listing 3-12.

Listing 3-12. com.apress.integration.movieweb.MovieController.java

```
package com.apress.integration.movieweb;

import org.slf4j.Logger;
import org.slf4j.LoggerFactory;
import org.springframework.http.HttpStatus;
```

```
import org.springframework.http.ResponseEntity;
import org.springframework.web.bind.annotation.RequestBody;
import org.springframework.web.bind.annotation.RequestMapping;
import org.springframework.web.bind.annotation.RequestMethod;
import org.springframework.web.bind.annotation.RestController;

@RestController
public class MovieController {

    private static final Logger log = LoggerFactory.getLogger(MovieController.class);

    @RequestMapping(method=RequestMethod.POST,value="/v1/movie")
    public ResponseEntity<String> movie(@RequestBody Movie body){
        log.info("Movie: " +  body);
        return new ResponseEntity<String>(HttpStatus.ACCEPTED);
    }

    @RequestMapping(method=RequestMethod.POST,value="/v1/movies")
    public ResponseEntity<String> movies(@RequestBody Movie[] body){
        for (Movie movie: body){
            log.info("Movie: " +  movie);
        }
        return new ResponseEntity<String>(HttpStatus.ACCEPTED);
    }

}
```

Listing 3-12 shows the `MovieController` class. This class is treated as a web controller due to its annotation. Spring Boot registers this controller and any URL mappings exposed; in this case, "`/v1/movie`" and "`/v1/movies`" (one is singular and the other plural). Let's look at the details.

- `@RestController`. This annotation is the marker for Spring Boot, so it is registered as an entry REST point.
- `@RequestMapping`. This annotation declares the REST API, the method that accepts incoming requests, and its path for accepting those requests. This annotation is necessary to be placed in the method that is the handler for the requests. You can use the `@GetMapping` annotation as well, an easy way to handle GET HTTP requests.
- `@RequestBody`. This annotation is used in both handlers, but look at the parameters—one is a single instance and the other is an array of `Movie` instances. Every time there is a request, the Spring MVC is in charge of automatically converting every JSON request into the correct instance; in this case, the `Movie` instance. (The `Movie` class is the same as in Part I).
- `ResponseEntity<String>`. Every handler returns a ResponseEntity status; in this case, a string that says `Accepted` with HTTP status code: `202`.

Now you can run the web application in a terminal by executing the following command.

```
$ ./mvnw spring-boot:run
```

You can do a small test and verify that your REST API is running. For example, you can open a terminal and use the `cURL` command, like in the following snippet, and get the same output.

```
$ curl -i -H "Content-Type:application/json" -X POST -d '[{"title":"The
Matrix","actor":"Keanu Reeves","year":1999},{"title":"Memento","actor":"Guy
Pearce","year":2000}]' http://localhost:8080/v1/movies

HTTP/1.1 202 Accepted
Server: Apache-Coyote/1.1
Content-Length: 0
```

You get the 202 Accepted display, and in the logs where you have run the web app, you see something similar to the following output.

```
INFO 8052 --- [.16-8080-exec-3] c.apress.integration.movieweb.MovieWebController   : Movie:
Movie(title: The Matrix, actor: Keanu Reeves, year: 1999)
INFO 8052 --- [.16-8080-exec-3] c.apress.integration.movieweb.MovieWebController   : Movie:
Movie(title: Memento, actor: Guy Pearce, year: 2000)
```

Well, you just created the REST API service, but you are missing the other requirements. Save a movie to the JDBC, and send an email about the new stored movie. In the rest controller's handler method, you can add the logic to do the JDBC and send the email, but the main idea is to see the power of Spring Integration.

You can run the Movie app (from Part I) to see how it communicates. You should see all the movies printed out in the MovieWeb console logs.

Spring Integration Through Declarative XML: Part II

Next, let's create the Spring bean context file shown in Listing 3-13.

Listing 3-13. src/main/resources/META-INF/spring/movie-webapp-integration.xml

```
<?xml version="1.0" encoding="UTF-8"?>
<beans xmlns="http://www.springframework.org/schema/beans"
       xmlns:xsi="http://www.w3.org/2001/XMLSchema-instance" xmlns:int="http://www.
       springframework.org/schema/integration"
       xmlns:int-http="http://www.springframework.org/schema/integration/http"
       xmlns:int-mail="http://www.springframework.org/schema/integration/mail"
       xmlns:jdbc="http://www.springframework.org/schema/jdbc" xmlns:int-jdbc="http://www.
       springframework.org/schema/integration/jdbc"
       xsi:schemaLocation="http://www.springframework.org/schema/jdbc http://www.
       springframework.org/schema/jdbc/spring-jdbc.xsd
        http://www.springframework.org/schema/integration/jdbc http://www.springframework.
        org/schema/integration/jdbc/spring-integration-jdbc.xsd
        http://www.springframework.org/schema/beans http://www.springframework.org/schema/
        beans/spring-beans.xsd
        http://www.springframework.org/schema/integration/http http://www.springframework.
        org/schema/integration/http/spring-integration-http.xsd
        http://www.springframework.org/schema/integration/mail http://www.springframework.
        org/schema/integration/mail/spring-integration-mail.xsd
        http://www.springframework.org/schema/integration http://www.springframework.org/
        schema/integration/spring-integration.xsd">
```

```
    <!-- Spring Integration -->
    <!-- Spring Integration: Http -->
    <int-http:inbound-channel-adapter id="movie"
                                      supported-methods="POST" channel="input" path="/v2/
                                      movie"
                                      request-payload-type="com.apress.integration.movieweb.
                                      Movie"
                                      status-code-expression="T(org.springframework.http.
                                      HttpStatus).ACCEPTED"
    />

    <int-http:inbound-channel-adapter id="movies"
                                      supported-methods="POST" channel="input" path="/v2/
                                      movies"
                                      request-payload-type="com.apress.integration.movieweb.
                                      Movie[]"
                                      status-code-expression="T(org.springframework.http.
                                      HttpStatus).ACCEPTED"
    />

    <!-- Spring Integration: Execution Channel -->
    <int:channel id="input"/>

    <!-- Spring Integration Service Activator. -->
    <int:service-activator input-channel="input" ref="movieEndpoint" />

</beans>
```

Listing 3-13 is the XML config file to use. This file should be created in `src/main/resources/META-INF/spring` directory.

■ **Note** All the source code is on the Apress web site (see the Source Code/Downloads tab at `www.apress.com`). You can copy/paste it.

Take a look at the following namespaces. Even though you are not going to use them right now, you will soon.

- `xmlns:int-mail` exposes some useful tags for email actions.
- `xmlns:jdbc` is useful for JDBC.

Let's review Listing 3-13 and see what is new.

- `<int-http:inbound-channel-adapter/>`. Even though you already created the `MovieController` class, this tag creates the same behavior. It creates two endpoints using version 2: `"/v2/movie"` and `"/v2/movies"`. The attributes are as follows.
    - `supported-methods="POST"` tells the endpoint to accept only POST requests.
    - `channel="input"` specifies where the request message is sent.

    - path="/v2/movie" is the request mapping path. There are two defined: one for a single movie and the other for a collection of movies.
    - request-payload-type="com.apress.integration.movieweb.Movie" is similar to declare the @RequestBody annotation. Spring MVC automatically converts the JSON format into the Movie object. For a collection of movies, you declare the Movie[] array.
    - status-code-expression="T(org.springframework.http.HttpStatus).ACCEPTED" shows a response type similar to the ResponseEntity<String> type.
- <int:channel id="input"/> creates a channel that produces and consumes a Message type.
- <int:service-activator input-channel="input" ref="movieEndpoint" /> exposes the name of the class where you declare the handler for this endpoint as a service activator.

You can create the same REST API endpoint programmatically (like the MovieWebController class) or without any code (declarative) using the XML configuration file.

The resulting graph of this XML configuration file is shown in Figure 3-11.

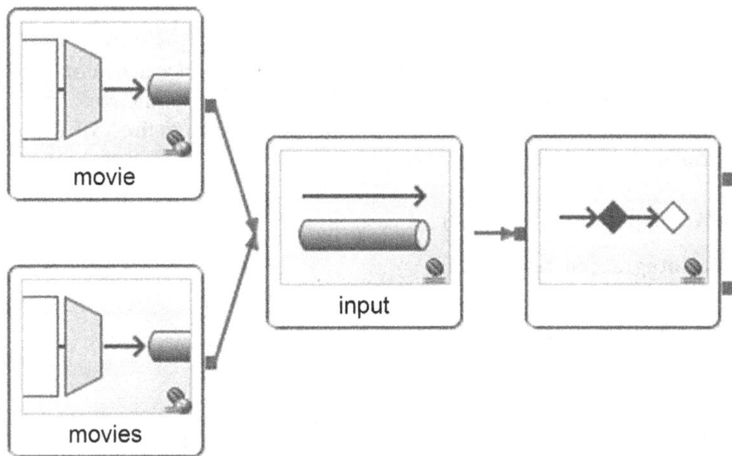

Figure 3-11. *Spring Integration graph part II (version 1)*

Spring Integration Development: Part II

Listing 3-14 is a service activator component, the MovieEndpoint class.

Listing 3-14. com.apress.integration.movieweb.MovieEndpoint.java

```
package com.apress.integration.movieweb;

import org.slf4j.Logger;
import org.slf4j.LoggerFactory;
import org.springframework.integration.annotation.MessageEndpoint;
import org.springframework.integration.annotation.ServiceActivator;
import org.springframework.messaging.handler.annotation.Headers;
```

```
import java.util.Map;

@MessageEndpoint
public class MovieEndpoint {

    private static final Logger log = LoggerFactory.getLogger(MovieEndpoint.class);

    @ServiceActivator
    public void processMovie(Movie movie, @Headers Map<String,Object> headers) throws
    Exception {
        log.info("Movie: " + movie);
    }

    @ServiceActivator
    public void processMovies(Movie[] movies, @Headers Map<String,Object> headers) throws
    Exception {
        for (Movie movie: movies){
            log.info("Movie: " +  movie);
        }
    }
}
```

Listing 3-14 shows the message endpoint. This class exposes two service activator handlers. Spring Integration decides which to choose when the message gets to the input channel.

Next, create the `MovieConfiguration` class because you need to include the XML file with the `@ImportResource` annotation (see Listing 3-15).

Listing 3-15. MovieWebApplication (version 2)

```
package com.apress.integration.movieweb;

import org.springframework.context.annotation.Configuration;
import org.springframework.context.annotation.ImportResource;

@Configuration
@ImportResource("META-INF/spring/movie-webapp-integration.xml")
public class MovieConfiguration {

}
```

Now, you can run the app. You should have now four REST endpoints—two handling requests by the `MovieController` class (`/v1/movie` and `/v1/movies`) and the others handling requests by Spring Integration and its `<int-http:inbound-channel-adapter/>` tag (`/v2/movie` and `/v2/movies`).

You can test it with cURL.

```
$ curl -i -H "Content-Type:application/json" -X POST -d '[{"title":"The
Matrix","actor":"Keanu Reeves","year":1999},{"title":"Memento","actor":"Guy
Pearce","year":2000}]' http://localhost:8080/v2/movies

HTTP/1.1 202 Accepted
Server: Apache-Coyote/1.1
Content-Length: 0
```

Again, note that you are using version 2 of the API.

Next, continuing with Part II requirements, it is necessary to add a way to store the movies in the database, and then, after that, send an email. One way to do this is by reusing the service activator handlers and creating a common function that stores the movies in the database. For that, you can use a regular JDBC code, the JDBCTemplate that Spring offers, or Hibernate with JPA.

Let's use Spring Integration! It has a component to insert directly into the database (see Listing 3-16).

Listing 3-16. movie-web-app-integration.xml version 2

```
<?xml version="1.0" encoding="UTF-8"?>
<beans xmlns="http://www.springframework.org/schema/beans"
       xmlns:xsi="http://www.w3.org/2001/XMLSchema-instance" xmlns:int="http://www.
       springframework.org/schema/integration"
       xmlns:int-http="http://www.springframework.org/schema/integration/http"
       xmlns:int-mail="http://www.springframework.org/schema/integration/mail"
       xmlns:jdbc="http://www.springframework.org/schema/jdbc" xmlns:int-jdbc="http://www.
       springframework.org/schema/integration/jdbc"
       xsi:schemaLocation="http://www.springframework.org/schema/jdbc http://www.
       springframework.org/schema/jdbc/spring-jdbc.xsd
        http://www.springframework.org/schema/integration/jdbc http://www.springframework.
        org/schema/integration/jdbc/spring-integration-jdbc.xsd
        http://www.springframework.org/schema/beans http://www.springframework.org/schema/
        beans/spring-beans.xsd
        http://www.springframework.org/schema/integration/http http://www.springframework.
        org/schema/integration/http/spring-integration-http.xsd
        http://www.springframework.org/schema/integration/mail http://www.springframework.
        org/schema/integration/mail/spring-integration-mail.xsd
        http://www.springframework.org/schema/integration http://www.springframework.org/
        schema/integration/spring-integration.xsd">

    <!-- Spring Integration -->
    <!-- Spring Integration: Http -->
    <int-http:inbound-channel-adapter id="movie"
                                      supported-methods="POST" channel="input" path="/v2/
                                      movie"
                                      request-payload-type="com.apress.integration.movieweb.
                                      Movie"
                                      status-code-expression="T(org.springframework.http.
                                      HttpStatus).ACCEPTED"
    />

    <int-http:inbound-channel-adapter id="movies"
                                      supported-methods="POST" channel="input" path="/v2/
                                      movies"
                                      request-payload-type="com.apress.integration.movieweb.
                                      Movie[]"
                                      status-code-expression="T(org.springframework.http.
                                      HttpStatus).ACCEPTED"
    />

    <!-- Spring Integration: Execution Channel -->
    <int:channel id="input"/>
```

```
    <!-- Spring Integration: JDBC -->
    <int-jdbc:outbound-channel-adapter
            query="insert into movies (title, actor, year) values ( :payload.title,
            :payload.actor, :payload.year)"
            data-source="dataSource" channel="input" />

</beans>
```

Listing 3-16 shows version 2 of `movie-webapp-integration.xml`. Note that *there is no* service activator anymore, meaning that you can pass a movie into the database directly from the `http:inbound` tag.

- `<int-jdbc:outbound-channel-adapter />` allows you to connect to any JDBC compliant database. (There is also one for NoSQL!) The following are the attributes.
    - `query` sets the SQL statement; the example is very basic one, but you can also do updates and deletes.
    - `data-source` is the name of the datasource, normally, it is a bean that contains all the necessary information to connect to the database, like username, password, URL, and so forth.
    - `channel` is where the tag gets the information.

You should have an integration graph like the one shown in Figure 3-12.

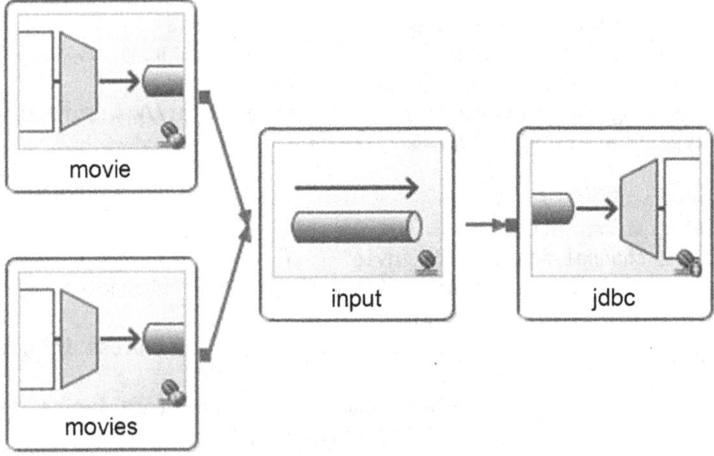

Figure 3-12. *Integration graph*

How is Figure 3-11 different from Figure 3-12? You just remove Service Activate and plug in the JDBC component.

Before you attempt to run the web application, you must make sure you have the SQL driver declared because one of the dependencies is H2. You can add a different one, but you need to make sure that your database engine is up and running.

Because you are using H2, Spring Boot uses the embedded database defaults. It has an in-memory database. If you are using any other database engine, modify the properties in `application.properties` accordingly.

You can add Listing 3-17 to the application.properties file to see if the data is being written into the H2 database engine.

Listing 3-17. src/main/resources/application.properties

```
# H2 Web Console
spring.h2.console.enabled=true

# External DataSource - MySQL
#spring.datasource.url=jdbc:mysql://localhost/testdb
#spring.datasource.username=scdf
#spring.datasource.password=scdf
#spring.datasource.driver-class-name=com.mysql.jdbc.Driver
```

Listing 3-17 shows the contents of the `application.properties` file. I commented some `DataSource` properties so that you can see that you are able to use MySQL or any other DB engine. Adding the `spring.datasource` property creates the `dataSource` bean (the value that you set in the datasource of the `<int-jdbc:outbound-channel-adapter/>` tag). Remember to add the correct credentials for database access, and change the driver class if you are using a different database engine. For now, just use H2.

Next, you need to create a schema to help the JDBC adapters send the data. Spring Boot can automatically generate the table and the database, but you need to use a different engine, like Hibernate/JPA. This example uses the JDBC driver (no JPA), so you need to provide a `src/main/resources/schema.sql` file that contains the table creation (see Listing 3-18).

Listing 3-18. src/main/resources/schema.sql

```
create table IF NOT EXISTS movies(
    id int not null auto_increment,
    title varchar(250),
    actor varchar(100),
    year smallint,
primary key(id));
```

Listing 3-18 is a very basic table where the main fields are declared.

Now, you can run the application, and use the cURL function like in the next snippet.

```
$ curl -i -H "Content-Type:application/json" -X POST -d '{"title":"The
Matrix","actor":"Keanu Reeves","year":1990}' http://localhost:8080/v2/movie

HTTP/1.1 202 Accepted
Server: Apache-Coyote/1.1
Content-Length: 0
```

Open your browser and point to `http://localhost:8080/h2-console/` to open the H2 console (see Figure 3-13).

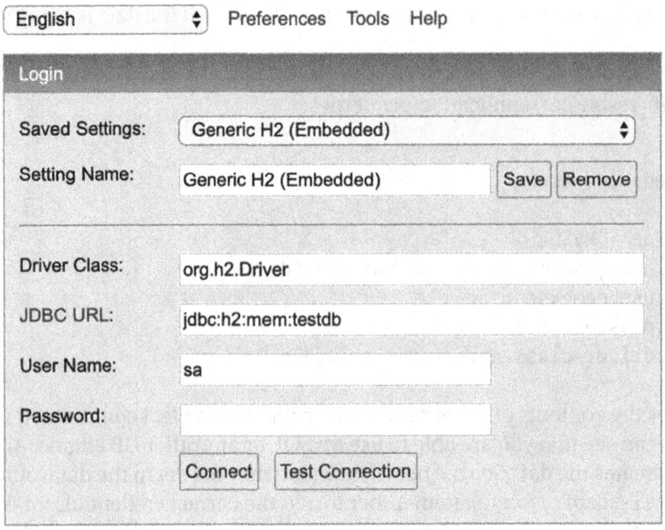

English Preferences Tools Help

Login

Saved Settings: Generic H2 (Embedded)

Setting Name: Generic H2 (Embedded) Save Remove

Driver Class: org.h2.Driver

JDBC URL: jdbc:h2:mem:testdb

User Name: sa

Password:

Connect Test Connection

Figure 3-13. *http://localhost:8080/h2-console*

You should be able to connect with the URL `jdbc:h2:mem:testdb`, the username `sa`, and an empty password. Click Connect. Figure 3-14 shows a defined Movies table, which includes the record that you posted.

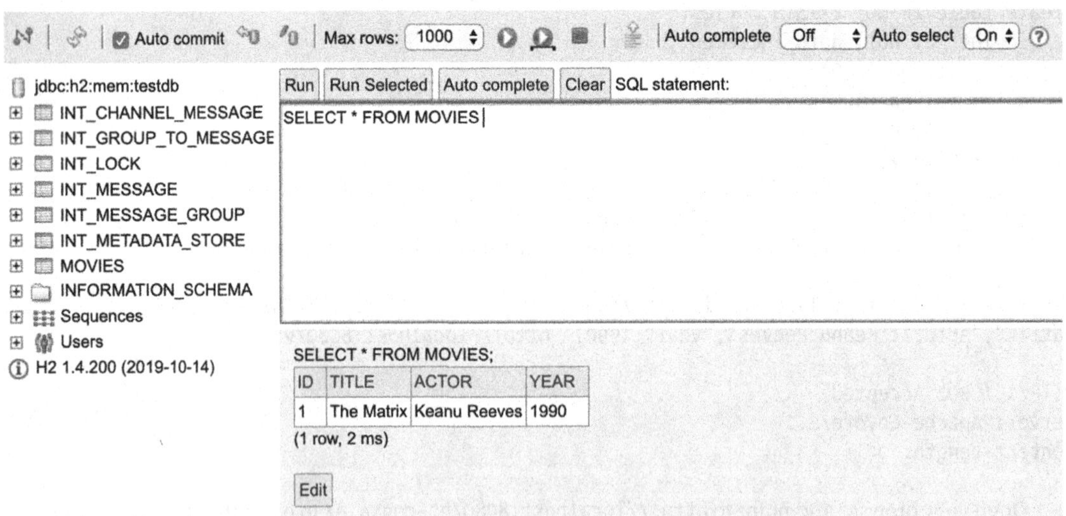

Figure 3-14. *H2 console*

Did you notice that the `curl` command was executed using the `/v2/movie` path and posted a single movie? How can you post a collection of movies and insert them in one call? There are many ways to implement this. For example, using a service activator that handles the collection (something like you saw in Listing 3-14) sends every movie by using another direct channel connected to the `<int-jdbc:outbout-channel-adapter/>` tag. Think about what would happen if you need to stop the insert and then resume or schedule for a specific day and time. It gets a little complicated using Spring Integration, right? The good part is that there is a way to do this kind of task, but that is your homework. Don't worry. I'll give you a hint—Spring Batch!

The next requirement is to send an email once the movie/movies are stored. Let's start with the final version of `movie-webapp-integration.xml` (see Listing 3-19).

Listing 3-19. src/main/resources/META-INF/spring/movie-webapp-integration.xml (version 3)

```
<?xml version="1.0" encoding="UTF-8"?>
<beans xmlns="http://www.springframework.org/schema/beans"
       xmlns:xsi="http://www.w3.org/2001/XMLSchema-instance" xmlns:int="http://www.
       springframework.org/schema/integration"
       xmlns:int-http="http://www.springframework.org/schema/integration/http"
       xmlns:int-mail="http://www.springframework.org/schema/integration/mail"
       xmlns:jdbc="http://www.springframework.org/schema/jdbc" xmlns:int-jdbc="http://www.
       springframework.org/schema/integration/jdbc"
       xsi:schemaLocation="http://www.springframework.org/schema/jdbc http://www.
       springframework.org/schema/jdbc/spring-jdbc.xsd
        http://www.springframework.org/schema/integration/jdbc http://www.springframework.
        org/schema/integration/jdbc/spring-integration-jdbc.xsd
        http://www.springframework.org/schema/beans http://www.springframework.org/schema/
        beans/spring-beans.xsd
        http://www.springframework.org/schema/integration/http http://www.springframework.
        org/schema/integration/http/spring-integration-http.xsd
        http://www.springframework.org/schema/integration/mail http://www.springframework.
        org/schema/integration/mail/spring-integration-mail.xsd
        http://www.springframework.org/schema/integration http://www.springframework.org/
        schema/integration/spring-integration.xsd">

    <!-- Spring Integration -->
    <!-- Spring Integration: Http -->
    <int-http:inbound-channel-adapter id="movie"
                                      supported-methods="POST" channel="publisher"
                                      path="/v2/movie"
                                      request-payload-type="com.apress.integration.movieweb.
                                      Movie"
                                      status-code-expression="T(org.springframework.http.
                                      HttpStatus).ACCEPTED"
    />

    <int-http:inbound-channel-adapter id="movies"
                                      supported-methods="POST" channel="publisher"
                                      path="/v2/movies"
                                      request-payload-type="com.apress.integration.movieweb.
                                      Movie[]"
                                      status-code-expression="T(org.springframework.http.
                                      HttpStatus).ACCEPTED"
    />

    <!-- Publish/Subscribe Channel -->
    <int:publish-subscribe-channel id="publisher" />
```

```
    <!-- Spring Integration: JDBC -->
    <int-jdbc:outbound-channel-adapter id="jdbc"
                                       query="insert into movies (title, actor, year) values
                                       ( :payload.title, :payload.actor, :payload.year)"
                                       data-source="dataSource" channel="publisher"
                                       order="1"  />

    <!-- Spring Integration: Mail -->
    <int-mail:outbound-channel-adapter channel="mail" mail-sender="mailSender" />
    <int:service-activator input-channel="publisher" output-channel="mail"
    ref="movieMailEndpoint" order="2" />
    <int:channel id="mail">
        <int:dispatcher task-executor="taskExecutor"/>
    </int:channel>

        <!-- More definitions in the next section ... -->

</beans>
```

Listing 3-19 shows is the final version of movie-webapp-integration.xml. What is new?

- <int:publish-subscribe-channel id="publisher"/> creates a channel using the Publish-Subscribe pattern. It sends the message to all the subscribers in the order specified (this is done by the subscriber adding the order attribute).
- <int-jdbc:outbound-channel-adapter/> stores the movie and now is a subscriber of the publisher channel. Let's look at the attributes and their values.
    - channel="publisher" is a subscriber of the publisher channel.
    - order="1" received the message first.
- <int:service-activator/> is a new service activator that creates the MailMessage instance to be delivered to the mail channel. The following are its attributes.
    - ref="movieMailEndpoint" is the bean reference class.
    - order="2" means that the service activator received the message after the storage.
    - output-channel="mail" is the name of the channel where the MailMessage instance is sent.
- <int-channel> is a new channel (executor channel) receiving the MailMessage instance. This channel is executed through a task executor, meaning that it can be an asynchronous call. The following are its attributes.
    - <int:dispatcher/> declares the class that makes the async call possible.
    - task-executor="taskExecutor" is the name of the bean implementation of the Task Executor class.

- `<int-mail:outbound-channel-adapter/>` is a new tag that sends email based on the parameters given in the `mailSender` properties (inside the `application.properties` file).
    - `mail-sender="mailSender"` is the name of the bean. The Spring container generates this bean based on the `application.properties` file looking at the `email.<props>`.

The Spring Integration graph of the final version is shown in Figure 3-15.

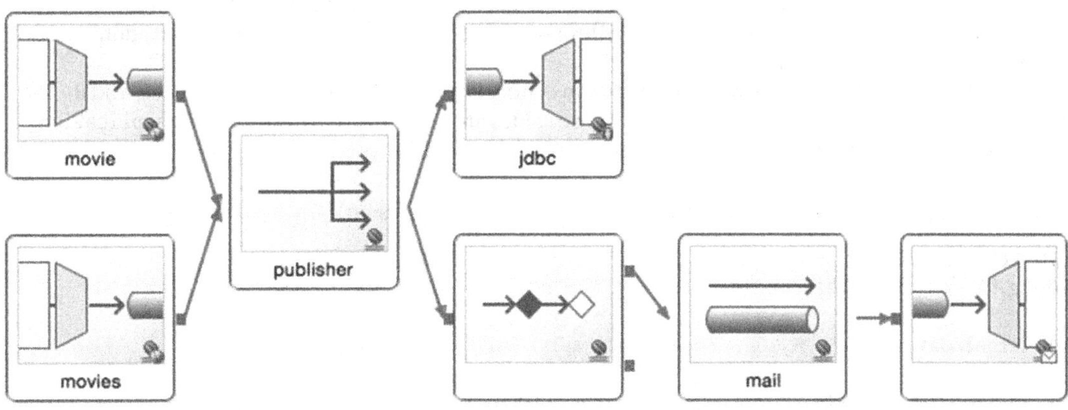

Figure 3-15. *Spring Integration graph*

Listing 3-19 shows that you have a dependency on two beans: `taskExecutor` and `emailSender`. Add the following bean declarations to `movie-webapp-integration.xml` (see Listing 3-20).

Listing 3-20. src/main/resources/META-INF/spring/movie-webapp-integration.xml (extra declaration dependencies)

```
<!-- Mail Properties -->
<bean id="mailSender" class="org.springframework.mail.javamail.JavaMailSenderImpl">
    <property name="host" value="${email.host}" />
    <property name="port" value="${email.port}" />
    <property name="username" value="${email.account.name}" />
    <property name="password" value="${email.account.password}" />
    <property name="javaMailProperties">
        <props>
            <prop key="mail.smtp.starttls.enable">true</prop>
            <prop key="mail.smtp.auth">true</prop>
        </props>
    </property>
</bean>

<!-- Helpers -->
<bean id="taskExecutor" class="org.springframework.scheduling.concurrent.
ThreadPoolTaskExecutor">
    <property name="corePoolSize" value="5" />
    <property name="maxPoolSize" value="10" />
    <property name="queueCapacity" value="25" />
</bean>
```

```
<!-- JSON Converter -->
<bean id="jsonConverter"
      class="org.springframework.http.converter.json.
      MappingJackson2HttpMessageConverter">
    <property name="supportedMediaTypes" value="application/json" />
</bean>
```

Listing 3-20 shows the `mailSender` bean definition and the `taskExecutor` definition that needs to be added to the *movie-webapp-integration.xml* file. The `taskExecutor` bean defines the `ThreadPoolTaskExecutor` class that acts as asynchronous handler for sending the email, so you don't need to way until the server responds.

`mailSender` has all the necessary information to connect to any SMTP provider you choose, and it offers a way to expose the values as properties. Those values are in the `src/main/resources/application.properties` file (see Listing 3-21).

Listing 3-21. src/main/resources/application.properties file (final version)

```
# H2 Web Console
spring.h2.console.enabled=true

# External DataSource - MySQL

#spring.datasource.url=jdbc:mysql://localhost/springxd
#spring.datasource.username=springxd
#spring.datasource.password=springxd
#spring.datasource.driver-class-name=com.mysql.jdbc.Driver
#spring.datasource.initialize=true

email.account.name=myuser@mydomain.com
email.account.password=mypassword
email.host=smtp.gmail.com
email.port=587
```

The properties shown in Listing 3-21 use the Gmail SMTP service provider. Listing 3-22 (`movie-webapp-integration.xml`) defines a reference of `movieWebMailEndpoint` in the service activator. Listing 3-22 shows this class.

Listing 3-22. com.apress.spring.integration.MovieWebMailEndpoint.java

```
package com.apress.integration.movieweb;

import org.slf4j.Logger;
import org.slf4j.LoggerFactory;
import org.springframework.integration.annotation.MessageEndpoint;
import org.springframework.integration.annotation.ServiceActivator;
import org.springframework.mail.MailMessage;
import org.springframework.mail.SimpleMailMessage;
import org.springframework.messaging.handler.annotation.Headers;

import java.util.Date;
import java.util.Map;
```

```
@MessageEndpoint
public class MovieMailEndpoint {

    private static final Logger log = LoggerFactory.getLogger(MovieMailEndpoint.class);

    @ServiceActivator
    public MailMessage process(Movie movie, @Headers Map<String,Object> headers) throws
    Exception {
        log.info("Movie: " + movie);

        SimpleMailMessage mailMessage = new SimpleMailMessage();
        mailMessage.setTo("myuser@mydomain.com");
        mailMessage.setSubject("A new Movie is in Town");
        mailMessage.setSentDate(new Date(0));
        mailMessage.setText(movie.toString());

        return mailMessage;
    }
}
```

Listing 3-22 shows the `Message` Endpoint and the service activator handler. This particular handler returns the `MailMessage` instance that is needed by the `<int-mail:outbound-channel-adapter/>` tag. This is where you add the To, Subject, and Text of the email message. The handler is using the `Movie` object and the header on the `Message` instance.

You can run a final test to see that the movie is stored, and then you get the message into your inbox. Make sure you have the right properties set, and you shouldn't have any issues. Remember that all the code in this chapter can be downloaded from the Apress web site.

Now it is time to run both parts. You can use Maven (in a separate window terminal), or you can choose to run your favorite IDE to see the complete flow!

■ **Note** If you are running STS and want to run both projects, you need to disable the Live Bean Support feature in the menu: Run ➤ Run Configurations, choose the configuration, and uncheck the Live Bean Support feature.

Congratulations! You just created a Spring Integration app that integrates two systems. In the end, you didn't use much code in it. Spring Integration does most of the heavy work. Even though this is a simple example, you know how to integrate systems like JMS, RabbitMQ, or SOAP, or to integrate with social media platforms like Facebook or Twitter.

Summary

This chapter introduced you to Spring Integration. You saw Spring Integration components and how it relies on messages, channels, and endpoints. You saw a few integration patterns and how Spring Integration facilitates the use of them.

You saw through an example how to use Spring Integration. And, you saw how easy it is to create apps with almost zero code and integrate them with other components or local/external systems.

Why is Spring Integration important? Spring Cloud Data Flow is based on Spring Integration, making it very reliable, scalable, and easy to extend. If you want to learn more about Spring Integration, Apress has very good titles.

CHAPTER 4

Spring Batch

In the previous chapter, I showed you what you can do with Spring Integration, a lightweight framework that connects external systems and processes to all kinds of data. But what happens when you need to do bulk processing? What happens when you need to perform business operations at a certain time in a mission-critical environment? How do you automate processing a large amount of data? How do you integrate an external system to process large data sets?

What is the typical system/scenario needed for a large data set? You probably need to **read** from a database or a file system (like HDFS), or maybe from message brokers with millions of messages queued. Then, you need to **process** that information based on business rules, and you need to split the data into multiple chunks that must be enhanced. Finally, you need to **write** the data to another engine/system (internal or external). Is there a framework that can execute such a scenario? Yes, Spring Batch!

Spring Batch

Spring Batch is a lightweight batch framework that allows you to create repeatable steps (read, write, process) for a large volume of data. It provides mechanisms for logging/tracing, job processing, job start/stop/restart, transaction management, sequential and partial processing, massive parallel processing, and more! One of the key benefits of using Spring Batch is that it follows the same principles as the Spring Framework, giving developers a way to create simple business classes based on POJOs (Plain Old Java Objects), a clear separation of concerns between infrastructures, a batch execution environment and a batch application, a default implementation of the core execution, an easy way to configure, customized and extend services, and an easy way to increase productivity. All this makes Spring Batch an ideal framework for batch processing.

Spring Batch is a collection of proven algorithms that support very high volumes of data, giving you the best performance through optimization logic and partition techniques. Spring Batch is a Spring ecosystem project that has become an IT standard for batch processing.

Programming Model

In Spring Batch, there are name conventions. You hear about declaring a job, steps, tasklets, chunks, read-process-write, and so forth, but you need to have some principles in mind.

1 Step = 1 Read-Process-Write = Tasklet

1 Job = Many Steps = Step 1 > Step 2 > Step 3 ... (Chained)

F. Gutierrez, *Spring Cloud Data Flow*, https://doi.org/10.1007/978-1-4842-1239-4_4

Figure 4-1 is a good picture of Spring Batch idioms.

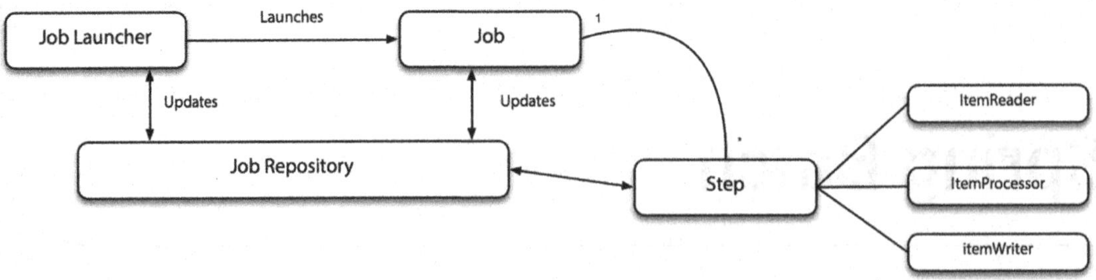

Figure 4-1. *Spring Batch stereotypes/idioms*

Batch processing (read-process-write) is the same as any other input-process-output or channel-process-channel pattern. You have jobs that contain defined steps, and these steps are chained. One of the benefits is that you can stop a job and resume it later, or at runtime, you can skip certain jobs based on an expression. Do you think that some of the patterns that Spring Batch offers are based on Spring Integration? Yes, they are!

Spring Batch Features

Spring Batch is a model based on customer use cases, and considers security, speed, performance, and reliability. The following are some Spring Batch features.

- Start/stop/restart jobs
- Retry/skip
- Declarative I/O
- Chunk-based processing
- Partition techniques
- Transaction management
- Web-based administration

Every Spring Batch application has an internal database that keeps track of the steps that are being executed, which ones are skipped, which jobs have been triggered, failures and successes, and more.

I think the best way to understand Spring Batch is with a simple example. The example is based on the Movie app from the previous chapter. You will use it later in the Spring Cloud Data Flow, batch, and cloud task processing.

Movie Batch App Using Declarative XML

The Movie Batch app reads from a CSV file and inserts each line as a record in the database. Again, this is a very simple example, but it is enough to demonstrate what you can do with Spring Batch. In this app, you use a declarative approach with an XML context. We use the programmatic approach not only for batch processing but with Spring Integration later in the chapter.

You can start by going to `https://start.spring.io` (see Figure 4-2).

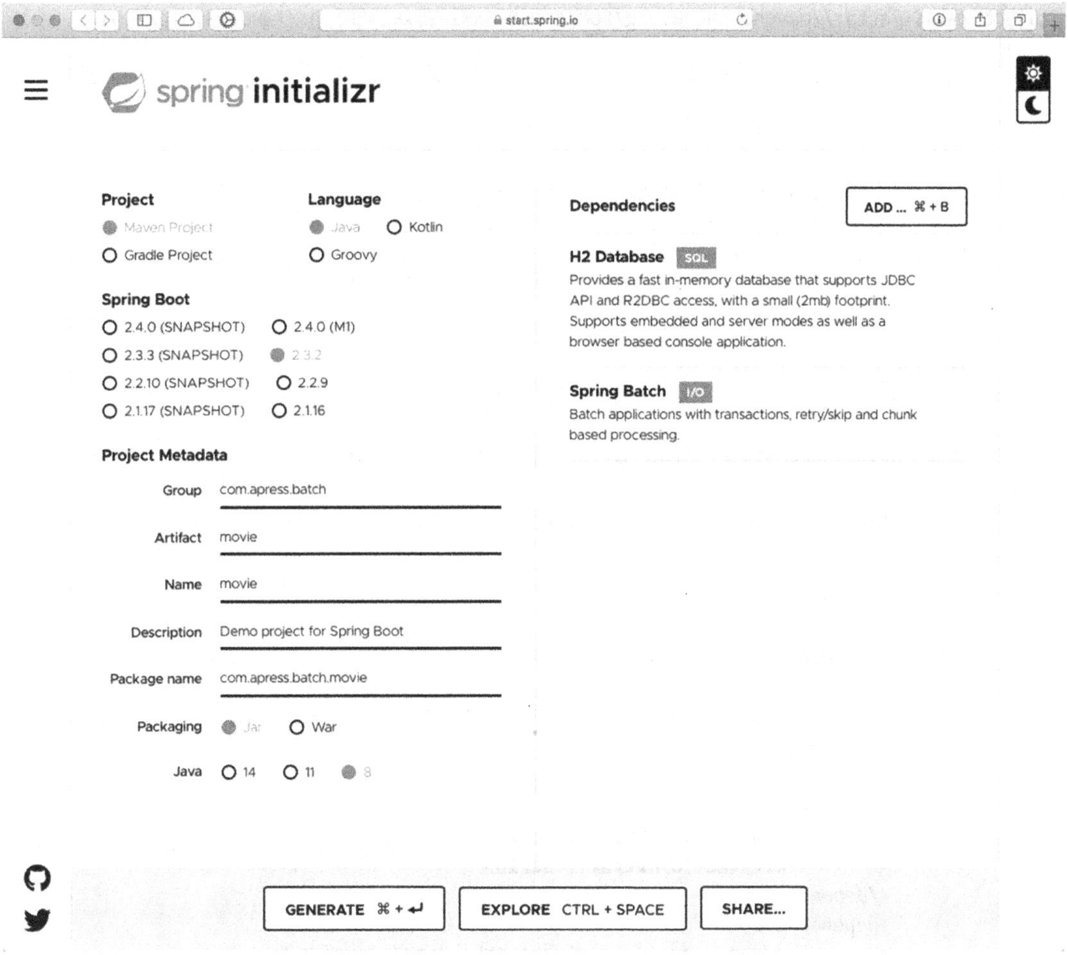

Figure 4-2. *`https://start.spring.io`—Spring Initializr*

You can use the following information to fill out the input fields.

- Group: `com.apress.batch`
- Artifact: `movie`
- Dependencies: Spring Batch, H2 Database

Press the Generate button to create a ZIP file for download. Once downloaded, you can unzip it and open it in your favorite IDE. Remember that Spring Batch keeps a record of any step, job, or execution, so it is necessary to include a DB engine driver; in this case, very useful for development, the H2 driver. Let's review the project. Open `pom.xml` (see Listing 4-1).

Listing 4-1. pom.xml

```
<?xml version="1.0" encoding="UTF-8"?>
<project xmlns="http://maven.apache.org/POM/4.0.0" xmlns:xsi="http://www.w3.org/2001/
XMLSchema-instance"
        xsi:schemaLocation="http://maven.apache.org/POM/4.0.0 https://maven.apache.org/xsd/
        maven-4.0.0.xsd">
        <modelVersion>4.0.0</modelVersion>
        <parent>
                <groupId>org.springframework.boot</groupId>
                <artifactId>spring-boot-starter-parent</artifactId>
                <version>2.2.2.RELEASE</version>
                <relativePath/> <!-- lookup parent from repository -->
        </parent>
        <groupId>com.apress.batch</groupId>
        <artifactId>movie</artifactId>
        <version>0.0.1-SNAPSHOT</version>
        <name>movie</name>
        <description>Demo project for Spring Boot</description>

        <properties>
                <java.version>1.8</java.version>
        </properties>

        <dependencies>
                <dependency>
                        <groupId>org.springframework.boot</groupId>
                        <artifactId>spring-boot-starter-batch</artifactId>
                </dependency>

                <dependency>
                        <groupId>com.h2database</groupId>
                        <artifactId>h2</artifactId>
                </dependency>
                <dependency>
                        <groupId>org.springframework.boot</groupId>
                        <artifactId>spring-boot-starter-test</artifactId>
                        <scope>test</scope>
                        <exclusions>
                                <exclusion>
                                        <groupId>org.junit.vintage</groupId>
                                        <artifactId>junit-vintage-engine</artifactId>
                                </exclusion>
                        </exclusions>
                </dependency>
                <dependency>
                        <groupId>org.springframework.batch</groupId>
                        <artifactId>spring-batch-test</artifactId>
                        <scope>test</scope>
                </dependency>
        </dependencies>
```

```
    <build>
        <plugins>
            <plugin>
                <groupId>org.springframework.boot</groupId>
                <artifactId>spring-boot-maven-plugin</artifactId>
            </plugin>
        </plugins>
    </build>

</project>
```

Listing 4-1 shows your `pom.xml` file. (You need to remove the default `<scope/>` tag that comes as the runtime for the H2 database.) Set the H2 database as the server. You could use any other client, such as MySQL, PostgreSQL, or any other DB engine; but in this case, we are using H2 as the server mode.

Next, create the `Movie` model class (see Listing 4-2).

Listing 4-2. com.apress.batch.movie.Movie.java

```java
package com.apress.batch.movie;

public class Movie {
    private String title;
    private String actor;
    private int year;

    public Movie(){}

    public Movie(String title, String actor, int year){
        this.title = title;
        this.actor = actor;
        this.year = year;
    }

    public String getTitle() {
        return title;
    }
    public void setTitle(String title) {
        this.title = title;
    }
    public String getActor() {
        return actor;
    }
    public void setActor(String actor) {
        this.actor = actor;
    }
    public int getYear() {
        return year;
    }
    public void setYear(int year) {
        this.year = year;
    }
```

```
    public String toString(){
        StringBuilder builder = new StringBuilder();
        builder.append("Movie(tile: ");
        builder.append(title);
        builder.append(", actor: ");
        builder.append(actor);
        builder.append(", year: ");
        builder.append(year);
        builder.append(")");
        return builder.toString();
    }
}
```

Listing 4-2 shows the Movie class (nothing changed from the previous chapter; it is a simple POJO class). Next, create the MovieConfiguration class to set up the H2 server and load the batch context file (see Listing 4-3).

Listing 4-3. com.apress.batch.movie.MovieConfiguration.java

```
package com.apress.batch.movie;

import org.h2.tools.Server;
import org.springframework.batch.core.configuration.annotation.EnableBatchProcessing;
import org.springframework.context.annotation.Bean;
import org.springframework.context.annotation.Configuration;
import org.springframework.context.annotation.ImportResource;

import java.sql.SQLException;

@Configuration
@EnableBatchProcessing
@ImportResource("META-INF/spring/movie-batch-context.xml")
public class MovieConfiguration {
   @Bean(initMethod = "start", destroyMethod = "stop")
    public Server h2Server() throws SQLException {
        return Server.createTcpServer("-tcp", "-ifNotExists","-tcpAllowOthers", "-tcpPort",
        "9092");
    }

}
```

Listing 4-3 shows the MovieConfiguration class. You already know about having a configuration class and how to import a context resource; the only thing new is @EnableBatchProcessing. This annotation does the following.

- Recognizes the DB engine. Because you added H2 as a dependency, Spring Batch does everything related to H2 or any other engine you add to your classpath through the pom.xml file.
- Initializes the internal SQL scripts to create the BATCH tables.
    - BATCH_JOB_EXECUTION
    - BATCH_JOB_EXECUTION_CONTEXT

- BATCH_JOB_EXECUTION_PARAMS
- BATCH_JOB_EXECUTION_SEQ
- BATCH_JOB_INSTANCE
- BATCH_JOB_SEQ
- BATCH_STEP_EXECUTION
- BATCH_STEP_EXECUTION_CONTEXT
- BATCH_STEP_EXECUTION_SEQ

- Discovers and configures any job
- Executes the job as defined

Listing 4-3 shows the @Bean annotation where we are creating h2Server. To set the H2 as a server mode, it is necessary to call createTcpServer with some options. Normally, those options are set as arguments when you execute the java -jar command to h2.jar; but here we are starting it within the app.

Let's import the movie-batch-context.xml file with the @ImportResource annotation. Next, let's create an XML configuration file because it drives every detail of this application (see Listing 4-4).

Listing 4-4. src/main/resources/META-INF/spring/movie-batch-context.xml

```
<?xml version="1.0" encoding="UTF-8"?>
<beans xmlns="http://www.springframework.org/schema/beans"
       xmlns:xsi="http://www.w3.org/2001/XMLSchema-instance"
       xmlns:jdbc="http://www.springframework.org/schema/jdbc"
       xmlns:batch="http://www.springframework.org/schema/batch"
       xsi:schemaLocation="
        http://www.springframework.org/schema/batch http://www.springframework.org/schema/
        batch/spring-batch.xsd
       http://www.springframework.org/schema/jdbc http://www.springframework.org/schema/
       jdbc/spring-jdbc.xsd
       http://www.springframework.org/schema/beans http://www.springframework.org/schema/
       beans/spring-beans.xsd">

    <bean id="movie" class="com.apress.batch.movie.Movie" scope="prototype"/>

    <batch:job id="movieJob">
        <batch:step id="step1">
            <batch:tasklet>
                <batch:chunk reader="movieFieldItemReader" writer="dbItemWriter" commit-
                interval="2"/>
            </batch:tasklet>
        </batch:step>
    </batch:job>

    <bean id="movieFieldItemReader" class="org.springframework.batch.item.file.
    FlatFileItemReader">
        <property name="resource" value="movies.txt"/>
        <property name="lineMapper">
            <bean class="org.springframework.batch.item.file.mapping.DefaultLineMapper">
                <property name="lineTokenizer">
```

```
                <bean class="org.springframework.batch.item.file.transform.
                DelimitedLineTokenizer">
                    <property name="names" value="title,actor,year"/>
                </bean>
            </property>
            <property name="fieldSetMapper">
                <bean class="org.springframework.batch.item.file.mapping.
                BeanWrapperFieldSetMapper">
                    <property name="prototypeBeanName" value="movie"/>
                </bean>
            </property>

        </bean>
    </property>

</bean>

<bean id="dbItemWriter"
      class="org.springframework.batch.item.database.JdbcBatchItemWriter">
    <property name="dataSource" ref="dataSource"/>
    <property name="sql">
        <value>
            <![CDATA[
            insert into movies(title,actor,year)
                    values (:title, :actor, :year)
        ]]>
        </value>
    </property>
    <property name="itemSqlParameterSourceProvider">
        <bean class="org.springframework.batch.item.database.
        BeanPropertyItemSqlParameterSourceProvider"/>
    </property>
</bean>

</beans>
```

Listing 4-4 shows all the required beans that you will use, but the important one is the namespace `xmlns:batch` tag. It provides the following.

- `<batch:job/>` defines the batch job with the name `movieJob`.
- `<batch:step/>` defines a step within the job.
- `<batch:tasklet/>` defines a particular task within the step (a tasklet).
- `<batch:chunk/>` defines the process (chunk), the reads (input), and the writes (output).

The following are to be reused.

- The movies text file: title, actor, and year (in a CSV format). This `movies.txt` file should be in your classpath so you can add it to the `src/main/resources` directory.
- You need to add in `src/main/resources` to the `schema.sql` file.

The other bean definitions are self-explanatory and easy to understand. If you want to know more about Spring Batch, I recommend *The Definitive Guide to Spring Batch* by Michael Minella (Apress, 2019).

Next, open the `application.properties` file and add the content shown in Listing 4-5.

Listing 4-5. src/main/resources/application.properties

```
# Local DB
spring.datasource.url=jdbc:h2:~/movies_db;AUTO_SERVER=TRUE
spring.datasource.username=sa
spring.datasource.password=
spring.datasource.initialization-mode=always
```

Listing 4-5 shows the properties that are required; because you set the H2 as server mode, Spring Boot does not execute its initialization of the in-memory database because it was overridden when we declared the Spring Bean `h2Server` (we are using a different URL: `jdbc:h2:~/movies_db;AUTO_SERVER=TRUE`). In this case, the H2 server created a file named `movie_db` (with `.lock.db` and `.mv.db` extensions) in your home directory. You can specify the path where you want the data stored.

Now, you can run your application. Open a terminal window and execute it.

```
$ ./mvnw clean spring-boot:run
```

Your output should look similar to the following.

```
]: Job: [FlowJob: [name=movieJob]] launched with the following parameters: [{}]
]: Executing step: [step1]
]: Step: [step1] executed in 65ms
]: Job: [FlowJob: [name=movieJob]] completed with the following parameters: [{}] and the
following status: [COMPLETED] in 91ms
```

The preceding output prints the job, the step execution, and when it was completed. You can see that the program keeps running, and that's because you set up the H2 as the server mode. You can review that Spring Batch read the file and dumped its contents in the database—a row per line from the `movies.txt` file. To verify this, you can use a UI like the SQuirreL SQL client (`https://sourceforge.net/projects/squirrel-sql/`) to see the contens (see Figure 4-3).

ID	TITLE	ACTOR	YEAR
1	The Matrix	Keanu Reeves	1999
2	Memento	Guy Pearce	2000
3	The Silence of the Lambs	Jodie Foster	1991
4	The Prestige	Christian Bale	2006
5	Disturbia	Shia LaBeouf	2007

Figure 4-3. *SQuirreL SQL client (`https://sourceforge.net/projects/squirrel-sql/`)*

Figure 4-3 shows the Squirrel SQL client. You need to use the same URL, `jdbc:h2:~/movies_db;AUTO_SERVER=TRUE`, to connect.

If you don't want to use an external UI, you can verify that the data is there by adding a small amount of code to your app. Create the `MovieQueryInfo` class shown in Listing 4-6.

Listing 4-6. com.apress.batch.movie.MovieQueryInfo.java

```
package com.apress.batch.movie;

import org.springframework.boot.CommandLineRunner;
import org.springframework.context.annotation.Bean;
import org.springframework.context.annotation.Configuration;
import org.springframework.jdbc.core.JdbcTemplate;

@Configuration
public class MovieQueryInfo {

    @Bean
    public CommandLineRunner getInfo(JdbcTemplate jdbcTemplate){
        return args -> {
            jdbcTemplate.query(
                    "select title,actor,year from movies",
                    (rs, rowNum) ->
                            new Movie(
                                    rs.getString("title"),
                                    rs.getString("actor"),
                                    rs.getInt("year")
                            )
            ).forEach(System.out::println);
        };
    }
}
```

Listing 4-6 shows a configuration file that is declaring the `getInfo` bean as `CommandLineRunner`, meaning that is run once the Spring container is configured and ready to run. You can re-run the app, and you should get the following output.

```
Movie(tile: The Matrix, actor: Keanu Reeves, year: 1999)
Movie(tile: Memento, actor: Guy Pearce, year: 2000)
Movie(tile: The Silence of the Lambs, actor: Jodie Foster, year: 1991)
Movie(tile: The Prestige, actor: Christian Bale, year: 2006)
Movie(tile: Disturbia, actor: Shia LaBeouf, year: 2007)
```

Congratulations, you created your first Spring Batch application!

Movie Batch App Using JavaConfig

Let's change our Movie app by using the JavaConfig approach. You are also going to read an XML file that lists movies. The idea is the same: read XML movies files, and save every movie into a row in a database.

Let's start by creating a new project. The only modification from the previous project is the `ArtifactId` name. Let's name it `movie-custom`, with the same dependencies: Spring Batch and the H2 database. This project has a different package name: `com.apress.batch.moviecustom`. It is based on the `ArtifactId` value. Figure 4-4 shows the structure and classes.

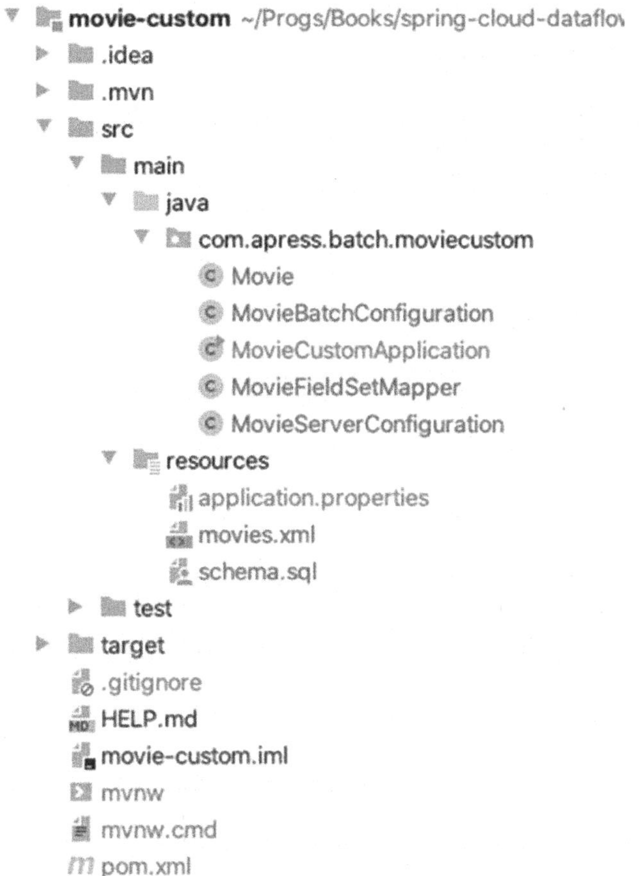

Figure 4-4. *Spring Batch project: movie-custom*

First, we need to add the dependencies in Listing 4-7to the `pom.xml` file.

Listing 4-7. pom.xml New Dependencies

```
<dependency>
        <groupId>org.springframework</groupId>
        <artifactId>spring-oxm</artifactId>
</dependency>
<dependency>
        <groupId>com.thoughtworks.xstream</groupId>
        <artifactId>xstream</artifactId>
        <version>1.4.11.1</version>
</dependency>
```

Listing 4-7 shows the new dependencies that read XML files and marshal them to the `Movie` object. Next, create a new `MovieServerConfiguration` class (see Listing 4-8).

Listing 4-8. com.apress.batch.moviecustom.MovieServerConfiguration.java

```
package com.apress.batch.moviecustom;

import org.h2.tools.Server;
import org.springframework.context.annotation.Bean;
import org.springframework.context.annotation.Configuration;

import java.sql.SQLException;

@Configuration
public class MovieServerConfiguration {

   @Bean(initMethod = "start", destroyMethod = "stop")
    public Server h2Server() throws SQLException {
        return Server.createTcpServer("-tcp", "-ifNotExists","-tcpAllowOthers", "-tcpPort",
        "9092");
    }

    @Bean(initMethod = "start", destroyMethod = "stop")
    public Server h2WebServer() throws SQLException {
        return Server.createWebServer("-web", "-ifNotExists","-webAllowOthers", "-webPort",
        "8092");
    }

}
```

Listing 4-8 shows the `MovieServerConfiguration` class. This class is declaring two beans—the `h2Server` bean from the previous app and the new `h2WebServer` that sets the H2 server as accessible from a web page. This comes in handy in development, and you don't need any extra SQL UI. Review the code. You see that it is very straightforward.

Next, let's create the `MovieFieldMapper` class (see Listing 4-9).

Listing 4-9. com.apress.batch.moviecustom.MovieFieldMapper.java

```
package com.apress.batch.moviecustom;

import org.springframework.batch.item.file.mapping.FieldSetMapper;
import org.springframework.batch.item.file.transform.FieldSet;
import org.springframework.validation.BindException;

public class MovieFieldSetMapper implements FieldSetMapper<Movie> {
    @Override
    public Movie mapFieldSet(FieldSet fieldSet) throws BindException {
        return new Movie(
                fieldSet.readString("title"),
                fieldSet.readString("actor"),
                fieldSet.readInt("year"));
    }
}
```

Listing 4-9 shows the MovieFieldSetMapper class, which is the declarative portion used in Listing 4-4 (movie-batch-context.xml), where we declared the movieFieldItemReader and the fieldSetMapper beans.

Next, create the MovieBatchConfiguration class (see Listing 4-10).

Listing 4-10. com.apress.batch.moviecustom.MovieBatchConfiguration.java

```
package com.apress.batch.moviecustom;

import org.springframework.batch.core.Job;
import org.springframework.batch.core.Step;
import org.springframework.batch.core.configuration.annotation.EnableBatchProcessing;
import org.springframework.batch.core.configuration.annotation.JobBuilderFactory;
import org.springframework.batch.core.configuration.annotation.StepBuilderFactory;
import org.springframework.batch.item.database.BeanPropertyItemSqlParameterSourceProvider;
import org.springframework.batch.item.database.JdbcBatchItemWriter;
import org.springframework.batch.item.xml.StaxEventItemReader;
import org.springframework.beans.factory.annotation.Autowired;
import org.springframework.context.annotation.Bean;
import org.springframework.context.annotation.Configuration;
import org.springframework.core.io.ClassPathResource;
import org.springframework.oxm.xstream.XStreamMarshaller;

import javax.sql.DataSource;
import java.util.HashMap;
import java.util.Map;

@Configuration
@EnableBatchProcessing
public class MovieBatchConfiguration {

    @Autowired
    public JobBuilderFactory jobBuilderFactory;

    @Autowired
    public StepBuilderFactory stepBuilderFactory;

    @Autowired
    public DataSource dataSource;

    @Bean
    public StaxEventItemReader<Movie> movieItemReader() {

        XStreamMarshaller unmarshaller = new XStreamMarshaller();

        Map<String, Class> aliases = new HashMap<>();
        aliases.put("movie", Movie.class);

        unmarshaller.setAliases(aliases);

        StaxEventItemReader<Movie> reader = new StaxEventItemReader<>();
```

```
        reader.setResource(new ClassPathResource("/movies.xml"));
        reader.setFragmentRootElementName("movie");
        reader.setUnmarshaller(unmarshaller);

        return reader;
    }

    @Bean
    public JdbcBatchItemWriter<Movie> movieItemWriter() {
        JdbcBatchItemWriter<Movie> itemWriter = new JdbcBatchItemWriter<>();

        itemWriter.setDataSource(dataSource);
        itemWriter.setSql("INSERT INTO movies (title,actor,year) VALUES (:title, :actor,
        :year)");
        itemWriter.setItemSqlParameterSourceProvider(new BeanPropertyItemSqlParameter
        SourceProvider());
        itemWriter.afterPropertiesSet();

        return itemWriter;
    }

    @Bean
    public Step step1() {
        return stepBuilderFactory.get("step1")
                .<Movie, Movie>chunk(10)
                .reader(movieItemReader())
                .writer(movieItemWriter())
                .build();
    }

    @Bean
    public Job job() {
        return jobBuilderFactory.get("job")
                .start(step1())
                .build();
    }
}
```

Listing 4-10 shows the MovieBatchConfiguration class, which is the same as the XML configuration. Let's review it.

- JobBuilderFactory. This class is a fluent API that allows you to create a Job (JobInstance). Job is a container for Step instances. It can combine multiple steps that belong together in a flow; it supports restartability for the steps. JobInstance is a logical job run, and it creates JobExecution, which keeps track of what's going on in every step. The job bean uses the JobBuilderFactory instance to start with a simple step and then add more. The following is an example.

```
@Bean
public Job consumerCreditCardJob() {
return this.jobBuilderFactory.get("consumerCreditCardJob")
        .start(consumerLoad())
        .next(processLoad())
        .next(applyInterest())
```

```
            .end()
            .build();
    }
```

The following is another example in which you can add transitions.

```
@Bean
public Job creditJob () {
return jobBuilderFactory.get("creditJob")
      .start(step1())
      .on("COMPLETED").to(step2())
      .from(step2()).on("COMPLETED").stopAndRestart(step3())
      .from(step3()).end()
      .build();
}
```

- `StepBuilderFactory`. This class provides a fluent API to create a `Step` definition. A `Step` is a domain object with a sequential phase of a batch job, meaning that every `job` is composed of one or more steps. The step defines the batch processing as a reader, a writer, or a processor.
- `movieItemReader`. This bean does the reading (by using the `StaxEventItemReader` class) and the marshaling from XML to the `Movie` object (by using the `XStreamMarshaller`). The `StaxEvenItemReader` has all the necessary logic to read the XML content and convert it into the `Movie` object. A lot of code is removed here.
- `movieItemWriter`. This bean uses `JdbcBatchItemWriter` to add a new record for every entry in the XML file. It uses `DataSource`, which, in this case, is instantiated by Spring Boot using the H2 server mode.

Figure 4-5 is a representation of `Job`, `JobInstance`, `JobExecution`, `Step`, and `StepExecution`.

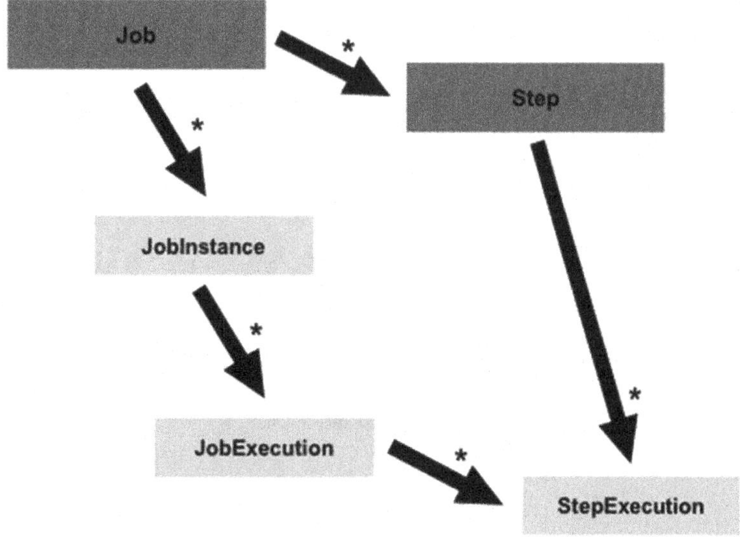

Figure 4-5. *Job-JobInstance-JobExecution-Step-Step Execution*

Finally, create the Movie class, which is the same as Listing 4-2.

Now, you can run the app. One of the new things is that you can use a web browser to access the H2 web portion using port 8092 and execute a SQL query to see the rows added to the Movies table (see Figures 4-6 and 4-7).

English Preferences Tools Help

Login

Saved Settings: Generic H2 (Embedded)

Setting Name: Generic H2 (Embedded) Save Remove

Driver Class: org.h2.Driver

JDBC URL: jdbc:h2:~/movies_db;AUTO_SERVER=TRUE

User Name: sa

Password:

Connect Test Connection

Figure 4-6. *H2 web console at http://localhost:8092 JDBC URL: jdbc:h2: ~/movies_db; AUTO_SERVER=TRUE*

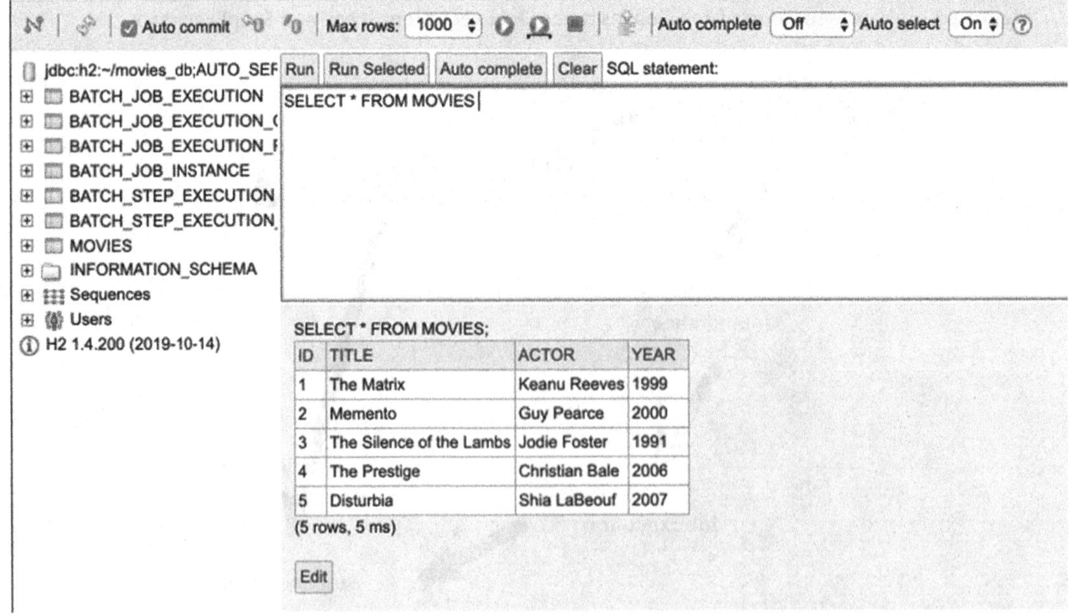

ID	TITLE	ACTOR	YEAR
1	The Matrix	Keanu Reeves	1999
2	Memento	Guy Pearce	2000
3	The Silence of the Lambs	Jodie Foster	1991
4	The Prestige	Christian Bale	2006
5	Disturbia	Shia LaBeouf	2007

Figure 4-7. *H2 web console—Movies table*

Figures 4-5 and 4-6 show the result of configuring the H2 web server in the `MovieServerConfiguration` class, which is useful in development. Of course, this can be managed by Spring Boot, but this example shows you another way to control and adapt the H2 server mode.

Summary

This chapter introduced Spring Batch. Even though the examples were simple, I showed you how easy it is to apply batch processing.

Spring Cloud Data Flow is based on Spring Integration and allows you to create batch processing. It is very reliable, scalable, and easy to extend. If you want to learn more about Spring Batch, I recommend The *Definitive Guide to Spring Batch* (Apress, 2019).

The next chapters revisit Spring Batch with Spring Task and look at how Spring Cloud Data Flow uses the power of these technologies to create flows that allow you to integrate batch processing into your systems.

CHAPTER 5

Spring Cloud

The words *cloud, cloud native, serverless,* and *containers* have been making noise in the IT industry for several years in relation to using new infrastructures, paradigms, and architectures to manage resources like storage, networking, memory, CPU, isolation, scalability, and microservices. What are *microservices*? In my opinion, they are an architectural pattern that structures a system in a collection of services with certain features, such as being loosely coupled, independently deployable, scalable, testable, maintainable, organized around business capabilities, and *owned by a small team.*

This chapter shows you how microservices play an important part in this new cloud-native era and discusses Spring Cloud's role in new architectural patterns. I'll show you some of the benefits of using Spring Cloud subprojects, like Spring Config Server, Spring Cloud Netflix, Spring Cloud Gateway, and Spring Cloud Stream. First, let's discuss what microservices are, the problems that you face when you develop under this new architecture, and how Spring Cloud's projects can solve these problems.

Microservices

The microservice architectural pattern is not new; in my opinion, it was created with the inception of the Unix operating system (around 1971) and its multitasking and multiuser capabilities. With the help of large *software tools* (small programs that work together using pipes (|), a simple symbol that allows information to pass to the next available program or command), you can create more robust systems.

Microservices have gained a lot of enthusiasm among architects, developers, and Ops teams, but why do we need them? I think time is an essential part of the puzzle. Our applications need to be fast, resilient, highly available, scalable, and have high performance to fit in this new cloud native era.

- *Speed.* You need the ability to innovate, experiment, and deliver faster. Use microservices and frameworks that help you achieve faster time to market scenarios.
- *Safety.* Move faster, do it in a way that maintains stability, availability, and durability in your whole development cycle through monitoring, isolation, tolerance, and autorecovery practices. Start thinking about continuous delivery and integration.
- *Scalable.* It has been proven that vertical scaling (buying more hardware) doesn't scale well. Use commodity hardware, reuse what you have and scale horizontally, and create multiple instances of the same application. Use a container to help you scale.
- *Mobility.* Prepare to support multiple devices from any location at any time. The number of mobile devices is growing, and they connect to the Internet, not only for social media, email, and chat, but for monitoring houses, engines, and more.

F. Gutierrez, *Spring Cloud Data Flow*, https://doi.org/10.1007/978-1-4842-1239-4_5

Let's talk about a cloud-native architecture and microservices, and creating a small app that is scalable, maintainable, secure, and robust. It needs to pass information. It needs to communicate and call some external services. Messaging is key! Most of the systems that I've seen at companies use RESTful APIs to communicate with other systems or programs to create decorators, translators, or facades. There are other communication options: HTTP, TCP (WebSocket, AMQP, MQTT), Reactive Streams, and so on. As you can see, there are a lot of ways to communicate, but to create microservices there should be a guide. Thankfully, there are the Twelve-Factor App principles. Even though I discussed them briefly in past chapters, it is necessary that you understand what they mean and how to apply them.

The Twelve-Factor App

Following what is needed to create a cloud-native architecture, the engineers at Heroku (a cloud PaaS company) identified many patterns, which became the Twelve-Factor Application guide. This guide explains how an application (a single unit) needs to be architected by focusing on declarative configuration, being stateless, and deployment independent; in other words, your application needs to be fast, safe, and scalable.

The following is a summary of the Twelve-Factor Application guide.

- *Codebase*. One codebase tracked in VCS; many deploys. One app has a single codebase, which is tracked by a version control system like Git, Subversion, or Mercurial. You can do many deployments (from the same code base) in development, testing, staging, and production environments.
- *Dependencies*. Explicitly declare and isolate dependencies. Sometimes an environment doesn't have an Internet connection (if it is a private system), so you need to think about packaging your dependencies (jars, gems, shared libraries, etc.), or if you have an internal repository of libraries, you can declare manifests like poms, gemfiles, and bundles. Never assume that you have everything in your final environment.
- *Configuration*. Store config in the environment. You shouldn't hardcode anything that varies. Use the environment variables or a configuration server.
- *Backing services*. Treat backing services as attached resources. Connect to services via URL or configuration.
- *Build, Release, Run*. Strictly separate build and run stages. This is related to a CI/CD (continuous integration, continuous delivery).
- *Processes*. Execute the app as one or more stateless processes. Processes should not store the internal state. Share nothing. Any necessary state should be considered a *backing service*.
- *Port binding*. Export services via port processes binding. Applications that are self-contained are exposed via port binding. An application can become another app's service.
- *Concurrency*. Scale out via the process model. Scale by adding more application instances. Individual processes are free to multithread.
- *Disposability*. Maximize robustness with fast startup and graceful shutdown. Processes should be disposable (they are stateless) and fault-tolerant.

- *Environment parity*. Keep development, staging, and production environments as similar as possible. This is a result of high quality and ensures continuous delivery.
- *Logs*. Treat logs as event streams. Your apps should write to standard output. Logs are streams of aggregated, time-ordered events.
- *Admin processes*. Run admin and management tasks as one-off processes. Run admin processes on the platform: DB migrations, one-time scripts, and so forth.

Some of my students ask me if you need to have a cloud infrastructure in place to create microservices. In my opinion, you don't need to have a huge infrastructure or a cloud environment to create microservices. If you follow the twelve-factor principles, you are ready to play in the game and compete with bigger companies. And when you are ready to move or switch to better infrastructure, you are already there.

If you want to create microservices and follow the twelve-factor principles, it is too much for a small team to create everything from scratch. You must face several changes.

- *Cultural*. You need to move away from people silos and create cross-functional teams; they work better and are dedicated to solving one business domain. Think about continuous delivery, decentralize the decision-making, and look for team autonomy.
- *Organizational*. Create business capability teams that are cross-functional. These teams have the autonomy to make their own decisions. Create platform team operations that are cross-functional.
- *Technical*. Move away from building monolith apps and adopt microservices architectures. Think in bounded contexts. Follow some of the principles and practices of domain-driven design. Start using containerization to gain the isolation, scalability, and high performance in your app, and look for service integrations that give you the control of distribution (see Figure 5-1).

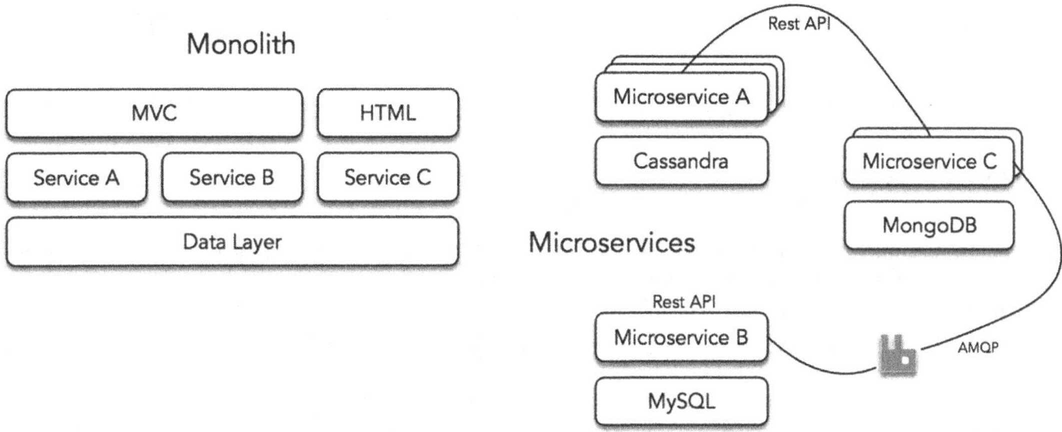

Figure 5-1. *Monolith vs. microservices*

Working in a microservices architecture can be challenging at first. And, it raises new problems that you need to control. What happens when one of the microservices is down? Who can restore the service? This means that you need to have resiliency in place. Also, if you have multiple instances of your microservice running, who balances them? If one of the instances is down, how do you discover new services or let the system know that the instance went down or is now up and running? If you have SSL in place, what is the best approach to save certificates or secrets and share them across multiple microservices? There are other concerns that a microservices architecture needs to handle, and it should be able to easily handle them.

In the next sections, I discuss how some Spring Cloud subprojects can help with these new challenges.

Spring Cloud

Spring Cloud is a set of tools/frameworks that develop microservices architectures easily, quickly, and safely. This section covers the most common Spring Cloud Services: Spring Cloud Config, service registry, and Circuit Breaker.

Spring Cloud Config

Spring Cloud Config provides server and client support for external configuration. It is a centralized configuration that can be used in *distributed systems*. The Config Server is an externalized application configuration service that provides a central place to manage your application's external properties across environments (see Figure 5-2).

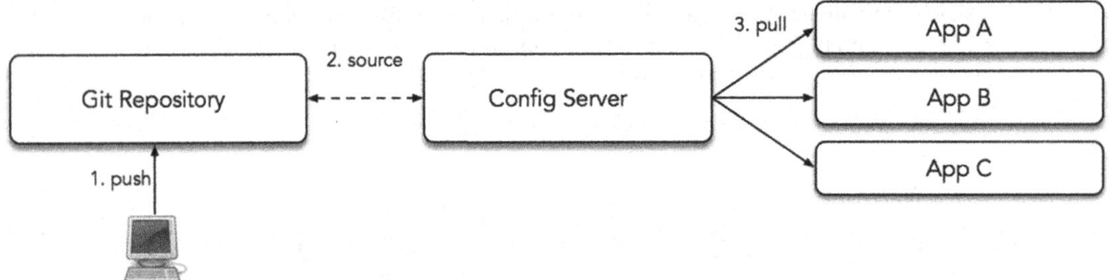

Figure 5-2. *Config Server*

You can use the Config Server during any phase of development, QA, production, or pipeline (continue delivery) because you can centrally manage every environment to access common external configuration without repackaging or redeploying. The following are some Spring Cloud Config Server features.

- Encrypt and decrypt property values (symmetric or asymmetric)
- HTTP API-based to allow name-value pairs or YAML configurations
- An embeddable server that is easy to set up in a Spring Boot app with the `@EnableConfigServer` annotation
- Connects to any version control (e.g., Git) and allows you to configure the access based on Spring profiles, branches, or tags

Spring Cloud Config Server

Let's create a Spring Cloud Config Server and discover what you need to configure it and make it accessible to clients. Open a browser and go to Spring Initializr at `https://start.spring.io` (see Figure 5-3).

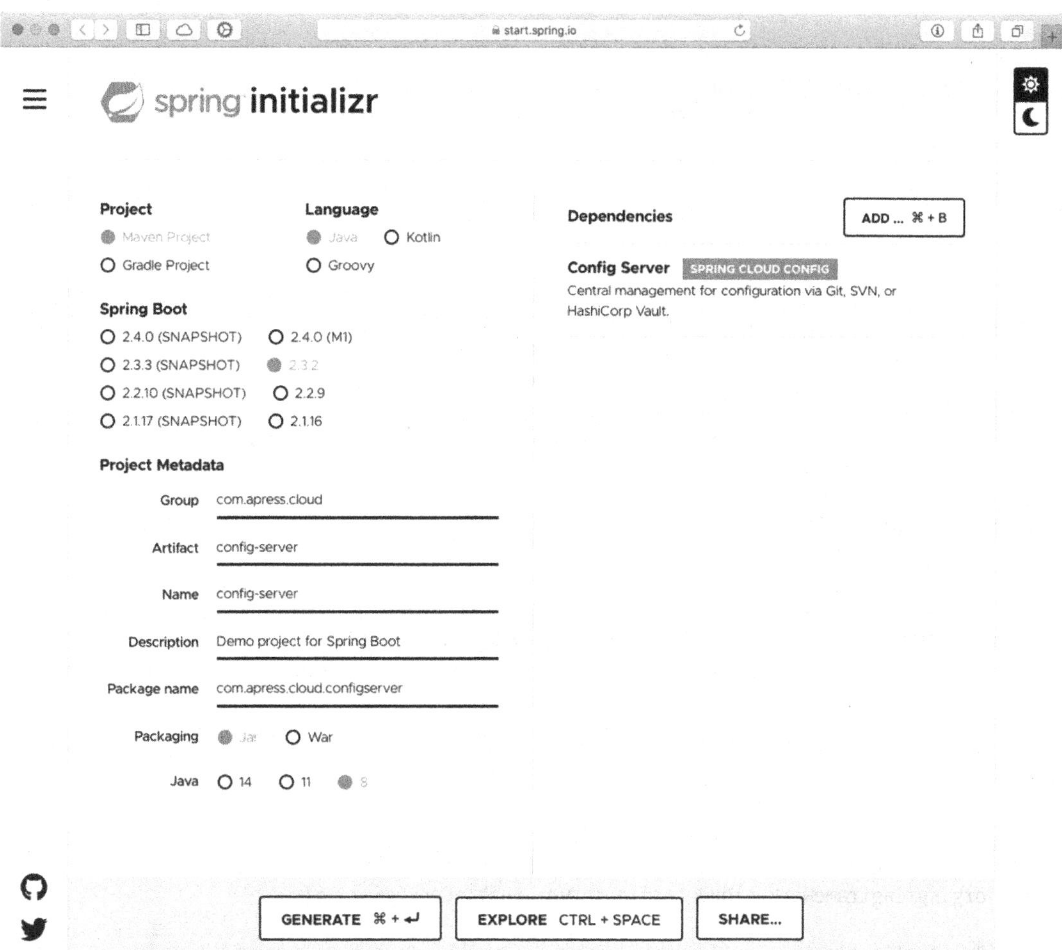

Figure 5-3. *`https://start.spring.io` at Spring Initializr*

Use the following data.

- Group: `com.apress.cloud`
- Artifact: `config-server`
- Package: `com.apress.cloud.configserver`
- Dependencies: Config Server

Next, click the Generate button to save a ZIP file. Uncompress it and open this project in your favorite IDE. Let's review it. Open the `pom.xml` file. To use all the Spring Cloud features, it is necessary to use dependency management to provide all the JARs needed in a cloud app (see Listing 5-1).

Listing 5-1. pom.xml Snippet

```
....
<properties>
        <java.version>1.8</java.version>
        <spring-cloud.version>Hoxton.SR6</spring-cloud.version>
</properties>

....
<dependencyManagement>
        <dependencies>
                <dependency>
                        <groupId>org.springframework.cloud</groupId>
                        <artifactId>spring-cloud-dependencies</artifactId>
                        <version>${spring-cloud.version}</version>
                        <type>pom</type>
                        <scope>import</scope>
                </dependency>
        </dependencies>
</dependencyManagement>
....
```

At the time this book was written, the current version was Hoxton.SR7. To remain updated, go to the main web project at `https://spring.io/projects/spring-cloud-config`.

Next, open the `ConfigServerApplication` class and complete the code with the content in Listing 5-2.

Listing 5-2. src/main/java/com/apress/cloud/configserver/ConfigServerApplication.java

```
package com.apress.cloud.configserver;

import org.springframework.boot.SpringApplication;
import org.springframework.boot.autoconfigure.SpringBootApplication;
import org.springframework.cloud.config.server.EnableConfigServer;

@SpringBootApplication
@EnableConfigServer
public class ConfigServerApplication {

        public static void main(String[] args) {
                SpringApplication.run(ConfigServerApplication.class, args);
        }

}
```

Listing 5-2 shows the ConfigServerApplication class. Even though I always recommend having any configuration class as a separate class, this can be the exception because you only need to use the @EnableConfigServer annotation. This annotation enables the Config Server, and it gets any new changes from the configuration settings, so it is necessary to tell the Cloud Config Server where to get the information.

Next, open your application.properties file and add the following content (see Listing 5-3).

Listing 5-3. src/main/resources/application.properties

```
# Default port
server.port=8888

# Spring Config Server
spring.cloud.config.server.git.uri=https://github.com/<github-username>/your-repo-app-
config.git
```

Listing 5-3 shows application.properties, where you define the Config Server port (normally, if you don't specify a particular port, 8888 is the default; again, this is on the client side) and the GIT repository in this case. Make sure you create a repo in GitHub or any other Git server.

That's it; you don't need to do anything else. Once you have your repo set (it can be empty for now), you can run your Config Server. You set up the Git server in the next sections.

Cloud Config Client

The following are some of the Spring Cloud Config Client features.

- Encrypt and decrypt property values (symmetric and asymmetric)
- Initialize the Spring environment with remote properties using the Cloud Config Server
- Pull any new changes and apply them to the Spring container without restarting the application. You benefit if you need to change logs, any ConfigProperties, or any @ Bean, @Value marked with the @RefreshScope annotation.

Let's create an example where you can use Spring Cloud Config Server and Spring Cloud Config Client. Let's review what we did in Chapter 3, but this time, you learn a programmatic approach rather than declarative XML.

Movie App

Let's re-create the Movie apps with the *movie* and the *movie-web* microservices. This time you'll use the Spring Integration DSL. Both applications use Spring Cloud Config Server, which means that you need to add the Spring Cloud Config Client dependency.

Let's start by creating the first movie project. Open a browser and go to https://start.spring.io. Use the following information.

- Group: com.apress.cloud
- Artifact: movie
- Dependencies: Config Client, Spring Integration, Spring Boot Actuator, Lombok

Press the Generate button to create a ZIP. Uncompress it and import it into your favorite IDE (see Figure 5-4).

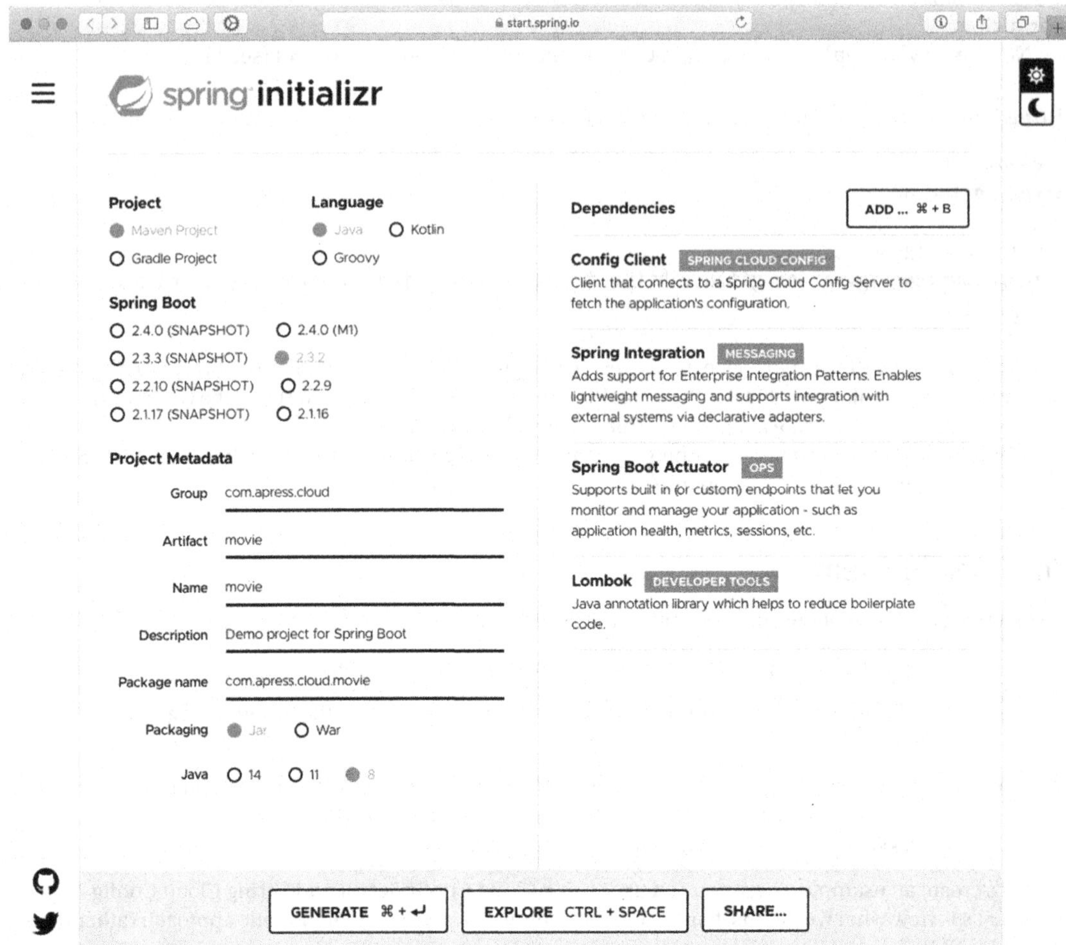

Figure 5-4. *Spring Initializr movie microservice*

Spring Boot Actuator and Lombok are the new dependencies. Spring Cloud Config Client allows the application to fetch any new changes in the configuration, and it can re-create Spring beans (`@Value`, `@Bean`, `@ConfigurationProperties`, log levels) without restarting. For this behavior, you must let the application know that it needs to pull any new configurations. To trigger this, you need the Spring Boot Actuator because it enables an endpoint in the JMX Bean exporter `refresh`.

Lombok removes the boilerplate from your main code, such as constructors or setters and getters. If you want to learn more about Lombok, go to `https://projectlombok.org`.

Let's start by adding the new dependencies (see Listing 5-4).

Listing 5-4. pom.xml Snippet

```
...
<dependency>
        <groupId>org.springframework.integration</groupId>
        <artifactId>spring-integration-file</artifactId>
</dependency>
<dependency>
        <groupId>org.springframework.integration</groupId>
        <artifactId>spring-integration-http</artifactId>
</dependency>
<dependency>
        <groupId>com.fasterxml.jackson.core</groupId>
        <artifactId>jackson-databind</artifactId>
</dependency>
...
```

Listing 5-4 shows some of the other dependencies. You are reading a file and then send it to another service through HTTP POST.

Let's create the Movie class (see Listing 5-5).

Listing 5-5. src/main/java/com/apress/cloud/movie/Movie.java

```
package com.apress.cloud.movie;

import lombok.AllArgsConstructor;
import lombok.Data;

@AllArgsConstructor
@Data
public class Movie {
    private String title;
    private String actor;
    private int year;
}
```

Listing 5-5 shows the new `Movie` class with no setters, getters, or constructors. Lombok provides this by using the `@AllArgsConstructors` and `@Data` (create getters, setters, toString, hashCode) annotations.

Next, let's create the `MovieProperties` class that holds information about the path that reads the files, the file pattern, preventing duplicates, a fixed delay in reading the path, and the remote server (see Listing 5-6).

Listing 5-6. src/main/java/com/apress/cloud/movie/MovieProperties.java

```
package com.apress.cloud.movie;

import lombok.Data;
import org.springframework.boot.context.properties.ConfigurationProperties;

@Data
@ConfigurationProperties(prefix = "movie")
public class MovieProperties {
```

```
    private String directory;
    private String filePattern;
    private Boolean preventDuplicates;
    private Long fixedDelay;

    private String remoteService = "http://localhost:8181/v1/movie";
}
```

Listing 5-6 shows the MovieProperties class that reaches the Config Server when the app starts. It has the values from the Git server.

Next, let's create the MovieConverter class, which has each line of the movie file. It needs to read a line and convert it into a Movie instance (see Listing 5-7).

Listing 5-7. src/main/java/com/apress/cloud/movie/MovieConverter.java

```
package com.apress.cloud.movie;

import lombok.extern.slf4j.Slf4j;
import org.springframework.core.convert.converter.Converter;
import org.springframework.stereotype.Component;

import java.util.List;
import java.util.stream.Collectors;
import java.util.stream.Stream;

@Slf4j
@Component
public class MovieConverter implements Converter<String,Movie> {

    @Override
    public Movie convert(String source) {
        log.debug(source);
        List<String> fields = Stream.of(source.split(",")).map(String::trim).
        collect(Collectors.toList());
        return new Movie(fields.get(0),fields.get(1),Integer.valueOf(fields.get(2)));
    }
}
```

Listing 5-7 shows MovieConverter, which gets the String (a single line from the movies CSV file), and it returns a Movie instance. Also, note that we set the logging level to DEBUG in this class.

Next, create the MovieIntegrationConfiguration class that uses the Spring Integration DSL (domain-specific language) that exposes a fluent API to configure all the integration flows. It is the same as using the XML from previous chapters (see Listing 5-8).

Listing 5-8. src/main/java/com/apress/cloud/movie/MovieIntegrationConfiguration.java

```
package com.apress.cloud.movie;

import lombok.AllArgsConstructor;
import org.springframework.boot.context.properties.EnableConfigurationProperties;
import org.springframework.context.annotation.Bean;
import org.springframework.context.annotation.Configuration;
```

```
import org.springframework.http.HttpMethod;
import org.springframework.integration.dsl.IntegrationFlow;
import org.springframework.integration.dsl.IntegrationFlows;
import org.springframework.integration.dsl.Pollers;
import org.springframework.integration.dsl.Transformers;
import org.springframework.integration.file.dsl.Files;
import org.springframework.integration.file.splitter.FileSplitter;
import org.springframework.integration.http.dsl.Http;

import java.io.File;
import java.net.URI;

@AllArgsConstructor
@EnableConfigurationProperties(MovieProperties.class)
@Configuration
public class MovieIntegrationConfiguration {

    private MovieProperties movieProperties;
    private MovieConverter movieConverter;

    @Bean
    public IntegrationFlow fileFlow() {
        return IntegrationFlows.from(Files
                        .inboundAdapter(new File(this.movieProperties.getDirectory()))
                        .preventDuplicates(true)
                        .patternFilter(this.movieProperties.getFilePattern()),
                e -> e.poller(Pollers.fixedDelay(this.movieProperties.getFixedDelay())))

                .split(Files.splitter().markers())
                .filter(p -> !(p instanceof FileSplitter.FileMarker))
                .transform(Transformers.converter(this.movieConverter))
                .transform(Transformers.toJson())
                .handle(Http
                        .outboundChannelAdapter(URI.create(this.movieProperties.
                        getRemoteService()))
                        .httpMethod(HttpMethod.POST))
                .get();
    }

}
```

Listing 5-8 shows the `MovieIntegrationConfiguration` class. Let's analyze it.

- `IntegrationFlow`. This class is a factory of the `IntegrationFlowBuilder` class that looks for any information about channels, handlers, routers, splitters, and any other integration pattern defined in a DSL. So, it creates the whole Spring Integration engine.
- `File.inboundAdapter`. Normally, a flow always starts with an inbound channel adapter. It could be a particular channel. In this case, we are using the inbound file to look for new files in the specified directory. One of the inbound adapter's features has pollers that allow you to look for new incoming `MessageSource` messages.

- `split`. This method creates a splitter that sets the payload as `Iterable`, `Interator`, `Array`, `Stream`, or a reactive `Publisher`, and it accepts an implementation of the splitter; in this case, we are using `Files.splitter.markers()`, which splits the file contents into lines and marks the start and end of the file.
- `filter`. This method filters the lines we are sending. It's important to have a filter because the first and last line of the file's content is a marker (`START - END`).
- `transform`. We are using two transformers. The first one calls the `Transformers.converter` method, where you pass the `movieConverter` bean. This class has the logic to get the file line, get comma-separated values, and create a `Movie` instance. The other transformer converts `Movie` to a JSON payload.
- `handle`. This handler is a service activator pattern endpoint. Here we are using an `Http.outboundChannelAdapter` that prepares a request to the external service and sends `Movie` in JSON format with the right headers.

You can say that this Java DSL is similar to the declarative XML from previous chapters, but which one should you choose? It depends on what you need and adds value to your organization, project, or yourself. From now on, we are going to use only Spring Integration DSL.

Next, prepare some text files (you can use those from previous chapters) and make them available in a known folder. When running this app, you can copy some of these movie text files into the `/tmp/movies` directory path; if this path is not in your system, you can create the folder. If you are using Windows OS, create it in `C:\tmp\movies`.

Next, rename `application.properties` to `bootstrap` with the `.yml` extension. It is important to know that by convention, you must use a `bootstrap.yml` file in your client because your main configuration now resides in the Git repository or any storage you used to centralize your configuration. From now on, we are going to use YAML files, which offer a simple hierarchy and are easy to read. Beware, though, that you need to have a least two-space indentations for any new property. Open the file and add the content from Listing 5-9.

Listing 5-9. src/main/resources/bootstrap.yml

```
spring:
  application:
    name: movies
  jmx:
    enabled: true
  cloud:
    config:
      uri:
        - http://localhost:8888
```

Listing 5-9 shows the `bootstrap.yml` file (exposing the `spring.cloud.config.uri` property where Spring Cloud Config Server is running). By default, the Spring Cloud Config Client always looks at that address if not specified, so you can remove it if you wish. Also, `application.yml` is exposing the `spring.application.name` property, which is useful when you have multiple microservices to identify the application. It is required to locate other microservices, so it is important to have it declared. Also, notice that you are enabling JMX through the `spring.jmx.enabled` property, which creates all the JMX endpoints. You use the refresh endpoint later.

Finally, let's create the configuration for this movie microservice. The next steps are based on using GitHub (`https://github.com`), but you can use any other Git server. I'm assuming that you know a little bit about Git commands. One of the benefits of using GitHub is that you can create files on the fly and commit them right away. So, follow these next steps.

1. Sign in to your GitHub account at `https://github.com` (if you don't have one, you can create one; it's free for public repositories/projects).
2. Create a new repository called `movies-config`.
3. Add/commit a `movies.yml` file with the following content. (There is a **Create new file** button in the Code tab to easily add a new file.) (See Figure 5-5.)

```
movie:
  directory: /tmp/movies
  file-pattern: "*.txt"
  prevent-duplicates: true
  fixed-delay: 5000
logging:
  level:
    com:
      apress:
        cloud: INFO
```

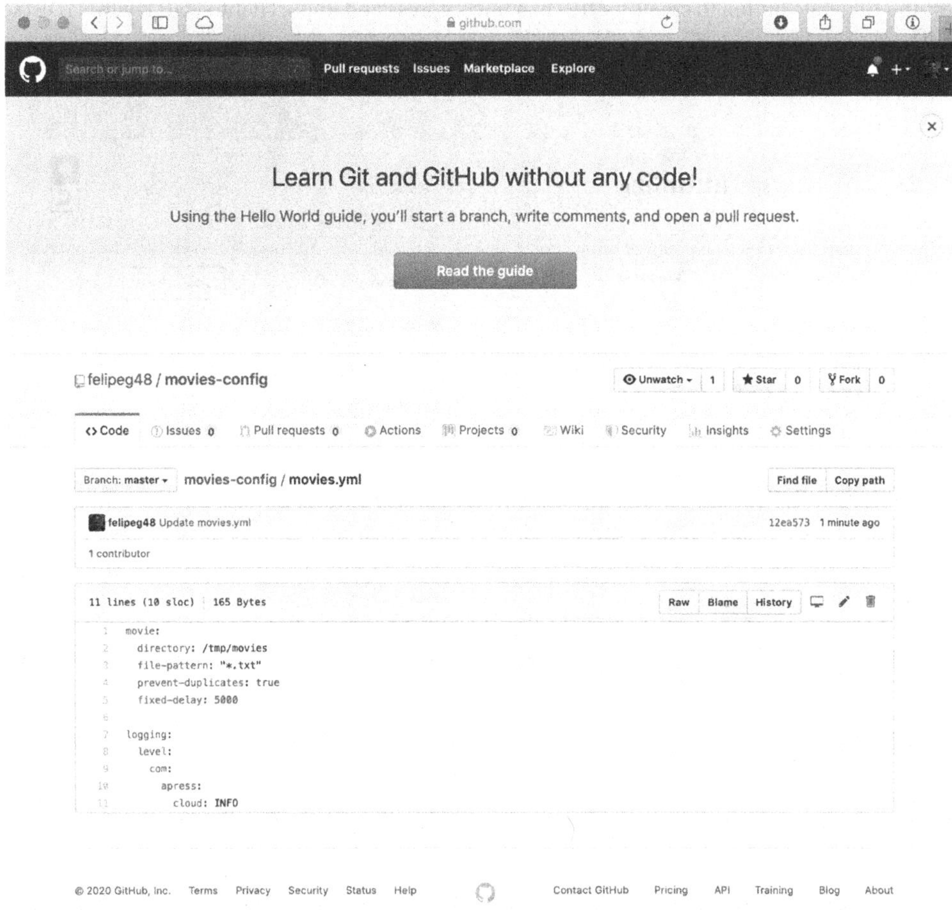

Figure 5-5. *`https://github.com` movies-config/movies.yml*

These properties are declared in the `MovieProperties` class (see Listing 5-6). Do not run the movie microservice yet (note that the `movie.directory` property points to `"/tmp/movies"`). If you are using Windows OS, use a value `like C:\\tmp\\movies` with the escape character. `movie.file-pattern` specifies that it look for any file that ends with the `.txt` extension. You'll run this microservice later.

Movie-Web App

Let's create the movie-web microservice. Remember that this microservice has an HTTP POST endpoint that allows JSON movie objects to be saved to the database. Open your browser and go to Spring Initializr at `https://start.spring.io`. Use the following information.

- Group: `com.apress.cloud`
- Artifact: `movie-web`
- Package: `com.apress.cloud.movieweb`
- Dependencies: Config Client, Spring Integration, Spring Web, Spring Actuator, H2, MySQL, Lombok

Press the Generate button to create a ZIP. Then uncompress and import it into your favorite IDE (see Figure 5-6).

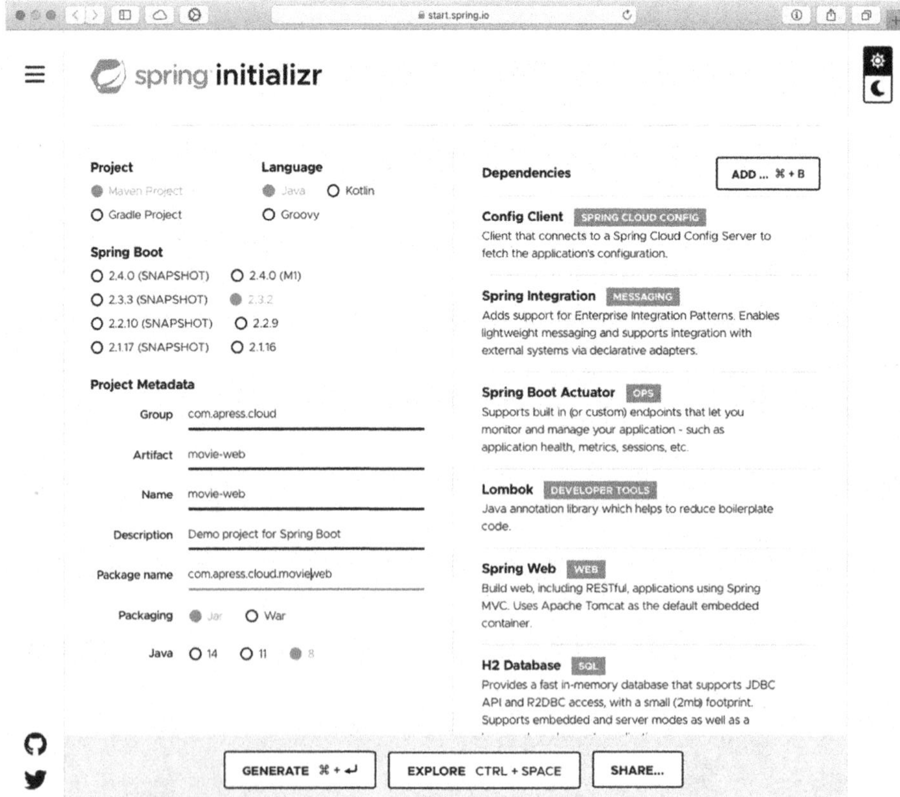

***Figure 5-6.** Spring Initializr movie-web microservice*

Let's add the new dependencies (see Listing 5-10).

Listing 5-10. pom.xml Snippet

```
...
<dependency>
        <groupId>org.springframework.integration</groupId>
        <artifactId>spring-integration-jdbc</artifactId>
</dependency>
<dependency>
        <groupId>org.springframework.integration</groupId>
        <artifactId>spring-integration-http</artifactId>
</dependency>
...
```

Next, let's create the `MovieWebProperties` class (see Listing 5-11).

Listing 5-11. src/main/java/com/apress/cloud/movieweb/MovieWebProperties.java

```
package com.apress.cloud.movieweb;

import lombok.Data;
import org.springframework.boot.context.properties.ConfigurationProperties;

@Data
@ConfigurationProperties(prefix = "movie-web")
public class MovieWebProperties {

    private String path;
}
```

Listing 5-11 shows the only property this microservice has, the endpoint path created to receive HTTP POST requests.

Next, you can create the `Movie` class, which is the same. The only difference is that there is a new Lombok annotation (see Listing 5-12).

Listing 5-12. src/main/java/com/apress/cloud/movieweb/Movie.java

```
package com.apress.cloud.movieweb;

import lombok.AllArgsConstructor;
import lombok.Data;
import lombok.NoArgsConstructor;

@NoArgsConstructor
@AllArgsConstructor
@Data
public class Movie {
    private String title;
    private String actor;
    private int year;
}
```

Listing 5-12 shows the Movie class, which used the @NoArgsConstructor annotation arguments that create a default constructor.

Next, let's create the MovieWebIntegrationConfiguration class, which has everything related to the Spring Integration flow using the Java DSL (see Listing 5-13).

Listing 5-13. src/main/java/com/apress/cloud/movieweb/MoviewWebIntegrationConfiguration.java

```
package com.apress.cloud.movieweb;

import lombok.AllArgsConstructor;
import org.springframework.boot.context.properties.EnableConfigurationProperties;
import org.springframework.context.annotation.Bean;
import org.springframework.context.annotation.Configuration;
import org.springframework.http.HttpMethod;
import org.springframework.integration.annotation.ServiceActivator;
import org.springframework.integration.dsl.IntegrationFlow;
import org.springframework.integration.dsl.IntegrationFlows;
import org.springframework.integration.dsl.MessageChannels;
import org.springframework.integration.handler.LoggingHandler;
import org.springframework.integration.http.dsl.Http;
import org.springframework.integration.jdbc.JdbcMessageHandler;
import org.springframework.messaging.MessageHandler;

import javax.sql.DataSource;

@AllArgsConstructor
@EnableConfigurationProperties(MovieWebProperties.class)
@Configuration
public class MovieWebIntegrationConfiguration {

    private MovieWebProperties movieWebProperties;

   @Bean
    public IntegrationFlow httpFlow() {
        return IntegrationFlows.from(Http
                    .inboundChannelAdapter(movieWebProperties.getPath())
                    .requestPayloadType(Movie.class)
                    .requestMapping(m -> m.methods(HttpMethod.POST)))
                .channel(MessageChannels.publishSubscribe("publisher"))
                .get();
    }

    @Bean
    public IntegrationFlow logFlow() {
        return IntegrationFlows.from("publisher")
                .log(LoggingHandler.Level.INFO,"Movie", m -> m)
                .get();
    }

    @Bean
    @ServiceActivator(inputChannel = "publisher")
    public MessageHandler process(DataSource dataSource){
```

```
        JdbcMessageHandler jdbcMessageHandler = new JdbcMessageHandler(dataSource,
                "INSERT INTO movies (title,actor,year) VALUES (?, ?, ?)");
        jdbcMessageHandler.setPreparedStatementSetter((ps, message) -> {
            ps.setString(1,((Movie)message.getPayload()).getTitle());
            ps.setString(2,((Movie)message.getPayload()).getActor());
            ps.setInt(3,((Movie)message.getPayload()).getYear());
        });
        jdbcMessageHandler.setOrder(1);
        return jdbcMessageHandler;
    }
}
```

Listing 5-13 shows the MovieWebIntegrationConfiguration class. Let's analyze it.

- Http.inboudChannelAdapter. Remember that our flow must start with some inbound adapters, and in this case, the Http.inboundChannelAdapter creates an endpoint that accepts any requests. It accepts only a Movie type in JSON format (default) using an HTTP POST method.
- channel. After receiving the request, it sends Movie to a publish/subscribe channel. Here, any other integration flow can be subscribed.
- log. The log method prints the message, but this should be a flow that sends an email.
- @ServiceActivator. This is another way to add a handler, a method marked with @ServiceActivator annotation. We are using JdbcMessageHandler, which automatically processes Movie/JSON and inserts it into the database engine—very straightforward. It returns a MessageHandler to close the flow.

Listing 5-13 is the same as the declarative XML from Chapter 3. The only difference is that you are not sending emails; here, you are using the log() call.

Next, you need to create the schema.sql file that initializes the database (see Listing 5-14).

Listing 5-14. src/main/resources/schema.sql

```
create table IF NOT EXISTS movies(
    id int not null auto_increment,
    title varchar(250),
    actor varchar(100),
    year smallint,
primary key(id));
```

As you can see, Listing 5-14 is the same file from previous chapters. Next, change the application's extension to bootstrap.yml and add the content from Listing 5-15.

Listing 5-15. src/main/resources/bootstrap.yml

```
server:
  port: 8181
spring:
  application:
    name: movie-web
```

Listing 5-15 shows the `bootstrap.yml` you be using, just the application's name and the `server.port`. Remember that we can still use the `spring.cloud.config.uri`, but it connects by default if this property is not set. Next, go to GitHub (or your Git Server) and add the `movie-web.yml` file with the following content (see Figure 5-7).

```
spring:
  h2:
    console:
      enabled: true
movie-web:
  path: /v1/movie
```

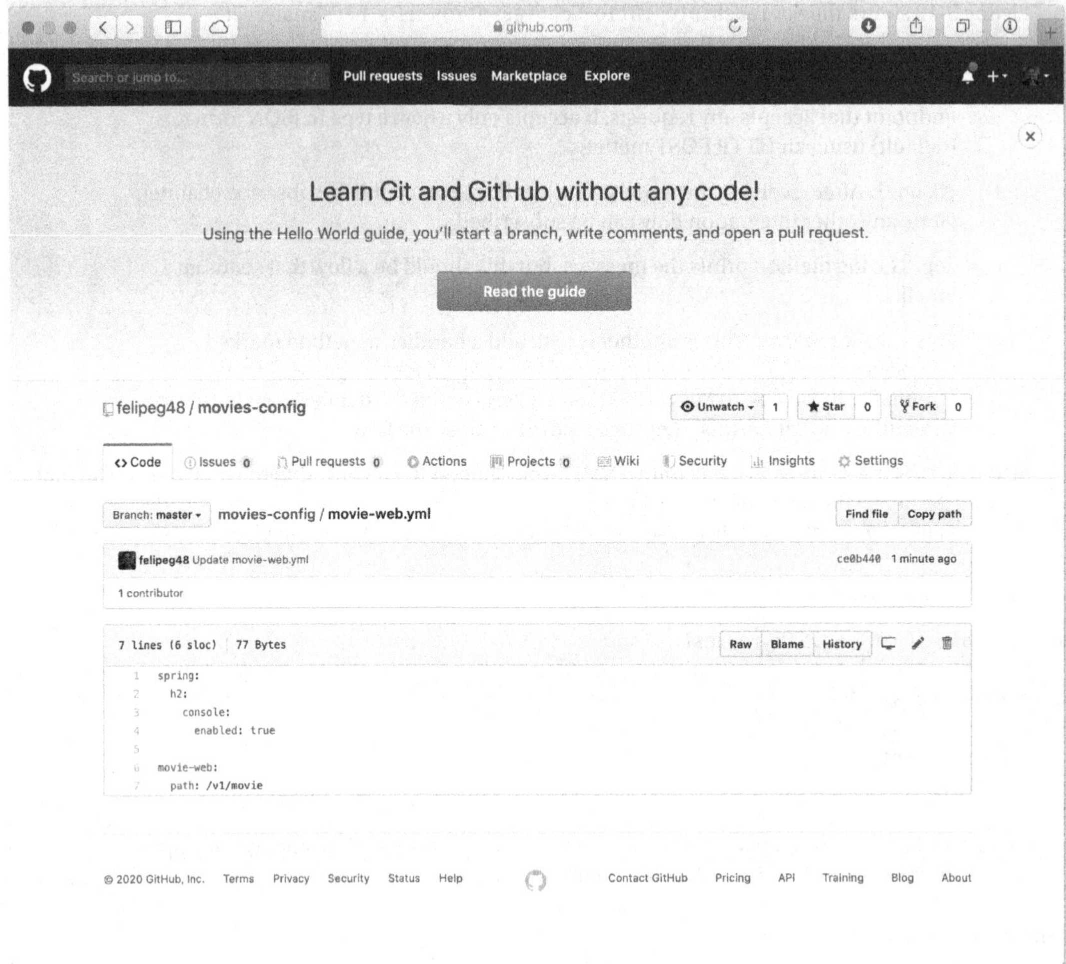

Figure 5-7. *`https://github.com` movies-config/movies-web.yml*

Running Config Server, Movie, and Movie Web Microservices

Now it's time to run these apps. Let's run the microservices in this order: (1) config-server, (2) movie-web, and (3) movie.

1. First, run the config-server microservice. If you are using Linux, open a terminal and run it with the following command.

   ```
   $ ./mvnw clean spring-boot:run
   ```

   If you are using Windows, run it with the following.

   ```
   > mvwn.bat clean spring-boot:run
   ```

   This is a `config-server` lookup for the GitHub account and repository that runs in port 8888.

2. Next, run the movie-web microservice. It runs in port 8181, based on the `movie-web.yml` configuration file created in the GitHub repository. You can use the same command to run the movie-web microservice. This microservice uses the config-server in port 8888, and it pulls the configuration based on the name of the app; so, in this case, it looks for `movie-web.yml` because it has the same name as the application set in the `spring.application.name` property.

   When running the movie-web app, look at the first logs printed. You see something like the following.

   ```
   Fetching config from server at : http://localhost:8888
   Located environment: name=movie-web, profiles=[default], label=null,
   version=a55fa1d67ebcc6f4d509f71ba9619f4fc2a116c8, state=null
   ```

   This means that it was successfully connected to the config-server microservice, and it loads the movie-web configuration from the GitHub server. It has the `/v1/movie` endpoint, runs in port 8181, and allows you to use the H2 console in the `/h2-console` endpoint.

3. Next, run the movie microservice. Before you run it, make sure you have the movie text files ready. (If you download the source code from Apress, note that I added them in the project's root, so you can easily reuse them).

   When run, it appears in the logs that are connecting to the config-server microservice at port 8888.

4. Now, it's time to send some movie files. If you are using the files that come from the book's source code, copy `movies-batch1.txt` to the `/tmp/movies` folder. This reads the files and posts the JSON to the movie-web microservice. In the movie-web microservice, you see in the logs that the movies were inserted into the H2 database. If you look at `http://localhost:8181/h2-console` (the movie-web microservice), you should see the movies are already inserted. The JDBC URL is `jdbc:h2:mem:testdb` (default values), the username is `sa`, and the password remains empty (see Figure 5-8).

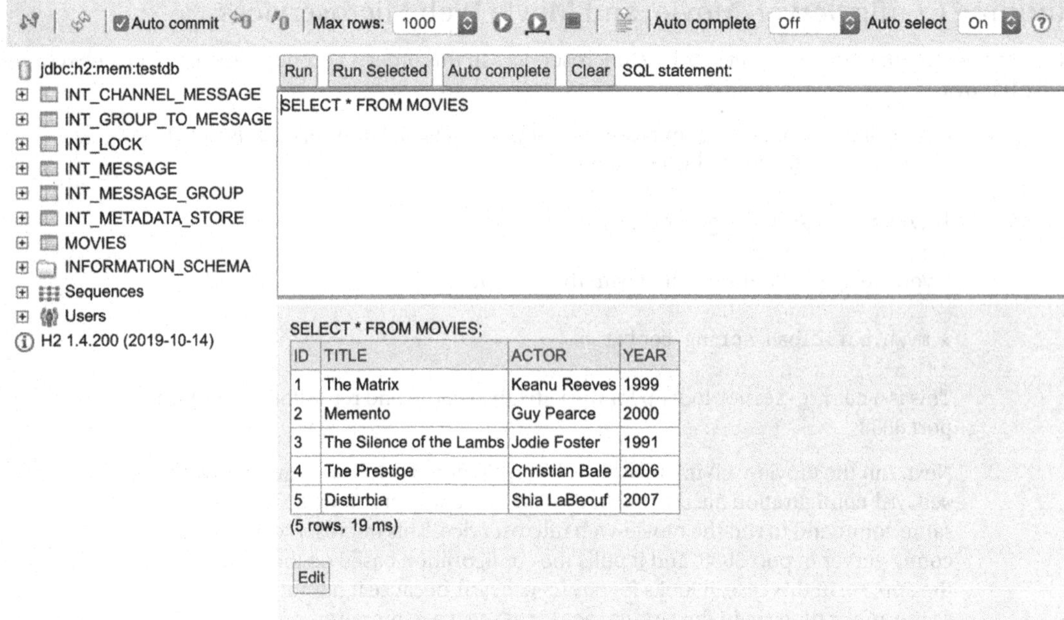

Figure 5-8. *`http://localhost:8181/h2-console` moview-web microservice*

Congratulations, you have just run config-server, which looks up the configuration based on your app's name, and the movie and movie-web microservices that use config-server to get their configuration.

Changing the Logging Level

If you paid attention to the movie microservice and its configuration, you saw that the logging level was set to INFO in the GitHub repository. What happens if you want to change the login level? Normally, you stop the application, change the logging level to DEBUG, and re-run the application. Well, Spring Cloud Config Client allows you to change the logging level without restarting your app—so don't stop the movie microservice. Let's look at how to apply these changes without restarting.

1. Modify the `movie.yml` file (from GitHub) and change the logging level from INFO to DEBUG. GitHub has a button (pencil icon) that allows you to modify the file online. Or, clone the repo in your computer and use Git commands to push this new change.

2. Once you commit the change, open a terminal and execute the `jconsole` command. This brings the JConsole that allows you to connect to a JMX protocol. Choose `com.apress.cloud.movie.MovieApp` from the list (see Figure 5-9).

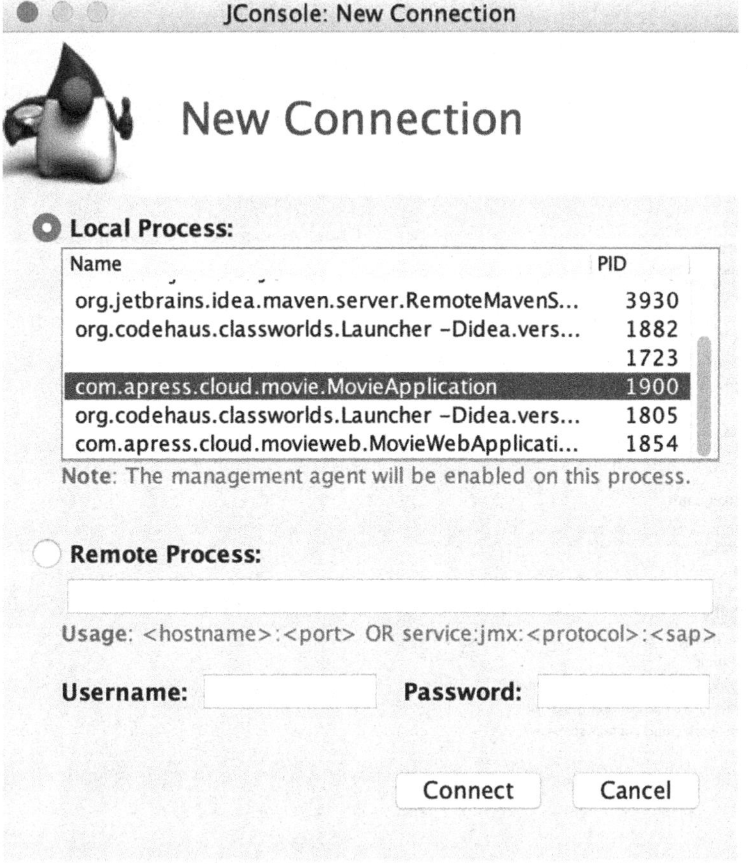

Figure 5-9. *JConsole*

3. Click the Insecure Connection button. Next, click the MBeans tab and expand org.springframework.boot ➤ Endpoint. Select the Operations/Refresh icon (see Figure 5-10).

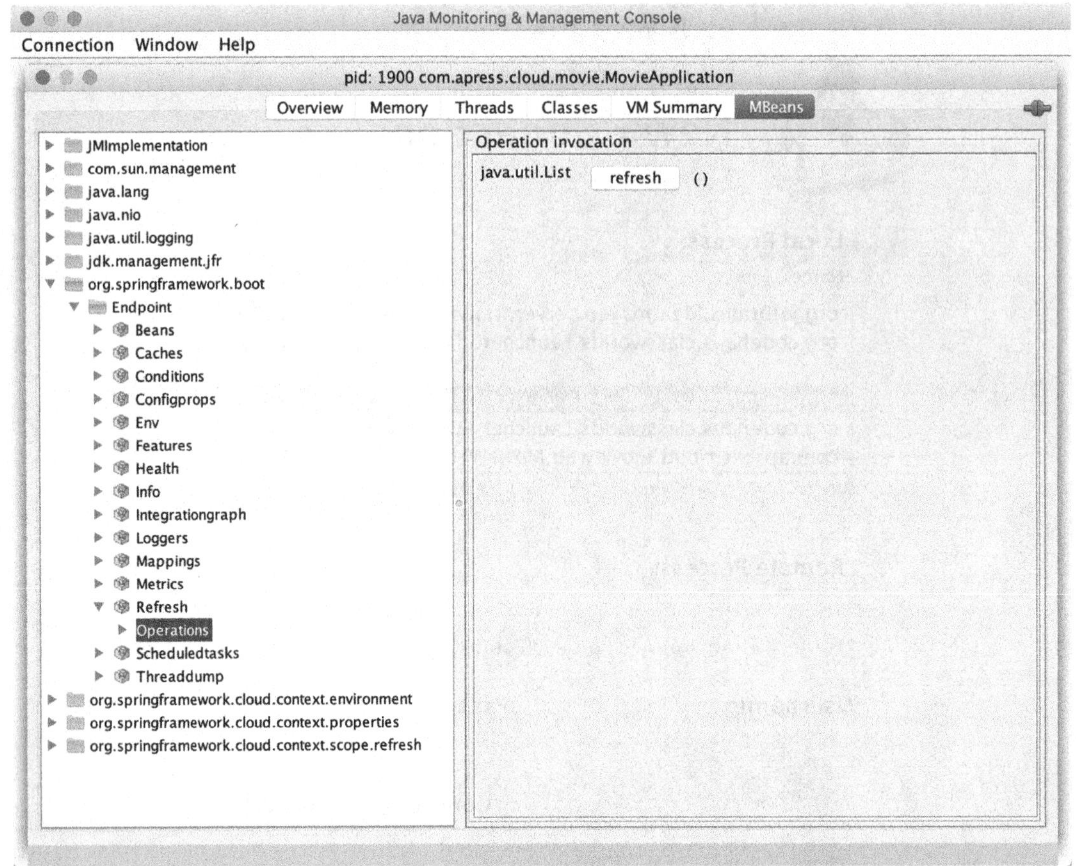

Figure 5-10. *MBeans org.springframework.boot ➤ Endpoint ➤ Refresh ➤ Operations*

4. Click the Refresh button. It appears that the `logging.level.com.apress.cloud` property changed. In the movie microservice logs, you see output about refreshing the scope and beans. This means that the logging level has changed as well.

5. Copy another file to the `/tmp/movies` folder (for example, `movies-batch2.txt`). Now you see the DEBUG in the movie microservice logs.

Congratulations! You changed the logging level without restarting the application, but there is more. You can change the logging and the `@ConfigurationProperties` marked classes and all `@Value` or `@Bean` marked with `@RefreshScope`. This tells the Spring container that those beans need to be re-created without restarting the app.

Of course, here we used JMX, but it also allows you to have a web endpoint, so you can do a POST to the `/actuator/refresh` endpoint. To enable the web endpoints, you need three things: spring-web and spring-actuator dependencies in your `pom.xml` file and the endpoint exposed with `management.endpoints.web.exposure.include=*`. Then any changes are made by using the following command.

```
$ curl localhost:8181/actuator/refresh -XPOST -H "Content-Type: application/json"
```

What happens if the movie-web microservice is down? One solution is to create several instances. If one is down, then we can access the other. But what do you need to do to get the list of available movie-web instances? What happens if one of them changes its port? Or, what would happen if one is down? How do you go to the next available?

These are new problems. You need something that allows you to keep a record of the available services and how to connect to them. You need a solution that allows you to register a service. The good thing is that there is a solution—the Eureka service registry.

Spring Cloud Netflix

Spring Cloud Netflix is the integration of Netflix OSS (`https://netflix.github.io/`) within Spring Boot apps. It supports autoconfiguration and wrapper classes based on the same patterns that the Spring Framework ecosystem offers developers. Spring Cloud Netflix has annotations with the functionality to create distributed applications. It provides pattern implementations like service discovery, circuit breaker, routing, and client-side load balancing. The following are some of its features.

- *Eureka Server* is the service discovery pattern implementation. Microservices instances can register and be discovered by other microservices. Is also provides a way to add multiple Eureka Servers that can register between them to provide the necessary redundancy. It provides the `@EnableEurekaServer` that enables an embedded service discovery.
- *Eureka Client* provides a discoverable pattern that registers Eureka Server and offers useful information, such as URL and ports. It provides the `@EnableDiscoveryClient` annotation that registers the microservice.
- *Circuit Breaker* is a pattern that offers a fault-tolerant scenario to your applications. It provides the `@EnableCircuitBreaker` and `@HistirixCommand` annotations, which are simple decorators with the functionality to create fault-tolerant microservices.
- *Eureka Ribbon* is an implementation of the client-side load-balancing patterns. It provides the `@LoadBalanced` annotation that normally goes in the `RestTemplate` instance; this creates the client load-balancing required for multiple microservices registered in Eureka Server.
- *Netflix Zuul* is an implementation of routing and filter patterns for creating proxies.
- *External Configuration* provides a way to communicate directly with Netflix Archaius to provide a Spring environment similar to Spring Cloud Config Server.

Service Discovery: Eureka Service Registry

The Eureka service registry provides the implementation of the service discovery pattern, which is one of the most important microservice architecture features (see Figure 5-11).

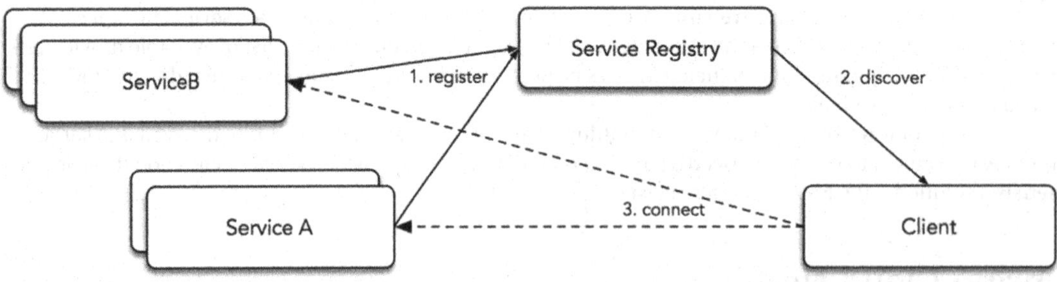

Figure 5-11. *Service registry*

When a client registers to the service registry, it provides metadata about its host and port; it also sends heartbeats to the service registry. Everything is in memory (metadata), from the server to the client.

Eureka Server

Let's create the eureka-server microservice. Go to your browser and open `https://start.spring.io`. Use the following information.

- Group: `com.apress.cloud`
- Artifact: `eureka-server`
- `Package: com.apress.cloud.eurekaserver`
- Dependencies: Eureka Server

Press the Generate button to create and download a ZIP file. You can uncompress it and import it into your favorite IDE (see Figure 5-12).

Figure 5-12. *`https://start.spring.io` eureka-server*

Review the `pom.xml` file. You have only one dependency—enough to create a service registry solution. Next, open the main class, `EurekaServerApplication.java`. Add the `@EnableEurekaServer` annotation (see Listing 5-16).

Listing 5-16. src/main/java/com/apress/cloud/eurekaserver/EurekaServerApplication.java

```
package com.apress.cloud.eurekaserver;

import org.springframework.boot.SpringApplication;
import org.springframework.boot.autoconfigure.SpringBootApplication;
import org.springframework.cloud.netflix.eureka.server.EnableEurekaServer;

@EnableEurekaServer
@SpringBootApplication
public class EurekaServerApplication {
```

```
        public static void main(String[] args) {
                SpringApplication.run(EurekaServerApplication.class, args);
        }

}
```

Listing 5-16 shows the main class. The only thing you need to have the service registry app do is use the @EnableEurekaServer annotation, and you need to configure it using the `application.properties` file.

Next, change the `application.properties` extension to `.yml` and open it. Add the content from Listing 5-17.

Listing 5-17. src/main/resources/application.yml

```
server:
  port: 8761

eureka:
  instance:
    hostname: localhost
  client:
    registerWithEureka: false
    fetchRegistry: false
    serviceUrl:
      defaultZone: http://${eureka.instance.hostname}:${server.port}/eureka/
```

Now, you are ready to run it. You can use the following command.

```
$ ./mvnw clean spring-boot:run
```

Open a new Browser tab and go to `http://localhost:8761` (see Figure 5-13).

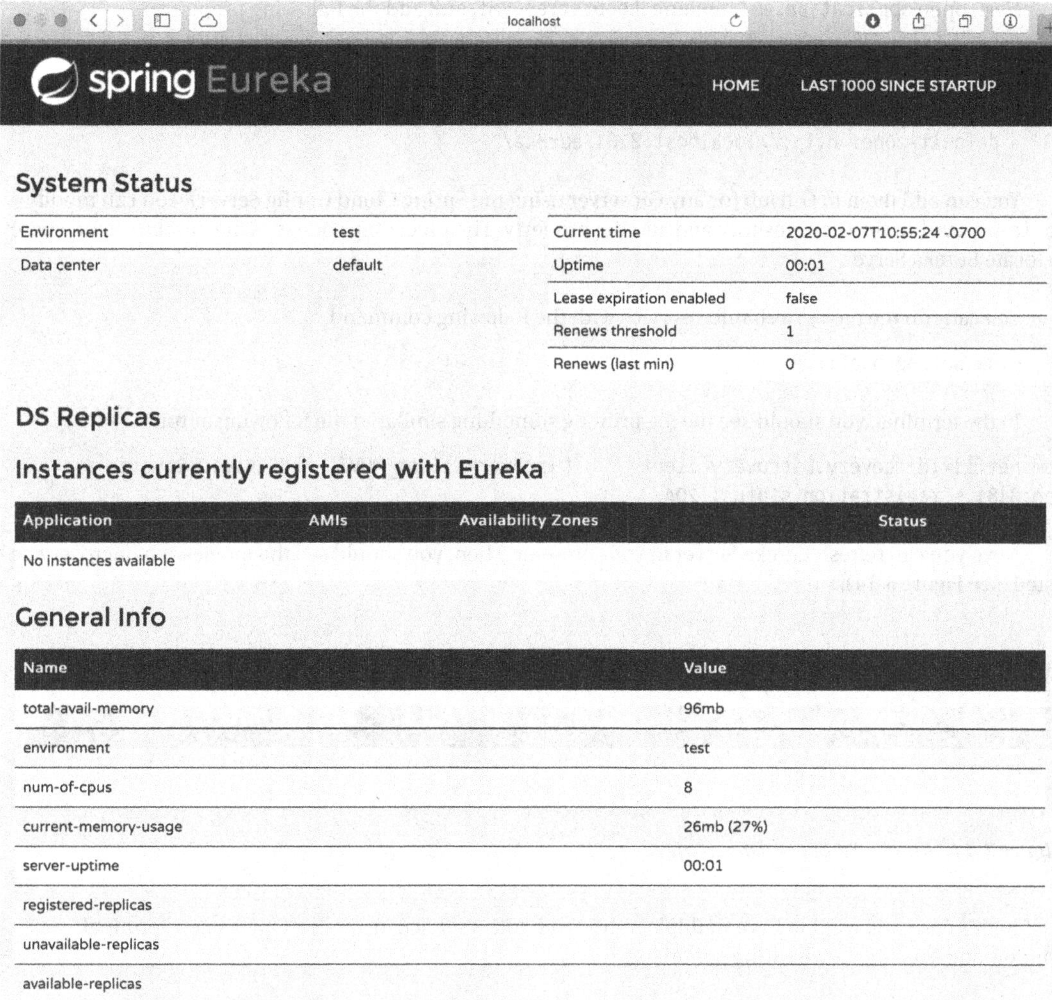

Figure 5-13. *Eureka Server at http://localhost:8761*

Eureka Client

Now that you have the service registry (Eureka Server) up and running, it is time to register it. First, add a dependency to become discoverable. Let's start with the *movie-web* microservice.

Service Discoverable: Movie Web Microservice

Open your movie-web microservice in your favorite IDE and open `pom.xml`. Add the following dependency.

```
<dependency>
        <groupId>org.springframework.cloud</groupId>
        <artifactId>spring-cloud-starter-netflix-eureka-client</artifactId>
</dependency>
```

Next, open `application.yml`, rename it `bootstrap.yml`, and add the following properties.

```
eureka:
  client:
    service-url:
      default-zone: http://localhost:8761/eureka/
```

You can add them to GitHub (or any Git server using the Spring Cloud Config Server). You can modify `movie-web.yml` in the Git repository and add the property. The preceding code tells the Eureka Client where to locate Eureka Server.

You can run the movie-web microservice with the following command.

```
$ ./mvnw spring-boot:run
```

In the terminal, you should see the log printing something similar to the following output.

```
com.netflix.discovery.DiscoveryClient     : DiscoveryClient_MOVIE-WEB/10.0.0.2:movie-
web:8181 - registration status: 204
```

Next, you can refresh Eureka Server in your browser. Then, you should see the movie-web microservice listed (see Figure 5-14).

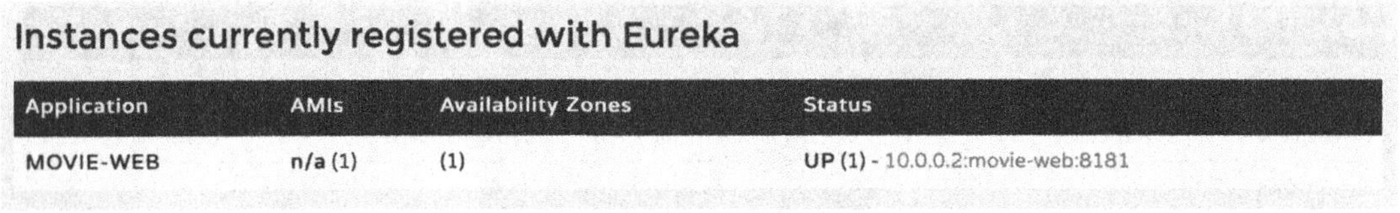

Instances currently registered with Eureka

Application	AMIs	Availability Zones	Status
MOVIE-WEB	n/a (1)	(1)	UP (1) - 10.0.0.2:movie-web:8181

Figure 5-14. *Eureka Server registered apps*

In this case, you want to have multiple movie-web microservice instances. Open a new terminal window and execute the following command.

```
$ ./mvnw spring-boot:run -Dspring-boot.run.jvmArguments="-Dserver.port=8282"
```

The preceding command runs another instance but using port 8282. Now, if you refresh Eureka Server again, you see the two instances up and running with their ports (see Figure 5-15).

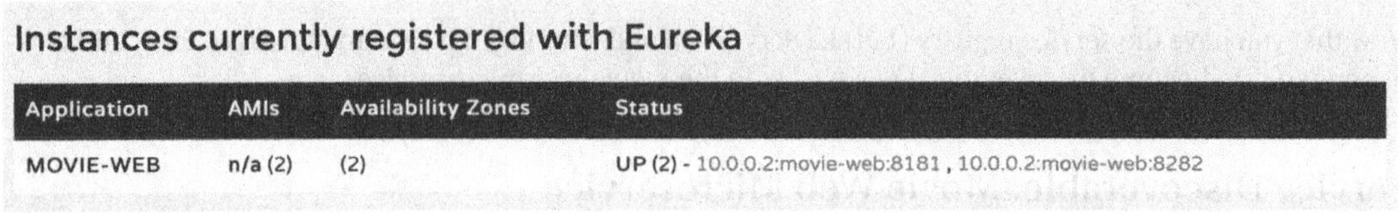

Instances currently registered with Eureka

Application	AMIs	Availability Zones	Status
MOVIE-WEB	n/a (2)	(2)	UP (2) - 10.0.0.2:movie-web:8181 , 10.0.0.2:movie-web:8282

Figure 5-15 *Eureka Server registered apps*

As you can see, this is easy for a client. You only need to add the eureka-client dependency and point to Eureka Server. Spring Boot runs all the autoconfiguration for you, and it registers within the Registry Server.

Discovering Services: Movie Microservice

Now that we have the movie-web microservice set to be discoverable, it is time for the movie microservice to use the service instances. So, let's modify the movie microservice project. Open the project in your favorite IDE, and let's make the modifications. Open the pom.xml file and add the following dependency.

```
<dependency>
        <groupId>org.springframework.cloud</groupId>
        <artifactId>spring-cloud-starter-netflix-eureka-client</artifactId>
</dependency>
```

As you can see, it is the same dependency that you added to the movie-web microservice. You need to connect to Eureka without registering because you only need to know the other instances. So, let's modify the bootstrap.yml file. Add the following property.

```
eureka:
  client:
    register-with-eureka: false
    service-url:
      default-zone: http://localhost:8761/eureka/
```

The register-with-eureka property is the only one you need. You can omit service-url because it connects by default to that URL unless you have the Eureka Server in a remote server and different port.

Next, let's open the MovieIntegrationConfiguration class. This is version 2 if you modify it with the content in Listing 5-18.

Listing 5-18. src/main/java/com/apress/cloud/movie/MovieIntegrationConfiguration.java Version 2

```
package com.apress.cloud.movie;

import com.netflix.appinfo.InstanceInfo;
import com.netflix.discovery.EurekaClient;
import lombok.AllArgsConstructor;
import org.springframework.boot.context.properties.EnableConfigurationProperties;
import org.springframework.context.annotation.Bean;
import org.springframework.context.annotation.Configuration;
import org.springframework.integration.dsl.IntegrationFlow;
import org.springframework.integration.dsl.IntegrationFlows;
import org.springframework.integration.dsl.Pollers;
import org.springframework.integration.dsl.Transformers;
import org.springframework.integration.file.dsl.Files;
import org.springframework.integration.file.splitter.FileSplitter;
import org.springframework.web.client.RestTemplate;

import java.io.File;

// Version 2 - Eureka Client
@AllArgsConstructor
@EnableConfigurationProperties(MovieProperties.class)
@Configuration
public class MovieIntegrationConfiguration {
```

```
    private MovieProperties movieProperties;
    private MovieConverter movieConverter;

    @Bean
    public IntegrationFlow fileFlow() {
        return IntegrationFlows.from(Files
                        .inboundAdapter(new File(this.movieProperties.getDirectory()))
                        .preventDuplicates(true)
                        .patternFilter(this.movieProperties.getFilePattern()),
                e -> e.poller(Pollers.fixedDelay(this.movieProperties.getFixedDelay())))
                .split(Files.splitter().markers())
                .filter(p -> !(p instanceof FileSplitter.FileMarker))
                .transform(Transformers.converter(this.movieConverter))
                .handle("movieHandler", "process")
                .get();
    }

    @Bean
    public RestTemplate restTemplate(){
        return new RestTemplate();
    }

    @Bean
    public MovieHandler movieHandler(EurekaClient discoveryClient){
        InstanceInfo instance = discoveryClient.getNextServerFromEureka("MOVIE-WEB", false);
        return new MovieHandler(restTemplate(),instance.getHomePageUrl() + "v1/movie");
    }

}
```

Listing 5-18 shows version 2 of the MovieIntegrationConfiguration class. Analyze it to compare the differences from Listing 5-8. Let's review it.

- handle. This method calls the MovieHandler bean, which is being declared. If you look at the class, you see the method process being passed as a second parameter.
- RestTemplate. This instance is useful for connecting to the microservice.
- MovieHandler. This bean uses the EurekaClient instance to get the next instance address available so that restTemplate can make the request.

Next, let's create the MovieHandler class (see Listing 5-19).

Listing 5-19. src/main/java/com/apress/cloud/movie/MovieHandler.java

```
package com.apress.cloud.movie;

import lombok.AllArgsConstructor;
import lombok.extern.slf4j.Slf4j;
import org.springframework.http.HttpStatus;
import org.springframework.http.ResponseEntity;
import org.springframework.web.client.RestTemplate;
```

```
@Slf4j
@AllArgsConstructor
public class MovieHandler {

    private RestTemplate restTemplate;
    private String serviceUrl;

    public void process(Movie movie){
        log.debug("Processing: {}", movie);
        log.debug("ServiceURL: {}", serviceUrl);

        ResponseEntity<Object> response = this.restTemplate.postForEntity(serviceUrl,movie,
        Object.class);
        if(response.getStatusCode().equals(HttpStatus.OK))
            log.debug("processed");
        else
            log.warn("Take a look of the logs...");
    }
}
```

Listing 5-19 shows the `MovieHandler` class, which uses `RestTemplate` and sends `Movie` as a JSON object to the service URL from Eureka Server.

Right now, it is not ideal to call the `getNextServerFromEureka` because you would need to call it again to get another available instance. Could it be simpler?

Ribbon: Client-Side Load Balancing Movie Microservice

To avoid directly using Eureka Client, the Spring Cloud team brings the Netflix Ribbon project to the next level. The Netflix Ribbon project is an IPC (interprocess communication) library created for the cloud for their services that allow them to have client-side load balancing with many features that probably a hardware load balancer is complicated to accomplish.

Ribbon provides *service discovery integration*, meaning that you need to have Eureka Server if you want to get all the available services; otherwise, you need to create a list of servers. Ribbon is *fault tolerant*, meaning that it knows when a server is up and running, and it can detect which servers are down. Ribbon offers *load-balancing* rules that can be extended. By default, it provides a round-robin rule, an availability filtering rule, and a weighted response-time rule.

To use Ribbon, you must add the `spring-cloud-starter-netflix-ribbon` dependency, but because you already added the `spring-cloud-starter-netflix-eureka-client` dependency, this is not necessary. Also, the Spring Cloud team offers a `@LoadBalanced` annotation that collects the list of servers and applies (unless configured) the round-robin rule.

Let's modify the `MovieIntegrationConfiguration` class. This is version 3 (see Listing 5-20).

Listing 5-20. src/main/java/com/apress/cloud/movie/MovieIntegrationConfiguration.java - version 3

```
package com.apress.cloud.movie;

import lombok.AllArgsConstructor;
import org.springframework.boot.context.properties.EnableConfigurationProperties;
import org.springframework.cloud.client.loadbalancer.LoadBalanced;
import org.springframework.context.annotation.Bean;
import org.springframework.context.annotation.Configuration;
```

```
import org.springframework.integration.dsl.IntegrationFlow;
import org.springframework.integration.dsl.IntegrationFlows;
import org.springframework.integration.dsl.Pollers;
import org.springframework.integration.dsl.Transformers;
import org.springframework.integration.file.dsl.Files;
import org.springframework.integration.file.splitter.FileSplitter;
import org.springframework.web.client.RestTemplate;

import java.io.File;

// Version 3 - With Load Balancer - Ribbon

@AllArgsConstructor
@EnableConfigurationProperties(MovieProperties.class)
@Configuration
public class MovieIntegrationConfiguration {

    private MovieProperties movieProperties;
    private MovieConverter movieConverter;

    @Bean
    public IntegrationFlow fileFlow() {
        return IntegrationFlows.from(Files
                        .inboundAdapter(new File(this.movieProperties.getDirectory()))
                        .preventDuplicates(true)
                        .patternFilter(this.movieProperties.getFilePattern()),
                e -> e.poller(Pollers.fixedDelay(this.movieProperties.getFixedDelay())))
                .split(Files.splitter().markers())
                .filter(p -> !(p instanceof FileSplitter.FileMarker))
                .transform(Transformers.converter(this.movieConverter))
                .handle("movieHandler", "process")
                .get();
    }

    @LoadBalanced
    @Bean
    public RestTemplate restTemplate(){
        return new RestTemplate();
    }

    @Bean
    public MovieHandler movieHandler(){
        return new MovieHandler(restTemplate());
    }
}
```

Listing 5-20 shows version 3 of the MovieIntegrationConfiguration class. The main change is that now the @LoadBalanced annotation is in the RestTemplate instance and MovieHandler only needs RestTemplate.

Next, let's modify the MovieHandler (version 2) class (see Listing 5-21).

Listing 5-21. src/main/java/com/apress/cloud/movie/MovieHandler.java (Version 2)

```
package com.apress.cloud.movie;

import lombok.AllArgsConstructor;
import lombok.extern.slf4j.Slf4j;
import org.springframework.http.HttpStatus;
import org.springframework.http.ResponseEntity;
import org.springframework.web.client.RestTemplate;

// Version 2 - Withe Ribbon

@Slf4j
@AllArgsConstructor
public class MovieHandler {

    private RestTemplate restTemplate;

    public void process(Movie movie){
        log.debug("Processing: {}", movie);
        ResponseEntity<Object> response = this.restTemplate.postForEntity("http://movie-web/
                                          v1/movie",movie,Object.class);
        if(response.getStatusCode().equals(HttpStatus.OK))
            log.debug("processed");
        else
            log.warn("Take a look of the logs...");
    }
}
```

Listing 5-21 shows version 2 of the `MovieHandler` class. The only difference is that it now uses only `RestTemplate`, and even though it is using a hard-coded URL (this can be set in the Config Server/Git Server), it is useful for our case. This explains a lot, but let's play with all the services.

Running All Together

Let's get all the services. You have the config-server, eureka-server, movie-web (two instances), and movie microservices that need to be up and running. You need to open several terminals, or if you are using any smart IDE, you can run them together.

1. Start the config-server and the eureka-server microservices. You can run them with the following command in separate terminal windows.

   ```
   ./mvnw clean spring-boot:run
   ```

2. Start the movie-web microservice instances. Run the version in which you added the Netflix Eureka Client as a dependency. You can run the first instance with the following.

   ```
   ./mvnw spring-boot:run -Dspring-boot.run.jvmArguments="-Dserver.
   port=8181"
   ```

Run the second one with the following in a different terminal window.

```
./mvnw spring-boot:run -Dspring-boot.run.jvmArguments="-Dserver.port=8282"
```

Wait until the two instances appear in Eureka Server. In your browser, go to `http://localhost:8761` (see Figure 5-15 to make sure they are registered).

3. Start the movie microservice. Use version 3 of the `MovieIntegrationConfiguration` class (see Listing 5-20) and version 2 of the `MovieHandler` (see Listing 5-21).

```
./mvnw clean spring-boot:run
```

4. You can add any movie text file (from the source code) to the `/tmp/movies` directory. You should see that movie-web instance 1 received some movies and instance 2 received other movies.

Congratulations! You have run several microservice with a cloud-native environment requirements, including independent deployment, multiple instances, service registery, service discovery, and centralized configuration.

Did you realize that each movie-web instance has its own movie databases? Here you need to add a centralized database, so keep everything in a persistence storage.

What would happen if all the movie-web instances were down or took too long to respond? You should have fault tolerance in mind.

Circuit Breaker

This is an implementation of the circuit breaker pattern that prevents cascading failures and provide fallback behavior until the failing service is in a normal state (see Figure 5-16).

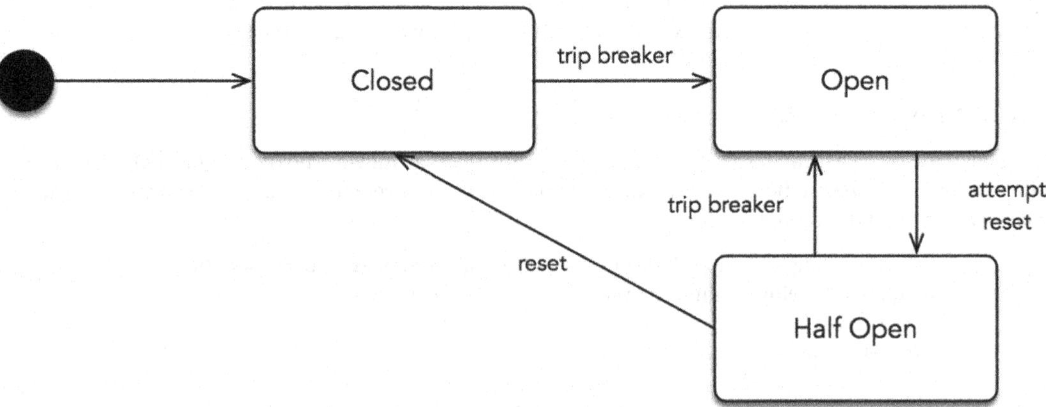

Figure 5-16. *Circuit breaker*

When you apply the circuit breaker to a service, it watches for failing calls. If these failures reach certain thresholds (this can be set programmatically), the circuit breaker opens and redirects the calls to the specified fallback operation. This gives the failing service time to recover. This pattern implementation is based on Netflix's Hystrix, and the Spring Cloud team enables this through annotations.

Hystrix: Movie Microservice

If you want to have fault tolerance in the movie microservice, it is necessary to add the right dependencies to the `pom.xml` file.

```
<dependency>
        <groupId>org.springframework.cloud</groupId>
        <artifactId>spring-cloud-starter-netflix-hystrix</artifactId>
</dependency>
```

Next, you need to add `@EnableCircuitBreaker` to the `MovieIntegrationConfiguration` class (see the following snippet).

```
@EnableCircuitBreaker
@AllArgsConstructor
@EnableConfigurationProperties(MovieProperties.class)
@Configuration
public class MovieIntegrationConfiguration {

    private MovieProperties movieProperties;
    private MovieConverter movieConverter;

    @Bean
    public IntegrationFlow fileFlow() {

        //....
```

There is another version of the `MovieHandler` class (version 3) (see Listing 5-22).

Listing 5-22. src/main/java/com/apress/cloud/movie/MovieHandler.java Version 3

```
package com.apress.cloud.movie;

import com.netflix.hystrix.contrib.javanica.annotation.HystrixCommand;
import lombok.AllArgsConstructor;
import lombok.extern.slf4j.Slf4j;
import org.springframework.http.HttpStatus;
import org.springframework.http.ResponseEntity;
import org.springframework.web.client.RestTemplate;

// Version 3 - With Circuit Breakers

@Slf4j
@AllArgsConstructor
public class MovieHandler {

    private RestTemplate restTemplate;
```

```
    public void process(Movie movie){
        log.debug("Processing: {}", movie);
        if(postMovie(movie))
            log.info("PROCESSED!");
    }

    @HystrixCommand(fallbackMethod = "defaultProcess")
    public boolean postMovie(Movie movie){
        ResponseEntity<Object> response = this.restTemplate.postForEntity("http://movie-web/
        v1/movie",movie,Object.class);
        if(response.getStatusCode().equals(HttpStatus.OK))
            return true;
        return false;
    }

    public boolean defaultProcess(Movie movie){
        log.error("COULD NOT process: {}, please try later.", movie);
        return false;
    }
}
```

Listing 5-22 shows version 3 of the `MovieHandler` class (note that we are using the `@HystrixCommand` annotation and using the `defaultProcess` method as a fallback method in case of any errors). If the service you try to use is not available, it uses the `defaultProcess` method instead until the service is up and running again. Behind the scenes, the `@HystrixCommand` annotation is an interceptor that has a try/catch implementation and creates monitor threads to keep pinging the service, so it knows when it is available again. Also, it creates a metrics stream that can be graphed to show the behavior. To use these real-time metrics, you need to add the following properties to `bootstrap.xml` in the movie microservice.

```
management:
  endpoints:
    web:
      exposure:
        include:
          - hystrix.stream
          - health
```

This exposes `/actuator/hystrix.stream`, which can present a graph based on the data. Before you run the movie microservice with these changes, you need to add `spring-boot-starter-web` because there is something missing in the configuration that requires a starter. So, add the `spring-boot-starter-web` dependency to your `pom.xml` file. If you're wondering whether there is a build UI to see these metrics—there is. It's called Hystrix Dashboard.

Hystrix Dashboard monitors and provides a lot of metrics about your services. You can create another microservice (at `https://start.spring.io`) and add only the `spring-boot-actuator` and the `spring-cloud-starter-hystrix-dashboard` dependencies, and use the `@EnableHystrixDashboard` annotation to enable it. Run it and then visit `/hystrix`. Point the dashboard to an individual instance's `/actuator/hystrix.stream` endpoint in a Hystrix client application (see Figures 5-17 and 5-18).

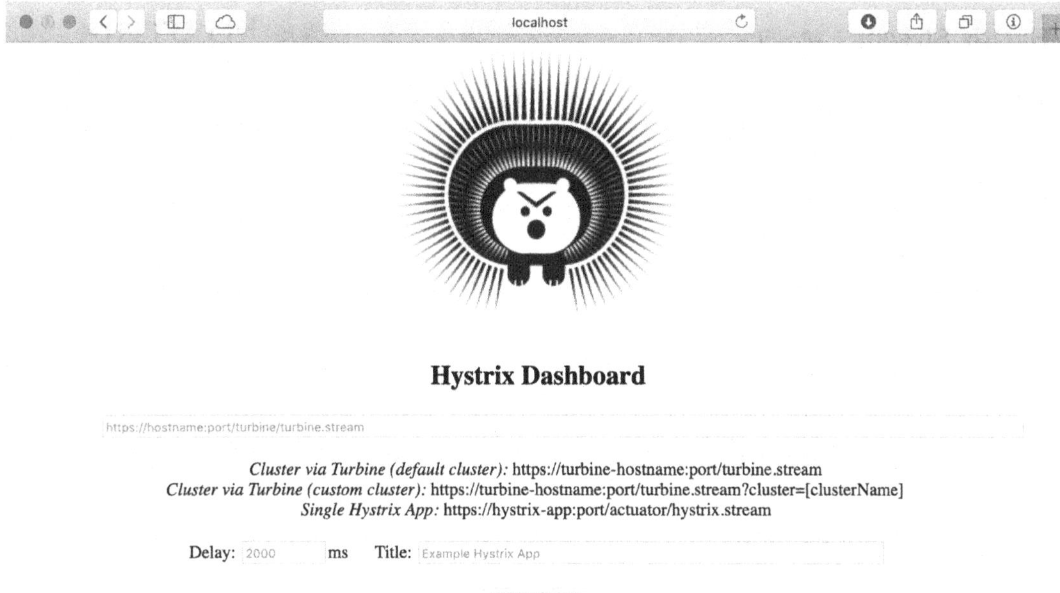

Figure 5-17. *Hystrix dashboard at http://localhost:8000/hystrix*

Here you add the microservice movie endpoint provided by the actuator, something like `http://localhost:8080/actuator/hystrix.stream`, and provide a title, like Movies, for example. To make it work, you need to send movies titles to the `/tmp/movies` folder. Then stop the movie-web instance and try again. You should see something similar to Figure 5-18. Open the circuit breaker.

Hystrix Stream: Movies

Circuit Sort: Error then Volume | Alphabetical | Volume | Error | Mean | Median | 90 | 99 | 99.5

Success | Short-Circuited | Timeout | Rejected | Failure | Error %

postMovie
0 | 0 | 0.0 %
0 | 0
0
Host: 0.0/s
Cluster: 0.0/s
Circuit Closed
Hosts 2 90th 0ms
Median 0ms 99th 0ms
Mean 0ms 99.5th 0ms

rateMovie
0 | 0 | 0.0 %
0 | 0
0
Host: 0.0/s
Cluster: 0.0/s
Circuit Closed
Hosts 2 90th 0ms
Median 0ms 99th 0ms
Mean 0ms 99.5th 0ms

trendMovie
0 | 0 | 0.0 %
0 | 0
0
Host: 0.0/s
Cluster: 0.0/s
Circuit Closed
Hosts 2 90th 0ms
Median 0ms 99th 0ms
Mean 0ms 99.5th 0ms

simpleMovie
0 | 0 | 0.0 %
0 | 0
0
Host: 0.0/s
Cluster: 0.0/s
Circuit Closed
Hosts 2 90th 0ms
Median 0ms 99th 0ms
Mean 0ms 99.5th 0ms

Thread Pools Sort: Alphabetical | Volume |

Movie Service
Host: 0.0/s
Cluster: 0.0/s
Active 0 Max Active 0
Queued 0 Executions 0
Pool Size 20 Queue Size 5

Figure 5-18. *Hystrix dashboard*

If you want more information about this dashboard, visit `https://spring.io/projects/spring-cloud`. Spring Cloud project offers other services, but that is for another book. You now have the tools to create microservices solutions.

About Reactive Programming

I've shown you some Spring Cloud subprojects that solve some of the twelve-factor guidelines and move toward microservices architectures, but where does reactive programming fit?

Remember that one of the important features of microservices is the ability to communicate with other microservices and legacy systems. Imagine that your microservice app needs to access several systems at once, and you already have a client that makes several calls to aggregate everything. At some point, this app becomes very chatty (network latency, concurrency, blocking, etc.), and you don't have only one client making this kind of request. You would have millions of requests.

Reactive programming solves this problem using a particular pattern: the API Gateway.

```
Observable<MarketExchangeRates> details = Observable.zip(
  localService.getExchangeRates("usd"),
  yahooFinancialService.getGlobalRates("mxn","jpy"),
  googleFinancialService.getEuropeExchangeRates(),
```

```
    (local, yahoo, google) -> {
          MarketExchangeRates exchangeRates = new
MarketExchangeRates();
          exchangeRates.setLocalMarket(local.getRates());
          exchangeRates.setEurope(google.getRates({"eur","gpb"}));
          exchangeRates.setGlobal(yahoo.getRate());
          return exchangeRates;
    }
);
```

With this code, you can do several parallel tasks and avoid resources like network hops and latency, concurrency, and blocking. Also, a service like Yahoo! Financial Services uses a config service, can register itself to a service registry, and use default methods in the event of a failure (e.g., circuit breaker).

Summary

This chapter discussed the microservices architecture and the challenges with designing cloud-native applications. I showed you how Spring Cloud subprojects help you create fast and easy cloud-native applications with the power of Spring Boot. It is an awesome technology that makes microservices easy to develop.

CHAPTER 6

Spring Cloud Stream

In previous chapters, I discussed some of the Spring Cloud projects, like Spring Cloud Config Server, Eureka Server, Ribbon, and Hystrix (an implementation of the circuit breaker pattern) to emphasize that microservices have to solve problems like externalized configuration, being discoverable in a failure, load balancing on the client side, fault tolerance, being reliable, and autorecovery after a crash. Thanks to Spring Cloud modules, you can resolve these issues and more.

So far, you have seen microservices that talk to each other through REST interfaces. In the previous chapters, you used `RestTemplate` to communicate from one microservice to another. But what happens if you need to communicate using a different protocol or middleware brokers like JMS, AMQP, WebSocket, STOMP, or MQTT? Do you need to learn every technology to do any integration? I mean, there are a lot of new technologies emerging that promote being fast, reliable, and fault-tolerant. Is there any solution or technology today that allows you to integrate applications or a system using middleware without learning it? Yes, Spring Cloud Stream!

In this chapter, you use Spring Cloud Stream Application Starters to see how easy it is to use any middleware broker without applying a single line of code. Then you see how Spring Cloud Stream works when you are introduced to the architecture and the programming model. It is very easy to create a custom stream that integrates with other technologies.

Spring Cloud Stream Application Starters

Spring Cloud Stream Application Starters are stand-alone executables that communicate with each other or an external system or application using messaging (e.g., HTTP), middleware (e.g., RabbitMQ, Apache Kafka, Kafka Stream, or Amazon Kinesis), or storage solutions (e.g., relational, non-relational, file system). Of course, other brokers are supported, including Google PubSub, Solace PubSub+, Azure Event Hubs, and Apache RocketMQ; the community provides all of them.

The following are some of the Application Starters features.

- Stand-alone runnable Spring Boot applications make them opinionated, robust, and flexible. Based on Spring Boot, these apps can override their default configuration through command lines, environment variables, YAML files, and Spring Cloud Configuration (this feature is already integrated within the app).
- These apps are based on enterprise integration patterns, meaning that they are based on Spring Integration, making them enterprise-ready.
- They can be used as Maven or Docker artifacts to create streaming pipelines with Spring Cloud Data Flow.

F. Gutierrez, *Spring Cloud Data Flow*, https://doi.org/10.1007/978-1-4842-1239-4_6

- They provide source, processor, and sink connectors that are used with any middleware technology (any broker), storage solutions (SQL, NoSQL, file system), or simply as HTTP request/responses. The *source* is ingesting data from any so source and forwards the payload to an *output channel*. The *processor* encapsulates both source and sink because it ingests data from an *input channel*, processes the payload, and sends it to an output channel. The *sink* gets the payload from the input channel.
- They provide adapters for various network protocols.
- These apps are based on Spring Web, so they open port 8080 by default, but this can be easily overridden by setting the `server.port` property at runtime using environment variables, in a command line, or in the `application.properties` file.
- They provide generic processors customized with SpEL (Spring Expression Language) or any other script language, like Groovy or Python.

Channels are the main method to expose the data to middleware messaging or storage. The middleware (regardless of the protocol) and the modules to connect the apps are called *binders*. RabbitMQ, Kafka, Kafka Streams, and Amazon Kinesis are the primary prebuilt binders supported by the Spring Cloud team.

Before we start with a simple example, you need to know some Application Starters naming conventions. You can find them in the Spring repositories, ready to be downloaded as JARs at `https://repo.spring.io/release/org/springframework/cloud/stream/app/`. The naming convention is *<functionality>-<type>-<binder>[-<version>]*. In the next example, you use a source (an HTTP application) and a sink (a log application) that is connected through RabbitMQ (our binder), so you need to find the following names.

- `http-source-rabbit` is an HTTP Spring Cloud Application Starter (source) that uses RabbitMQ as a binder. It opens an HTTP port that listens for incoming requests and forwards the payload to RabbitMQ (output channel).
- `log-sink-rabbit` is a log-sink Spring Cloud Application Starter that uses RabbitMQ as a binder to listen for new incoming messages (input channel) and logs them into the console.

In this chapter, you are using several of these out-of-the-box Spring Cloud Application Starters.

You also can use also Docker, and the naming convention is the same: *springcloudstream/<functionality>-<type>-<binder>:<version>*.

There are about 70 proven Application Starters that are divided into sources, processors, and sinks, and some of them can connect with external systems like Hadoop, GemFire, TensorFlow, Python, and Groovy scripts; but let's start with our first example.

HTTP Source | Log-Sink Example

Let's start by using out-of-the-box apps that work. There are different ways to get these apps; one is to go directly to GitHub at `https://github.com/spring-cloud-stream-app-starters` to download the source code and built them.

```
./mvnw clean install -PgenerateApps
```

In this example, you send a JSON message to an HTTP source application that sends it to the binder (RabbitMQ), and the message is consumed by the log-sink app, and it logs the message into the console (see Figure 6-1).

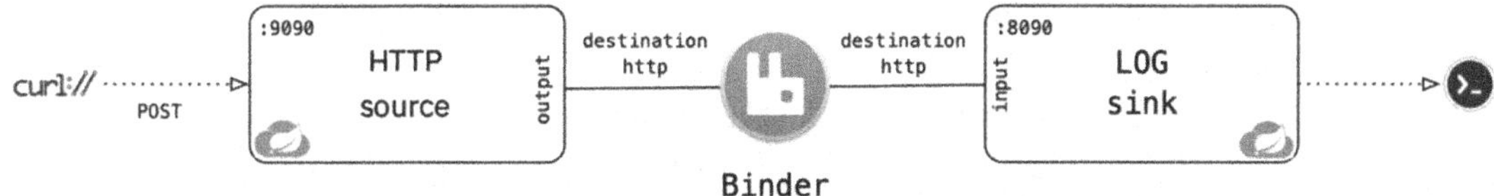

Figure 6-1. *Spring Cloud App Starters HTTP|log*

Using Uber-Jars

You are using the prebuilt uber-jars. Let's go through it step by step.

1. Make sure you have Java 8 at a minimum on your system. I run Java 8 for all the examples in this book.

2. Download the JARs from `https://repo.spring.io/release/org/springframework/cloud/stream/app/`. Look for the `http-source-rabbit` and `log-sink-rabbit` folders. You can use the latest version (when writing this book, the version was 2.1.1.RELEASE and 2.1.2.RELEASE, respectively). Save them in a workspace directory.

3. You need to use RabbitMQ as a binder, so if you have one already installed, you can use that one, or if you need to install it, you can download it from `www.rabbitmq.com/download.html`. It depends on Erlang, so make sure you have that as well. In this book, I use Docker for some of the technologies. If you need to install Docker, I recommend installing Docker Desktop from `www.docker.com/products/docker-desktop` if you are using Mac or Windows. If you are using Linux, follow the installation information at `https://runnable.com/docker/install-docker-on-linux`.

   To use a RabbitMQ Docker image, open a terminal window and execute the following command.

   ```
   $ docker run -d --rm --name rabbit -p 15672:15672 -p 5672:5672
   rabbitmq:3.8.3-management-alpine
   ```

   Make sure you have RabbitMQ up and running by going to `https://localhost:15672` with the username/password `guest/guest`.

4. Next, let's run the HTTP app with the following command (make sure you are in the directory where the two uber-jars are).

   ```
   $ java -jar http-source-rabbit-2.1.1.RELEASE.jar \
         --spring.cloud.stream.bindings.output.destination=http \
         --server.port=9090
   ```

   The preceding command starts the HTTP source app that listens for incoming data in port 9090. Note that you are adding a property: `spring.cloud.stream.bindings.output.destination=http`. This property tells the app to use the `http` output channel as a destination where it forwards the incoming payload. I discuss these properties later. If you don't add the `destination` property, the app uses the `output` property by default.

5. Open a new terminal window and run the log-sink app by using the following command.

```
$ java -jar log-sink-rabbit-2.1.2.RELEASE.jar \
      --spring.cloud.stream.bindings.input.destination=http \
      --server.port=8090
```

   The preceding command runs the log-sink app in port 8090, and its destination is `http` (the same as the HTTP source app). If you don't add this property, then it takes the default, `input`, but you are never going to get the messages because no one is sending it to the input destination. That's why it needs to be the same as the HTTP source (see Figure 6-1).

6. Next, open a new terminal to post some messages. Execute the following command.

```
$ curl -XPOST -H "Content-Type: application/json" -d '
{"msg": "Hello App Starters"}}' http://localhost:9090
$ curl -XPOST -H "Content-Type: application/json" -d '
{"msg": "This is awesome"}}' http://localhost:9090
$ curl -XPOST -H "Content-Type: application/json" -d '
{"msg": "Hello Spring Cloud"}}' http://localhost:9090
```

You should see the message in the log-sink terminal.

Congratulations! You have run your first Spring Cloud Application Starters solution! Even though this is a simple example, you can use the Application Starter in common day-to-day solutions, such as reading from a file system or processing a message and saving it to a database. Yes, you can do this with Application Starters!

There are many ways to run Application Starters. They are based on Spring Boot, which means that you can override defaults like use command-line arguments, environment variables, `application.properties` files, and the Spring Cloud Config server. When you run Spring Cloud Application Starters apps, you find the following output in the logs (at the beginning).

```
Fetching config from server at : http://localhost:8888
```

This means that if you run the following *Config Server* from the previous chapter, and create the properties for these apps, it is easier running them without using any extra parameter, only `java -jar`.

```
$ cd ch05/config-server
$ ./mvnw spring-boot:run
```

For example, for the `http-source-rabbit` app starter, you can create `http-source.yml` file in GitHub with the following properties.

```
spring:
  cloud:
    stream:
      bindings:
        output:
          destination: http
server:
  port: 9090
```

For the `log-sink-rabbit` app starter, you need to create the `log-sink.yml` file within your GitHub repository, with the following content.

```
spring:
  cloud:
    stream:
      bindings:
        input:
          destination: http
server:
  port: 8090
```

Run the apps as follows with no parameters at all.

```
$ java -jar http-source-rabbit-2.1.1.RELEASE.jar
$ java -jar log-sink-rabbit-2.1.2.RELEASE.jar
```

You are using the power of Spring Cloud and its modules.

Using Docker

Application Starters is used for this next example. (I use Unix commands. If you are using Windows OS, look for the right translation when using paths.) First, take a look at Figure 6-2 to see how to create it. You need Docker images because you are adding processors. A *filter processor* filters your message if the `msg` key contains a `Hello` value. Then it uses the Groovy Transform processor to set the value in uppercase (you create a Groovy script to transform the `msg` value).

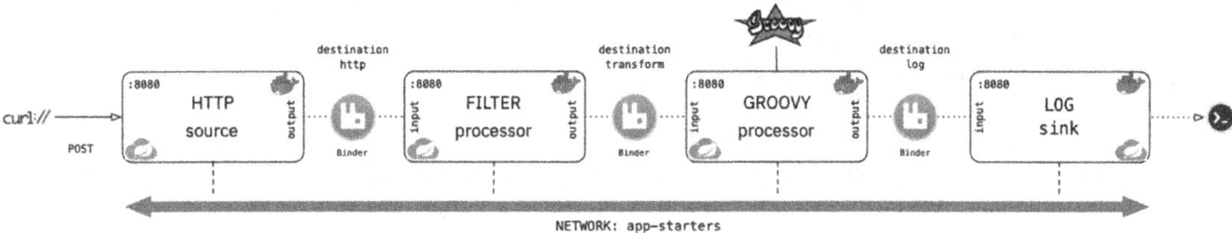

Figure 6-2. *Using Docker HTTP | FILTER | TRANSFORM | LOG*

Figure 6-2 shows the solution for this example. Let's go through it step by step.

1. First, make sure your RabbitMQ has stopped. If you are using Docker, make sure you is removed from the docker process list. In this scenario, you need to make sure RabbitMQ runs in the same network as the Application Starters.

2. Create a Docker network with the following command.

   ```
   $ docker network create app-starters
   ```

3. Next, put the RabbitMQ Docker image in the same network. Execute the following command.

   ```
   $ docker run -d --rm \
     --name rabbit \
   ```

```
  --network app-starters \
  --hostname rabbit \
  rabbitmq:3.8.3-management-alpine
```

Note that this is the app-starters network. I used the \ symbol to specify that there is another line before executing the command.

4. Next, run the HTTP source.

```
docker run -d \
  -p 8080:8080 \
  --name http \
  --rm \
  --network app-starters \
  --env SPRING.CLOUD.STREAM.BINDINGS.OUTPUT.DESTINATION='http' \
  --env SPRING.RABBITMQ.HOST='rabbit' \
  springcloudstream/http-source-rabbit:2.1.1.RELEASE
```

Note that the properties are used as environment variables. This is the only container that exposes 8080 to our host, so it's easy to post messages.

5. Next, run the filter processor.

```
docker run -d \
  --name filter \
  --rm \
  --network app-starters \
  --env SPRING.CLOUD.STREAM.BINDINGS.INPUT.DESTINATION='http' \
  --env SPRING.CLOUD.STREAM.BINDINGS.OUTPUT.DESTINATION='transform' \
  --env FILTER.EXPRESSION="#jsonPath(payload,'$.msg').contains('Hello')" \
  --env SPRING.RABBITMQ.HOST='rabbit' \
  springcloudstream/filter-processor-rabbit:2.1.1.RELEASE
```

The filter processor lets the messages that contain (camel case) the word "Hello" pass. It's using *SpEL* with the built-in jsonPath object that can manipulate JSON objects. We are also declaring the properties for INPUT and OUTPUT destinations; the processor always needs both.

6. Next, in your working directory, create the transform.groovy script with the following content.

```
import groovy.json.JsonSlurper
import groovy.json.JsonOutput

def jsonSlurper = new JsonSlurper()
def json = jsonSlurper.parseText(new String(payload))

json.msg = json.msg.toUpperCase()

JsonOutput.toJson(json)
```

This code is Groovy script, which is very similar to Java. (In my opinion, it's less verbose. Learn more about it at https://groovy-lang.org/. I think it is very straightforward; it gets the payload and uppercases the msg value. In a Groovy script, the last line is considered a return value.

7. Next, execute the Groovy Transform processor app with the following command.

```
docker run -d \
  --name transform \
  --rm \
  --network app-starters \
  --env SPRING.CLOUD.STREAM.BINDINGS.INPUT.DESTINATION='transform' \
  --env SPRING.CLOUD.STREAM.BINDINGS.OUTPUT.DESTINATION='log' \
  --env SPRING.RABBITMQ.HOST='rabbit' \
  --env GROOVY-TRANSFORMER.SCRIPT=file:///mnt/transform.groovy \
  --volume $PWD/:/mnt \
  springcloudstream/groovy-transform-processor-rabbit:2.1.1.RELEASE
```

   Note that you are still using the input and output destinations. The important part here is that you are using the `groovy-transformer.script` property, which looks for the `transform.groovy` in the `/mnt` path. Also look at the `--volume` argument from Docker, where you are using our current path and where you saved the `transform.groovy` script; its content is mounted in the `/mnt` folder. It's important for Windows OS users to use the full path, something like `--volume C:\workspace\:/mnt` or wherever you have your `transform.groovy` script file. After running this command, make sure the script is in the `/mnt` folder by executing the following.

```
$ docker exec transform bash -c 'ls -lrt /mnt'
```

   `transform.groovy` should be listed.

8. Next, execute log-sink with the following command.

```
docker run -d \
  --name log \
  --rm \
  --network app-starters \
  --env SPRING.CLOUD.STREAM.BINDINGS.INPUT.DESTINATION='log' \
  --env SPRING.RABBITMQ.HOST='rabbit' \
  springcloudstream/log-sink-rabbit:2.1.2.RELEASE
```

9. Next, view the log-sink app's logs with the following command.

```
$ docker logs -f log
```

10. Finally, send some messages.

```
$ curl -XPOST -H "Content-Type: application/json" -d '{"msg": "Hello App
Starters"}}' http://localhost:8080
$ curl -XPOST -H "Content-Type: application/json" -d '{"msg": "This is
awesome"}}' http://localhost:8080
$ curl -XPOST -H "Content-Type: application/json" -d '{"msg": "Hello Spring
Cloud"}}' http://localhost:8080
```

The log-sink app logs that the messages were converted to uppercase when the msg value contains the word `Hello`. Congrats!! You created a solution using Docker as your main infrastructure.

Remember that you can still use Spring Cloud Config Server with the same files (`http-source.yml`, `filter-processor.yml`, `groovy-transformer-processor.yml`, and `log-sink.yml`) and avoid all the environment variable definitions. Remember, there are many ways to run these apps.

Later, you will orchestrate all these containers with Kubernetes to have a reliable, scalable, and fault-tolerant solution using Spring Cloud Data Flow!

Using Docker Compose

Instead of executing all these commands, you can run Docker Compose. Copy the following `docker-compose.yaml` file into your workspace directory (see Listing 6-1).

Listing 6-1. docker-compose.yaml

```
version: '3'
services:
  rabbit:
    image: "rabbitmq:3.8.3-management-alpine"
    container_name: rabbit
    networks:
      - app-starters

  http:
    image: "springcloudstream/http-source-rabbit:2.1.1.RELEASE"
    container_name: http
    environment:
      - spring.cloud.stream.bindings.output.destination=http
      - spring.rabbitmq.host=rabbit
    ports:
      - "8080:8080"
    networks:
      - app-starters

  filter:
    image: "springcloudstream/filter-processor-rabbit:2.1.1.RELEASE"
    container_name: filter
    environment:
      - spring.cloud.stream.bindings.input.destination=http
      - spring.cloud.stream.bindings.output.destination=transform
      - spring.rabbitmq.host=rabbit
      - filter.expression=#jsonPath(payload,'$$.msg').contains('Hello')
    networks:
      - app-starters

  transform:
    image: "springcloudstream/groovy-transform-processor-rabbit:2.1.1.RELEASE"
    container_name: transform
    environment:
      - spring.cloud.stream.bindings.input.destination=transform
      - spring.cloud.stream.bindings.output.destination=log
      - spring.rabbitmq.host=rabbit
      - groovy-transformer.script=file:///mnt/transform.groovy
```

```
    volumes:
      - "$PWD/:/mnt"
    networks:
      - app-starters

  log:
    image: "springcloudstream/log-sink-rabbit:2.1.2.RELEASE"
    container_name: log
    environment:
      - spring.cloud.stream.bindings.input.destination=log
      - spring.rabbitmq.host=rabbit
    networks:
      - app-starters

networks:
  app-starters:
```

Listing 6-1 shows the `docker-compose.yaml` file. Note that it is the same as the Docker commands, but look closely at the `filter.expression` property. Because you are using jsonPath to look for the `$.msg` value, the `$` must be escaped, and here you use the double `$$`.

■ **Note** You can download all the source code for this chapter in the Apress web site.

I said that you can use different binders. Well, you can choose whatever Uber-JARs or Docker method you wish to run App Starters using Kafka. You need to use the correct *<functionality>-<type>-<binder>* naming convention, so if you want to test HTTP | LOG, you must download `http-source-kafka` and `log-sink-kafka`.

Spring Cloud Stream

In this section, you learn more about Spring Cloud Stream, its main concepts, and a programming model that changed in 3.x, and I talk more about binders. In later chapters, you create a custom binder to be a communication channel between microservices without using a specific API.

First, let's look at a small example that illustrates the power of this technology and how you can use the same code regardless of the binder.

Movie Cloud Stream Using Kafka: movie-sink-kafka

Let's create a simple microservice that does a sink's role: logs movies by producer (see Figure 6-3).

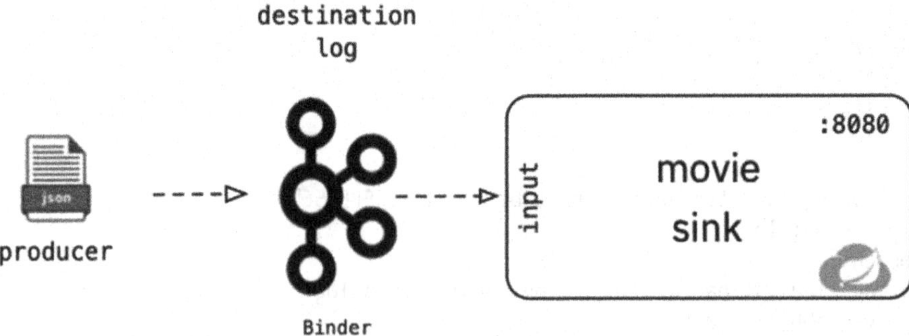

Figure 6-3. Movie Cloud Stream using Kafka (sink - movie-sink-kafka)

Open your browser and point to `https://start.spring.io`. Add the following metadata.

- Group: `com.apress.cloud.stream`
- Artifact: `movie`
- Dependencies: Cloud Stream, Spring for Apache Kafka Streams, Lombok

Click the Generate button to download a ZIP file. Uncompress and import it into your favorite IDE (see Figure 6-4).

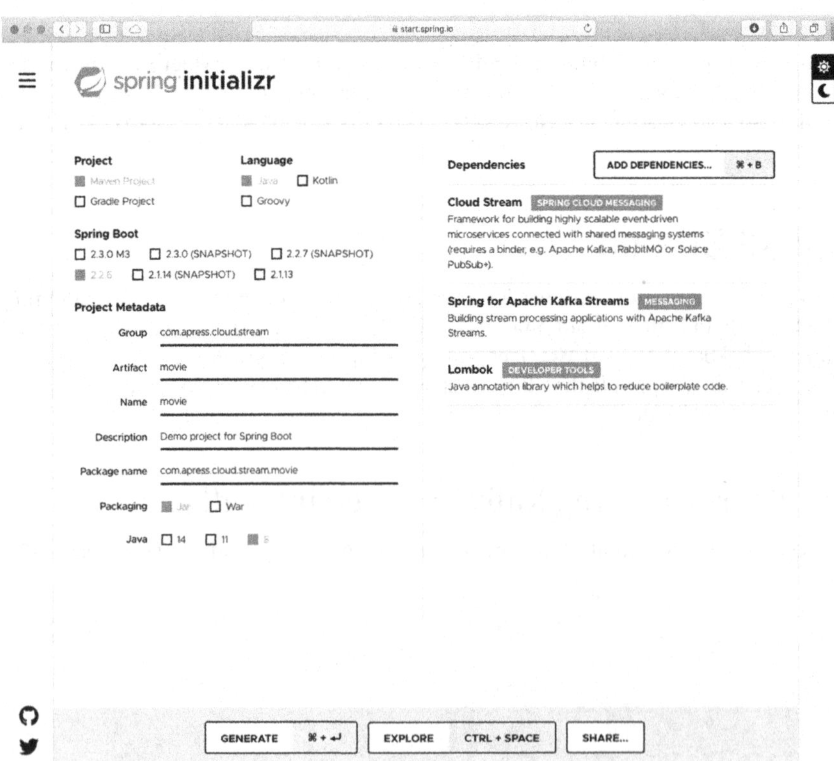

Figure 6-4. `https://start.spring.io` *- Spring Initializr - Movie Cloud Stream - Sink*

Let's start by opening the `pom.xml` file. Note that you have two Kafka dependencies in place, but you need to add a third one (see Listing 6-2).

Listing 6-2. pom.xml Snippet

```
...

<!-- Kafka Streams : Binder -->
<dependency>
        <groupId>org.apache.kafka</groupId>
        <artifactId>kafka-streams</artifactId>
</dependency>
<dependency>
        <groupId>org.springframework.cloud</groupId>
        <artifactId>spring-cloud-stream-binder-kafka-streams</artifactId>
</dependency>
<dependency>
        <groupId>org.springframework.cloud</groupId>
        <artifactId> spring-cloud-stream-binder-kafka</artifactId>
</dependency>
...
```

Listing 6-2 shows a snippet of `pom.xml` that adds the dependencies that Spring Cloud Stream needs to use a Kafka broker. Remember to add the `spring-cloud-stream-binder-kafka` dependency.

Next, create the `Movie` class. You can use the one from previous chapters (see Listing 6-3).

Listing 6-3. src/main/java/com/apress/cloud/stream/movie/Movie.java

```
package com.apress.cloud.stream.movie;

import lombok.AllArgsConstructor;
import lombok.Data;
import lombok.NoArgsConstructor;

@AllArgsConstructor
@NoArgsConstructor
@Data
public class Movie {
    private String title;
    private String actor;
    private int year;
}
```

Listing 6-3 shows the `Movie` class. Note that you are using the Lombok annotations to avoid boilerplate setters and getters and the `toString` override.

Next, create the `MovieStream` class. This is the sink (see Listing 6-4).

Listing 6-4. src/main/java/com/apress/cloud/stream/movie/MovieStream.java

```
package com.apress.cloud.stream.movie;

import lombok.extern.log4j.Log4j2;
```

```java
import org.springframework.context.annotation.Bean;
import org.springframework.context.annotation.Configuration;

import java.util.function.Consumer;

@Log4j2
@Configuration
public class MovieStream {

    @Bean
    public Consumer<Movie> log() {
        return movie -> {
            log.info("Movie received: {}",movie);
        };
    }
}
```

Listing 6-4 shows the `MovieStream` class, a sink with a method named log, and it returns a `Consumer` interface. And yes, this is part of reactive/functional programming, which I discuss in the next sections. It is one of the programming models that Spring Cloud Stream offers.

Next, let's modify `application.properties` with the content from Listing 6-5.

Listing 6-5. src/main/resources/application.properties

```
# Bindings for Kafka
spring.cloud.stream.bindings.log-in-0.destination=log
```

Listing 6-5 shows the `application.properties` file that defines a `log-in-0` binding with the destination named log. `log-in-0` is part of what Kafka does. You can have several consumers within a group, and you identify them with the `name-in-#` format, meaning that you have `log-in-1`, `log-in-2`, and so forth; in this case, it is `log-in-0`. This is also necessary for the programming model you are using here, but don't worry; this becomes clearer in the next sections.

The Spring Cloud Stream Application Starter log (log-sink-rabbit) is the same code (more or less) because the Spring Cloud team added more functionality to it. Now, you can call this microservice the *movie-sink-kafka* app starter.

Let's test it. Use Docker Compose to run Kafka. If you are familiar with this technology, it uses Zookeeper to create clusters, so I think it is easier to use Docker in this case. Use the `docker-compose.yml` file that comes in the companion source code (see Listing 6-6).

Listing 6-6. docker-compose.yml

```yaml
version: '3'

services:
  zookeeper:
    image: 'bitnami/zookeeper:latest'
    container_name: zookeeper
    networks:
      - kafka-net
    ports:
      - '2181:2181'
    environment:
```

```
      - ALLOW_ANONYMOUS_LOGIN=yes

  kafka:
    image: 'bitnami/kafka:latest'
    container_name: kafka
    networks:
      - kafka-net
    ports:
      - '9092:9092'
    environment:
      - KAFKA_CFG_ZOOKEEPER_CONNECT=zookeeper:2181
      - KAFKA_CFG_ADVERTISED_LISTENERS=PLAINTEXT://localhost:9092
      - ALLOW_PLAINTEXT_LISTENER=yes
    depends_on:
      - zookeeper

networks:
  kafka-net:
```

Listing 6-6 shows the `docker-compose.yml`. Note that you are using the Zookeeper Bitnami images and Kafka. To start Kafka, open a terminal window and execute the following.

```
$ docker-compose up
```

Run the application in your IDE or execute the following command in the terminal window with your microservices.

```
$ ./mvnw spring-boot:run
```

Next, send some movies to the `movie-sink-kafka` stream. Open a terminal window and execute the following command. This command is interactive, so you can add the JSON object.

```
$ docker exec -it kafka /opt/bitnami/kafka/bin/kafka-console-producer.sh --broker-list
127.0.0.1:9092 --topic log
> {"title":"The Matrix","actor":"Keanu Reeves","year":1999}
> {"title":"Memento","actor":" Guy Pearce ","year":2000}
```

After executing these commands, you should see something similar to the following in the logs.

```
Movie received: Movie(title=The Matrix, actor=Keanu Reeves, year=1999)
Movie received: Movie(title=Memento, actor= Guy Pearce , year=2000)
```

Congratulations, you created your own Cloud Stream sink!

Stop the Docker producer by pressing Ctrl+C, and then stop Docker Compose by executing `docker-compose down` in the same directory where it was started.

Movie Cloud Stream Using RabbitMQ: movie-sink-rabbit

Now its time to create a sink using the RabbitMQ binder. What do you need to create movie-sink-rabbit? You are modifying the same project. Let's get started (see Figure 6-5).

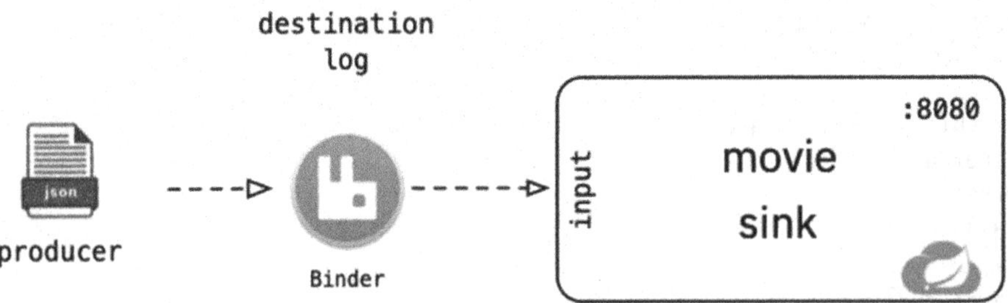

Figure 6-5. *Movie Cloud Stream using RabbitMQ (sink - movie-sink-rabbit)*

Open your `pom.xml` file, comment the three Kafka dependencies, and add the `spring-cloud-starter-stream-rabbit` dependency (see Listing 6-7).

Listing 6-7. pom.xml Snippet

```
...
<!-- RabbitMQ Streams - Binder-->
<dependency>
        <groupId>org.springframework.cloud</groupId>
        <artifactId>spring-cloud-starter-stream-rabbit</artifactId>
</dependency>
...
```

That's all you need to do. Let's test it.

First, use the following command to make sure RabbitMQ is up and running.

```
$ docker run -d --rm \
  --name rabbit \
  -p 15672:15672 -p 5672:5672 \
  rabbitmq:3.8.3-management-alpine
```

Next, run the application.

Open your browser and point to `http://localhost:15672`. Access the RabbitMQ console with `guest/guest`. Go to the Queues tabs. You find something like `log.anonymous.xxxx` queue. Click the queue (see Figure 6-6).

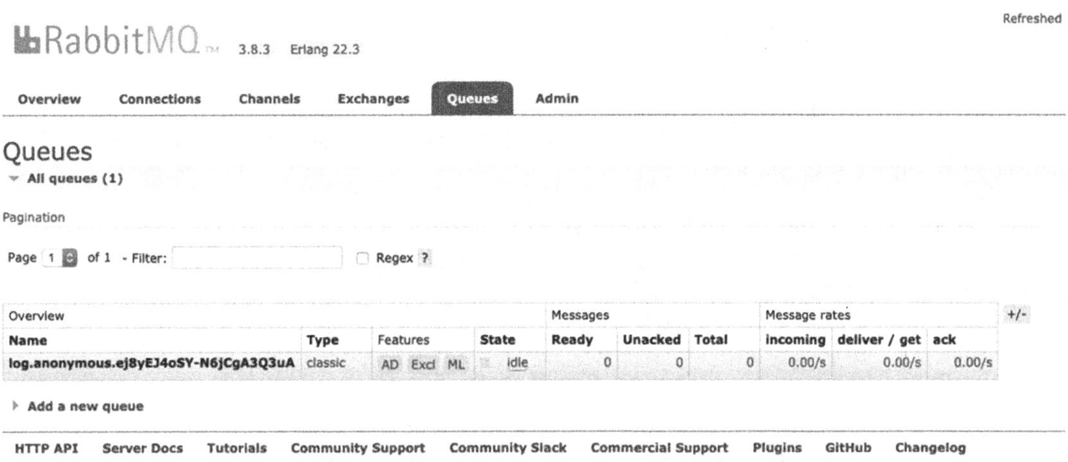

Figure 6-6. *http://localhost:15672/#/queues - log.anonymous.xxxx*

Once you click the queue, go to the **Publish message** section. In the Properties field, add `content_type` with an `application/json` value and add a movie in JSON format (see Figure 6-7).

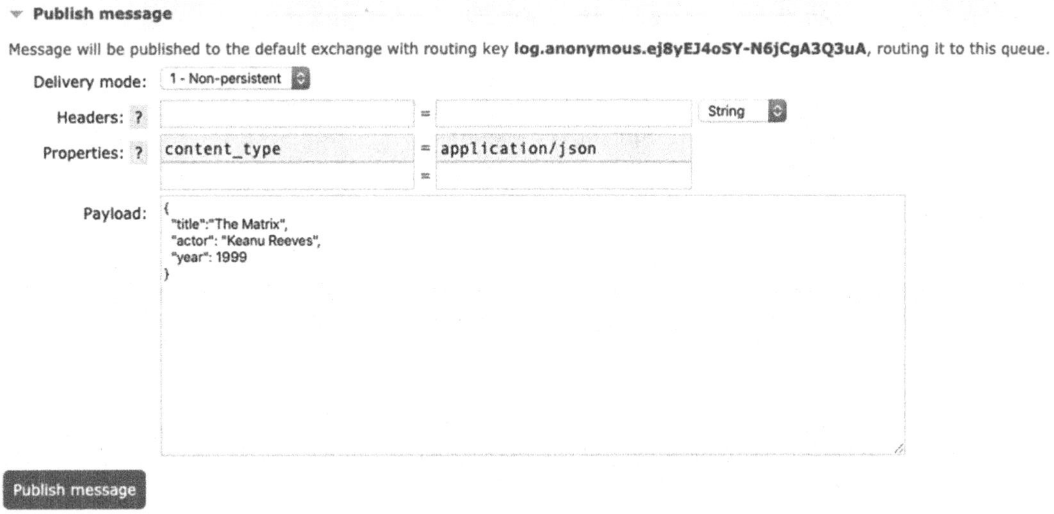

Figure 6-7. *Queue publish message*

Click the **`Publish message`** button. You see something like the following in the application logs.

```
Movie received: Movie(title=The Matrix, actor=Keanu Reeves, year=1999)
```

Congratulations! You have created the movie-sink-rabbit app starter! You may be wondering why you did not change the `application.properties`. Well, this is the beauty of Spring Cloud Stream and the way Spring Boot does autoconfiguration. It knows how to treat those properties. I discuss them later.

Spring Cloud Stream

Spring Cloud Stream is a message-driven framework for creating microservices apps. It is built on top of Spring Boot, which makes it possible to create enterprise-ready microservices with ease. It uses Spring Integration to expose enterprise integration patterns and provides an easy way to communicate (through channels) with any messaging broker.

One of the main features (in my opinion, the key feature) of Spring Cloud Stream is that it provides an opinionated configuration for *any* middleware broker by using the Java Service Provider Interface (SPI), making implementation and integration very easy. It uses messaging patterns like publish-subscribe, consumer groups, and partitions (see Figure 6-8).

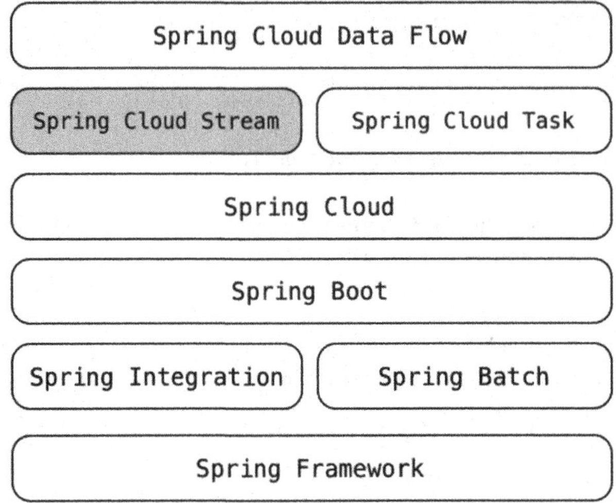

Figure 6-8. *Spring ecosystem*

Because Spring Cloud Stream is based on Spring Boot, you can convert an existing Spring Boot application into a Spring Cloud Stream app by adding the following dependencies.

```
...
              <dependency>
                <groupId>org.springframework.cloud</groupId>
                <artifactId>spring-cloud-stream</artifactId>
        </dependency>

...
<dependencyManagement>
        <dependencies>
                <dependency>
                        <groupId>org.springframework.cloud</groupId>
                        <artifactId>spring-cloud-dependencies</artifactId>
                        <version>${spring-cloud.version}</version>
                        <type>pom</type>
                        <scope>import</scope>
```

```
        </dependency>
    </dependencies>
</dependencyManagement>
```

I used the Horsham.SR7 version of Spring Cloud dependencies when writing this book; you can check the main page for the latest GA version (`https://spring.io/projects/spring-cloud-stream`).

You also need to add the right binder dependencies, which are based on your supported brokers; the Spring Cloud Stream homepage shows the brokers supported. In this book, you use either Kafka or RabbitMQ. For Kafka, you need to add the following binder dependencies.

```
<dependency>
    <groupId>org.apache.kafka</groupId>
    <artifactId>kafka-streams</artifactId>
</dependency>
<dependency>
    <groupId>org.springframework.cloud</groupId>
    <artifactId>spring-cloud-stream-binder-kafka-streams</artifactId>
</dependency>
<dependency>
    <groupId>org.springframework.cloud</groupId>
    <artifactId>spring-cloud-stream-binder-kafka</artifactId>
</dependency>
```

The preceding dependencies help when using Kafka and Kafka Stream model programming. And if you need the RabbitMQ broker, you need to add the following binder dependencies.

```
<dependency>
    <groupId>org.springframework.cloud</groupId>
    <artifactId>spring-cloud-starter-stream-rabbit</artifactId>
</dependency>
```

If you need to do unit and integration testing, you can add the following dependencies.

```
<dependency>
    <groupId>org.springframework.boot</groupId>
    <artifactId>spring-boot-starter-test</artifactId>
    <scope>test</scope>
    <exclusions>
        <exclusion>
            <groupId>org.junit.vintage</groupId>
            <artifactId>junit-vintage-engine</artifactId>
        </exclusion>
    </exclusions>
</dependency>
<dependency>
    <groupId>org.springframework.cloud</groupId>
    <artifactId>spring-cloud-stream-test-support</artifactId>
    <scope>test</scope>
</dependency>
```

Spring Cloud Stream Features

Spring Cloud Stream provides several features that allow you to create and extend message-driven microservice applications.

- It provides a middleware-neutral core, meaning that your microservice can communicate with other microservices and external services through middleware-specific binder implementations. You need to use destinations (input and output channels) in your code (see Figure 6-9).

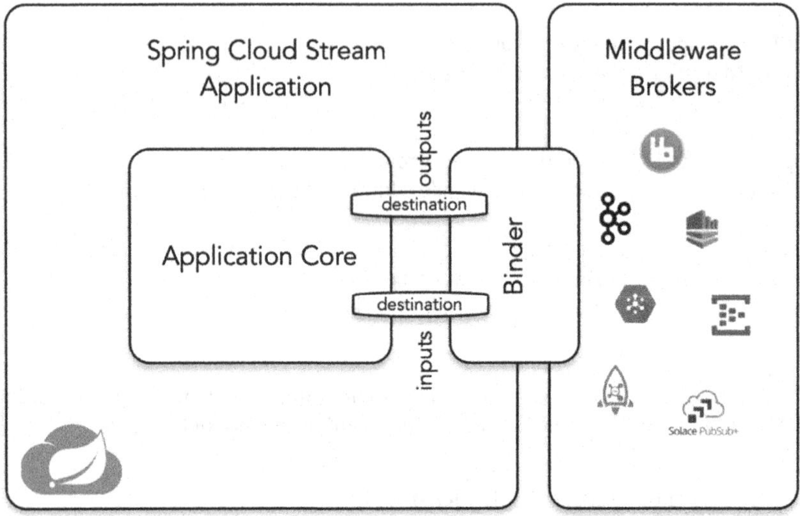

Figure 6-9. *Spring Cloud Stream application model*

- You can run stand-alone Spring Cloud Stream apps using any build tool, including Maven or Gradle, to produce runnable JARs.
- Spring Cloud Stream provides binder implementations for Kafka and RabbitMQ (with the Spring Cloud team). Other binders are supported by the community (Amazon Kinesis, Google PubSub, Solace PubSub+, Azure Event Hubs, and Apache RocketMQ). If you are not using any of these binder implementations, you can create your own. Spring Cloud Stream provides the binder abstraction based on the Java Service Provider Interface, so it's easy to write your own plug-and-play binder. You create a binder implementation later.

  With this binder abstraction, it is easy to dynamically choose the mapping to external destinations (input and output channels) at runtime through your application properties when you declare the `spring.cloud.stream.bindings.[input|output].destination` property. Spring Cloud Stream creates a **topic** if you are using Kafka or a **queue** if you are using RabbitMQ. Because Spring Cloud Stream is opinionated, it configures your binder based on what you have in your classpath. Because of this abstraction, you can easily add multiple binders to your Cloud Stream app. You probably need to consume (input destination) from RabbitMQ and process and send the payload (output destination) to a Kafka broker (see Figure 6-10).

- It provides a testing framework for unit and integrations testing for your Cloud Stream applications. It provides a specialized binder implementation for testing purposes.
- It provides a publish-subscribe communication that reduce the complexity of producers and consumers, making a more flexible, scalable, decoupled, and fault-tolerant environment. This publish-subscribe messaging pattern is not new but is simple to implement across different middleware brokers.
- It provides a way to create consumer groups; with this, it implements by default the worker messaging pattern (round-robin style), which allows you to scale up your application and ensures that the consumers in a group receive one message at a time. To create consumer groups in your application, you need to set the `spring.cloud.stream.bindings.<binding-name>.group` property. If you don't specify a group, Spring Cloud Streams generates an anonymous consumer group and subscribes your consumers to it (see Figure 6-10).

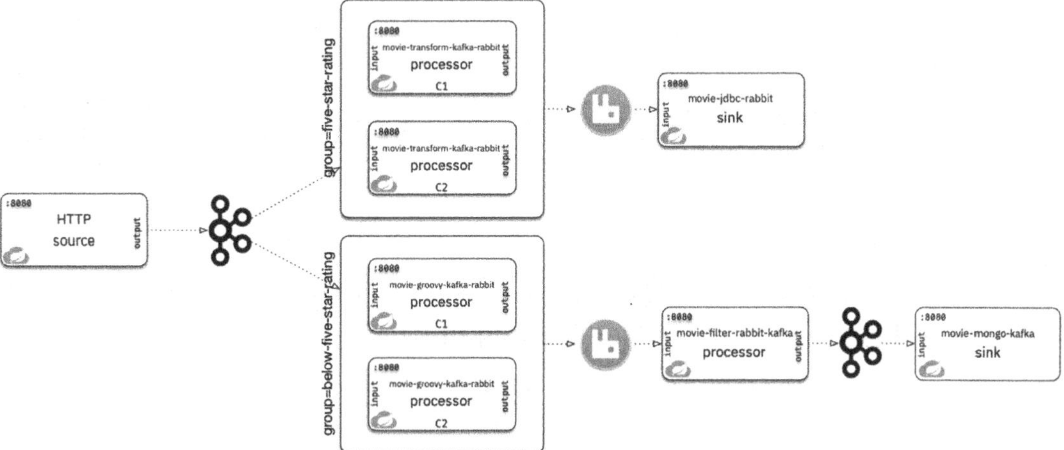

Figure 6-10. *Consumer groups: multiple binders*

- It provides durability by making consumer group subscriptions durable even if a consumer is down. When it recovers from the failure, the message is waiting, but you need to know that if you don't add a group, it creates an anonymous subscription, which is not durable. So, as a good practice, I recommend setting a group and a destination within your applications.
- It provides two different types of consumers: asynchronous (normally message-driven patterns) and synchronous (polling patterns).
- It provides partitioning support, where you can partition data between multiple instances. This feature allows you to have super speed for processing data in real time and allows you to have partition within brokers that don't support this feature, like RabbitMQ; on the other hand, Kafka uses partitions by default. It's important to know that if you want to use the partition feature, you need to configure both ends—the producer and the consumer.

During the next couple of sections, you use some of these features.

Programming Model

Let's review the programming model to learn how to create Spring Cloud Stream applications (a.k.a. App Starters that can be used out of the box).

- *Message*. This data structure normally contains headers (sometimes even footers) and payload and is used by producers and consumers.
- *Destination binders*. Some components provide integration with middleware systems. These binders take care of connectivity, data type conversion, developer code execution, delegation, routing of messages to and from producers and consumers, and more. Even though these binders are capable of integration, they require the developer to provide configuration related to the bindings. I discuss destination binders and how to implement your own binder in later chapters.
- *Binding*. This is a bridge between your application and middleware systems (bridge to topics and queues). Destination binders create these bindings (see Figure 6-11).

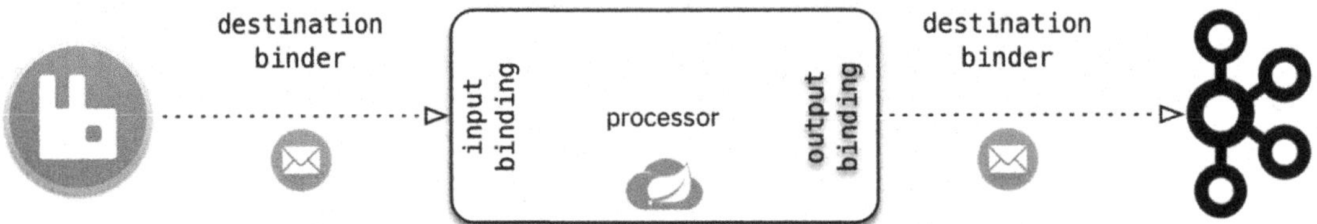

Figure 6-11. *Destination binder*

Annotation-Based Bindings Version 2.x and Below

Developers need to follow these easy steps to create a Spring Cloud Stream application in version 2.x and lower.

1. Add the necessary dependencies: `spring-cloud-stream` and `spring-cloud-stream-binder-*`.
2. Use the `@EnableBinding` annotation to specify if your binding is a source, processor, or sink interface. When this annotation is added to your class, Spring Cloud wires up all the necessary components to create your Stream app.
3. If you want to create a source, you need to declare an output channel and use it to send the payload. If you want to create a processor, you need to declare the input and output channels and use them to consume and produce the payload. If you want to create a sink, you need to declare an input channel and use it to consume the payload.

    a. To consume messages (input channel), you can use legacy Spring Integration Flows or the `@StreamListener` annotation, which makes it easier to consume messages. For sending messages (output channel), you can use legacy Spring Integration Flows or the `@SendTo` annotation.

Let's look at the binding interfaces that create Cloud Stream apps. Spring Cloud Stream provides binding interfaces that create easy contracts between microservices.

- Source defines a contract to produce messaging by providing a destination where the produced message is sent. The following code defines the Source interface.

  ```
  public interface Source {

    String OUTPUT = "output";

    @Output(Source.OUTPUT)
    MessageChannel output();
  }
  ```

  The Source interface uses a functional interface. org.springframework.messaging.MessageChannel provides an overload send method and is marked by the @Output annotation. This marker identifies the type of binding, destination, and behavior by wiring up all the necessary logic.

- Processor defines an encapsulation of the Source and the Sink interfaces, which provides an easy way to consume and produce messages. The following code defines the Processor interface.

  ```
  public interface Processor extends Source, Sink {}
  ```

- Sink defines a contract for a message consumer by providing a destination where the message is consumed. The following code defines the Sink interface.

  ```
  public interface Sink {

    String INPUT = "input";

    @Input(Sink.INPUT)
    SubscribableChannel input();
  }
  ```

  The Sink interface uses an org.springframework.messaging.SubscribableChannel interface that extends from the MessageChannel interface, and it's marked with the @Input annotation. Again, this helps Spring Cloud Stream wire up all the necessary logic for your application.

Newer versions of Spring Cloud Stream have backward compatibility, so you can still use these interfaces with Spring Cloud Stream version 3.x. Let's start with an example of how to use 2.x and lower versions. Version 2.x and below were used on top of Spring Web. You needed to be careful with your local environment because if you were developing several apps, you had to change the server.port property for each app. The Spring Cloud team turned this off in version 3.x. My recommendation is that if you want to use 2.x or below bindings, choose the latest version of Spring Cloud Stream so the web is turned off, and you won't need to worry about it.

File | Transform | Log (Rabbit) Example

Let's start with a simple stream. Let's read movies.txt (in a CSV format) and put the title in uppercase and log the movie in the console. You are using RabbitMQ as a binder, and you are creating three small apps (see Figure 6-12).

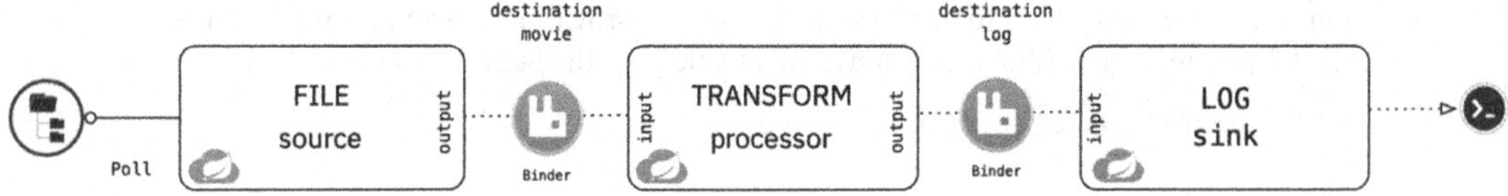

Figure 6-12. *File | Transform | Log: RabbitMQ binder*

movie-file-source-rabbit

The first source microservice reads `movie.txt` from the file system. Open a browser that points to `https://start.spring.io`. Add the following metadata.

- Group: `com.apress.cloud.stream`
- Artifact: `movie-file-source-rabbit`
- Package name: `com.apress.cloud.stream.movie`
- Dependencies: Cloud Stream, Lombok

■ **Note** We are changing the package name.

You can click the Generate button to download a ZIP file. You can uncompress and import it into your favorite IDE (see Figure 6-13).

Figure 6-13. *`https://start.spring.io`: Spring Initializr*

Because you are using the RabbitMQ binder, open your `pom.xml` file and add the following dependencies.

```
<!-- RabbitMQ Binder -->
<dependency>
        <groupId>org.springframework.cloud</groupId>
        <artifactId>spring-cloud-starter-stream-rabbit</artifactId>
</dependency>

<!-- Spring Integration -->
<dependency>
        <groupId>org.springframework.integration</groupId>
        <artifactId>spring-integration-file</artifactId>
</dependency>
```

You are adding `spring-integration-file` because you are reading from the file system. Next, create your `Movie` model class. You can use what's listed in Listing 6-3.

Next, create the `MovieStreamProperties` class. This class holds two properties that are read from the `application.properties` file (see Listing 6-8).

Listing 6-8. src/main/java/com/apress/cloud/stream/movie/MovieStreamProperties.java

```
package com.apress.cloud.stream.movie;

import lombok.Data;
import org.springframework.boot.context.properties.ConfigurationProperties;

@Data
@ConfigurationProperties(prefix = "movie.stream")
public class MovieStreamProperties {

    private String directory;
    private String namePattern;
}
```

You need to convert the CSV file into a `Movie` object. This means that you need to create a `MovieConverter` class that does the conversion (see Listing 6-9).

Listing 6-9. src/main/java/com/apress/cloud/stream/movie/MovieConverter.java

```
package com.apress.cloud.stream.movie;

import org.springframework.core.convert.converter.Converter;
import org.springframework.stereotype.Component;

import java.util.List;
import java.util.stream.Collectors;
import java.util.stream.Stream;

@Component
public class MovieConverter implements Converter<String,Movie> {
    @Override
    public Movie convert(String s) {
        List<String> fields = Stream.of(s.split(",")).map(String::trim).collect(Collectors.
        toList());
        return new Movie(fields.get(0),fields.get(1),Integer.valueOf(fields.get(2)));
    }
}
```

Listing 6-9 shows the `MovieConverter` class that implements the `Converter<S,T>` interface that accepts a String and returns a `Movie` object.

Next, create the `MovieStream` class, which has everything necessary to create a Stream app (see Listing 6-10).

Listing 6-10. src/main/java/com/apress/cloud/stream/movie/MovieStream.java

```
package com.apress.cloud.stream.movie;

import lombok.AllArgsConstructor;
import org.springframework.boot.context.properties.EnableConfigurationProperties;
```

```
import org.springframework.cloud.stream.annotation.EnableBinding;
import org.springframework.cloud.stream.messaging.Source;
import org.springframework.context.annotation.Bean;
import org.springframework.integration.dsl.IntegrationFlow;
import org.springframework.integration.dsl.IntegrationFlows;
import org.springframework.integration.dsl.Pollers;
import org.springframework.integration.dsl.Transformers;
import org.springframework.integration.file.dsl.Files;
import org.springframework.integration.file.splitter.FileSplitter;

import java.io.File;

@EnableConfigurationProperties(MovieStreamProperties.class)
@AllArgsConstructor
@EnableBinding(Source.class)
public class MovieStream {

    private MovieStreamProperties movieStreamProperties;
    private MovieConverter movieConverter;

    @Bean
    public IntegrationFlow fileFlow(){
        return IntegrationFlows.from(Files
                        .inboundAdapter(new File(this.movieStreamProperties.getDirectory()))
                        .preventDuplicates(true)
                        .patternFilter(this.movieStreamProperties.getNamePattern()),
                e -> e.poller(Pollers.fixedDelay(5000L)))

                .split(Files.splitter().markers())
                .filter(p -> !(p instanceof FileSplitter.FileMarker))
                .transform(Transformers.converter(movieConverter))
                .transform(Transformers.toJson())
                .channel(Source.OUTPUT)
                .get();
    }

}
```

Listing 6-10 shows the `MovieStream` class. Let's analyze it.

- `@EnableBinding`. This annotation tells the Spring Cloud Stream what configuration to apply, and because you are passing `Source.class` as a parameter, it is configured as a source binding. This marker is the only thing you need to create a Spring Cloud Stream app. The rest is up to the Spring Cloud Stream framework (how to connect, send the message, etc.).
- `IntegrationFlow`. This part you already know from Chapter 3. Note that you are declaring an `IntegrationFlow`, and you are using `inboundAdapter` to read files from the file system in the specific directory and specific pattern. You are polling every 5 seconds, and you are prevented from reading the same file twice. Also, you are reading the content of the file and using `MovieConverter` to create a `Movie` object that is converted into a JSON format that is sent to the output channel.

- channel(Source.OUTPUT). This part of the code belongs to IntegrationFlow, which is the last part that you send to the output channel (a destination that is declaring very soon).

You are using Spring Integration here, and you are using the Spring Integration DSL (you can use the XML as well). Remember, to create a Spring Cloud Stream (with version 2.x and below), it is necessary to declare the @EnableBinding annotation and the type of binding, in this case, a source binding; and second, the output channel, because this is a source binding type is necessary to tell where the message is sent; it is accomplished by adding channel(Source.OUTPUT) to the flow in the last part. I know that I'm repetitive here, but I want to make sure you understand what is happening with this code and how easy it is to create Streams.

Finally, you need to open application.properties and add the content from Listing 6-11.

Listing 6-11. src/main/resources/application.properties

```
# Bindings
spring.cloud.stream.bindings.output.destination=movie

# Movie Stream
movie.stream.directory=.
movie.stream.name-pattern=movies.txt
```

The important part in Listing 6-11 is the declaration of the spring.cloud.stream.bindings.output.destination property. This means that the Source.OUTPUT channel creates a destination named movie as a topic exchange in RabbitMQ.

movie-transform-processor-rabbit

Now let's work on the next processor microservice, which consumes a Movie object. It changes the title to uppercase. Open a browser pointing to https://start.spring.io. Add the following metadata.

- Group: com.apress.cloud.stream
- Artifact: movie-transform-processor-rabbit
- Package name: com.apress.cloud.stream.movie
- Dependencies: Cloud Stream, Lombok

■ **Note** We are changing the package name.

You can click the Generate button to download a ZIP file. Uncompress it and import it into your favorite IDE. This is the same as Figure 6-13, but make sure to change the artifact and the package names accordingly.

First, make sure you add the RabbitMQ binder (only the binder). Then, create the Movie class (the same as in Listing 6-3).

Next, create the MovieStream class that contains the transformation code. Remember, it sets the movie title in uppercase (see Listing 6-12).

Listing 6-12. src/main/java/com/apress/cloud/stream/movie/MovieStream.java

```
package com.apress.cloud.stream.movie;

import org.springframework.cloud.stream.annotation.EnableBinding;
import org.springframework.cloud.stream.annotation.StreamListener;
import org.springframework.cloud.stream.messaging.Processor;
import org.springframework.messaging.handler.annotation.SendTo;

@EnableBinding(Processor.class)
public class MovieStream {

    @StreamListener(Processor.INPUT)
    @SendTo(Processor.OUTPUT)
    public Movie process(Movie movie){
        movie.setTitle(movie.getTitle().toUpperCase());
        return movie;
    }
}
```

Listing 6-12 shows the `MovieStream` class. Let's analyze the annotations.

- `@EnableBinding` tells Spring Cloud Stream that the app is a stream and a processor type. This means that it needs to set the input and output channels.
- `@StreamListener` connects to a queue (RabbitMQ) or a topic (Kafka); it sets the input channel.
- `@SendTo` sends the payload to the output channel.

As you can see, this is very straightforward; in fact, you could use the transform-processor-rabbit app starter instead. You can do this as homework.

Finally, you need to open `application.properties` and add the content from Listing 6-13.

Listing 6-13. src/main/resources/application.properties

```
# Bindings - RabbitMQ
spring.cloud.stream.bindings.input.destination=movie
spring.cloud.stream.bindings.output.destination=log
```

Note that you are using the INPUT channel that connects to a `movie` (destination) queue, and it uses the output channel to send the payload to a topic named `log` (destination) in RabbitMQ.

movie-log-sink-rabbit

The next sink microservice receives a `Movie` object, and it logs it into the console. Let's start by opening a browser pointing to `https://start.spring.io`. Add the following metadata.

- Group: `com.apress.cloud.stream`
- Artifact: `movie-log-sink-rabbit`
- Package name: `com.apress.cloud.stream.movie`
- Dependencies: Cloud Stream, Lombok

■ **Note** We are changing the package name.

You can click the Generate button. This downloads a ZIP file. You can uncompress and import it into your favorite IDE (see Figure 6-13), but make sure to change the artifact and the package names accordingly.

First, make sure you add the RabbitMQ binder (only the binder). Then, you need to create the `Movie` class (see Listing 6-3).

Next, create the `MovieStream` class that logs the `Movie`, and it should show the `title` in uppercase (see Listing 6-14).

Listing 6-14. src/main/java/com/apress/cloud/stream/movie/MovieStream.java

```
package com.apress.cloud.stream.movie;

import lombok.extern.log4j.Log4j2;
import org.springframework.cloud.stream.annotation.EnableBinding;
import org.springframework.cloud.stream.annotation.StreamListener;
import org.springframework.cloud.stream.messaging.Sink;

@Log4j2
@EnableBinding(Sink.class)
public class MovieStream {

    @StreamListener(Sink.INPUT)
    public void process(Movie movie){
        log.info("Movie processed: {}",movie);
    }
}
```

Listing 6-14 shows the `MovieStream` class. Let's analyze the annotations.

- `@EnableBinding` tells Spring Cloud Stream that this app is a stream, and it is a sink type. This means that it needs to set the input channel.
- `@StreamListener` connects to a queue (RabbitMQ) or a topic (Kafka); it sets the input channel.

Finally, you need to open `application.properties` and add the content from Listing 6-15.

Listing 6-15. src/main/resources/application.properties

```
# Bindings - RabbitMQ
spring.cloud.stream.bindings.input.destination=log
```

Note that you are using the input channel that connects to a `log` (destination) queue to get the `Movie` payload, and the title should be uppercase.

Running All of Them Together

Before you run your apps, it is important to make sure you have RabbitMQ running and listening in port 5672. You can run RabbitMQ using Docker, as before, with the following command.

```
$ docker run -d --rm \
  --name rabbit \
  -p 15672:15672 -p 5672:5672 \
  rabbitmq:3.8.3-management-alpine
```

Next, run the apps with the following.

```
$ ./mvnw spring-boot:run
```

I suggest you start with `movie-log-sink-rabbit`, then `movie-transform-processor-rabbit`, and finally, `movie-file-source-rabbit`, in that order. Also, make sure that `movies.txt` is reachable to the app. You can find a copy of `movies.txt` in the root folder of the `movie-file-source-rabbit` app.

You should see the following output in the `movie-log-sink-rabbit` console or terminal.

```
Movie processed: Movie(title=THE MATRIX, actor=Keanu Reeves, year=1999)
Movie processed: Movie(title=MEMENTO, actor=Guy Pearce, year=2000)
Movie processed: Movie(title=THE SILENCE OF THE LAMBS, actor=Jodie Foster, year=1991)
Movie processed: Movie(title=THE PRESTIGE, actor=Christian Bale, year=2006)
Movie processed: Movie(title=DISTURBIA, actor=Shia LaBeouf, year=2007)
```

More About Bindings

As you saw in the examples, Spring Cloud Stream components are based on Spring Messaging's `MessageChannel` (outbound) and `SubscribableChannel` (inbound). These interfaces make Spring Cloud Stream more extensible. You can have a similar interface in which you define multiple outputs, perhaps for a dynamic scenario.

```
public interface MovieGenre {
    String INPUT = "movie-genre";
    String GENRE_SCIENCE_FICTION = "science-fiction";
    String GENRE_ROMANCE = "romance";
    String GENRE_HORROR = "horror";
    String GENRE_DEFAULT = "default-output";

    @Input(INPUT)
    SubscribableChannel movie();

    @Output(GENRE_HORROR)
    MessageChannel horror();

    @Output(GENRE_SCIENCE_FICTION)
    MessageChannel scienceFiction();

    @Output(GENRE_ROMANCE)
    MessageChannel romance();
}
```

Your `Stream` class can be written as follows.

```
@Log4j2
@EnableBinding(MovieGenre.class)
public class MovieStream {
```

```
    //Acts as Processor
    @Bean
    @ServiceActivator(inputChannel = MovieGenre.INPUT)
    public AbstractMappingMessageRouter destinationRouter(@Qualifier("binderAwareChannel
    Resolver") DestinationResolver<MessageChannel> channelResolver) {
        AbstractMappingMessageRouter router = new ExpressionEvaluatingRouter
        (new SpelExpressionParser().parseExpression("#jsonPath(payload,'$.genre')"));
        router.setDefaultOutputChannelName(MovieGenre.GENRE_DEFAULT);
        router.setChannelResolver(channelResolver);
        return router;
    }

    //Sinks
    @StreamListener(MovieGenre.GENRE_SCIENCE_FICTION)
    public void genreScienceFiction(Movie movie){
        log.info("Science Fiction: {}",movie);
    }

    @StreamListener(MovieGenre.GENRE_HORROR)
    public void genreHorror(Movie movie){
        log.info("Horror: {}",movie);
    }

    //...
}
```

The processor is using `@ServiceActivator` (another way to create a processor or sink). You can find the complete code within the `movie-multiple-rabbit` project in the companion source code or on the Apress web site. You need to manually send a JSON object in the `movie-genre` anonymous queue in the RabbitMQ console (don't forget to add `content-type:application/json` in the Properties field when publishing the message). The JSON should be as follows.

```
{
  "title":"The Matrix",
  "actor":"Keanu Reeves",
  "year":1999,
  "genre":"science-fiction"
}
```

Also, you can use multiple bindings, something like the following.

```
@EnableBinding(value={MovieGenre.class, MovieEvents.class})
```

These examples are more likely to use event-based message consumption because you define multiple `MessageChannels` and use `DestinationResolver` to route the message to the right destination. Still, sometimes you need some control, such as controlling the rate of what you are consuming. You can create `PollableMessageSource`, like in the following snippet.

```
public interface MovieEvent {
     @Input
     PollableMessageSource ratingChanged();
}
```

Channel/Bindings Naming Conventions

When you use the default binding implementation, the marked channel takes the method name only by adding the `@Input` or `@Output` annotation. In other words, if you have code like the following.

```
public interface MovieGenre {
    @Input
    SubscribableChannel movie();
}
```

The binding/destination (the topic in the broker) is named `movie`. You can override this behavior if you pass the parameter's value to the `@Input` annotation; for example, if you have the following code.

```
public interface MovieGenre {
    @Input("new-movie")
    SubscribableChannel movie();
}
```

The binding/destination (the topic in the broker) is named `newMovie`. A very simple name convention. Also, you can override the behavior using the `spring.cloud.stream.bindings` properties. This is the expression:

```
spring.cloud.stream.bindings.[channel-name].destination=[new-channel-name]
```

If you are using our first example, `@Input` (with no parameters), it takes the name of the method. If you want to override it, you need the following.

```
#application.properties
spring.cloud.stream.bindings.movie.destination=newMovie
```

The preceding command overrides the name `movie`. It creates the `newMovie` binding/destination in the broker. If you are using an annotation like `@Input("newMovie")`, you want to override it. You should put the following in `application.properties`.

```
#application.properties
spring.cloud.stream.bindings.new-movie.destination=new-movie-event
```

This overrides the `new-movie` binding/destination for the `new-movie-event` binding/destination in the broker. More about these naming conventions later.

Bindings Version 3.x

One of the main additions to version 3.x is the ability to use functions to produce or consume messages when working with bindings. You don't need to add or use any extra annotation like `@EnableBinding` or `@StreamListener`. The new opinionated runtime can look at your code and create the right stream type (source, processor, or sink) on the fly.

By using POJOs (Plain Old Java Objects), version 3.x offers a clearer way to create a Stream app and use context beans types like `java.util.function.Supplier<T>` (for a source), `java.util.function.Function<T,R>` (for a processor), and `java.util.function.Consumer<T>` (for a sink). It creates Reactive Streams, which means that you can use reactive programming right away by using this new programming model.

Let's review the new ways to create Stream applications using version 3.x. If you want to use the latest version of Spring Cloud Stream (Horsham.SR7), you need to do the following.

1. Add the right dependencies to `pom.xml`: `spring-cloud-stream`, `spring-cloud-stream-binder-kafka-streams`, and `spring-cloud-stream-binder-kafka`.
2. Declare your beans type: Supplier, Function, Consumer.
3. With these types of beans, you can start writing with Spring Cloud Function, create function composition, and expose the functions you need. For this feature, you can use the `spring.cloud.function.definition` property to provide the names of the functions you want to use. You can use Unix-like pipes to define several functions (function composition); Again, this method is used in the Spring Cloud Function framework to create serverless apps within AWS Lambda, OpenWhisk, and so forth. You see this in more detail later.

Next, create a source, processor, and sink using Kafka as a binder and version 3.x features. Remember that it has backward compatibility, and since version 2.1, you can use cloud functions to create Stream apps.

movie-source-kafka

This Cloud Stream app sends movies, acting as a source. Open a browser pointing to `https://start.spring.io`. Add the following metadata.

- Group: `com.apress.cloud.stream`
- Artifact: `movie-source-kafka`
- Package name: `com.apress.cloud.stream.movie`
- Dependencies: Cloud Stream, Spring for Apache Kafka Streams, Lombok

---

■ **Note** We are changing the **package name**.

You can click the Generate button to download a ZIP file. You can uncompress and import it into your favorite IDE (see Figure 6-14).

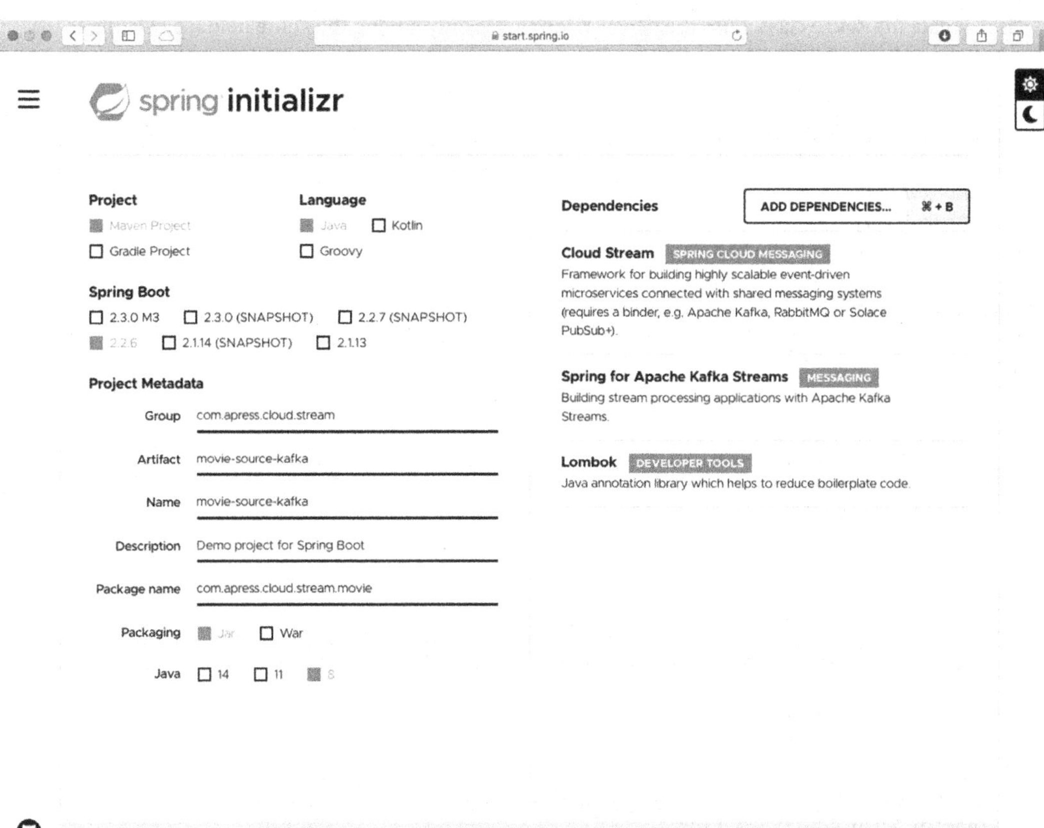

Figure 6-14. *`https://start.spring.io`: Spring Initializr*

Open your `pom.xml` file and make sure you have the necessary dependencies.

```
...
<dependency>
        <groupId>org.springframework.cloud</groupId>
        <artifactId>spring-cloud-stream</artifactId>
</dependency>

<dependency>
        <groupId>org.apache.kafka</groupId>
        <artifactId>kafka-streams</artifactId>
</dependency>
<dependency>
        <groupId>org.springframework.cloud</groupId>
        <artifactId>spring-cloud-stream-binder-kafka-streams</artifactId>
</dependency>
<dependency>
        <groupId>org.springframework.cloud</groupId>
        <artifactId>spring-cloud-stream-binder-kafka</artifactId>
</dependency>
```

Next, create the Movie class. I use the new version that is only adding the genre field (see Listing 6-16).

Listing 6-16. src/main/java/com/apress/cloud/stream/movie/Movie.java

```
package com.apress.cloud.stream.movie;

import lombok.AllArgsConstructor;
import lombok.Data;
import lombok.NoArgsConstructor;

@AllArgsConstructor
@NoArgsConstructor
@Data
public class Movie {
    private String title;
    private String actor;
    private int year;
    private String genre;
}
```

Next, create the MovieStream class (see Listing 6-17).

Listing 6-17. src/main/java/com/apress/cloud/stream/movie/MovieStream.java

```
package com.apress.cloud.stream.movie;

import org.springframework.context.annotation.Bean;
import org.springframework.context.annotation.Configuration;
import reactor.core.publisher.Flux;

import java.util.function.Supplier;

@Configuration
public class MovieStream {

    @Bean
    public Supplier<Flux<Movie>> movie() {
        return () -> Flux.just(
                new Movie("The Matrix","Keanu Reves",1999,"science-fiction"),
                new Movie("It","Bill Skarsgård",2017,"horror")
        );
    }
}
```

Listing 6-17 shows the MovieStream class. Note that the class is no longer using @Binding, but uses the @Configuration annotation to help Spring Cloud Stream identify any declared beans. In this class, you are using java.util.function.Supplier and Flux (from https://projectreactor.io) that send two Movie objects. Also note that it is important to mark this method with @Bean so the framework wires up all the necessary logic for publishing messages. That's it, very simple. Next, open application.properties and add the content from Listing 6-18.

Listing 6-18. sr/main/resources/application.properties

```
## Kafka Binders
spring.cloud.stream.bindings.movie-out-0.destination=uppercase
```

movie-processor-kafka

This Cloud Stream app sends the `Movie` object, and it does an uppercase on the title field, acting as a processor. Open a browser pointing to `https://start.spring.io`. Add the following metadata.

- Group: `com.apress.cloud.stream`
- Artifact: `movie-processor-kafka`
- Package name: `com.apress.cloud.stream.movie`
- Dependencies: Cloud Stream, Spring for Apache Kafka Streams, Lombok

---

■ **Note** We are changing the **package name**.

You can click the Generate button to download a ZIP file. You can uncompress and import it into your favorite IDE.

Make sure you have the Kafka and Cloud Stream dependencies in your `pom.xml` file. Create your `Movie` class; it is the same as Listing 6-16. Next, create the `MovieStream` class (see Listing 6-19).

Listing 6-19. src/main/java/com/.apress/cloud/stream/movie/MovieStream.java

```
package com.apress.cloud.stream.movie;

import lombok.extern.log4j.Log4j2;
import org.springframework.context.annotation.Bean;
import org.springframework.context.annotation.Configuration;

import java.util.function.Function;

@Log4j2
@Configuration
public class MovieStream {

    @Bean
    public Function<Movie, Movie> uppercase() {
        return movie -> {
            log.info("Processing: {}", movie);
            movie.setTitle(movie.getTitle().toUpperCase());
            return movie;
        };
    }
}
```

Listing 6-19 shows the `MovieStream` class that acts as a processor because it uses the `Function` functional interface that receives `Movie`, and it returns a modified `Movie` object. Note that the class is being marked with `@Configuration` and the uppercase method with `@Bean` annotations.

Next, add the content from Listing 6-20 to the `application.properties` file.

Listing 6-20. sr/main/resources/application.properties

```
## Kafka Binders
spring.cloud.stream.bindings.uppercase-in-0.destination=uppercase
spring.cloud.stream.bindings.uppercase-out-0.destination=log
```

movie-sink-kafka

This Cloud Stream App logs the movie, acting as sink. Open a browser pointing to `https://start.spring.io`. Add the following metadata.

- Group: `com.apress.cloud.stream`
- Artifact: `movie-sink-kafka`
- Package name: `com.apress.cloud.stream.movie`
- Dependencies: Cloud Stream, Spring for Apache Kafka Streams, Lombok

---

■ **Note** We are changing the **package name**.

You can click the Generate button to download a ZIP file. You can uncompress and import it into your favorite IDE.

Make sure you have the Kafka and Cloud Stream dependencies in `pom.xml`. Create a `Movie` class; it is the same as Listing 6-16. Next, create the `MovieStream` class (see Listing 6-21).

Listing 6-21. src/main/java/com/.apress/cloud/stream/movie/MovieStream.java

```
package com.apress.cloud.stream.movie;

import lombok.extern.log4j.Log4j2;
import org.springframework.context.annotation.Bean;
import org.springframework.context.annotation.Configuration;

import java.util.function.Consumer;

@Log4j2
@Configuration
public class MovieStream {

    @Bean
    public Consumer<Movie> log(){
        return movie -> {
            log.info("Movie Processed: {}", movie);
        };

    }
}
```

Listing 6-21 shows the MovieStream class. In this case, it is using the Consumer interface that logs a Movie object. Remember that you are using a marked class with @Configuration and the log method marked with the @Bean annotation for the framework to recognize them and do the heavy lifting of wiring up everything up and listening for new incoming messages from the declared topic.

Next, add the content from Listing 6-22 to the application.properties file.

Listing 6-22. sr/main/resources/application.properties

```
## Kafka Binders
spring.cloud.stream.bindings.log-in-0.destination=log
```

Running All of Them Together

It's time to run the applications. You are using the docker-compose.yml file from Listing 6-6. Open a terminal, go to the docker-compose.yml file, and run your environment with

```
$ docker-compose up
```

Afterward, run your application with your IDE or the following command in the root folder of every app.

```
$ ./mvnw spring-boot:run
```

You should see the movie titles in uppercase in the movie-sink-kafka app console.

```
Movie Processed: Movie(title=THE MATRIX, actor=Keanu Reves, year=1999, genre=science-fiction)
Movie Processed: Movie(title=IT, actor=Bill Skarsgård, year=2017, genre=horror)
```

Congratulations! You created a Spring Cloud Stream app using the new version 3.x features.

Binding Naming Convention

Are you wondering why you used spring.cloud.stream.bindings in that format in the previous examples? In version 3.x., the naming conventions for the bindings are as follows.

- for an input binding: <function-name> + -in + <index>
- for an output binding: <function-name> + -out + <index>

The index always starts at 0, which has to do with the functions with multiple input and output arguments. You see this later. That's why in the movie-source-kafka app, the function name is movie, meaning that it creates the binding name, movie-out-0, which you overwrite in uppercase.

In the movie-processor-kafka app, the function name is uppercase. It generates (because it is a Function processor) two bindings (uppercase-in-0 and uppercase-out-0) that you overwrite with uppercase and log, respectively.

Finally, in the movie-sink-kafka app, the function name is log, so the generated binding is log-in-0, and you overwrite it with log. Why do you need to overwrite them? Because it is easier for the developer and any other external system to access a business-defined name.

Producing and Consuming

There are different ways to produce and consume messages, and version 3.x brings more ways to accomplish this. You can still use Spring Integration using XML or annotations or/and a mix with the Spring Integration DSL (`IntegrationFlow`). With the new features of version 3.x, the recommended way is to use functional and reactive programming depending on your system or application needs.

Using Spring Integration, you can produce messages to the output channel with the following code.

```
@Bean
@InboundChannelAdapter(value = Source.OUTPUT, poller = @Poller(fixedRate = "5000",
maxMessagesPerPoll = "1"))
    public MessageSource<Movie> movieMessageSource() {
        return () -> new GenericMessage<>(new Movie("The Matrix","Keanu Reeves",1999));
    }
```

The preceding code shows the `@InboundChannelAdapter` that executes every 5 seconds the method `movieMessageSource` sending one `Movie` object. This code is impractical, but you get the idea of sending a message to the Source.OUTPUT channel.

■ **Note** You can find the code of this section the projects: `movie-file-source-rabbit`, `movie-transform-processor-rabbit`, and `movie-log-sink-rabbit`.

The same can be accomplished by using the Source interface with the following code.

```
@Bean
public ApplicationRunner movieMessage(Source source){
        return args -> {
            source.output().send(new GenericMessage<>(new Movie("The Matrix","Keanu
            Reeves",1999)));
        };
    }
```

Here you are using the `source` and the defined method `output()` to send only one time a `Movie` object. Or you can use `MessageChannel` directly as well. And the same behavior can be accomplished using the `java.util.function.*` functional interfaces.

```
@Bean  // Every second send this movie.
 public Supplier<Movie> movieSupplier() {
      return () -> new Movie("The Matrix", "Keanu Reves", 1999);
 }
```

The preceding method has a Poller every second, and you can use instead of `@Bean` you can use `@PollableBean` annotation and overwrite any default polling settings. Remember that with the functional interfaces, you need to take care of the `spring.cloud.stream.bindings.<function-[in|out]-<index>>.destination` properties names.

To consume messages using Spring Integration using the @ServiceActivator annotation with the following code.

```
@ServiceActivator(inputChannel = Sink.INPUT)
 public void movieProcess(Movie movie){
      log.info("Movie processed: {}",movie);
 }
```

Also, you already know that you can execute the same behavior using the @StreamListener annotation.

```
@StreamListener(Sink.INPUT)
 public void process(Movie movie){
      log.info("Movie processed: {}",movie);
 }
```

And if you want to use the java.util.function.* functional interfaces.

```
@Bean
    public Consumer<Movie> log(){
        return movie -> {
            log.info("Movie Processed: {}", movie);
        };
    }
```

Remember that with the functional interfaces, you need to take care of the spring.cloud.stream.bindings.<function-[in|out]-<index>>.destination properties names.

If you need to consume, process, and then produce a message (a *processor*) and if you are using Spring Integration, you can use the @Transformer annotation.

```
@Transformer(inputChannel = Processor.INPUT, outputChannel = Processor.OUTPUT)
public Movie transform(Movie movie){
      movie.setTitle(movie.getTitle().toUpperCase());
      return movie;
}
```

See that you are using the processor.INPUT and Processor.OUTPUT channels. The same behavior can be accomplished with the @ServiceActivator annotation.

```
@ServiceActivator(inputChannel = Processor.INPUT, outputChannel = Processor.OUTPUT)
public Movie transformServiceActivator(Movie movie){
     movie.setTitle(movie.getTitle().toUpperCase());
     return movie;
}
```

You can use other annotations, such as @Splitter, @Aggregator, and @Filter; and of course, you can use the dedicated @StreamListener and @SendTo annotation for the same behavior.

```
@StreamListener(Processor.INPUT)
@SendTo(Processor.OUTPUT)
public Movie process(Movie movie){
     movie.setTitle(movie.getTitle().toUpperCase());
     return movie;
}
```

If you want to use the `java.util.function.*` functional interfaces.

```
@Bean
public Function<Movie, Movie> uppercase() {
      return movie -> {
          movie.setTitle(movie.getTitle().toUpperCase());
          return movie;
      };
}
```

Remember that with the functional interfaces, you need to take care of the `spring.cloud.stream.bindings.<function-[in|out]-<index>>.destination` properties names.

■ **Note** It is important to know that you cannot have `@EnableBinding` and any other `@Bean` with `java.util.function.*` interfaces. They must be in separate classes if you want to mix them.

@StreamListener Features

This annotation has some interesting features that can help when business logic requires some routings based on the message content or the message `headers`. In other words, you can use conditional statements to help you with the routing. If you want to use this feature, you need to satisfy two conditions.

- It must be an individual message (this means that reactive API methods are not supported).
- It must not return a value.

You will use SpEL to set the expression to be evaluated. If you need to add a condition expression with a header, you can do something like the following.

```
@StreamListener(value = Sink.INPUT, condition = "headers['genre']=='science-fiction'")
 public void processScienceFiction(Movie movie){
      log.info("Science Fiction Movie processed: {}",movie);
  }

 @StreamListener(value = Sink.INPUT, condition = "headers['genre']=='drama'")
 public void processDrama(Movie movie){
      log.info("Drama  Movie processed: {}",movie);
  }
```

If you need to evaluate an expression against the payload's content, then you can do something like this.

```
@StreamListener(value = Sink.INPUT, condition = "#jsonPath(payload,'$.year') < 2000")
 public void processTwoThousandAndBelow(Movie movie){
     log.info("1990-2000 Movie processed: {}",movie);
 }

 @StreamListener(value = Sink.INPUT, condition = "#jsonPath(payload,'$.year') >= 2000")
 public void processTwoThousandAndAbove(Movie movie){
     log.info("2000-Present Movie processed: {}",movie);
 }
```

More Features

Many features are covered in the upcoming chapters, but when it comes to producing and consuming messages, you can get the message in different formats and have access to the headers and security.

Mapping Method Arguments

If you want access to the Payload, you already know that you can use the instance object or a representation, depending on the contentType header. Also, you can have access to other parts of the message, like.

```
@StreamListener(Sink.INPUT)
    public void process(@Payload String payload, @Header("contentType") String contentType,
    @Headers Map<String, Object> map){
        log.info("Payload processed: {} - ContentType: {} - Headers:
        {}",payload,contentType,map);
    }
```

See the usage of the @Payload, @Header, and @Headers annotations. Also, you can get the Message with.

```
@StreamListener(Sink.INPUT)
 public void process(Message message){
      log.info("Message processed: {} ",message);
 }
```

Reactive and Functions

Another cool feature is that now you can use Reactive programming, something that you saw in previous examples. You can have a Reactive Consumer interface that uses a Flux or Mono data types from project reactor (https://projectreactor.io/). You can apply all the operations for any Flux or Mono types.

```
public Function<Flux<Movie>, Mono<Movie>> movieConsumer() {
        return flux -> flux
                                    .map(..).filter(..).then();
}
```

With the preceding code you can have control on all the Pollable properties, like fixedDelay and maxMessagePerPoll.

```
spring.cloud.stream.poller.fixed-delay=5000
```

also, you can use instead of the @Bean for your Supplier, you can use the @PollableBean annotation and use the preceding properties to configure it.

```
@PollableBean
public Supplier<Flux<Movie>> stringSupplier() {
        return () -> Flux.just(new Movie("The Matrix","Keanu Reeves",1999));
}
```

Sometimes you require to connect from a common Web Microservice to a Reactive Microservice or have several functions that you need to use at once, so, how can I connect and use functions with Spring Cloud Stream? Spring Cloud Stream introduce a final org.springframework.cloud.stream.function.StreamBridge class and it provides a *Function Composition* that allows to run several functions as one.

For example, you can have a basic RestController class that accept incoming POST requests to /movies path.

```
@AllArgsConstructor
@RestController
public class MovieController {

    private StreamBridge streamBridge;

    @PostMapping("/movies")
    @ResponseStatus(HttpStatus.ACCEPTED)
    public void toMovieBinding(@RequestBody Movie movie) {
        streamBridge.send("movie-out-0", movie);
    }
}
```

If you try to run this app, it fails because it needs to know what binding to use to send the `Movie` object; so, it is necessary to add the following properties.

```
spring.cloud.stream.source=movie
spring.cloud.stream.bindings.movie-out-0.destination=movie
```

The key property is `spring.cloud.stream.source`, which is required to create the binding. With the movie value, it creates **movie-out-0** (following the binding naming convention). The second property you are already are familiar with: it internally renames `movie-out-0` to `movie`.

If you need to do the same behavior using a Reactor API, you can use the following code.

```
@RestController
public class MovieController{
    EmitterProcessor<Movie> processor = EmitterProcessor.create();

    @PostMapping("/movies")
    @ResponseStatus(HttpStatus.ACCEPTED)
    public void toMovieSupplier(@RequestBody Movie movie) {
        processor.onNext(movie);
    }

    @Configuration
    class MovieSupplier {
        @Bean
        public Supplier<Flux<Movie>> movie() {
            return () -> processor;
        }
    }
}
```

Note that the class is using `EmitterProcessor`, and the `toMovieSupplier` method controller is invoking the `onNext` method; that's why you need to declare the `@Bean` annotation and use the supplier by invoking the same `EmitterProcessor` instance (in this case, the `processor` object).

Look at the following code.

```
@Configuration
public class MovieStream {
    String GENRE_SCIENCE_FICTION = "science-fiction";
```

```
    @Bean
    public Function<Flux<Movie>, Flux<Movie>> onlyScienceFiction() {
        return flux -> flux.filter( movie -> movie.getGenre().equals(GENRE_SCIENCE_
        FICTION));
    }

    @Bean
    public Function<Flux<Movie>, Flux<Movie>> titleUpperCase() {
        return flux -> flux.map( movie -> {
            movie.setTitle(movie.getTitle().toUpperCase());
            return movie;
        });
    }
}
```

You use Spring Cloud Function syntax with Project Reactor, so it won't run because you need to have only one function defined. If you need more than one, you need to create a function composition.

You need to declare the name of your composition by using the `spring.cloud.function.definition` property and using the | (pipe) symbol for the function methods. In this example, `application.properties` looks like the following.

```
spring.cloud.function.definition=onlyScienceFiction|titleUpperCase
spring.cloud.stream.bindings.onlyScienceFictiontitleUpperCase-in-0.destination=movie
spring.cloud.stream.bindings.onlyScienceFictiontitleUpperCase-out-0.destination=log
```

Note that `spring.cloud.function.definition` is set to `onlyScienceFiction|titleUpp erCase`, the name of the function methods. The Spring Cloud Stream configuration generates `onlyScienceFictiontitleUpperCase-in-0` and the `onlyScienceFictiontitleUpperCase-out-0` binders; in this case, they are renamed `movie` and `log`, respectively.

If you need both because you are using in a different stream, use a ; (semicolon) instead of the | (pipe). It should be as follows.

```
spring.cloud.function.definition=onlyScienceFiction;titleUpperCase
```

The preceding property generates `onlyScienceFiction-in-0` and `onlyScienceFiction-out-0`, and the `titleUpperCase-in-0` and `titleUpperCase-out-0` bindings.

Sometimes you receive different types of data that you need to process as composite logic. Spring Cloud Stream allows you to have multiple input and output arguments, like the following class.

```
@Configuration
public class MovieStream {
    String GENRE_SCIENCE_FICTION = "science-fiction";

    @Bean
    public Function<Tuple2<Flux<Integer>,Flux<Movie>>, Flux<Message<Movie>>> movieTuple() {
        return tuple -> {
            Flux<Integer> integerFlux = tuple.getT1();
            Flux<Movie> movieFlux = tuple.getT2();
```

```
            return Flux.just(
                    MessageBuilder.withPayload(movieFlux.blockFirst()).
                    setHeader("stars",integerFlux.map(m -> m.toString())).build());
        };
    }
}
```

In this example, you receive a `Flux` of `Integer` type and a `Flux<T>` of `Movie<T>` type, and you return a `Message<Movie>` object. This means that the bindings created are `movieTuple-in-0`, `movieTuple-in-1`, and `movieTuple-out-0`. Note the index in the bindings naming convention. And if a tuple is the return value, you have `<method-name>-out-0`, `<method-name>-out-1`, and so on, depending on the tuple arguments.

Another feature lets you go from `Function` to `IntegrationFlow`. You accomplish this as follows.

```
@Configuration
public class MovieStream {
    @Bean
    public IntegrationFlow movieFlow() {
        return IntegrationFlows.from(MovieFunction.class)
                .transform(Transformers.toJson())
                .channel(Source.OUTPUT)
                .get();
    }
    public interface MovieFunction extends Function<Movie, Movie> { }
}
```

The important part is the declaration of the `MovieFunction` interface that is referencing a gateway pattern, which Spring Integration generates. Since the method name is `movieFlow`, it creates the `movieFlow.gateway-in-0` and `movieFlow.gateway-out-0` bindings.

Spring Cloud Stream, Project Reactor, and Spring Cloud Function make an incredible team for creating amazing enterprise-ready applications using the latest technologies!

■ **Note** All the code in this section is in the `ch06/function-bridge` directory structure in the book's companion source code. It uses the Kafka binder.

Routing

Routing is another feature. You can route messages to a particular function to process it based on the payload content or the message headers. To use this feature, you need to set the `spring.cloud.stream.function.routing.enabled` value to equal `true` and set the `spring.cloud.function.routing-expression` properties.

By default, it creates the `functionRouter-in-0` and `functionRouter-out-0` bindings (the same naming convention for functions/Reactive Streams) if you are creating a processor stream. If you are creating a sink, it creates the `functionRouter-in-0` binding.

The following snippet is an example.

```
@Log4j2
@Configuration
public class MovieStream {

    @Bean
    public Function<Movie, Movie> drama() {
        return movie -> {
            log.info("Drama: {}",movie);
            movie.setGenre(movie.getGenre().toUpperCase());
            return movie;
        };
    }

    @Bean
    public Function<Movie, Movie> fiction() {
        return movie -> {
            log.info("Science Fiction: {}", movie);
            movie.setTitle(movie.getTitle().toUpperCase());
            return movie;
        };
    }
}
```

There are two functions: `drama` and `fiction`. Note that each has its logic in uppercase: the `drama` uppercase function in the genre field, and the `fiction` uppercase function the title field. Let's look at the `application.properties` file.

```
# Rabbit Binding
spring.cloud.stream.bindings.functionRouter-in-0.destination=movie
spring.cloud.stream.bindings.functionRouter-out-0.destination=log

# Routing Function
spring.cloud.stream.function.routing.enabled=true
spring.cloud.function.routing-expression=headers['genre']
```

Note that the expression evaluates the header `genre`, and depending on the value, it calls the name of the method. This means that the `Movie` object should have a header genre with `drama` or `fiction` value. Also, note that there are two functions. You are enabling the routing feature. This means that the configuration creates `functionRouter-in-0` and `functionRouter-out-0`. In this example, you are renaming `functionRouter-[in|out]-0` to the `movie` and `log` bindings, respectively. This is easy to follow.

■ **Note** All the code of this section is in the `ch06/routing` directory structure in the book's companion source code. It's using the RabbitMQ binder.

Summary

This chapter described how Spring Cloud Stream works and how you can create Stream apps with ease. With the power of Spring Integration and the opinionated engine of Spring Boot, you can build enterprise systems that connect to legacy systems or any middleware broker using the binding feature—without learning a new API. The chapter introduced the Stream types: source, processor, and sink. You saw how easy it is to start a Stream project by adding the right dependencies from Kafka or RabbitMQ.

In the next chapter, you see more features and learn how to create a binder to plug in to your Stream apps.

You still have a lot of work to do because this chapter was just the beginning.

CHAPTER 7

Spring Cloud Stream Binders

In the previous chapter, I showed you how Spring Cloud Stream Application Starters work as stand-alone apps that can deliver an enterprise-ready solution with ease. I showed you the Spring Cloud Stream model application and how the main core is based on Spring Integration and Spring Boot for its easy configuration. You saw how to use Spring Cloud Functions and Spring Integration to create streams very easily. I also showed you a feature (the best, in my opinion) called a *binder* that allows your solution to use any physical destination or any middleware messaging broker. This chapter covers how to create a custom binder.

You will use the NATS server (`https://nats.io`), a broker for building distributed applications to provide real-time streaming and big data use-cases (see Figure 7-1). Are wondering why did I chose NATS over other technologies? I used to work on Cloud Foundry (`www.cloudfoundry.org`) projects, and one of the main components to keep alive some of the VMs are to use NATS, a fast and reliable messaging broker, that is easy to use. As an experiment, I decided to create a prototype as a binder implementation. It took me a few hours. Yes, it is very easy to create a custom binder.

Let's get started by discussing what's behind the NATS technology and how to implement it.

Figure 7-1. `https://nats.io`

Binder

A binder uses the Service Provider Interface (SPI) pattern, which allows you to extend or add extra functionality to your system by enabling features or replacing components. This pattern has been around since the first iterations of the Java programming language and adds plugin functionality.

Spring Cloud Stream exposes several interfaces and abstract and utility classes; it also provides discovery strategies that allow you to plug in external middleware. These interfaces and classes help you create binders very easily. A typical scenario features a producer and consumer using a binder to produce and consume messages. The binder takes care of the connection, retries, sessions, or anything that allows the publisher and consumer to use the broker with knowing how it is done. It hides boilerplate coding and avoids the need to learn a specific API.

F. Gutierrez, *Spring Cloud Data Flow*, https://doi.org/10.1007/978-1-4842-1239-4_7

Let's start by reviewing the main interface: `org.springframework.cloud.stream.binder.Binder<T,C,P>`. This interface provides input and output bind targets. It adds properties to both the producer and the consumer; these properties offer support to the required broker-specific properties (if any) in a type-safe manner (see Listing 7-1).

Listing 7-1. org.springframework.cloud.stream.binder.Binder Interface

```
public interface Binder<T, C extends ConsumerProperties, P extends ProducerProperties> {
    Binding<T> bindConsumer(
                                String bindingName, String group, T inboundBindTarget, C
                                consumerProperties);
    Binding<T> bindProducer(String bindingName, T outboundBindTarget, P producerProperties);
}
```

Let's review Listing 7-1.

- `binderConsumer`. This method's first parameter is the destination name that internally creates the necessary channels and whatever purpose object is needed in the broker, such as queue, topic, and so forth. The next parameter is a group in which the consumers accept messages (a worker style or publish/subscribe patterns). The third parameter is the destination/channel instance where the consumer listens/subscribes to new incoming messages. The fourth parameter is a broker (specific) and business properties that belongs to the message.
- `binderProducer`. This method's first parameter is the destination name that creates the necessary channels and whatever purpose object is needed in the broker, like a topic, exchange, and so forth. The next parameter is the destination/channel instance where the producer sends the messages. The last parameter is any property that contains broker-specific and business properties.

I think these signatures are very straightforward to follow. Figure 7-2 shows an example of a binder.

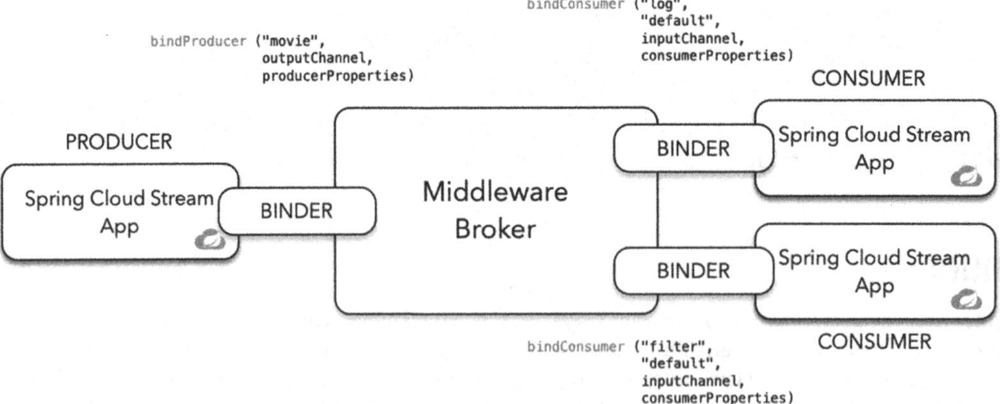

Figure 7-2. *Binder abstraction*

Implementing a Binder

If you want to implement a binder, you must follow these simple rules.

- A class must implement the Binder interface.
- A @Configuration marked class defines a binder bean and the steps for creating the middleware broker infrastructure; it may be a connection, or session, some credentials, and so forth.
- It is necessary to create a META-INF/spring.binders file that is found in the classpath and contains one or more binder definitions.

As you can see, it is very simple to implement a binder, so let's start creating a custom binder using the NATS brokers.

NATS Binder

Creating a custom binder helps developers speed up development; as a binder developer, you need to know how this broker works.

Before you start implementing the binder, I think it is necessary to create a library that allows you to produce and consume messages so you can reuse it later. At the end of the chapter, you create a nats-binder project with three modules: nats-messaging (NATS client), nats-messaging-binder (NAT binder implementation), and nats-messaging-test (NATS binder test).

Download the NATS server (https://nats.io/) and install it. This chapter uses a NATS Docker image. You can pull it using the following command.

```
$ docker pull nats
```

This command downloads a 10 MB image.

Project: nats-binder

To make development easier, let's create a directory structure for the main pom.xml file and its modules. Create a folder called nats-binder and add the pom.xml file in Listing 7-2.

Listing 7-2. nats-binder/pom.xml

```
<?xml version="1.0" encoding="UTF-8"?>
<project xmlns="http://maven.apache.org/POM/4.0.0" xmlns:xsi="http://www.w3.org/2001/
XMLSchema-instance"
    xsi:schemaLocation="http://maven.apache.org/POM/4.0.0 https://maven.apache.org/xsd/
    maven-4.0.0.xsd">
    <modelVersion>4.0.0</modelVersion>

    <groupId>com.apress.nats</groupId>
    <artifactId>nats-binder</artifactId>
    <version>0.0.1</version>
    <packaging>pom</packaging>

    <properties>
        <java.version>1.8</java.version>
```

```
        <maven.compiler.target>1.8</maven.compiler.target>
        <maven.compiler.source>1.8</maven.compiler.source>
        <project.build.sourceEncoding>UTF-8</project.build.sourceEncoding>
        <project.reporting.outputEncoding>UTF-8</project.reporting.outputEncoding>
    </properties>

    <modules>
        <module>nats-messaging-binder</module>
        <module>nats-messaging</module>
        <module>nats-messaging-test</module>
    </modules>

    <dependencies>
        <dependency>
            <groupId>org.springframework.boot</groupId>
            <artifactId>spring-boot-starter</artifactId>
        </dependency>
        <dependency>
            <groupId>org.springframework</groupId>
            <artifactId>spring-messaging</artifactId>
        </dependency>
        <dependency>
            <groupId>org.projectlombok</groupId>
            <artifactId>lombok</artifactId>
            <optional>true</optional>
        </dependency>
        <dependency>
            <groupId>org.springframework.boot</groupId>
            <artifactId>spring-boot-configuration-processor</artifactId>
            <optional>true</optional>
        </dependency>
        <dependency>
            <groupId>org.springframework.boot</groupId>
            <artifactId>spring-boot-starter-test</artifactId>
            <scope>test</scope>
            <exclusions>
                <exclusion>
                    <groupId>org.junit.vintage</groupId>
                    <artifactId>junit-vintage-engine</artifactId>
                </exclusion>
            </exclusions>
        </dependency>
    </dependencies>

    <dependencyManagement>
        <dependencies>
            <dependency>
                <groupId>org.springframework.boot</groupId>
                <artifactId>spring-boot-dependencies</artifactId>
                <version>2.2.6.RELEASE</version>
                <type>pom</type>
```

```
                <scope>import</scope>
            </dependency>
        </dependencies>
    </dependencyManagement>

    <build>
        <plugins>
            <plugin>
                <groupId>org.apache.maven.plugins</groupId>
                <artifactId>maven-compiler-plugin</artifactId>
                <configuration>
                    <source>8</source>
                    <target>8</target>
                </configuration>
            </plugin>
        </plugins>
    </build>
</project>
```

Analyze `pom.xml` and the dependencies.

Next, create the modules, and because you are using Spring Initializr, you can uncompress the ZIP file in the `nats-binder` folder.

NATS Client: nats-messaging

Open a browser and point to `https://start.spring.io`. Use the following metadata.

- Group: `com.apress.nats`
- Artifact: `nats-messaging`
- Package: `com.apress.nats`
- Dependencies: Lombok

Press the Generate button to download a ZIP file. Uncompress it into the `nats-binder` directory and import it into your favorite IDE (see Figure 7-3).

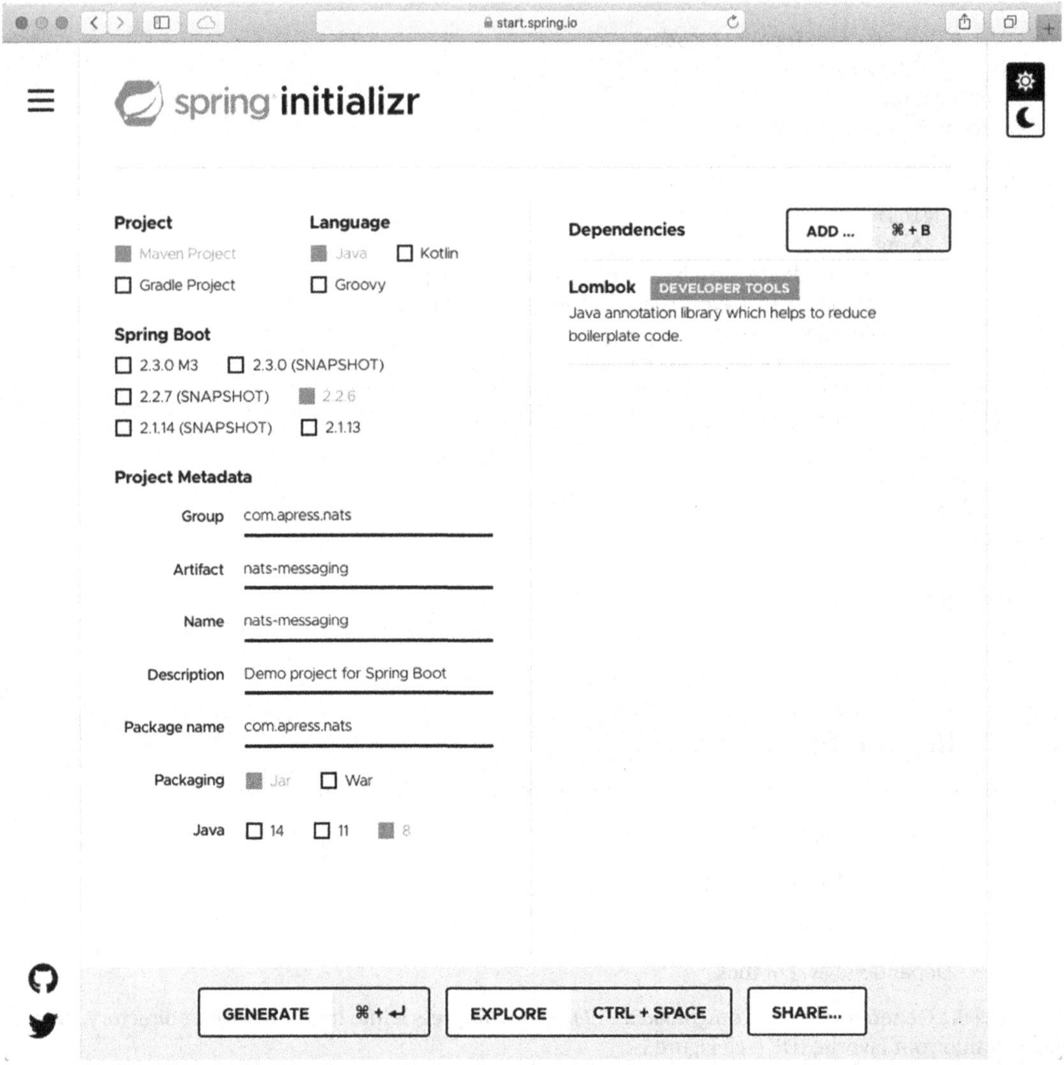

Figure 7-3. *Spring Initializr nats-messaging*

Next, let's add the dependencies needed to use the NATS server. One of the benefits of using open source technology is that it is open to the community. This case requires the NAT Java client (`https://nats.io/download/nats-io/nats.java/` and `https://github.com/nats-io/nats.java`).

Open `pom.xml` and replace it with the content in Listing 7-3.

Listing 7-3. nats-binder/nats-messaging/pom.xml

```
<?xml version="1.0" encoding="UTF-8"?>
<project xmlns="http://maven.apache.org/POM/4.0.0" xmlns:xsi="http://www.w3.org/2001/
XMLSchema-instance"
        xsi:schemaLocation="http://maven.apache.org/POM/4.0.0 https://maven.apache.org/xsd/
        maven-4.0.0.xsd">
        <modelVersion>4.0.0</modelVersion>
```

```
        <parent>
                <groupId>com.apress.nats</groupId>
                <artifactId>nats-binder</artifactId>
                <version>0.0.1</version>
                <relativePath>..</relativePath>
        </parent>

        <packaging>jar</packaging>

        <groupId>com.apress.nats</groupId>
        <artifactId>nats-messaging</artifactId>
        <version>0.0.1-SNAPSHOT</version>
        <name>nats-messaging</name>
        <description>Demo project for Spring Boot</description>

        <dependencies>
                <dependency>
                        <groupId>io.nats</groupId>
                        <artifactId>jnats</artifactId>
                        <version>2.6.6</version>
                </dependency>

                <dependency>
                        <groupId>com.fasterxml.jackson.core</groupId>
                        <artifactId>jackson-databind</artifactId>
                </dependency>
        </dependencies>

</project>
```

Take a look at pom.xml and note that the parent is declaring the nats-binder main project. Remember, the nats-messaging library is a module. Review it, and let's continue.

At the time of this writing, the Java NATS client version was 2.6.6. Let's start by creating the NatsProperties class. This class holds all the information about the server, port, and so forth (see Listing 7-4).

Listing 7-4. src/main/java/com/apress/nats/NatsProperties.java

```
package com.apress.nats;

import lombok.Data;
import org.springframework.boot.context.properties.ConfigurationProperties;

@Data
@ConfigurationProperties("spring.nats")
public class NatsProperties {

    private String host = "localhost";
    private Integer port = 4222;
}
```

Listing 7-4 shows the NatsProperties class; as you can see, it is very simple and has default values. Remember that you can override these properties in the application.properties/yml file, command line or environment variables, and so forth.

Next, create the NatsConnection class (see Listing 7-5).

Listing 17-5. src/main/java/com/apress/nats/NatsConnection.java

```
package com.apress.nats;

import io.nats.client.Connection;
import io.nats.client.Nats;
import lombok.Data;

import java.io.IOException;

@Data
public class NatsConnection {
    private Connection connection;
    private NatsProperties natsProperties;
    private NatsConnection(){}

    public NatsConnection(NatsProperties natsProperties) throws IOException,
    InterruptedException {
        this.natsProperties = natsProperties;
        this.connection =
Nats.connect("nats://" + natsProperties.getHost() + ":" + natsProperties.getPort().
toString());
    }

}
```

Listing 7-5 shows the NatsConnection class. This class has the NATS Connection instance. Here you are calling NatProperties to use the default values or those provided by the developer when using spring.nats.* properties. As you can see, the Nats class is static. You can call the connect method passing the schemed (nats://), the host, and the port, which is a very simple way to connect to the NATS server.

Next, let's create the NatsTemplate class (see Listing 7-6).

Listing 7-6. src/main/java/com/apress/nats/NatsTemplate.java

```
package com.apress.nats;

import lombok.AllArgsConstructor;
import lombok.Data;
import lombok.extern.log4j.Log4j2;
import org.springframework.messaging.Message;
import org.springframework.util.SerializationUtils;

import java.nio.charset.StandardCharsets;

@Log4j2
@AllArgsConstructor
@Data
```

```
public class NatsTemplate {

    private NatsConnection natsConnection;

    public void send(String subject, String message){
        assert this.natsConnection != null && subject != null && !subject.isEmpty() &&
        message != null && !message.isEmpty();
        log.debug("Sending: {}", message);
        this.natsConnection.getConnection().publish(subject, message.
        getBytes(StandardCharsets.UTF_8));
    }

    public void send(String subject,Message<?> message){
        assert this.natsConnection != null && subject != null && !subject.isEmpty() &&
        message != null;
        log.debug("Sending: {}", message);
        this.natsConnection.getConnection().publish(subject, SerializationUtils.
        serialize(message));
    }

}
```

Listing 7-6 shows the `NatsTemplate` class. This class removes all the boilerplate and provides all the operations that deal with the NATS server. This is an implementation of the template design pattern; if you are using the Spring Framework, you can find several of these, including `JmsTemplate`, `RabbitTemplate`, `KafkaTemplate`, and `JdbcTemplate`.

You are declaring only two overload methods, where you always receive the subject (similar to a topic) and the message. You are using the `org.springframework.messaging.Message` interface. Also note that you need the `NatsConnection` instance. To publish a message, you use the connection (with the `getConnection()` method call) and invoke the `publish` method. In the `send(String subject, Message<?> message)` method, you use a Spring serialization utils to serialize your message into a byte array. The NATS protocol requires that messages are the `byte[]` type.

Next, let's create the `NatMessageListener` interface (see Listing 7-7).

Listing 7-7. src/main/java/com/apress/nats/NatsMessageListener.java

```
package com.apress.nats;

public interface NatsMessageListener  {
    void onMessage(byte[] message);
}
```

Listing 7-7 shows the `NatsMessageListener` interface, which has the `onMessage` method with a `byte[]` type as a parameter.

Next, let's create at least one implementation to delegate the listener. This class subscribes to the subject (the same a topic) in the NATS server.

Create the `NatsMessageListenerAdapter` class (see Listing 7-8).

Listing 7-8. src/main/java/com/apress/nats/NatsMessageListenerAdapter.java

```
package com.apress.nats;
```

```
import io.nats.client.Dispatcher;
import io.nats.client.Subscription;
import lombok.Data;
import lombok.extern.log4j.Log4j2;

@Log4j2
@Data
public class NatsMessageListenerAdapter {

    private NatsConnection natsConnection;
    private String subject;
    private NatsMessageListener adapter;
    private Subscription subscription;
    private Dispatcher dispatcher;

    public void start(){
        assert natsConnection != null && natsConnection.getConnection() != null && subject
        != null && adapter != null;
        log.debug("Creating Message Listener...");
        dispatcher = this.natsConnection.getConnection().createDispatcher((msg) -> {});
        subscription = dispatcher.subscribe(this.subject, (msg) -> {
            adapter.onMessage(msg.getData());
        });
        log.debug("Subscribed to: {}",this.subject);
    }

    public void stop(){
        assert dispatcher != null && subject != null;
        log.debug("Unsubscribing from: {}", subject);
        dispatcher.unsubscribe(subject,300);
    }
}
```

Listing 7-8 shows the NatMessageListenerAdapter class that implements NatsMessageListener. Analyze this class before continuing. In the Java NATS client, there are two ways to get messages: synchronous and asynchronous. You are implementing the asynchronous way. To use it, you need to create a Dispatcher instance (based on the connection) and subscribe to the subject (the same as a topic). When you need to remove the subscription, you only need to call the unsubscribe method from the Dispatcher instance.

■ **Note** The code uses the @Log4j2 annotation from Lombok to inject the logging. Normally, you don't use it like that. You need to use AOP to create your cross-cutting concern for logging.

Now that you have the producer (NatsTemplate) and the consumer (NatsMessageListener), let's create the configuration. Create the NatsConfiguration class (see Listing 7-9).

Listing 7-9. src/main/java/com/apress/nats/NatsConfiguration.java

```
package com.apress.nats;
```

```
import org.springframework.boot.autoconfigure.condition.ConditionalOnMissingBean;
import org.springframework.boot.context.properties.EnableConfigurationProperties;
import org.springframework.context.annotation.Bean;
import org.springframework.context.annotation.Configuration;

import java.io.IOException;

@EnableConfigurationProperties(NatsProperties.class)
@Configuration
public class NatsConfiguration {

    @Bean
    @ConditionalOnMissingBean
    public NatsConnection natsConnection(NatsProperties natsProperties) throws IOException,
    InterruptedException {
        return new NatsConnection(natsProperties);
    }

    @Bean
    @ConditionalOnMissingBean
    public NatsTemplate natsTemplate(NatsConnection natsConnection){
        return new NatsTemplate(natsConnection);
    }

}
```

Listing 7-9 shows the `NatsConfiguration` class, which creates `NatsConnection` and `NatsTemplate` Spring beans. Note that you are using the `@ConditionalOnMissingBean`, which is useful when another class that uses this library creates its own beans with different implementations or values, so you avoid having several beans with the same type.

So that's it. This is the nats-messaging library that connects, produces, and consumes messages. Now, you can test it with the code in Listing 7-10. You can create the `NatsProducerConsumer` class, or you can add this code to the `NatsMessagingApplicationTest` class.

Listing 7-10. src/main/java/com/apress/nats/NatsProducerConsumer.java

```
package com.apress.nats;

import lombok.extern.log4j.Log4j2;
import org.springframework.boot.ApplicationRunner;
import org.springframework.context.annotation.Bean;
import org.springframework.context.annotation.Configuration;

import java.nio.charset.StandardCharsets;

@Log4j2
@Configuration
public class NatsProducerConsumer {

    @Bean(initMethod = "start",destroyMethod = "stop")
    public NatsMessageListenerAdapter natsMessageListenerAdapter(NatsConnection
    natsConnection){
```

```
        NatsMessageListenerAdapter adapter = new NatsMessageListenerAdapter();
        adapter.setNatsConnection(natsConnection);
        adapter.setSubject("test");
        adapter.setAdapter( message -> {
            log.info("Received: {}", new String(message, StandardCharsets.UTF_8));
        });
        return adapter;
    }
    @Bean
    public ApplicationRunner sendMessage(NatsTemplate natsTemplate){
        return args -> {
            natsTemplate.send("test","Hello There!");
        };
    }

}
```

To run this app, you need to have the NATS server up and running. You can run it with the following command (I used Docker).

```
$ docker run -d --rm --name nats -p 4222:4222 nats
```

Now you can execute the app in your IDE or by using the following command line.

```
$ ./mvnw spring-boot:run
```

You should see the following in your logs.

```
                NatsTemplate      : Sending: Hello There!
NatsProducerConsumer      : Received: Hello There!
```

Congratulations! You have created your `nats-messaging` library that is used in the next module. Now, you can stop your NATS server with the following.

```
$ docker stop nats
```

Stop your app.

■ **Warning** Before continuing, **comment out all** the code of the `NatProducerConsumer.java` class.

NATS Binder Implementation: nats-messaging-binder

Let's start with the binder implementation. Open a browser and point to `https://start.spring.io`. Use the following metadata.

- Group: `com.apress.nats`
- Artifact: `nats-messaging-binder`
- Package: `com.apress.nats`
- Dependencies: Lombok

Press the Generate button to download a ZIP file. Uncompress it into the `nats-binder` directory and import it into your favorite IDE (see Figure 7-4).

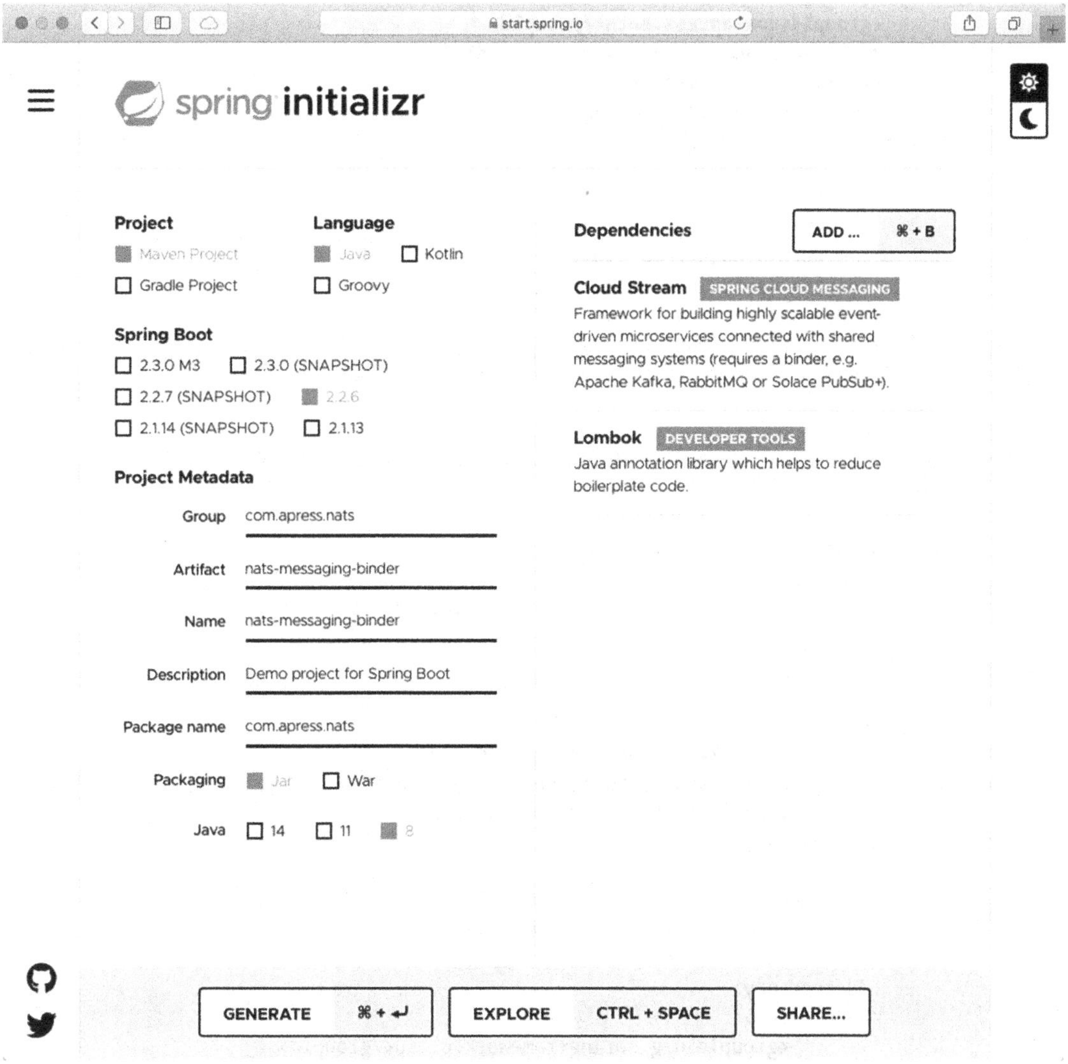

Figure 7-4. *Spring Initializr nats-messaging-binder*

Let's start by opening the `pom.xml` file replacing it with the content in Listing 7-11.

Listing 7-11. nats-binder/nats-messaging-binder/pom.xml

```
<?xml version="1.0" encoding="UTF-8"?>
<project xmlns="http://maven.apache.org/POM/4.0.0" xmlns:xsi="http://www.w3.org/2001/
XMLSchema-instance"
```

```
xsi:schemaLocation="http://maven.apache.org/POM/4.0.0 https://maven.apache.org/xsd/
maven-4.0.0.xsd">
<modelVersion>4.0.0</modelVersion>
<parent>
        <groupId>com.apress.nats</groupId>
        <artifactId>nats-binder</artifactId>
        <version>0.0.1</version>
        <relativePath>..</relativePath>
</parent>

<packaging>jar</packaging>

<groupId>com.apress.nats</groupId>
<artifactId>nats-messaging-binder</artifactId>
<version>0.0.1-SNAPSHOT</version>
<name>nats-messaging-binder</name>
<description>Demo project for Spring Boot</description>

<properties>
        <spring-cloud.version>Hoxton.SR3</spring-cloud.version>
</properties>

<dependencies>
        <dependency>
                <groupId>org.springframework.cloud</groupId>
                <artifactId>spring-cloud-stream</artifactId>
        </dependency>

        <dependency>
                <groupId>com.apress.nats</groupId>
                <artifactId>nats-messaging</artifactId>
                <version>0.0.1-SNAPSHOT</version>
        </dependency>

        <dependency>
                <groupId>org.projectlombok</groupId>
                <artifactId>lombok</artifactId>
        </dependency>
        <dependency>
                <groupId>org.springframework.cloud</groupId>
                <artifactId>spring-cloud-stream-test-support</artifactId>
                <scope>test</scope>
        </dependency>

</dependencies>

<dependencyManagement>
        <dependencies>
                <dependency>
                        <groupId>org.springframework.cloud</groupId>
                        <artifactId>spring-cloud-dependencies</artifactId>
```

```
                    <version>${spring-cloud.version}</version>
                    <type>pom</type>
                    <scope>import</scope>
                </dependency>
            </dependencies>
        </dependencyManagement>

</project>
```

Listing 7-11 shows the pom.xml file for the nats-messaging-binder module. Note that you are declaring the nats-messaging module as a dependency.

Next, let's follow the steps to create a new binder

Implement the Binder Interface

If you review the Binder interface, you see that you need several classes before you can implement it (see Listing 7-1). One of the parameters that you need to pass is the *inbound* and *outbound binding targets* for the consumer and producer methods, respectively. You can create all the logic for that and follow the practices for creating the different types of channels, messaging support, message converters, and so forth, but that takes too long. What if you rely on some of the abstract implementations that already takes out the underlying infrastructure that needs to be done with channels and so forth.

You can use the org.springframework.cloud.stream.binder.AbstractMessageChannelBinder class, which extends org.springframework.cloud.stream.binder.AbstractBinder class that implements the org.springframework.cloud.stream.binder.Binder interface. The AbstractMessageChannelBinder class brings all the logic needed to create the infrastructure for channels, connections, retry logic, destination creation, and so forth. So, that's the main class to extend. If you look at its signature, you see the code in Listing 7-12.

Listing 7-12. org.springframeworl.cloud.stream.binder.AbstractMessageChannelBinder.java

```
public abstract class AbstractMessageChannelBinder<C extends ConsumerProperties, P extends
ProducerProperties, PP extends ProvisioningProvider<C, P>>
                extends AbstractBinder<MessageChannel, C, P> implements
                PollableConsumerBinder<MessageHandler, C>, ApplicationEventPublisherAware
{
        // ...
}
```

Listing 7-12 is a snippet of the AbstractMessageChannelBinder class, which requires ConsumerProperties, ProducerProperties, and ProvisioningProvider classes. Let's start by creating the ProvisionProvider implementation. Create the NatsMessageBinderProvisioningProvider class (see Listing 7-13).

Listing 7-13. src/main/java/com/apress/nats/NatsMessageBinderProvisioningProvider.java

```
package com.apress.nats;

import org.springframework.cloud.stream.binder.ConsumerProperties;
import org.springframework.cloud.stream.binder.ProducerProperties;
import org.springframework.cloud.stream.provisioning.ConsumerDestination;
import org.springframework.cloud.stream.provisioning.ProducerDestination;
```

```
import org.springframework.cloud.stream.provisioning.ProvisioningException;
import org.springframework.cloud.stream.provisioning.ProvisioningProvider;

public class NatsMessageBinderProvisioningProvider implements ProvisioningProvider<ConsumerP
roperties, ProducerProperties> {

    @Override
    public ProducerDestination provisionProducerDestination(String name, ProducerProperties
    properties) throws ProvisioningException {
        return new NatsMessageBinderDestination(name);
    }

    @Override
    public ConsumerDestination provisionConsumerDestination(String name, String group,
    ConsumerProperties properties) throws ProvisioningException {
        return new NatsMessageBinderDestination(name);
    }
}
```

Listing 7-13 shows the `NatsMessageBinderProvisioningProvider` class that implements `ProvisioningProvider` with `ConsumerProperties` and `ProducerProperties` concrete classes as parameters. These classes help all the `spring.cloud.stream.bindings.[destinationName].[consumer|producer]` properties. Note that in the implementation, you are sending a new instance of the `NatsMessageBinderDestination` class. So, let's create it (see Listing 7-14).

Listing 7-14. src/main/java/com/apress/nats/NatsMessageBinderDestination.java

```
package com.apress.nats;

import lombok.AllArgsConstructor;
import lombok.Data;
import org.springframework.cloud.stream.provisioning.ConsumerDestination;
import org.springframework.cloud.stream.provisioning.ProducerDestination;

@AllArgsConstructor
@Data
public class NatsMessageBinderDestination implements ProducerDestination,
ConsumerDestination {

    private final String destination;

    @Override
    public String getName() {
        return this.destination.trim();
    }

    @Override
    public String getNameForPartition(int partition) {
        throw new UnsupportedOperationException("Partition not yet implemented for Nats
        Binder");
    }
}
```

Listing 7-14 shows the NatsMessageBinderDestination that implements both the ProducerDestination and the ConsumerDestination interfaces. The ProducerDestination interface declares getName() and getNameForPartition, and the ConsumerDestination interface declares getName(). This creates the destination and all the wiring for the underlying channel and integration infrastructure. Note that you are not implementing the partition feature for now.

Now that you have the ProvisioningProvider interface implementation, you must take care of consuming the incoming messages from the NATS server by creating a consumer endpoint and listeners. This means that you override the createConsumerEndpoint method in AbstractMessageChannelBinder, and this method needs to return MessageProducer. Let's use a class that implements all the necessary logic and overrides the methods needed. One of these classes is MessageProducerSupport, which is a support class for producer endpoints that creates the output channels; it has a method for sending messages. So, let's create the NatsMessageBinderProducer class (see Listing 7-15).

Listing 7-15. src/main/java/com/apress/nats/NatsMessageBinderProducer.java

```
package com.apress.nats;

import lombok.extern.log4j.Log4j2;
import org.springframework.cloud.stream.provisioning.ConsumerDestination;
import org.springframework.integration.endpoint.MessageProducerSupport;
import org.springframework.messaging.Message;
import org.springframework.messaging.support.MessageBuilder;
import org.springframework.util.SerializationUtils;

import java.nio.charset.StandardCharsets;

@Log4j2
public class NatsMessageBinderProducer extends MessageProducerSupport {

    private ConsumerDestination destination;
    private NatsMessageListenerAdapter adapter = new NatsMessageListenerAdapter();

    public NatsMessageBinderProducer(ConsumerDestination destination, NatsConnection
    natsConnection){
        assert destination != null && natsConnection != null;
        adapter.setSubject(destination.getName());
        adapter.setNatsConnection(natsConnection);
        adapter.setAdapter(messageListener);
    }

    @Override
    protected void doStart() {
        adapter.start();
    }

    @Override
    protected void doStop() {
        adapter.stop();
        super.doStop();
    }
```

```
    private NatsMessageListener messageListener = message -> {
        log.debug("[BINDER] Message received from NATS: {}",message);
        log.debug("[BINDER] Message Type received from NATS: {}",message.getClass().
        getName());
        this.sendMessage((Message<?>)SerializationUtils.deserialize(message));
    };
}
```

Listing 7-15 shows the `NatsMessageBinderProducer` class that is extending the `MessageProducerSupport` class. The only methods that you override are `doStart()` and `doStop()`. Let the class business logic handle the rest. In this class, you need to set up the listener that is connected to the NATS server. Look at the constructor where you need a `NatsConnection` instance. You start listening when the underlying bootstrap calls the `doStart()` method. When you receive the message, use the `sendMessage` method that deserializes it into a `Messager<?>` type, which is a wrapper class containing headers and the payload.

Now it's time to extend the `AbstractMessageChannelBinder` class (binder implementation). Create the `NatsMessageBinder` class (see Listing 7-16).

Listing 7-16. src/main/java/com/apress/nats/NatsMessageBinder.java

```
package com.apress.nats;

import lombok.extern.log4j.Log4j2;
import org.springframework.cloud.stream.binder.AbstractMessageChannelBinder;
import org.springframework.cloud.stream.binder.ConsumerProperties;
import org.springframework.cloud.stream.binder.ProducerProperties;
import org.springframework.cloud.stream.provisioning.ConsumerDestination;
import org.springframework.cloud.stream.provisioning.ProducerDestination;
import org.springframework.integration.core.MessageProducer;
import org.springframework.messaging.MessageChannel;
import org.springframework.messaging.MessageHandler;

@Log4j2
public class NatsMessageBinder extends AbstractMessageChannelBinder<ConsumerProperties, Prod
ucerProperties,NatsMessageBinderProvisioningProvider> {

    private NatsTemplate natsTemplate;

    public NatsMessageBinder(String[] headersToEmbed, NatsMessageBinderProvisioningProvider
    provisioningProvider, NatsTemplate natsTemplate) {
        super(headersToEmbed, provisioningProvider);
        this.natsTemplate = natsTemplate;
    }

    @Override
    protected MessageHandler createProducerMessageHandler(ProducerDestination destination,
    ProducerProperties producerProperties, MessageChannel errorChannel) throws Exception {
        return message -> {
            assert natsTemplate != null;
            log.debug("[BINDER] Sending to NATS: {}",message);
            natsTemplate.send(destination.getName(),message);
        };
    }
```

```
    @Override
    protected MessageProducer createConsumerEndpoint(ConsumerDestination destination, String
    group, ConsumerProperties properties) throws Exception {
        assert natsTemplate != null;
        return new NatsMessageBinderProducer(destination, this.natsTemplate.
        getNatsConnection());
    }
}
```

Listing 7-16 shows the `NatsMessageBinder` class, our main binder implementation. Take a look at the constructor, where it is necessary to call the base class (`AbstractMessageChannelBinder`) passing the headers of the message (e.g., custom headers or the broker-related headers), the `ProvisioningProvider` (`NatsMessageBinderProvisioningProvider` class), and the `NatsTemplate` that sends the messages.

We override `createProducerMessageHandler`, which returns `MessageHandler`. It has the message to send to the NATS server. That's why the `NatsTemplate` instance is used to get the destination name and the message. Also, we override `createConsumerEndPoint`, which returns an instance of the `NatMessageBinderProducer` class. Remember that this class starts with the listener for incoming messages.

Create the @Configuration Beans

Now that we have our binder implementation, it is time to create the configuration and the Spring beans that do the binder's autoconfiguration. Create the `NatsMessageBinderConfiguration` class (see Listing 7-17).

Listing 7-17. src/main/java/com/apress/nats/NatsMessageBinderConfiguration.java

```
package com.apress.nats;

import org.springframework.boot.context.properties.EnableConfigurationProperties;
import org.springframework.context.annotation.Bean;
import org.springframework.context.annotation.Configuration;
import org.springframework.context.annotation.Import;

@EnableConfigurationProperties(NatsProperties.class)
@Import(NatsConfiguration.class)
@Configuration
public class NatsMessageBinderConfiguration {

    @Bean
    public NatsMessageBinderProvisioningProvider natsMessageBinderProvisioningProvider(){
        return new NatsMessageBinderProvisioningProvider();
    }

    @Bean
    public NatsMessageBinder natsMessageBinder(NatsMessageBinderProvisioningProvider
    natsMessageBinderProvisioningProvider, NatsTemplate natsTemplate){
        return new NatsMessageBinder(null,natsMessageBinderProvisioningProvider,
        natsTemplate);
    }
}
```

Listing 7-17 shows the NatsMessageBinderConfiguration class. This class is importing the NatsConfiguration class that contains NatsTemplate and NatsConnection (see Listing 7-9). Here we are defining the binder, the natsMessageBinderProvisioningProvider, and the natsMessageBinder that the Spring beans need to wire up everything for the binder to work. In the natsMessageBinder method, we return a new instance of the NatsMessageBinder class that has several parameters. For now, you are passing null to the headers. You can deal with them later.

Create the META-INF/spring.binders

Next, you need to add the configuration to the spring.binders file. Create the META-INF folder in the src/main/resources path and create the spring.binders file with the content in Listing 7-18.

Listing 7-18. src/main/resources/META-INF/spring.binders

```
nats:\
com.apress.nats.NatsMessageBinderConfiguration
```

Listing 7-18 shows the spring.binders file, which is required for the autoconfiguration to work. This means that if you add this module as a dependency, it uses spring.binders to find every class with the @Configuration annotated class and executes the autoconfiguration logic to set up the binder or any other configuration.

Note that you are naming this binder nats, which is important when using multiple binders in one stream, which is discussed in later sections.

NATS Binder Test

Now that you have the nats-messaging and the nats-messaging-binder modules, it's time to test it. Of course, there are specialized test classes for that, but I want to show you how easy it is to use this binder and save the unit/integration testing for later.

Open a browser and point to https://start.spring.io. Use the following metadata.

- Group: com.apress.nats
- Artifact: nats-messaging-test
- Package: com.apress.nats

Press the Generate button to download a ZIP file. Uncompress it into the nats-binder directory and import it into your favorite IDE (see Figure 7-5).

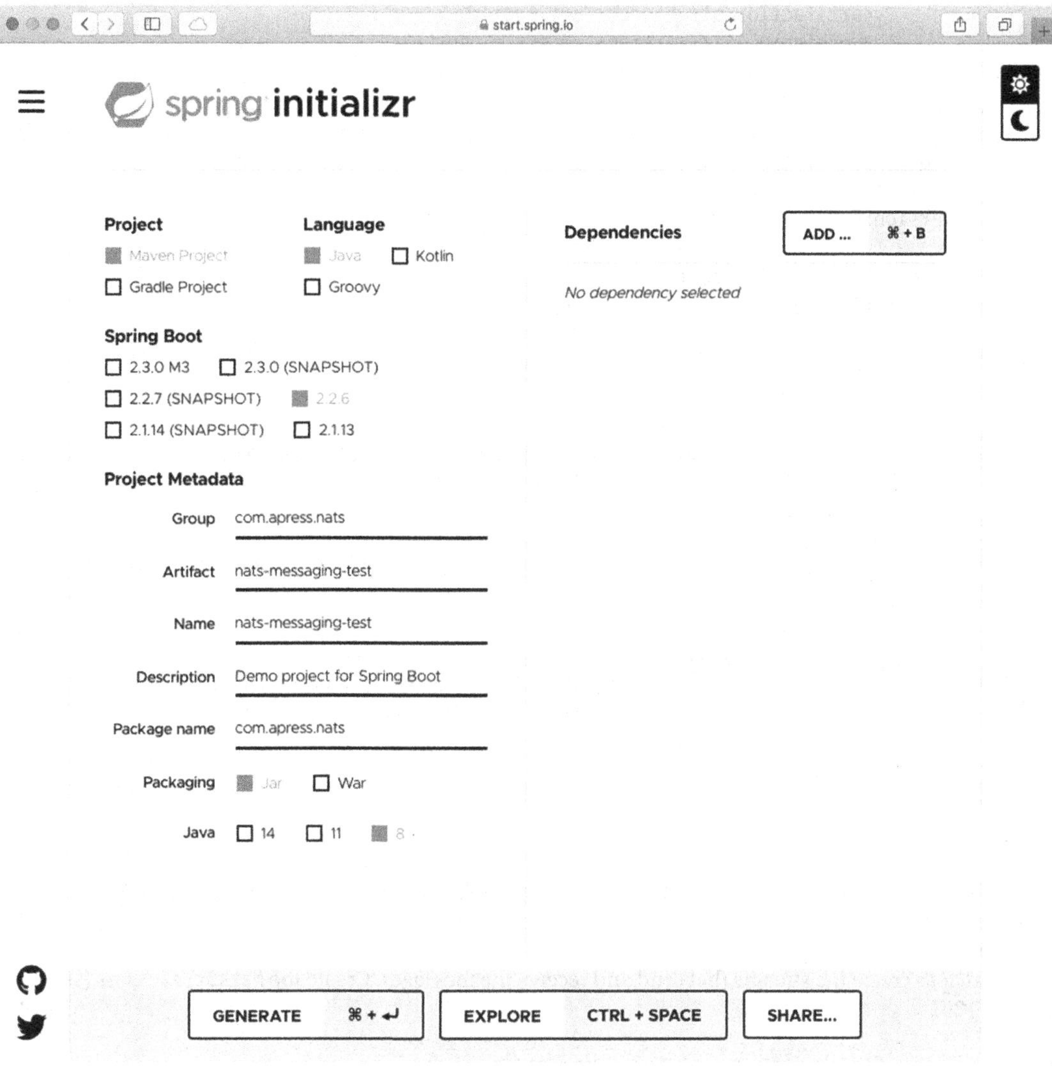

***Figure 7-5** Spring Initializr nats-messaging-test*

Open pom.xml and replace it with the content in Listing 7-19.

Listing 7-19. nats-messaging-test/pom.xml

```
<?xml version="1.0" encoding="UTF-8"?>
<project xmlns="http://maven.apache.org/POM/4.0.0" xmlns:xsi="http://www.w3.org/2001/
XMLSchema-instance"
        xsi:schemaLocation="http://maven.apache.org/POM/4.0.0 https://maven.apache.org/xsd/
        maven-4.0.0.xsd">
        <modelVersion>4.0.0</modelVersion>
        <parent>
                <groupId>com.apress.nats</groupId>
```

```
            <artifactId>nats-binder</artifactId>
            <version>0.0.1</version>
            <relativePath>..</relativePath><!-- lookup parent from repository -->
    </parent>

    <groupId>com.apress.nats</groupId>
    <artifactId>nats-messaging-test</artifactId>
    <version>0.0.1-SNAPSHOT</version>

    <name>nats-messaging-test</name>
    <description>Demo project for Spring Boot</description>

    <dependencies>
            <dependency>
                    <groupId>com.apress.nats</groupId>
                    <artifactId>nats-messaging-binder</artifactId>
                    <version>0.0.1-SNAPSHOT</version>
            </dependency>
    </dependencies>

    <build>
            <plugins>
                    <plugin>
                            <groupId>org.springframework.boot</groupId>
                            <artifactId>spring-boot-maven-plugin</artifactId>
                    </plugin>
            </plugins>
    </build>
</project>
```

Listing 7-19 shows `pom.xml`. Note that you are only using `nats-messaging-binder` and no other dependency because `nats-messaging-binder` provides everything that you need, including the `nats-messaging` module.

Next, let's create the streams that send and receive the messages. Create the `NatsStream` class (see Listing 7-20).

Listing 7-20. src/main/java/com/apress/nats/NatsStream.java

```
package com.apress.nats;

import lombok.extern.log4j.Log4j2;
import org.springframework.cloud.stream.annotation.EnableBinding;
import org.springframework.cloud.stream.annotation.StreamListener;
import org.springframework.cloud.stream.messaging.Sink;
import org.springframework.cloud.stream.messaging.Source;
import org.springframework.context.annotation.Bean;
import org.springframework.integration.annotation.InboundChannelAdapter;
import org.springframework.integration.annotation.Poller;
import org.springframework.integration.core.MessageSource;
import org.springframework.messaging.support.GenericMessage;
```

```
@Log4j2
@EnableBinding({Source.class, Sink.class})
public class NatsStream {

    @Bean
    @InboundChannelAdapter(value = Source.OUTPUT, poller = @Poller(fixedRate = "10000",
maxMessagesPerPoll = "1"))
    public MessageSource<String> timerMessageSource() {
        return () -> new GenericMessage<>("Hello Spring Cloud Stream");
    }

    @StreamListener(Sink.INPUT)
    public void process(Object message){
        log.info("Received and ProcessedClass: {}", message.getClass().getName());
        log.info("Received and Processed: {}", message);
    }
}
```

Listing 7-20 shows the NatsStream class. Take a look at the @EnableBinding declaration. We are using a 2.x programming style with the Source and Sink interfaces. To produce messages, you use the Spring Integration @InboundChannelAdapter annotation adapter. The underlying implementation of this adapter contains a pollable logic that calls and executes the method every 10 seconds based on the fixedRated parameter from the @Poller annotation. Note that this adapter uses the output channel to send a message; in this case, a GenericMessage<> type (a String). If you are curious, this is the same logic used for the Time Source Application Starter. It uses @InboundChannelAdapter to send a message every *T* seconds.

The @StreamListener annotation marks a method that receives all the incoming messages from the input channel.

Next, let's help the binder name the channels/destinations and connect them. If this isn't done, input and output channels/destinations are created but won't be connected.

Open application.properties and use the content in Listing 7-21.

Listing 7-21. src/main/resources/application.properties

```
# Nats Bindings
spring.cloud.stream.bindings.output.destination=movie
spring.cloud.stream.bindings.input.destination=movie

# Debugging
logging.level.org.springframework.cloud.stream.messaging=DEBUG
logging.level.com.apress.nats=DEBUG
```

Listing 7-21 shows application.properties. Note that we are using the 2.x programming model, and the naming convention is based on input/output channels/destinations. So, the input and output channels must have the same name to produce (source) and consume (sink); in this case, you are calling the channels/destinations movie. Note that you use the debug logging level to get insight into what is happening.

Before you run the test, make sure you have the Docker NATS server image container up and running. If it's not running, you can run it with the following.

```
$ docker run -d --rm --name nats -p 4222:4222 nats
```

Now you can run it from your IDE. If your IDE is smart, it already knows about the configuration. But if you want to run it from the command line, you need to add the following files in the root project (nats-binder).

```
$ cp -r nats-messaging/.mvn .
$ cp nats-messaging/mvnw* .
```

Copy the Maven wrapper that compiles, installs, and executes the test. Next, in the project (nats-binder) execute the following.

```
$ ./mvnw clean compile install
$ ./mvnw spring-boot:run -pl nats-messaging-test
```

If everything went well, you should get the following output every 10 seconds.

```
Received and Processed: Hello Spring Cloud Stream
```

Also look at the beginning of the logs, where you have the debug information from the other classes. You should see the Creating Message Listener and Subscribed to: movie messages.

Congratulations! You have created a NATS server binder. Now you can use it everywhere you need to use NATS without worrying about any API.

Don't forget to stop your NAT server.

■ **Notes** You can find all the source code in the `ch07/nats-binder` folder in this book's companion code.

Multiple Binders

It was fun to create a NATS binder, right? Now, let's look at solving a particular requirement when you need more than one binder. So far, you are using either Rabbit or Kafka, but not together or maybe with multiple Rabbit brokers or a Rabbit for a source and a Kafka for a processor.

In this section, you learn how to use multiple binders, particularly, the NATS and RabbitMQ binders. You create three separated projects: `movie-file-source-nats`, which exposes JSON movie messages to the NATS server, `movie-filter-processor-nats-rabbit`, which listens from NATS and sends messages to Rabbit, and finally, `movie-log-sink-rabbit`, which logs messages from RabbitMQ (see Figure 7-6).

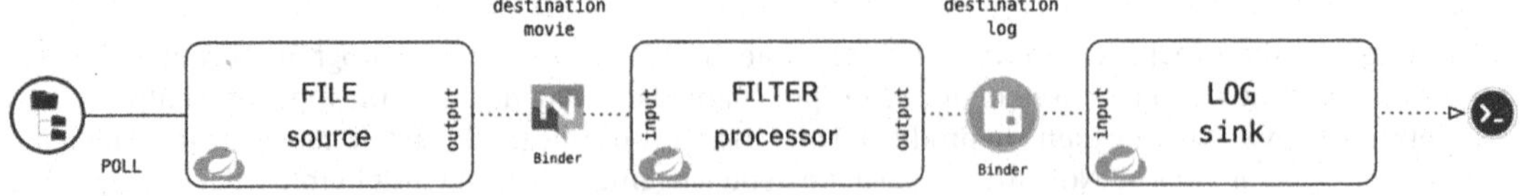

Figure 7-6. *Multiple binders*

movie-file-source-nats

This stream reads all the JSON movies from a file, and it sends them to the next stream using the NATS binder. Open a browser and point to `https://start.spring.io`. Use the following metadata.

- Group: `com.apress.cloud.stream`
- Artifact: `movie-file-source-nats`
- Package: `com.apress.cloud.stream.movie`
- Dependencies: Lombok

Press the Generate button to download a ZIP file. Uncompress it and import it into your favorite IDE. Note the package name (see Figure 7-7).

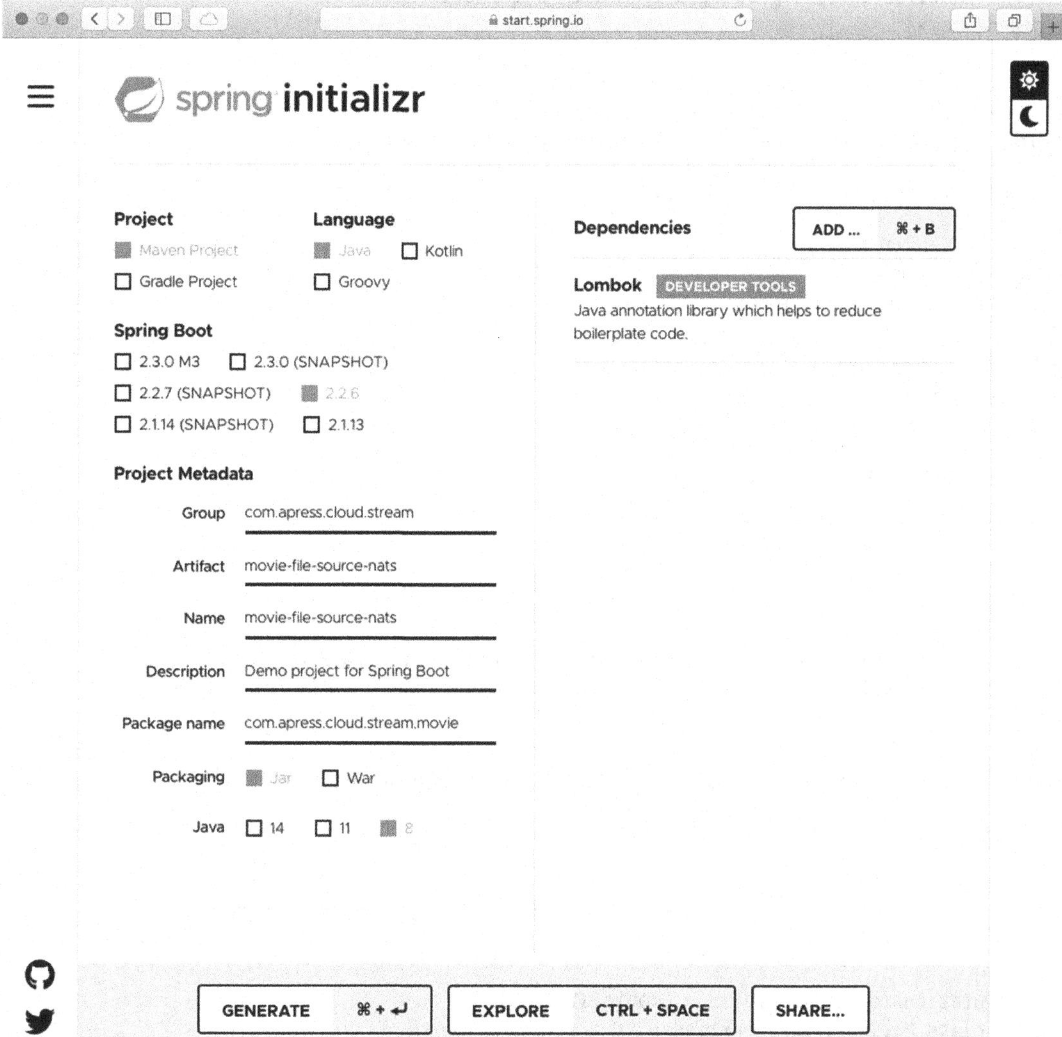

Figure 7-7. Spring Initializr movie-file-source-nats

Open your `pom.xml` file and add the following two dependencies.

```
<!-- NATS -->
<dependency>
        <groupId>com.apress.nats</groupId>
        <artifactId>nats-messaging-binder</artifactId>
        <version>0.0.1-SNAPSHOT</version>
</dependency>
<!-- Spring Integration -->
<dependency>
        <groupId>org.springframework.integration</groupId>
        <artifactId>spring-integration-file</artifactId>
</dependency>
```

Next, create the Movie class (see Listing 7-22).

Listing 7-22. src/main/java/com/apress/cloud/stream/movie/Movie.java

```
package com.apress.cloud.stream.movie;

import lombok.AllArgsConstructor;
import lombok.Data;
import lombok.NoArgsConstructor;

@AllArgsConstructor
@NoArgsConstructor
@Data
public class Movie {
    private String title;
    private String actor;
    private int year;
    private String genre;
}
```

As you can see, the Movie class is the same as in previous chapters. Next, create the MovieStreamProperties class. This class holds the information about the directory (where the JSON movies are) and the name pattern (see Listing 7-23).

Listing 7-23. src/main/java/com/apress/cloud/stream/movie/MovieStreamProperties.java

```
package com.apress.cloud.stream.movie;

import lombok.Data;
import org.springframework.boot.context.properties.ConfigurationProperties;

@Data
@ConfigurationProperties(prefix = "movie.stream")
public class MovieStreamProperties {

    private String directory;
    private String namePattern;
}
```

As you can see, it is the same class that is in other chapters; nothing special about it. Next, create the MovieStream class (see Listing 7-24).

Listing 7-24. src/main/java/com/apress/cloud/stream/movie/MovieStream.java

```
package com.apress.cloud.stream.movie;

import lombok.AllArgsConstructor;
import org.springframework.boot.context.properties.EnableConfigurationProperties;
import org.springframework.cloud.stream.annotation.EnableBinding;
import org.springframework.cloud.stream.messaging.Source;
import org.springframework.context.annotation.Bean;
import org.springframework.integration.dsl.IntegrationFlow;
import org.springframework.integration.dsl.IntegrationFlows;
import org.springframework.integration.dsl.Pollers;
import org.springframework.integration.dsl.Transformers;
import org.springframework.integration.file.dsl.Files;
import org.springframework.integration.file.splitter.FileSplitter;

import java.io.File;

@AllArgsConstructor
@EnableConfigurationProperties(MovieStreamProperties.class)
@EnableBinding(Source.class)
public class MovieStream {

    private MovieStreamProperties movieStreamProperties;

    @Bean
    public IntegrationFlow fileFlow(){
        return IntegrationFlows.from(Files
                        .inboundAdapter(new File(this.movieStreamProperties.getDirectory()))
                        .preventDuplicates(true)
                        .patternFilter(this.movieStreamProperties.getNamePattern()),
                        e -> e.poller(Pollers.fixedDelay(5000L)))
                .split(Files.splitter().markers())
                .filter(p -> !(p instanceof FileSplitter.FileMarker))
                .transform(Transformers.fromJson(Movie.class))
                .channel(Source.OUTPUT)
                .get();
    }
}
```

Listing 7-24 shows the MovieStream class. Note that you are using the version 2.x model programming where you need to use the @EnableBinding annotation and provide the type, in this case, a Source type. Next, open your application.properties file and add the content from Listing 7-25.

Listing 7-25. src/main/resources/application.properties

```
# Nats Bindings
# Programming Style version 2.x
spring.cloud.stream.bindings.output.destination=movie
```

```
# Movie Stream Properties
movie.stream.directory=.
movie.stream.name-pattern=movies-json.txt

# Debugging
logging.level.com.apress.nats=DEBUG
logging.level.org.springframework.cloud.stream.messaging.DirectWithAttributesChannel=DEBUG
```

Note that you are renaming the output destination movie.

That's is for this stream. I know that the code seems repetitive, but it helps you understand the concept better. How can you do this using reactive programming? You need to make a small change. First, you can return Publisher<Message<Movie>> in fileFlow, and instead of calling the get() method (to get the IntegrationFlow instance), use toReactivePublisher(). Second, you need to create a supplier. Remember that you need to subscribe to the publisher. You need to declare a Supplier method for that. And third, you need to use the spring.cloud.stream.bindings.[suplier-method-name]-out-0.destination property.

For this stream, I added movies-json.txt at the root of the project. It contains the following content.

```
{"title":"The Matrix","actor":"Keanu Reeves","year":1999,"genre":"fiction"}
{"title":"Memento","actor":"Guy Pearce","year":2000,"genre":"drama"}
{"title":"The Prestige","actor":"Christian Bale","year":2006,"genre":"drama"}
{"title":"Disturbia","actor":"Shia LaBeouf","year":2007,"genre":"drama"}
```

■ **Note** You can find all the source code in the ch07/multiple folder. You find commented out the reactive version.

---

movie-filter-processor-nats-rabbit

Next, let's create the processor that filters a movie based on its genre value. This stream uses the NATS (for input) and RabbitMQ (for output) binders. Open a browser and point to https://start.spring.io. Use the following metadata.

- Group: com.apress.cloud.stream
- Artifact: movie-filter-processor-nats-rabbit
- Package: com.apress.cloud.stream.movie
- Dependencies: Cloud Stream, Lombok

Press the Generate button to download a ZIP file. Uncompress it and import it into your favorite IDE. Note the package name.

Open the pom.xml file and add the following dependencies.

```
<!-- NATS -->
<dependency>
        <groupId>com.apress.nats</groupId>
        <artifactId>nats-messaging-binder</artifactId>
```

```
        <version>0.0.1-SNAPSHOT</version>
</dependency>

<!-- RabbitMQ Binder -->
<dependency>
        <groupId>org.springframework.cloud</groupId>
        <artifactId>spring-cloud-starter-stream-rabbit</artifactId>
</dependency>
```

Next, create the Movie class. You can use the same code as in Listing 7-22. Next, you need to create the MovieStream class (see Listing 7-26).

Listing 7-26. src/main/java/com/apress/cloud/stream/movie/MovieStream.java

```
package com.apress.cloud.stream.movie;

import org.springframework.cloud.stream.annotation.EnableBinding;
import org.springframework.cloud.stream.messaging.Processor;
import org.springframework.integration.annotation.Filter;

@EnableBinding(Processor.class)
public class MovieStream {

    String GENRE_DRAMA = "drama";

    @Filter(inputChannel = Processor.INPUT,outputChannel = Processor.OUTPUT)
    public boolean onlyDrama(Movie movie) {
        return movie.getGenre().equals(GENRE_DRAMA);
    }
}
```

Here you are still using the version 2.x model in which you need to declare @EnableBinding with its type, in this case, the processor with the input and output processor. Also note that you are using the Spring Integration @Filter annotations that need to return a boolean depending on the evaluated expression. In this case, you are evaluating if the genre is DRAMA; if so, let it pass. Also note that the @Filter annotation requires two parameters: inputChannel and outputChannel; in this case, they are processor type members.

You can find the reactive version in the source code for this project.

Next, let's rename application.properties as application.yaml. Add the content from Listing 7-27.

Listing 7-27. src/main/resources/application.yaml

```
spring:
  cloud:
    stream:
      bindings:
        input:
          binder: nats
          destination: movie
        output:
          binder: rabbit
          destination: log
```

In this case, you are using YAML because it is more legible and understandable than the properties. Note that you are using the `spring.cloud.stream.binding.input.binder` set to `nats` (this name is from the `META-INF/spring.binders` from the `nats-messaging-binder` module). And you are setting `spring.cloud.stream.binding.input.destination` to `movie`. Set `output.binder` to `rabbit` and set `output.destination` to `log`.

If you enable the reactive part from the `MovieStream` class, you need to use the naming convention for bindings. You can find this code commented out in the `application.yaml` file.

movie-log-sink-rabbit

Next, is the movie-log-sink-rabbit Stream. For this stream log, you use an old style and a Spring Integration XML file to create the log-sink. Open a browser and point to `https://start.spring.io`. Use the following metadata.

- Group: `com.apress.cloud.stream`
- Artifact: `movie-log-sink-rabbit`
- Package: `com.apress.cloud.stream.movie`
- Dependencies: Cloud Stream, Lombok

You can press the Generate button to download a ZIP file. Uncompress it and import it into your favorite IDE. Note the package name.

Open the `pom.xml` file and add the following dependency.

```
<!-- RabbitMQ Binder -->
<dependency>
        <groupId>org.springframework.cloud</groupId>
        <artifactId>spring-cloud-starter-stream-rabbit</artifactId>
</dependency>
```

Next, create the `Movie` class. You can use the code in Listing 7-22. Then, create the `MovieStream` class (see Listing 7-28).

Listing 7-28. src/main/java/com/apress/cloud/stream/movie/MovieStream.java

```
package com.apress.cloud.stream.movie;

import org.springframework.cloud.stream.annotation.EnableBinding;
import org.springframework.cloud.stream.messaging.Sink;
import org.springframework.context.annotation.Configuration;
import org.springframework.context.annotation.ImportResource;

@Configuration
@ImportResource({"/META-INF/spring/movie-log.xml"})
@EnableBinding(Sink.class)
public class MovieStream {
}
```

You are using `@EnableBinding` with the sink type as parameter. Note that you are using the `@ImportResource` annotation to load a legacy XML file. Next, create the `META-INF/spring/movie-log.xml` file (see Listing 7-29).

Listing 7-29. src/main/resources/META-INF/spring/movie-log.xml

```
<?xml version="1.0" encoding="UTF-8"?>
<beans xmlns="http://www.springframework.org/schema/beans"
       xmlns:xsi="http://www.w3.org/2001/XMLSchema-instance"
       xmlns:int="http://www.springframework.org/schema/integration"

       xsi:schemaLocation="http://www.springframework.org/schema/beans
    https://www.springframework.org/schema/beans/spring-beans.xsd
    http://www.springframework.org/schema/integration
    https://www.springframework.org/schema/integration/spring-integration.xsd">

    <int:json-to-object-transformer
            input-channel="input"
            output-channel="logger"
            type="com.apress.cloud.stream.movie.Movie"/>

    <int:logging-channel-adapter id="logger"
                                 logger-name="LOG"
                                 level="INFO"
                                 expression="payload"/>
</beans>
```

Listing 7-29 shows the legacy XML Spring Integration. I think that any legacy Spring system that still uses the XML approach can be modernized to Spring Boot very easily because you can reuse your XML and take advantage of the performance (this topic is for another time).

As you can see, you are using the `json-to-object-transformer` component (because the data from RabbitMQ is an application/JSON type) just to convert to an object and getting the `toString()` format logged into the console. Note that the transformer sets the `input-channel` attribute to `input` (the name of the binding) and the `output-channel` attribute to `logger`, which is the `logging-channel-adapter` component's ID.

Finally, open `application.properties` and add the following content.

```
# Binding RabbitMQ
spring.cloud.stream.bindings.input.destination=log
```

Running Them All Together

You are ready to run everything, but to run all the streams, you need to make sure the NATS server and the RabbitMQ broker are up and running. I added a `docker-compose.yml` file in the source code. It contains both servers. Instead of manually starting them, you can use Docker Compose (see Listing 7-30).

Listing 7-30. docker-compose.yml

```
version: '3'

services:
  nats:
    image: 'nats:latest'
    container_name: nats
```

```
    ports:
      - '4222:4222'
      - '8222:8222'

  rabbit:
    image: 'rabbitmq:3.8.3-management-alpine'
    container_name: rabbit
    ports:
      - '15672:15672'
      - '5672:5672'
```

Open a terminal window and go to this file. Run the following command to start the servers.

```
$ docker-compose up
```

Go to your IDE and run your streams, starting with the log and processor; or you can run this stream using the following well-known Maven command.

```
$ ./mvnw spring-boot-run.
```

You need to run `movie-file-source-nats` last to read the `movies-json.txt` file, which is the well-known root of the project. After running it, the movie-log-sink-rabbit should only stream the three drama-genre movies.

```
Movie(title=Memento, actor=Guy Pearce, year=2000, genre=drama)
Movie(title=The Prestige, actor=Christian Bale, year=2006, genre=drama)
Movie(title=Disturbia, actor=Shia LaBeouf, year=2007, genre=drama)
```

Congrats! You used multiple brokers!

What happens when you have multiple brokers of the same type? In other words, you have a processor that is listening from a RabbitMQ server located on the East Coast, and you need to process the message and send it to a RabbitMQ server on the West Coast. Using the same principle and naming convention, use the following configuration in `application.yaml`.

```
spring:
  cloud:
    stream:
      bindings:
        input:
          destination: movie
          binder: rabbit1
        output:
          destination: log
          binder: rabbit2
      binders:
        rabbit1:
          type: rabbit
          environment:
            spring:
              rabbitmq:
                host: east-coast.mydomain.com
        rabbit2:
          type: rabbit
```

```
environment:
  spring:
    rabbitmq:
      host: west-coast.mydomain.com
username: admin
      password: {cipher}c789b2ee5bd
```

As you can see, it is very easy to add multiple binders of the same type.

Extra Configuration

Even though I discussed configurations from the previous chapter, there are other properties that are worth mentioning. Check out the `org.springframework.cloud.stream.config.BindingServiceProperties` class and the Javadoc for more information on these properties.

Summary

In this chapter, I showed you how to create a custom binder by following the three steps: implement from the `Binder` interface, add the configuration that creates the `binder`, and finally, add the binder configuration to the `spring.binders` file. This is used when the Spring Boot autoconfiguration starts due to the findings in the classpath.

You created a NATS binder and used it in the multiple binders. This chapter used different ways to create streams: using version 2.x, where you need to declare the `@Binding` annotation with its type (source, processor, or sink), using version 3.x, where you can use functional and reactive programming, or using some of the code from old Spring Integration annotations and legacy XML.

In the next chapter, I discuss Spring Cloud Data Flow and how Spring Cloud Stream and the binder technology fit into our solutions.

CHAPTER 8

Spring Cloud Data Flow: Introduction and Installation

In previous chapters, you saw Spring Cloud Stream applications that run as stand-alone microservices. You can create a composite of Cloud Stream apps to make a complete, robust, and scalable system. You can run them by downloading the latest Uber-JAR and executing the `java -jar` command. You can run them with Docker Compose by using the app's Docker images. You learned how to create custom Cloud Stream apps in versions 1.x to 2.x by using annotations and in version 3.x using functional or reactive programming.

Now that you have multiple Cloud Stream apps, a technology should manage them. You need the ability to run your apps, coordinate them when one is down, manage versions of the composite stream, orchestrate them with triggers, add hooks that respond to a particular event, add security to securely connect to external systems, schedule batch jobs, and more.

Since you have used Docker Compose, Docker Swarm may be a good solution. It is, but you need something to manage the app life cycle and the whole composite stream. You need something to handle versions when new parameters are set or multiple deployments to different platforms. You need a way to gather information about your stream, like logs and metrics and to manage every aspect of your solution. Speaking of scalability, resilience, and high availability, you can depend on a cloud platform like Cloud Foundry or Kubernetes or, even better, Red Hat OpenShift.

This chapter discusses Spring Cloud Data Flow, a stream life cycle technology that offers all that you need to create robust, stream-based microservices and batch data processing solutions.

Spring Cloud Data Flow

Spring Cloud Data Flow is an open source technology that composes complex topologies for streaming and batch data pipelines. It uses the prebuilt microservices covered in previous chapters and allows you to develop and test microservices for data integration. It can be used stand-alone or in any cloud platform, like Cloud Foundry or Kubernetes, and even better, you can use all the added features in Red Hat OpenShift.

F. Gutierrez, *Spring Cloud Data Flow*, https://doi.org/10.1007/978-1-4842-1239-4_8

Features

Let's go over some of the main features that Spring Cloud Data Flow provides to solve complex topologies for streaming.

- *Programming model.* You saw this in previous chapters, where you used the Spring Cloud Stream framework to create Stream apps. Even though you haven't seen it in action yet, you can use the Spring Cloud Task framework to create or trigger a batch solution that defines ETL (extract, transform, load) jobs using Spring Batch. As you already know, there are the old-fashioned Spring Integration (through channels), functional (using Java 8+), and reactive programming (Kafka Streams) programming models.
- *Polyglot.* One of the benefits of creating Stream apps as microservices is that you can use Python, Groovy, .NET, or any other language. Spring Cloud Data Flow can launch your app to connect to your stream.
- *Message broker binders.* You can use the same code with a pluggable binder regardless of the message middleware broker you use. The Spring Cloud Stream team supports RabbitMQ and Kafka out of the box, but you can find multiple binder implementations in the community. Based on what you learned in previous chapters, you can create a binder and use it with Spring Cloud Data Flow.
- *Application Starters.* Spring Cloud Data Flow uses Spring Cloud Stream Application Starters with Docker or Maven artifacts to create stream solutions. You see that you can register your custom stream with ease and use it in the dashboard, so you have a visual representation of the stream.
- *Security.* I haven't covered security yet, but Spring Cloud Data Flow allows you to secure not only the dashboard but all your microservices using security standards such as OAuth2 or OpenID Connect for authentication and authorization.
- *Continuous delivery.* One of the benefits of using Spring Cloud Data Flow is avoiding downtime when you upgrade your stream. This is done by applying canary or blue-green deployment practices to your streams and adding continuous delivery and continuous integrations tools.
- *Batch processing.* In Spring Cloud Data Flow, you can manage the execution of any batch job with a detailed status report and a way to restart failed jobs, and because it can be installed in any flavor of Cloud Foundry and Kubernetes, you can schedule any batch job from within the Spring Cloud Data Flow dashboard.
- *Domain-specific language.* Spring Cloud Data Flow provides a domain-specific language (DSL) that visually displays the connection to the next app using | pipelines.

Spring Cloud Data Flow is a choreographer for stream topologies/apps. It creates robust integration solutions. It offers ways to visualize, run, deploy, change, and manage versions of your streams by using the REST API, a shell tool, or a GUI dashboard. Let's jump in with a local installation so that you can see Spring Cloud Data Flow in action.

Local Installation

You can run Spring Cloud Data Flow in your local or development environment. The instructions in this section are not suitable for a production environment. Remember that if you need production-grade instructions, you need to rely on a platform that brings scalability, resiliency, fault tolerance, high availability, storage, monitoring, and more, such as Kubernetes, Cloud Foundry, Mesos, or Yarn.

Single Machine/Server

In the next sections, I describe how to use RabbitMQ and Kafka as binders. In other chapters, you can reuse the NATs binder from previous chapters; for now, choose either RabbitMQ or Kafka. It's worth mentioning that the server used here (Skipper and Data Flow) use H2 as a persistence engine by default. This DB engine is an in-memory database, meaning that once you finish, any stream created, or job or app registered is gone. So, the following sections use MySQL as a persistence engine. You can use PostgreSQL or Oracle if you prefer; it is a matter of changing the Spring Data Source properties.

Using RabbitMQ as a Binder and MySQL for Persistence

To make things easier, create a folder named `workspace-rabbit-mysql`.

The following steps are required to get Spring Cloud Data Flow up and running on a single machine. `workspace-rabbit-mysql` is the directory, RabbitMQ is the binder, and MySQL is the persistence. Some of the steps are optional, but they set your environment for future testing.

1. Create a `download.sh` script in the `workspace-rabbit-mysql` folder, with the following content.

    ```
    #!/bin/sh
    wget https://repo.spring.io/release/org/springframework/cloud/
    spring-cloud-dataflow-server/2.6.0/spring-cloud-dataflow-server-
    2.6.0.jar
    wget https://repo.spring.io/release/org/springframework/cloud/
    spring-cloud-dataflow-shell/2.6.0/spring-cloud-dataflow-shell-
    2.6.0.jar
    wget https://repo.spring.io/release/org/springframework/cloud/
    spring-cloud-skipper-server/2.5.0/spring-cloud-skipper-server-
    2.5.0.jar
    ```

    When writing this book, I used 2.6.0 version for the Data Flow server and shell and version 2.50 for the Skipper server. Make the script executable and execute it. Note that you download three JARs, Skipper, and the Data Flow server and shell.

2. In the `workspace-rabbit-mysql` folder, create the `docker-compose.yml` file with the following content.

    ```
    version: '3'

    services:
      mysql:
        image: mysql:5.7.25
        container_name: dataflow-mysql
        environment:
          MYSQL_DATABASE: dataflow
          MYSQL_USER: root
    ```

```
      MYSQL_ROOT_PASSWORD: rootpw
    ports:
      - "3306:3306"

  rabbitmq:
    image: rabbitmq:3.8.3-alpine
    container_name: dataflow-rabbitmq
    ports:
      - "5672:5672"
```

3. In the `workspace-rabbit-mysql` folder, create the `startup-skipper.sh` script file with the following content and make it executable.

```
#!/bin/sh
java -jar spring-cloud-skipper-server-2.5.0.jar \
--spring.datasource.url=jdbc:mysql://localhost:3306/dataflow \
--spring.datasource.username=root \
--spring.datasource.password=rootpw \
--spring.datasource.driver-class-name=org.mariadb.jdbc.Driver
```

   Note that you are declaring the Spring datasource. If you don't add these properties, the Skipper and Data Flow servers will use the H2 embedded engine as the default persistence mechanism. Note that for now, I use `localhost` in every property, meaning that you can change it if you have a remote server.

4. In the `workspace-rabbit-mysql` folder, create the `startup-dataflow.sh` script file with the following content and make it executable.

```
#!/bin/sh
java -jar spring-cloud-dataflow-server-2.6.0.jar \
--spring.datasource.url=jdbc:mysql://localhost:3306/dataflow \
--spring.datasource.username=root \
--spring.datasource.password=rootpw \
--spring.datasource.driver-class-name=org.mariadb.jdbc.Driver \
--spring.cloud.dataflow.applicationProperties.stream.spring.
rabbitmq.host=localhost
```

   Note that you are adding the `stream.spring.rabbitmq` properties. If you don't specify them, then it uses Kafka as default binder.

5. Execute the `docker-compose` command in the `workspace-rabbit-mysql` folder.

```
$ docker-compose up -d
```

   The `-d` option sends the `docker-compose` processes to the background. Just remember that you need to come back here later because to shut down the services.

6. In another terminal window, execute the following command. Start the Skipper server first.

```
$ ./startup-skipper.sh
```

7. In the new terminal, start the Spring Cloud Data Flow server.

```
$ ./startip-dataflow.sh
```

Using Kafka as a Binder and MySQL for Persistence

If you want to use Kafka as a binder, create a `workspace-kafka-mysql` folder to hold the configuration.

The following steps are required to get Spring Cloud Data Flow up and running on a single machine using the `workspace-kafka-mysql` directory structure, Kafka as the binder, and MySQL for persistence.

1. Reuse the `download.sh` script from before; you can copy it here. If you already executed it, move the JARs to the `workspace-kafka-mysql` folder structure.

2. In the `workspace-kafka-mysql` folder, create the `docker-compose.yml` file with the following content.version: '3'

```
services:
  mysql:
    image: mysql:5.7.25
    container_name: dataflow-mysql
    environment:
      MYSQL_DATABASE: dataflow
      MYSQL_USER: root
      MYSQL_ROOT_PASSWORD: rootpw
    ports:
      - "3306:3306"

  zookeeper:
    image: 'bitnami/zookeeper:latest'
    container_name: zookeeper
    networks:
      - kafka-net
    ports:
      - '2181:2181'
    environment:
      - ALLOW_ANONYMOUS_LOGIN=yes

  kafka:
    image: 'bitnami/kafka:latest'
    container_name: kafka
    networks:
      - kafka-net
    ports:
      - '9092:9092'
    environment:
      - KAFKA_CFG_ZOOKEEPER_CONNECT=zookeeper:2181
      - KAFKA_CFG_ADVERTISED_LISTENERS=PLAINTEXT://localhost:9092
      - ALLOW_PLAINTEXT_LISTENER=yes
    depends_on:
      - zookeeper

networks:
  kafka-net:
```

3. In the `workspace-kafka-mysql` folder, create the `startup-skipper.sh` script file. It is the same as the `workspace-rabbit-mysql`, so you can copy it here.

4. In the `workspace-kafka-mysql` folder, create the `startup-dataflow.sh` script file with the following content and make it executable.

```
java -jar spring-cloud-dataflow-server-2.6.0.jar \
--spring.datasource.url=jdbc:mysql://localhost:3306/dataflow \
--spring.datasource.username=root \
--spring.datasource.password=rootpw \
--spring.datasource.driver-class-name=org.mariadb.jdbc.Driver \
--spring.cloud.dataflow.applicationProperties.stream.spring.cloud.
stream.kafka.binder.brokers=PLAINTEXT://localhost:9092 \
--spring.cloud.dataflow.applicationProperties.stream.spring.cloud.
stream.kafka.streams.binder.brokers=PLAINTEXT://localhost:9092 \
--spring.cloud.dataflow.applicationProperties.stream.spring.cloud.
stream.kafka.binder.zkNodes=localhost:2181 \
--spring.cloud.dataflow.applicationProperties.stream.spring.cloud.
stream.kafka.streams.binder.zkNodes=localhost:2181
```

   See that you are passing all the necessary information for the Kafka binder.

5. Execute the `docker-compose` command in the `workspace-kafka-mysql` folder.

```
$ docker-compose up -d
```

6. The `-d` option sends the `docker-compose` processes to the background. Just remember that you need to return later because to shut down the services.

7. In another terminal window, execute the following command to start the Skipper server.

```
$ ./startup-skipper.sh
```

8. In the new terminal, start the Spring Cloud Data Flow server.

```
$ ./startup-dataflow.sh
```

Did you notice that whether you chose Rabbit or Kafka as a binder, the same persistence mechanism is declared? Did you notice the logs on both servers? Did you see that is trying to connect to a Spring Cloud Config server in port 8888? How can you solve the MySQL duplication if you need to use both binders?

You can use Spring Cloud Config to set common configurations, such as MySQL for persistence and a binder-specific configuration. Instead of using the command line or `application.properties/yaml` files, you can use a centralized server so the Skipper and Data Flow servers can have those configurations when booting up.

Using Spring Boot Config Features

Choose either RabbitMQ or Kafka to avoid putting all the properties in the command line. You can always use the Spring Boot config features to put your application's properties in the current directory or a `config/` directory.

I used the structure shown in Figure 8-1 with Uber-JARs.

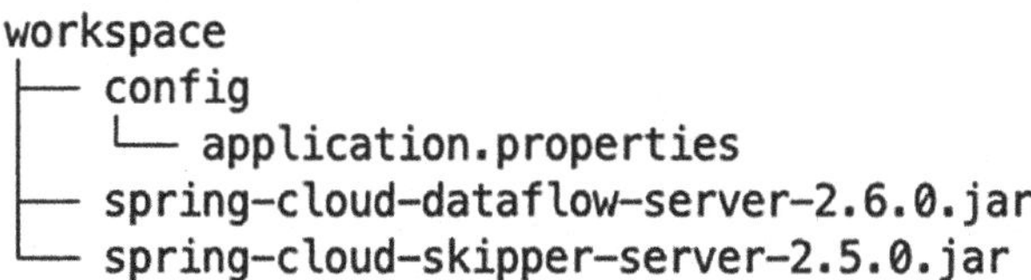

Figure 8-1. *Workspace with config/application.properties and Uber-JARs*

The `config/application.properties` have the following content.

```
## DataSource
spring.datasource.url=jdbc:mysql://localhost:3306/dataflow
spring.datasource.username=root
spring.datasource.password=rootpw
spring.datasource.driver-class-name=org.mariadb.jdbc.Driver

## Binder
spring.cloud.dataflow.applicationProperties.stream.spring.rabbitmq.host=localhost
spring.cloud.dataflow.applicationProperties.stream.spring.rabbitmq.username=guest
spring.cloud.dataflow.applicationProperties.stream.spring.rabbitmq.password=guest
```

You can run either JAR with the following.

```
$ java -jar spring-cloud-skipper-server-2.6.0.jar
```

Spring Boot takes the `config/application.properties` and uses its content to connect to MySQL and Rabbit in this example.

Spring Cloud Data Flow Dashboard

Once you complete setting up your local environment, open a browser and point to `http://localhost:9393/dashboard`. Your screen should look something like Figure 8-2.

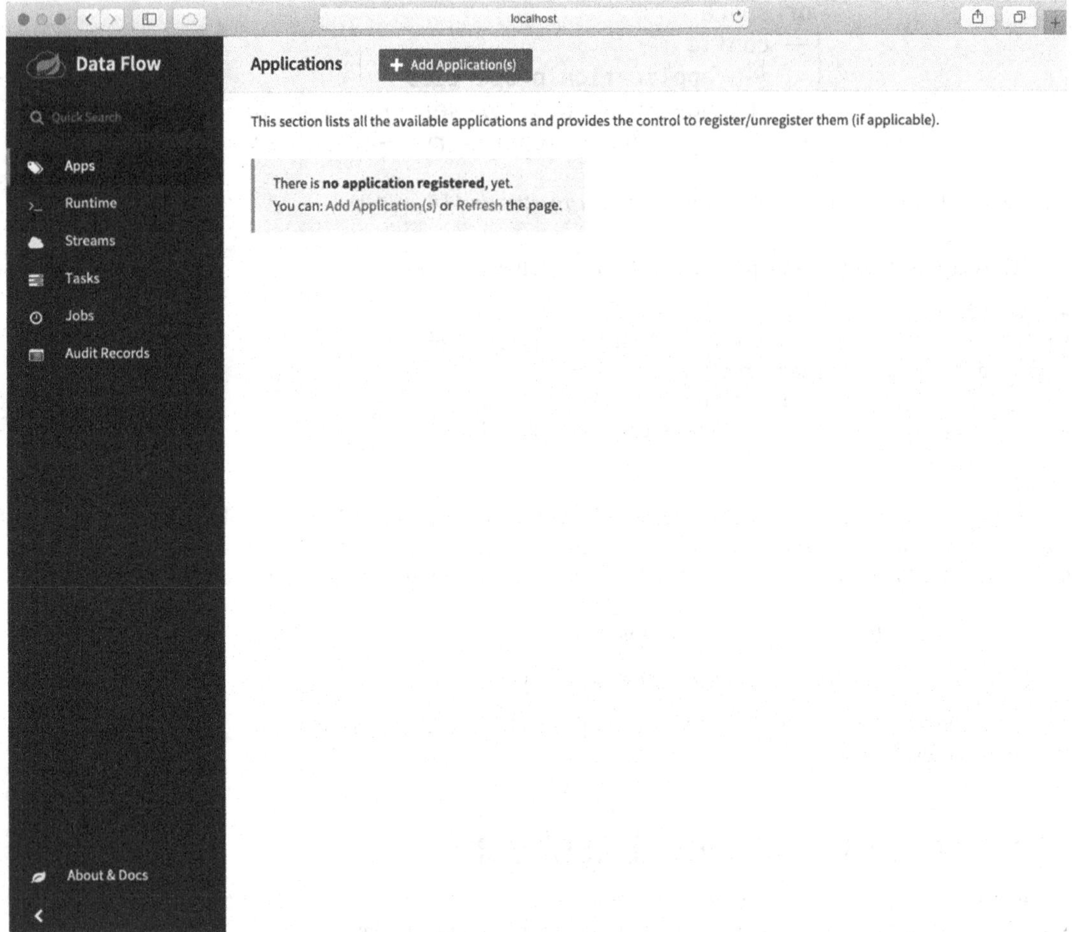

Figure 8-2 *Spring Cloud Data Flow dashboard: http://localhost:9393/dashboard*

Figure 8-2 shows the dashboard. Everything went okay. Don't worry about the tabs or other links displayed. I discuss them when you create your first stream flow.

Registering Cloud Stream Applications Starters

Once the server is up and running, it is time to register the Cloud Stream Application Starters. In the main dashboard, click the + Add Application(s) button. Next, select **Bulk import application** (see Figure 8-3).

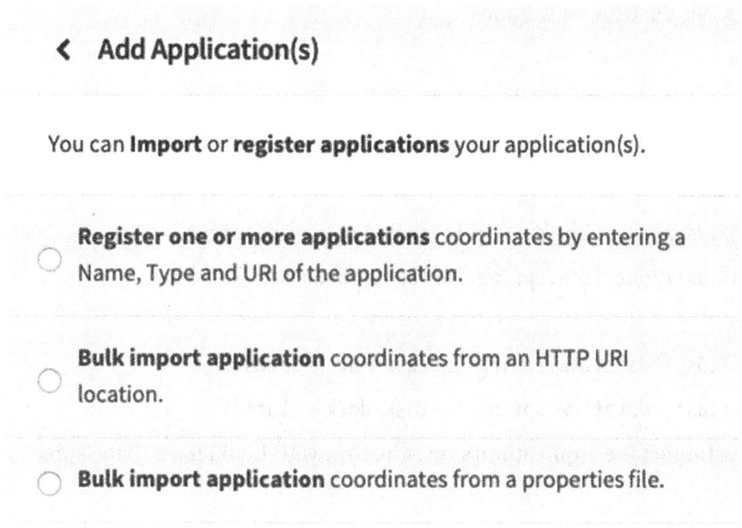

< **Add Application(s)**

You can **Import** or **register applications** your application(s).

○ **Register one or more applications** coordinates by entering a Name, Type and URI of the application.

○ **Bulk import application** coordinates from an HTTP URI location.

○ **Bulk import application** coordinates from a properties file.

Figure 8-3. *Add applications: http://localhost:9393/dashboard/#/apps/add*

Next, add the URI. The easiest way is to click the section where are all the Stream apps are listed. For example, click **Stream Apps (RabbitMQ/Maven)** if you are using RabbitMQ (see Figure 8-4).

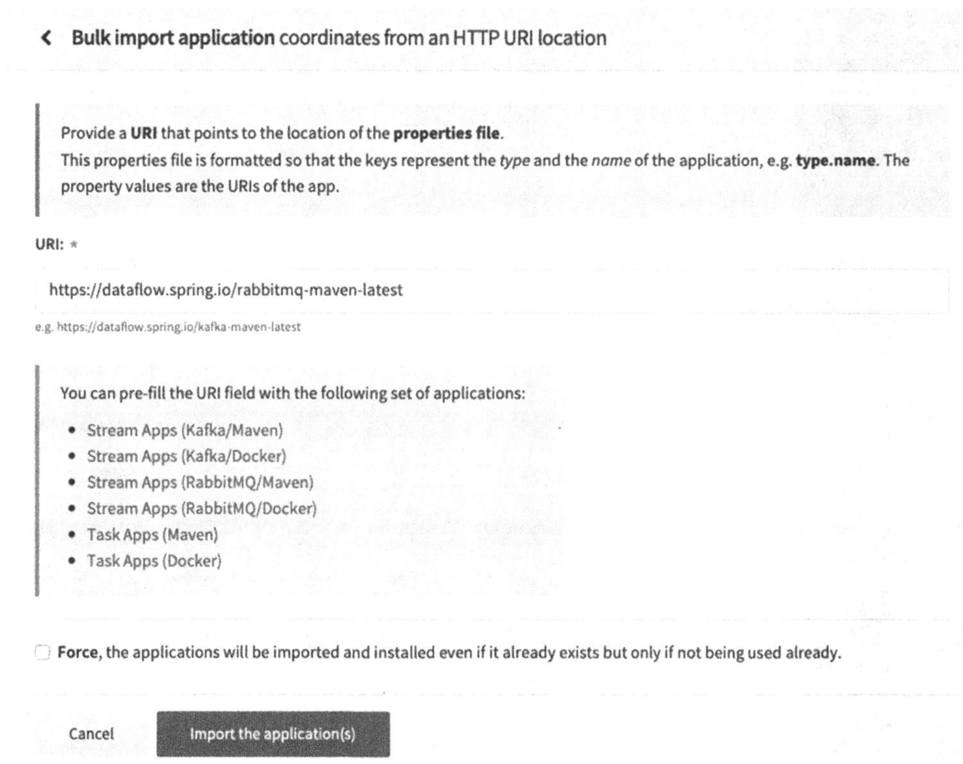

< **Bulk import application** coordinates from an HTTP URI location

Provide a **URI** that points to the location of the **properties file**.
This properties file is formatted so that the keys represent the *type* and the *name* of the application, e.g. **type.name**. The property values are the URIs of the app.

URI: *

https://dataflow.spring.io/rabbitmq-maven-latest

e.g. https://dataflow.spring.io/kafka-maven-latest

You can pre-fill the URI field with the following set of applications:

- Stream Apps (Kafka/Maven)
- Stream Apps (Kafka/Docker)
- Stream Apps (RabbitMQ/Maven)
- Stream Apps (RabbitMQ/Docker)
- Task Apps (Maven)
- Task Apps (Docker)

☐ **Force**, the applications will be imported and installed even if it already exists but only if not being used already.

Cancel | Import the application(s)

Figure 8-4. *Add Bulk apps from URI: http://localhost:9393/dashboard/#/apps/add/import-from-uri*

The following lists the URIs for the apps.

- Kafka
  - `https://dataflow.spring.io/kafka-maven-latest`
  - `https://dataflow.spring.io/kafka-docker-latest`
- RabbitMQ
  - `https://dataflow.spring.io/rabbitmq-maven-latest`
  - `https://dataflow.spring.io/rabbitmq-docker-latest`
- Tasks
  - `https://dataflow.spring.io/task-maven-latest`
  - `https://dataflow.spring.io/task-docker-latest`

Next, click the **Import the application(s)** button. Now you should have all the apps imported (see Figure 8-5).

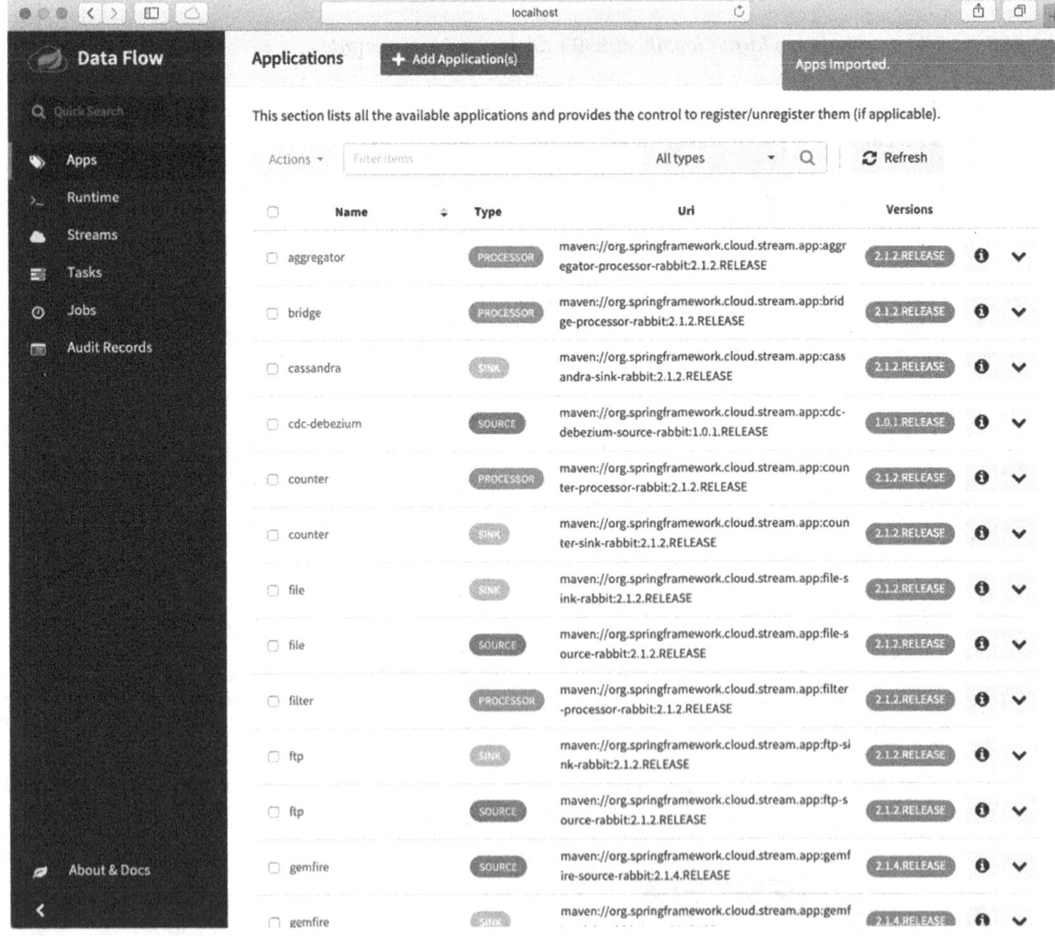

***Figure 8-5.** Apps Imported: http://localhost:9393/dashboard/#/apps*

■ **Note** I added some scripts to the source code that start up locally on a single machine and the Spring Cloud Data Flow servers. I'm assuming you have `docker-compose`, `curl`, and `wget` commands.

Separated Server or a Proxy

If you want a separated machine to run individually, you can do so, but you need to tell the Data Flow server where the Skipper server is with the `spring.cloud.skipper.client.serverUri` property. Set this property as a parameter in the command line.

```
$ java -jar spring-cloud-dataflow-server-2.6.0.jar \
   --spring.cloud.skipper.client.serverUri=https://my-other-server:7577/api
```

If you are behind a proxy, you need to set `server.use-forward-headers` to `true`, or start the Data Flow server with the following parameters.

```
$ java -jar spring-cloud-dataflow-server-2.6.0.jar \
   --spring.cloud.skipper.client.serverUri=https://192.51.100.1:7577/api  \
   --server.use-forward-headers=true
```

These are the paths and URLs that you need to use in your proxy configuration.

```
securityinfo:
  path: /security/**
  url: http://data-flow-server:9393/security
about:
  path: /about/**
  url: http://data-flow-server:9393/about
apps:
  path: /apps/**
  url: http://data-flow-server:9393/apps
dashboard:
  path: /dashboard/**
  url: http://data-flow-server:9393/dashboard
audit-records:
  path: /audit-records/**
  url: http://data-flow-server:9393/audit-records
jobs:
  path: /jobs/**
  url: http://data-flow-server:9393/jobs
streams:
  path: /streams/**
  url: http://data-flow-server:9393/streams
tasks:
  path: /tasks/**
  url: http://data-flow-server:9393/tasks
tools:
  path: /tools/**
  url: http://data-flow-server:9393/tools
runtime:
```

```
  path: /rutime/**
  url: http://data-flow-server:9393/runtime
completions:
  path: /completions/**
  url: http://data-flow-server:9393/completions
```

Using Docker Compose

Docker creates the infrastructure you need for local development and testing. It's easy to use and very effective. So, let's start by creating two docker-compose files. I recommend creating a folder that holds these files. One file uses Rabbit and the other uses the Kafka binders.

Create docker-compose-rabbitmq.yml with the content in Listing 8-1.

Listing 8-1. docker-compose-rabbitmq.yml

```
version: '3'

services:
  mysql:
    image: mysql:5.7.25
    container_name: dataflow-mysql
    environment:
      MYSQL_DATABASE: dataflow
      MYSQL_USER: root
      MYSQL_ROOT_PASSWORD: rootpw
    expose:
      - 3306

  rabbitmq:
    image: rabbitmq:3.8.3-alpine
    container_name: dataflow-rabbitmq
    expose:
      - '5672'

  dataflow-server:
    image: springcloud/spring-cloud-dataflow-server:${DATAFLOW_VERSION:?DATAFLOW_VERSION
    variable needs to be set!}
    container_name: dataflow-server
    ports:
      - "9393:9393"
    environment:
      - spring.cloud.dataflow.applicationProperties.stream.spring.rabbitmq.host=rabbitmq
      - spring.cloud.skipper.client.serverUri=http://skipper-server:7577/api
      - SPRING_DATASOURCE_URL=jdbc:mysql://mysql:3306/dataflow
      - SPRING_DATASOURCE_USERNAME=root
      - SPRING_DATASOURCE_PASSWORD=rootpw
      - SPRING_DATASOURCE_DRIVER_CLASS_NAME=org.mariadb.jdbc.Driver
    depends_on:
      - rabbitmq
```

```
    entrypoint: "./wait-for-it.sh mysql:3306 -- java -jar /maven/spring-cloud-dataflow-
    server.jar"
    volumes:
      - ${HOST_MOUNT_PATH:-.}:${DOCKER_MOUNT_PATH:-/root/scdf}

  skipper-server:
    image: springcloud/spring-cloud-skipper-server:${SKIPPER_VERSION:?SKIPPER_VERSION
    variable needs to be set!}
    container_name: skipper
    ports:
      - "7577:7577"
      - "20000-20105:20000-20105"
    volumes:
      - ${HOST_MOUNT_PATH:-.}:${DOCKER_MOUNT_PATH:-/root/scdf}

  app-import:
    image: springcloud/openjdk:2.0.0.RELEASE
    container_name: dataflow-app-import
    depends_on:
      - dataflow-server
    command: >
      /bin/sh -c "
        ./wait-for-it.sh -t 180 dataflow-server:9393;
        wget -qO- 'http://dataflow-server:9393/apps' --post-data='uri=${STREAM_APPS_URI:-
        https://dataflow.spring.io/rabbitmq-maven-latest&force=true}';
        echo 'Stream apps imported'
        wget -qO- 'http://dataflow-server:9393/apps' --post-data='uri=${TASK_APPS_URI:-
        https://dataflow.spring.io/task-maven-latest&force=true}';
        echo 'Task apps imported'"
```

Note that you are using the `DATAFLOW_VERSION` and `SKIPPER_VERSION` environment variables, and they need to be set to get the image version. With this approach, you find a reusable Docker Compose file for any version. Of course, you can add Rabbit and MySQL versions in the same form. Each service uses environment variables that point to the service name, which is useful because Docker Compose creates a DNS, making it easier for the DevOps guys to use names instead of IPs.

If you look at Listing 8-1, you see the `app-import` declaration at the end. Even though you haven't seen the components of the Spring Cloud Stream Cloud Data Flow yet, the Data Flow server provides an API that allows you to connect to it. In this case, you are posting a URI to register the applications when you use this Docker Compose file.

Next, you can create the `docker-compose-kafka.yml` file with the content in Listing 8-2.

Listing 8-2. docker-compose-kafka.yml

```
version: '3'

services:
  mysql:
    image: mysql:5.7.25
    container_name: dataflow-mysql
    environment:
      MYSQL_DATABASE: dataflow
      MYSQL_USER: root
```

```
      MYSQL_ROOT_PASSWORD: rootpw
    expose:
      - 3306

  kafka-broker:
    image: confluentinc/cp-kafka:5.3.1
    container_name: dataflow-kafka
    expose:
      - "9092"
    environment:
      - KAFKA_ADVERTISED_LISTENERS=PLAINTEXT://kafka-broker:9092
      - KAFKA_ZOOKEEPER_CONNECT=zookeeper:2181
      - KAFKA_ADVERTISED_HOST_NAME=kafka-broker
      - KAFKA_OFFSETS_TOPIC_REPLICATION_FACTOR=1
    depends_on:
      - zookeeper

  zookeeper:
    image: confluentinc/cp-zookeeper:5.3.1
    container_name: dataflow-kafka-zookeeper
    expose:
      - "2181"
    environment:
      - ZOOKEEPER_CLIENT_PORT=2181

  dataflow-server:
    image: springcloud/spring-cloud-dataflow-server:${DATAFLOW_VERSION:?DATAFLOW_VERSION
    variable needs to be set!}
    container_name: dataflow-server
    ports:
      - "9393:9393"
    environment:
      - spring.cloud.dataflow.applicationProperties.stream.spring.cloud.stream.kafka.binder.
        brokers=PLAINTEXT://kafka-broker:9092
      - spring.cloud.dataflow.applicationProperties.stream.spring.cloud.stream.kafka.
        streams.binder.brokers=PLAINTEXT://kafka-broker:9092
      - spring.cloud.dataflow.applicationProperties.stream.spring.cloud.stream.kafka.binder.
        zkNodes=zookeeper:2181
      - spring.cloud.dataflow.applicationProperties.stream.spring.cloud.stream.kafka.
        streams.binder.zkNodes=zookeeper:2181
      - spring.cloud.skipper.client.serverUri=http://skipper-server:7577/api
      - SPRING_DATASOURCE_URL=jdbc:mysql://mysql:3306/dataflow
      - SPRING_DATASOURCE_USERNAME=root
      - SPRING_DATASOURCE_PASSWORD=rootpw
      - SPRING_DATASOURCE_DRIVER_CLASS_NAME=org.mariadb.jdbc.Driver
    depends_on:
      - kafka-broker
    entrypoint: "./wait-for-it.sh mysql:3306 -- java -jar /maven/spring-cloud-data
    flow-server.jar"
    volumes:
      - ${HOST_MOUNT_PATH:-.}:${DOCKER_MOUNT_PATH:-/root/scdf}
```

```
  app-import:
    image: springcloud/openjdk:2.0.0.RELEASE
    container_name: dataflow-app-import
    depends_on:
      - dataflow-server
    command: >
      /bin/sh -c "
        ./wait-for-it.sh -t 180 dataflow-server:9393;
        wget -qO- 'http://dataflow-server:9393/apps' --post-data='uri=${STREAM_APPS_URI:-
        https://dataflow.spring.io/kafka-maven-latest&force=true}';
        echo 'Stream apps imported'
        wget -qO- 'http://dataflow-server:9393/apps' --post-data='uri=${TASK_APPS_URI:-
        https://dataflow.spring.io/task-maven-latest&force=true}';
        echo 'Task apps imported'"

  skipper-server:
    image: springcloud/spring-cloud-skipper-server:${SKIPPER_VERSION:?SKIPPER_VERSION
    variable needs to be set!}
    container_name: skipper
    ports:
      - "7577:7577"
      - "20000-20105:20000-20105"
    environment:
      - SPRING_CLOUD_SKIPPER_SERVER_PLATFORM_LOCAL_ACCOUNTS_DEFAULT_PORTRANGE_LOW=20000
      - SPRING_CLOUD_SKIPPER_SERVER_PLATFORM_LOCAL_ACCOUNTS_DEFAULT_PORTRANGE_HIGH=20100
      - SPRING_DATASOURCE_URL=jdbc:mysql://mysql:3306/dataflow
      - SPRING_DATASOURCE_USERNAME=root
      - SPRING_DATASOURCE_PASSWORD=rootpw
      - SPRING_DATASOURCE_DRIVER_CLASS_NAME=org.mariadb.jdbc.Driver
    entrypoint: "./wait-for-it.sh mysql:3306 -- java -Djava.security.egd=file:/dev/./
    urandom -jar /spring-cloud-skipper-server.jar"
    volumes:
      - ${HOST_MOUNT_PATH:-.}:${DOCKER_MOUNT_PATH:-/root/scdf}
```

Listing 8-2 shows the `docker-compose-kafka.yml` file; note that it is similar to RabbitMQ, using Kafka and Zookeeper. Also review the properties and identify that you are using service names.

Next, start your infrastructure by using the following for RabbitMQ.

```
$ export DATAFLOW_VERSION=2.6.0
$ export SKIPPER_VERSION=2.5.0
$ docker-compose -f docker-compose-rabbitmq.yml up
```

Or you use the following for Kafka.

```
$ export DATAFLOW_VERSION=2.6.0
$ export SKIPPER_VERSION=2.5.0
$ docker-compose -f docker-compose-kafka.yml up
```

Next, go to your browser and open `http://localhost:9393/dashboard`. Your screen should be the same as Figure 8-5. It should have already imported the apps.

To shutdown, execute the following if you are using RabbitMQ.

```
$ export DATAFLOW_VERSION=2.6.0
$ export SKIPPER_VERSION=2.5.0
$ docker-compose -f docker-compose-rabbitmq.yml down
```

Execute the following if you are using Kafka.

```
$ export DATAFLOW_VERSION=2.6.0
$ export SKIPPER_VERSION=2.5.0
$ docker-compose -f docker-compose-kafka.yml down
```

Remember that the shutdown command must be run in the same directory that the YAML file is located.

Kubernetes Installation

You haven't seen the power of Spring Cloud Data Flow and what it is capable of. In the upcoming chapters, you create streams that can take more than a single machine. At some point, you need to scale up and have the ability to get insights into what's going on with your stream flow. What happens when some of the apps (within the flow) start to fail? You should be able to create multiple instances and monitor them, and if one instance is down, re-create it. Of course, you can do that manually but when you have a flow with 100 microservices, you need to rely on a platform that provides resiliency, high availability, scalability, and visibility.

Before you start, you need to have a Kubernetes installation up and running. You can use your computer if you have enough RAM to run Spring Cloud Data Flow or have resources in any public cloud (IBM Cloud, Google, Amazon, or Microsoft Azure).

Personal Computer with Docker Desktop

Mac or Windows users can install Docker Desktop. It can enable Kubernetes, but you need at least 16 GB of RAM on your computer. You can install it from `www.docker.com/products/docker-desktop`.

Next, you need to make some modifications. Open Docker Desktop Preferences, go to Resources, and modify the settings. You also need to enable Kubernetes (see Figures 8-6 and 8-7).

- CPUs: 4
- RAM: 8 GB
- Swap: 1.5 GB
- Disk image size: 30 GB

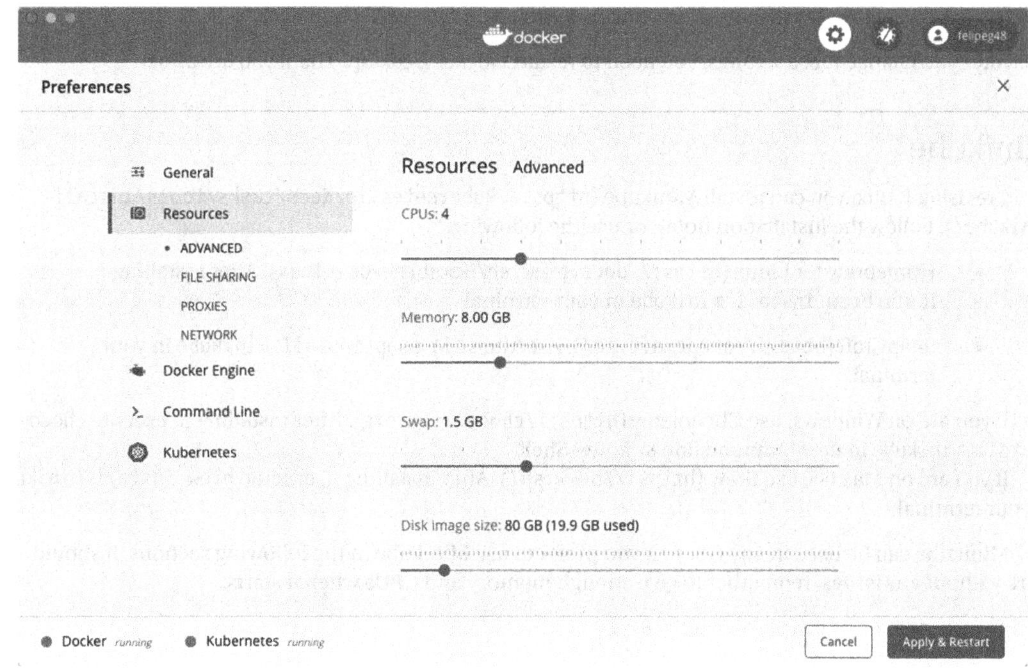

Figure 8-6. *Docker Desktop: Preferences ➤ Resources*

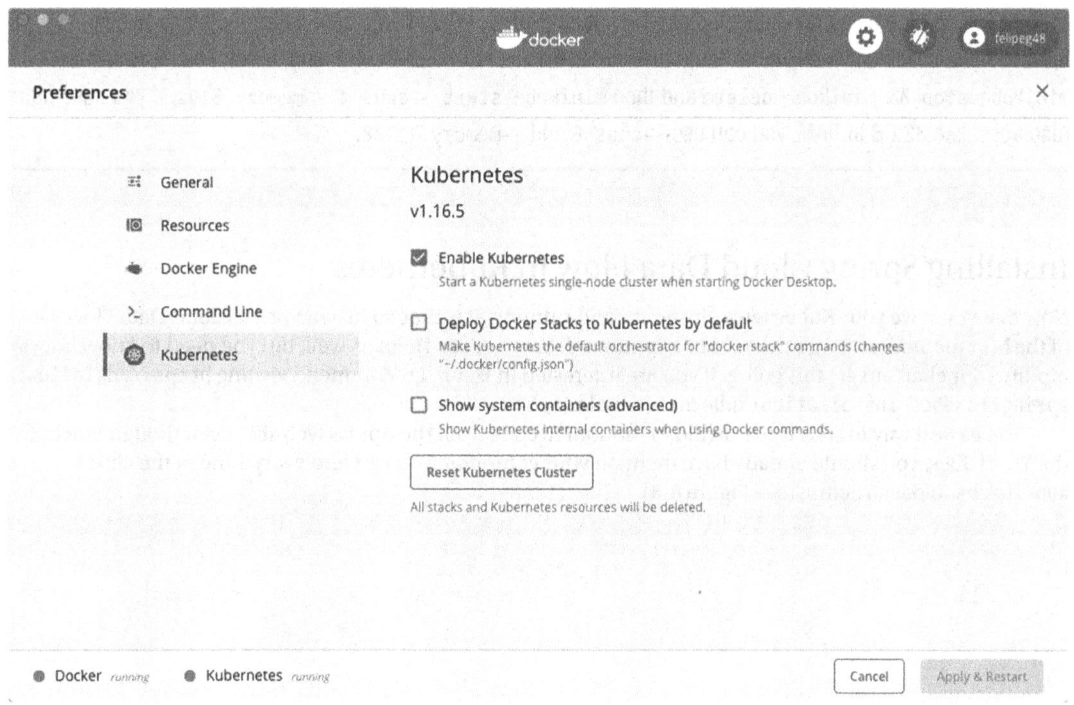

Figure 8-7. *Docker Desktop: Preferences ➤ Kubernetes*

If you have the resources on your computer, add more RAM and CPU.

After you change these settings, you need to restart Docker Desktop. Then, you are all set.

Minikube

If you're using Linux, you can install Minikube (`https://kubernetes.io/docs/tasks/tools/install-minikube/`). Follow the installation notes, or use the following.

- Homebrew for Linux (`https://docs.brew.sh/Homebrew-on-Linux`). After installing it, run `brew install minikube` in your terminal.
- SnapCraft (`https://snapcraft.io/`). Execute `sudo snap install minikube` in your terminal.

If you are on Windows, use Chocolatey (`https://chocolatey.org`). After installing it, execute `choco install minikube` in the command line or PowerShell.

If you are on Mac OS, use Brew (`https://brew.sh/`). After installing it, execute `brew install minikube` in your terminal.

Minikube can be used in any OS, so if you prefer to use Minikube in the following sections, it should work without any issues; remember to give enough memory and CPUs when it starts.

```
$ minikube start --cpus 4 --memory 8192
```

Read the documentation on what other parameters can be passed; for example, the driver to use.

■ **Note** If you are using Minikube, look at the `kubectl describe nodes` command. You should have the CPUs you specified when you execute the `minikube start --cpus` command; if not, you can execute `minikube stop && minikube delete` and then `minikube start --cpus 4 --memory 8192`. If you have more resources, like 32 GB in RAM, you can use `--cpus 6` and `--memory 12288`.

Installing Spring Cloud Data Flow in Kubernetes

Now that you have your Kubernetes cluster up and running, it is time to install Spring Cloud Data Flow. One of the best methods is to use the `kubectl` command. You can use Helm as well, but you need to know how to modify your charts to get this going; if you are interested in Helm, I recommend visiting `https://dataflow.spring.io/docs/installation/kubernetes/helm/`.

The easiest way to start is to download the source code from the Apress web site. Even though I include the YAML files, you should already have them on your computer. You can find everything in the `ch08/kubernetes` folder structure (see Figure 8-8).

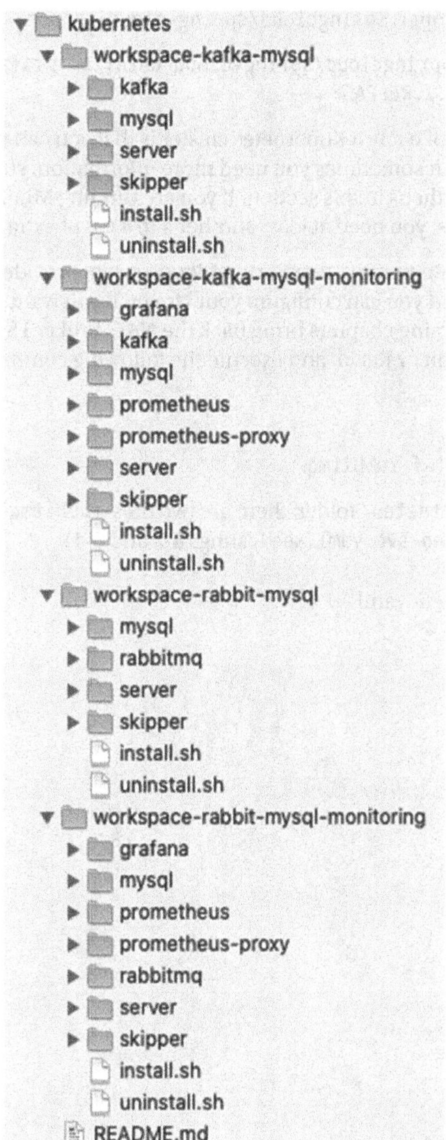

Figure 8-8. *Source Code: ch08/kubernetes*

Using kubectl

Let's go through step-by-step instructions to install each component. I'm assuming your cluster is running, and you have downloaded the companion book's source code.

1. It is important to know the versions that you are going to work on. When this book was written, the following versions were available.

    a. Spring Cloud Data Flow: `springcloud/spring-cloud-dataflow-server:2.6.0`

b. Spring Cloud Skipper: `springcloud/spring-cloud-skipper-server:2.5.0`

c. Grafana Image: `springcloud/spring-cloud-dataflow-grafana-prometheus:2.5.2.RELEASE`

One of the benefits of using a Kubernetes cluster is that you can use its monitoring tools, but sometimes you need more information, so let's plug in Grafana and Prometheus in this section. If you are running Minikube or Docker Desktop Kubernetes, you need at least another 2 to 4 GB of extra memory.

2. Choose the broker. Remember that Spring Cloud Stream provides RabbitMQ and Kafka as brokers, and you can configure your stream if you want to use multiple binders. (The upcoming chapters bring back the NATs broker.) Select one of the binders, either Rabbit or Kafka, and execute the following commands.

a. RabbitMQ

```
kubectl create -f rabbitmq/
```

In the `ch08/kubernetes/` folder, there are two files: `rabbitmq-deployment.yaml` and `rabbitmq-svc.yaml` (see Listings 8-3 and 8-4).

Listing 8-3. rabbitmq-deployment.yaml

```
apiVersion: apps/v1
kind: Deployment
metadata:
  name: rabbitmq
  labels:
    app: rabbitmq
spec:
  replicas: 1
  selector:
    matchLabels:
      app: rabbitmq
  template:
    metadata:
      labels:
        app: rabbitmq
    spec:
      containers:
      - image: rabbitmq:3.8.3-alpine
        name: rabbitmq
        ports:
        - containerPort: 5672
```

Note that you are using the `rabbitmq:3.8.3-alpine` image, and the port is the 5672. The app is named rabbitmq, an easy mechanism in Kubernetes to find, edit, and delete, if necessary, the pod, service, or deployment.

Listing 8-4. rabbitmq-svc.yaml

```
apiVersion: v1
kind: Service
metadata:
  name: rabbitmq
  labels:
    app: rabbitmq
spec:
  ports:
  - port: 5672
  selector:
    app: rabbitmq
```

You are naming the service rabbitmq, so it is easier to locate the RabbitMQ server by name. Remember that Kubernetes has a DNS, a power tool for locating services.

b. Kafka

```
kubectl create -f kafka/
```

There are four files. Kafka depends on Zookeeper, so you must add its deployment and service (see Listings 8-5, 8-6, 8-7, and 8-8).

Listing 8-5. kafka-zk-deployment.yaml

```
apiVersion: apps/v1
kind: Deployment
metadata:
  name: kafka-zk
  labels:
    app: kafka
    component: kafka-zk
spec:
  replicas: 1
  selector:
    matchLabels:
      app: kafka-zk
  template:
    metadata:
      labels:
        app: kafka-zk
        component: kafka-zk
    spec:
      containers:
      - name: kafka-zk
        image: digitalwonderland/zookeeper
        ports:
        - containerPort: 2181
        env:
        - name: ZOOKEEPER_ID
          value: "1"
        - name: ZOOKEEPER_SERVER_1
          value: kafka-zk
```

Listing 8-6. kafla-zk-svc.yaml

```
apiVersion: v1
kind: Service
metadata:
  name: kafka-zk
  labels:
    app: kafka
    component: kafka-zk
spec:
  ports:
  - name: client
    port: 2181
    protocol: TCP
  - name: follower
    port: 2888
    protocol: TCP
  - name: leader
    port: 3888
    protocol: TCP
  selector:
    app: kafka-zk
    component: kafka-zk
```

Listing 8-7. kafka-deployment.yaml

```
apiVersion: apps/v1
kind: Deployment
metadata:
  name: kafka-broker
  labels:
    app: kafka
    component: kafka-broker
spec:
  replicas: 1
  selector:
    matchLabels:
      app: kafka
  template:
    metadata:
      labels:
        app: kafka
        component: kafka-broker
    spec:
      containers:
      - name: kafka
        image: wurstmeister/kafka:2.12-2.3.0
        ports:
        - containerPort: 9092
        env:
          - name: ENABLE_AUTO_EXTEND
```

```
          value: "true"
        - name: KAFKA_RESERVED_BROKER_MAX_ID
          value: "999999999"
        - name: KAFKA_AUTO_CREATE_TOPICS_ENABLE
          value: "false"
        - name: KAFKA_PORT
          value: "9092"
        - name: KAFKA_ADVERTISED_PORT
          value: "9092"
        - name: KAFKA_ADVERTISED_HOST_NAME
          valueFrom:
            fieldRef:
              fieldPath: status.podIP
        - name: KAFKA_ZOOKEEPER_CONNECT
          value: kafka-zk:2181
```

Listing 8-8. kafka-svc.yaml

```
apiVersion: v1
kind: Service
metadata:
  name: kafka
  labels:
    app: kafka
    component: kafka-broker
spec:
  ports:
  - port: 9092
    name: kafka-port
    targetPort: 9092
    protocol: TCP
  selector:
    app: kafka
    component: kafka-broker
```

Remember to choose either Rabbit or Kafka (for now). The next chapter mixes RabbitMQ, Kafka, and NATs brokers.

c. Install MySQL (you can whatever fits your environment or your business logic; remember to change the properties in the YAML files to reflect the new DB engine).

```
kubectl create -f mysql/
```

In this folder, there are four files. To use a MySQL server, you must define the storage. In this case, use the default Storage class (you can modify it to one that suits your needs, like an SSD or elastic storage that can grow if needed). It is necessary to add a username and password, so you must create a Kubernetes secret object (see Listings 8-9, 8-10, 8-11, and 8-12).

Listing 8-9. mysql-pvc.yaml

```
apiVersion: v1
kind: PersistentVolumeClaim
metadata:
  name: mysql
  labels:
    app: mysql
  annotations:
    volume.alpha.kubernetes.io/storage-class: default
spec:
  accessModes:
    - ReadWriteOnce
  resources:
    requests:
      storage: 8Gi
```

For now, you are using the `storage-class:default` and 8 GB of storage. You can modify it if you want.

Listing 8-10. mysql-secrets.yaml

```
apiVersion: v1
kind: Secret
metadata:
  name: mysql
  labels:
    app: mysql
data:
  mysql-root-password: eW91cnBhc3N3b3Jk
```

Of course, you can change the password to one that fits your solution.

Listing 8-11. mysql-deployment.yml

```
apiVersion: apps/v1
kind: Deployment
metadata:
  name: mysql
  labels:
    app: mysql
spec:
  replicas: 1
  selector:
    matchLabels:
      app: mysql
  template:
    metadata:
      labels:
        app: mysql
    spec:
      containers:
```

```
      - image: mysql:5.7.25
        name: mysql
        env:
          - name: MYSQL_ROOT_PASSWORD
            valueFrom:
              secretKeyRef:
                key: mysql-root-password
                name: mysql
        ports:
          - containerPort: 3306
            name: mysql
        volumeMounts:
          - name: data
            mountPath: /var/lib/mysql
        args:
          - "--ignore-db-dir=lost+found"
      volumes:
      - name: data
        persistentVolumeClaim:
          claimName: mysql
```

One of the main properties from the preceding file is the `secretKeyRef` pointing to the `mysql-root-password` secret object.

Listing 8-12. mysql-svc.yaml

```
apiVersion: v1
kind: Service
metadata:
  name: mysql
  labels:
    app: mysql
spec:
  ports:
    - port: 3306
  selector:
    app: mysql
```

3. If you need monitoring, install Grafana and Prometheus. Spring Cloud Data Flow is uses *Micrometer Application Monitoring* (`http://micrometer.io/`) to send stats about your stream, such as memory and CPU consumption and the number of threads.

   a. Prometheus

```
kubectl create -f prometheus/prometheus-clusterroles.yaml
kubectl create -f prometheus/prometheus-clusterrolebinding.yaml
kubectl create -f prometheus/prometheus-serviceaccount.yaml
kubectl create -f prometheus-proxy/
kubectl create -f prometheus/prometheus-configmap.yaml
kubectl create -f prometheus/prometheus-deployment.yaml
kubectl create -f prometheus/prometheus-service.yaml
```

As you can see, cluster roles, bindings, and a service account need to be added. You must add a proxy to send information to Grafana, and then the `ConfigMap`, deployment, and service (see Listings 8-13, 8-14, 8-15, 8-16, 8-17, 8-18, 8-19, 8-20, 8-21, and 8-22).

Listing 8-13. prometheus-clusterroles.yaml

```
kind: ClusterRole
apiVersion: rbac.authorization.k8s.io/v1
metadata:
  name: prometheus
  labels:
    app: prometheus
rules:
- apiGroups: [""]
  resources:
  - nodes
  - nodes/proxy
  - services
  - endpoints
  - pods
  verbs: ["get", "list", "watch"]
- apiGroups:
  - extensions
  resources:
  - ingresses
  verbs: ["get", "list", "watch"]
- nonResourceURLs: ["/metrics"]
  verbs: ["get"]
```

Listing 8-14. prometheus-clusterrolebinding.yaml

```
kind: ClusterRoleBinding
apiVersion: rbac.authorization.k8s.io/v1
metadata:
  name: prometheus
  labels:
    app: prometheus
roleRef:
  apiGroup: rbac.authorization.k8s.io
  kind: ClusterRole
  name: prometheus
subjects:
- kind: ServiceAccount
  name: prometheus
  namespace: default
```

Listing 8-15. prometheus-serviceaccount.yaml

```
kind: ServiceAccount
apiVersion: v1
metadata:
  name: prometheus
  labels:
    app: prometheus
  namespace: default
```

Here you are assigning the service account to the default namespace, but you can change it to suit your environment.

Listing 8-16. prometheus-proxy-clusterrolebinding.yaml

```
apiVersion: rbac.authorization.k8s.io/v1beta1
kind: ClusterRoleBinding
metadata:
  name: prometheus-proxy
  labels:
    app: prometheus-proxy
subjects:
  - kind: ServiceAccount
    name: prometheus-proxy
    namespace: default
roleRef:
  kind: ClusterRole
  name: cluster-admin
  apiGroup: rbac.authorization.k8s.io
```

Listing 8-17. prometheus-proxy-serviceaccount.yaml

```
apiVersion: v1
kind: ServiceAccount
metadata:
  name: prometheus-proxy
  labels:
    app: prometheus-proxy
  namespace: default
```

Listing 8-18. prometheus-proxy-deployment.yaml

```
apiVersion: apps/v1
kind: Deployment
metadata:
  name: prometheus-proxy
  labels:
    app: prometheus-proxy
spec:
#  replicas: 3
  selector:
```

```
    matchLabels:
      app: prometheus-proxy
  template:
    metadata:
      labels:
        app: prometheus-proxy
    spec:
      serviceAccountName: prometheus-proxy
      containers:
        - name: prometheus-proxy
          image: micrometermetrics/prometheus-rsocket-proxy:latest
          imagePullPolicy: Always
          ports:
            - name: scrape
              containerPort: 8080
            - name: rsocket
              containerPort: 7001
          resources:
            limits:
              cpu: 1.0
              memory: 2048Mi
            requests:
              cpu: 0.5
              memory: 1024Mi
      securityContext:
        fsGroup: 2000
        runAsNonRoot: true
        runAsUser: 1000
```

You are using the latest image for the Prometheus proxy: `micrometermetrics/prometheus-rsocket-proxy`.

Listing 8-19. prometheus-proxy-service.yaml

```
apiVersion: v1
kind: Service
metadata:
  name: prometheus-proxy
  labels:
    app: prometheus-proxy
spec:
  selector:
    app: prometheus-proxy
  ports:
    - name: scrape
      port: 8080
      targetPort: 8080
    - name: rsocket
      port: 7001
      targetPort: 7001
  type: LoadBalancer
```

Even though kubectl -f prometheus-proxy/ is used here, you don't need to care about the order. The Prometheus proxy communicates with and gets all the metrics from our Stream apps.

Listing 8-20. prometheus-configmap.yaml

```
apiVersion: v1
kind: ConfigMap
metadata:
  name: prometheus
  labels:
    app: prometheus
data:
  prometheus.yml: |-
    global:
      scrape_interval: 10s
      scrape_timeout: 9s
      evaluation_interval: 10s

    scrape_configs:
    - job_name: 'proxied-applications'
      metrics_path: '/metrics/connected'
      kubernetes_sd_configs:
        - role: pod
          namespaces:
            names:
              - default
      relabel_configs:
        - source_labels: [__meta_kubernetes_pod_label_app]
          action: keep
          regex: prometheus-proxy
        - source_labels: [__meta_kubernetes_pod_container_port_number]
          action: keep
          regex: 8080
    - job_name: 'proxies'
      metrics_path: '/metrics/proxy'
      kubernetes_sd_configs:
        - role: pod
          namespaces:
            names:
              - default
      relabel_configs:
        - source_labels: [__meta_kubernetes_pod_label_app]
          action: keep
          regex: prometheus-proxy
        - source_labels: [__meta_kubernetes_pod_container_port_number]
          action: keep
          regex: 8080
        - action: labelmap
          regex: __meta_kubernetes_pod_label_(.+)
```

```
        - source_labels: [__meta_kubernetes_pod_name]
          action: replace
          target_label: kubernetes_pod_name
```

ConfigMap tells Prometheus where to get the information for the metrics.

Listing 8-21. prometheus-deployment.yaml

```
apiVersion: apps/v1
kind: Deployment
metadata:
  labels:
    app: prometheus
  name: prometheus
spec:
  selector:
    matchLabels:
      app: prometheus
  template:
    metadata:
      labels:
        app: prometheus
    spec:
      serviceAccountName: prometheus
      containers:
        - name: prometheus
          image: prom/prometheus:v2.12.0
          args:
            - "--config.file=/etc/prometheus/prometheus.yml"
            - "--storage.tsdb.path=/prometheus/"
            - "--web.enable-lifecycle"
          ports:
            - name: prometheus
              containerPort: 9090
          volumeMounts:
            - name: prometheus-config-volume
              mountPath: /etc/prometheus/
            - name: prometheus-storage-volume
              mountPath: /prometheus/
      volumes:
        - name: prometheus-config-volume
          configMap:
            name: prometheus
        - name: prometheus-storage-volume
          emptyDir: {}
```

Listing 8-22. prometheus-service.yaml

```
apiVersion: v1
kind: Service
metadata:
```

```
  name: prometheus
  labels:
    app: prometheus
  annotations:
      prometheus.io/scrape: 'true'
      prometheus.io/path:   /
      prometheus.io/port:   '9090'
spec:
  selector:
    app: prometheus
  ports:
    - port: 9090
      targetPort: 9090
```

It is important to give that order instead of `kubectl -f prometheus/` because it could start the deployment without assigning the cluster roles.

b. Grafana

```
kubectl create -f grafana/
```

With Grafana, you must add configuration that knows about Prometheus and a username and password to connect it (see Listings 8-23, 8-24, 8-25, and 8-26).

Listing 8-23. grafana-configmap.yaml

```
apiVersion: v1
kind: ConfigMap
metadata:
  name: grafana
  labels:
    app: grafana
data:
  datasources.yaml: |
    apiVersion: 1
    datasources:
    - name: ScdfPrometheus
      type: prometheus
      access: proxy
      org_id: 1
      url: http://prometheus:9090
      is_default: true
      version: 5
      editable: true
      read_only: false
```

Listing 8-24. grafana-secret.yaml

```
apiVersion: v1
kind: Secret
type: Opaque
```

```
metadata:
  name: grafana
  labels:
    app: grafana
data:
  admin-username: YWRtaW4=
  admin-password: cGFzc3dvcmQ=
```

Listing 8-25. grafana-deployment.yaml

```
apiVersion: apps/v1
kind: Deployment
metadata:
  labels:
    app: grafana
  name: grafana
spec:
  selector:
    matchLabels:
      app: grafana
  template:
    metadata:
      labels:
        app: grafana
    spec:
      containers:
        - image: springcloud/spring-cloud-dataflow-grafana-prometheus:2.5.2.RELEASE
          name: grafana
          env:
            - name: GF_SECURITY_ADMIN_USER
              valueFrom:
                secretKeyRef:
                  name: grafana
                  key: admin-username
            - name: GF_SECURITY_ADMIN_PASSWORD
              valueFrom:
                secretKeyRef:
                  name: grafana
                  key: admin-password
          ports:
            - containerPort: 3000
          resources:
            limits:
              cpu: 500m
              memory: 2500Mi
            requests:
              cpu: 100m
              memory: 100Mi
          volumeMounts:
            - name: config
              mountPath: "/etc/grafana/provisioning/datasources/datasources.yaml"
```

```
            subPath: datasources.yaml
      volumes:
        - name: config
          configMap:
            name: grafana
```

Listing 8-26. grafana-service.yaml

```
apiVersion: v1
kind: Service
metadata:
  name: grafana
  labels:
    app: grafana
spec:
  selector:
    app: grafana
  type: LoadBalancer
  ports:
    - port: 3000
      targetPort: 3000
```

4. Add the Data Flow server roles, bindings, and service account.

    a. Data Flow roles, bindings, and service account

    ```
    kubectl create -f server/server-roles.yaml
    kubectl create -f server/server-rolebinding.yaml
    kubectl create -f server/service-account.yaml
    ```

    See Listings 8-27, 8-28, and 8-29.

Listing 8-27. server-roles.yaml

```
kind: Role
apiVersion: rbac.authorization.k8s.io/v1
metadata:
  name: scdf-role
rules:
  - apiGroups: [""]
    resources: ["services", "pods", "replicationcontrollers", "persistentvolumeclaims"]
    verbs: ["get", "list", "watch", "create", "delete", "update"]
  - apiGroups: [""]
    resources: ["configmaps", "secrets", "pods/log"]
    verbs: ["get", "list", "watch"]
  - apiGroups: ["apps"]
    resources: ["statefulsets", "deployments", "replicasets"]
    verbs: ["get", "list", "watch", "create", "delete", "update", "patch"]
  - apiGroups: ["extensions"]
    resources: ["deployments", "replicasets"]
    verbs: ["get", "list", "watch", "create", "delete", "update", "patch"]
```

```
  - apiGroups: ["batch"]
    resources: ["cronjobs", "jobs"]
    verbs: ["create", "delete", "get", "list", "watch", "update", "patch"]
```

Listing 8-28. server-rolebinding.yaml

```
kind: RoleBinding
apiVersion: rbac.authorization.k8s.io/v1beta1
metadata:
  name: scdf-rb
subjects:
- kind: ServiceAccount
  name: scdf-sa
roleRef:
  kind: Role
  name: scdf-role
  apiGroup: rbac.authorization.k8s.io
```

Listing 8-29. service-account.yaml

```
apiVersion: v1
kind: ServiceAccount
metadata:
  name: scdf-sa
```

5. Add the cloud Skipper server. It is a key component because it deploys, keeps track of the Stream version, and much more.

    a. Skipper

        i. If you use Rabbit, execute the following.

        ```
        kubectl create -f skipper/skipper-config-rabbit.yaml
        ```

        ii. If you use Kafka, execute the following.

        ```
        kubectl create -f skipper/skipper-config-kafka.yaml
        ```

        Remember that you need to select only one (for now) (see Listings 8-30 and 8-31).

Listing 8-30. skipper-config-rabbit.yaml

```
apiVersion: v1
kind: ConfigMap
metadata:
  name: skipper
  labels:
    app: skipper
data:
  application.yaml: |-
```

```
    spring:
      cloud:
        skipper:
          server:
            platform:
              kubernetes:
                accounts:
                  default:
                    environmentVariables: 'SPRING_RABBITMQ_HOST=${RABBITMQ_SERVICE_
                    HOST},SPRING_RABBITMQ_PORT=${RABBITMQ_SERVICE_PORT}'
                    limits:
                      memory: 1024Mi
                      cpu: 500m
                    readinessProbeDelay: 120
                    livenessProbeDelay: 90
      datasource:
        url: jdbc:mysql://${MYSQL_SERVICE_HOST}:${MYSQL_SERVICE_PORT}/skipper
        username: root
        password: ${mysql-root-password}
        driverClassName: org.mariadb.jdbc.Driver
        testOnBorrow: true
        validationQuery: "SELECT 1"
```

Note that you are adding the datasource and the RabbitMQ server and port in ConfigMap; all are environment variables. Kubernetes creates an environment variable for each service and adds them to every container, so it's easy to know where the other services are; it normally sets the IP and port.

Listing 8-31. skipper-config-kafka.yaml

```
apiVersion: v1
kind: ConfigMap
metadata:
  name: skipper
  labels:
    app: skipper
data:
  application.yaml: |-
    spring:
      cloud:
        skipper:
          server:
            platform:
              kubernetes:
                accounts:
                  default:
                    environmentVariables: 'SPRING_CLOUD_STREAM_KAFKA_BINDER_BROKERS=${KAFKA_
                    SERVICE_HOST}:${KAFKA_SERVICE_PORT},SPRING_CLOUD_STREAM_KAFKA_BINDER_ZK_
                    NODES=${KAFKA_ZK_SERVICE_HOST}:${KAFKA_ZK_SERVICE_PORT}'
                    limits:
                      memory: 1024Mi
```

```
                  cpu: 500m
                readinessProbeDelay: 120
                livenessProbeDelay: 90
    datasource:
      url: jdbc:mysql://${MYSQL_SERVICE_HOST}:${MYSQL_SERVICE_PORT}/skipper
      username: root
      password: ${mysql-root-password}
      driverClassName: org.mariadb.jdbc.Driver
      testOnBorrow: true
      validationQuery: "SELECT 1"
```

After selecting the broker, add the deployment and service.

```
gkubectl create -f skipper/skipper-deployment.yaml
kubectl create -f skipper/skipper-svc.yaml
```

See Listings 8-32 and 8-33.

Listing 8-32. skipper-deployment.yaml

```
apiVersion: apps/v1
kind: Deployment
metadata:
  name: skipper
  labels:
    app: skipper
spec:
  selector:
    matchLabels:
      app: skipper
  replicas: 1
  template:
    metadata:
      labels:
        app: skipper
    spec:
      containers:
      - name: skipper
        image: springcloud/spring-cloud-skipper-server:2.6.0
        imagePullPolicy: Always
        ports:
        - containerPort: 80
        livenessProbe:
          httpGet:
            path: /actuator/health
            port: 7577
          initialDelaySeconds: 45
        readinessProbe:
          httpGet:
            path: /actuator/info
            port: 7577
          initialDelaySeconds: 45
        resources:
```

```
        limits:
          cpu: 1.0
          memory: 1024Mi
        requests:
          cpu: 0.5
          memory: 640Mi
      env:
      - name: SPRING_CLOUD_KUBERNETES_CONFIG_NAME
        value: skipper
      - name: SPRING_CLOUD_KUBERNETES_SECRETS_ENABLE_API
        value: 'true'
      - name: SPRING_CLOUD_KUBERNETES_SECRETS_NAME
        value: mysql
    initContainers:
    - name: init-mysql-wait
      image: busybox
      command: ['sh', '-c', 'until nc -w3 -z mysql 3306; do echo waiting for mysql; sleep
      3; done;']
    - name: init-mysql-database
      image: mysql:5.6
      env:
      - name: MYSQL_PWD
        valueFrom:
          secretKeyRef:
            name: mysql
            key: mysql-root-password
      command: ['sh', '-c', 'mysql -h mysql -u root -e "CREATE DATABASE IF NOT EXISTS
      skipper;"']
    serviceAccountName: scdf-sa
```

Listing 8-33. skipper-svc.yaml

```
apiVersion: v1
kind: Service
metadata:
  name: skipper
  labels:
    app: skipper
    spring-deployment-id: scdf
spec:
  type: LoadBalancer
  ports:
  - port: 80
    targetPort: 7577
  selector:
    app: skipper
```

Skipper can be accessed from the outside when you the type is set to `LoadBalancer`, but if you don't need it, you can use `NodePort` instead. `NodePort` is useful when using Minikube or Docker Desktop Kubernetes.

6. Finally, add the Data Flow server.

```
kubectl create -f server/server-config.yaml
kubectl create -f server/server-deployment.yaml
kubectl create -f server/server-svc.yaml
```

Note that you need a config declaration (see Listings 8-34, 8-35, and 8-36).

Listing 8-34. server-config.yaml

```
apiVersion: v1
kind: ConfigMap
metadata:
  name: scdf-server
  labels:
    app: scdf-server
data:
  application.yaml: |-
    spring:
      cloud:
        dataflow:
          applicationProperties:
            stream:
              management:
                metrics:
                  export:
                    prometheus:
                      enabled: true
                      rsocket:
                        enabled: true
                        host: prometheus-proxy
                        port: 7001
            task:
              management:
                metrics:
                  export:
                    prometheus:
                      enabled: true
                      rsocket:
                        enabled: true
                        host: prometheus-proxy
                        port: 7001
          grafana-info:
            url: 'https://grafana:3000'
          task:
            platform:
              kubernetes:
                accounts:
                  default:
                    limits:
                      memory: 1024Mi
```

```
    datasource:
      url: jdbc:mysql://${MYSQL_SERVICE_HOST}:${MYSQL_SERVICE_PORT}/mysql
      username: root
      password: ${mysql-root-password}
      driverClassName: org.mariadb.jdbc.Driver
      testOnBorrow: true
      validationQuery: "SELECT 1"
```

Note that the Prometheus and Grafana sections are in `ConfigMap`, but if you are deploying without these monitoring tools, you should remove the stream (the whole block), task (the entire block with `prometheus-proxy`) and `grafana-info` (the whole block).

Listing 8-35. server-deployment.yaml

```
apiVersion: apps/v1
kind: Deployment
metadata:
  name: scdf-server
  labels:
    app: scdf-server
spec:
  selector:
    matchLabels:
      app: scdf-server
  replicas: 1
  template:
    metadata:
      labels:
        app: scdf-server
    spec:
      containers:
      - name: scdf-server
        image: springcloud/spring-cloud-dataflow-server:2.4.2.RELEASE
        imagePullPolicy: Always
        volumeMounts:
          - name: database
            mountPath: /etc/secrets/database
            readOnly: true
        ports:
        - containerPort: 80
        livenessProbe:
          httpGet:
            path: /management/health
            port: 80
          initialDelaySeconds: 45
        readinessProbe:
          httpGet:
            path: /management/info
            port: 80
          initialDelaySeconds: 45
        resources:
          limits:
```

```
            cpu: 1.0
            memory: 2048Mi
          requests:
            cpu: 0.5
            memory: 1024Mi
        env:
        - name: KUBERNETES_NAMESPACE
          valueFrom:
            fieldRef:
              fieldPath: "metadata.namespace"
        - name: SERVER_PORT
          value: '80'
        - name: SPRING_CLOUD_CONFIG_ENABLED
          value: 'false'
        - name: SPRING_CLOUD_DATAFLOW_FEATURES_ANALYTICS_ENABLED
          value: 'true'
        - name: SPRING_CLOUD_DATAFLOW_FEATURES_SCHEDULES_ENABLED
          value: 'true'
        - name: SPRING_CLOUD_KUBERNETES_SECRETS_ENABLE_API
          value: 'true'
        - name: SPRING_CLOUD_KUBERNETES_SECRETS_PATHS
          value: /etc/secrets
        - name: SPRING_CLOUD_KUBERNETES_CONFIG_NAME
          value: scdf-server
        - name: SPRING_CLOUD_DATAFLOW_SERVER_URI
          value: 'http://${SCDF_SERVER_SERVICE_HOST}:${SCDF_SERVER_SERVICE_PORT}'
          # Provide the Skipper service location
        - name: SPRING_CLOUD_SKIPPER_CLIENT_SERVER_URI
          value: 'http://${SKIPPER_SERVICE_HOST}:${SKIPPER_SERVICE_PORT}/api'
          # Add Maven repo for metadata artifact resolution for all stream apps
        - name: SPRING_APPLICATION_JSON
          value: "{ \"maven\": { \"local-repository\": null, \"remote-repositories\": {
          \"repo1\": { \"url\": \"https://repo.spring.io/libs-snapshot\"} } } }"
      initContainers:
      - name: init-mysql-wait
        image: busybox
        command: ['sh', '-c', 'until nc -w3 -z mysql 3306; do echo waiting for mysql; sleep
        3; done;']
      serviceAccountName: scdf-sa
      volumes:
        - name: database
          secret:
            secretName: mysql
```

Listing 8-36. server-svc.yaml

```
kind: Service
apiVersion: v1
metadata:
  name: scdf-server
  labels:
```

```
    app: scdf-server
    spring-deployment-id: scdf
spec:
  # If you are running k8s on a local dev box or using minikube, you can use type NodePort
instead
  type: LoadBalancer
  ports:
    - port: 80
      targetPort: 80
      name: scdf-server
  selector:
    app: scdf-server
```

You can use `NodePort` (if you are using Minikube or Docker Desktop Kubernetes) for a local environment and `LoadBalancer` for production.

Those are the steps to create Spring Cloud Data Flow and its components. Once you have deployed it, you can get access by using the following command.

```
kubectl get svc scdf-server
```

Look for the external IP. If you are using `NodePort`, look at the port(s) to go to your local IP. If you are using Minikube, execute the following.

```
minikube service scdf-server --url
```

If you are using Docker Desktop Kubernetes, access `kubernetes.docker.internal`, which points to 127.0.0.1.

After you get the IP from `scdf-server`, open a browser, use the IP with the port (if you used `NodePort`) and the `/dashboard` path. You should see the same dashboard shown in Figure 8-2.

Let's start testing your Spring Cloud Data Flow server.

■ **Note** I added `install.sh` and `uninstall.sh` scripts in the book's source code. You can find them in the `ch08/kubernetes` folder. These scripts are for Unix/Linux only, and you need a jq tool (`https://stedolan.github.io/jq/`) installed.

Testing Your Installation with a Simple Stream

In this section, you create a small stream. It is a sneak peek of what you can do. It is very simple and makes sure your installation and binder are working as expected.

I use Docker Compose (local) in the first part and a Kubernetes cluster (production) for infrastructure, but you can use whatever method you wish for this example.

Using Docker Compose

In this section, let's use Docker Compose to set up the Spring Cloud Data Flow infrastructure with RabbitMQ and MySQL. If you want to download the code, the YAML files are in the `ch08/docker-compose` folder. Execute the following.

```
export DATAFLOW_VERSION=2.6.0
export SKIPPER_VERSION=2.5.0
docker-compose -f docker-compose-rabbitmq.yml up -d
```

Note that you are sending this to the background. Open your browser and go to `http://localhost:9393/dashboard`. If you used the YAML file, you should already have the apps registered. If you don't have the apps, follow the previous sections to register them. Remember that they should be based on RabbitMQ, and either Maven or Docker.

Next, click the Streams pane in the left sidebar (see Figure 8-9).

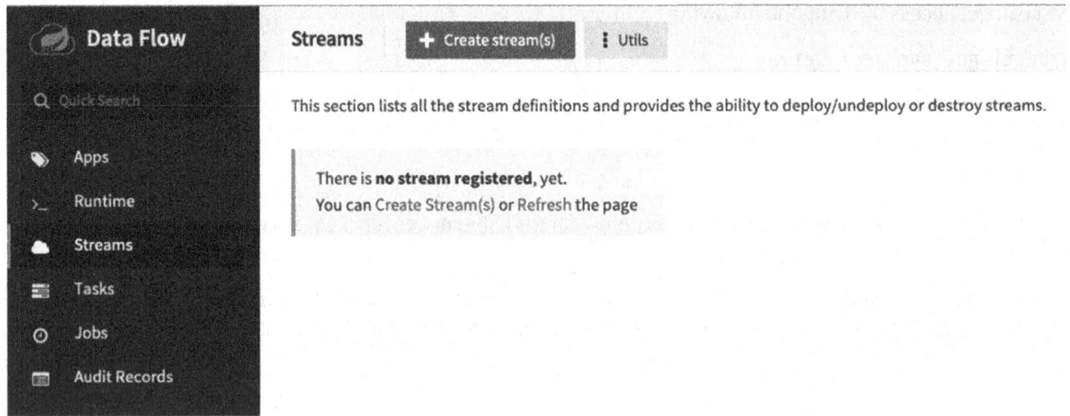

Figure 8-9. *Streams: http://localhost:9393/dashboard/#/streams/definitions*

Next, click **+ Create stream(s)**. This opens the page where you add your stream definition. Here you can use the source, processor, and sink apps to drag-and-drop and connect them. In this case, go to the text area (where it says "Enter stream definition") and enter the following.

```
time | log
```

The app blocks form as shown in Figure 8-10.

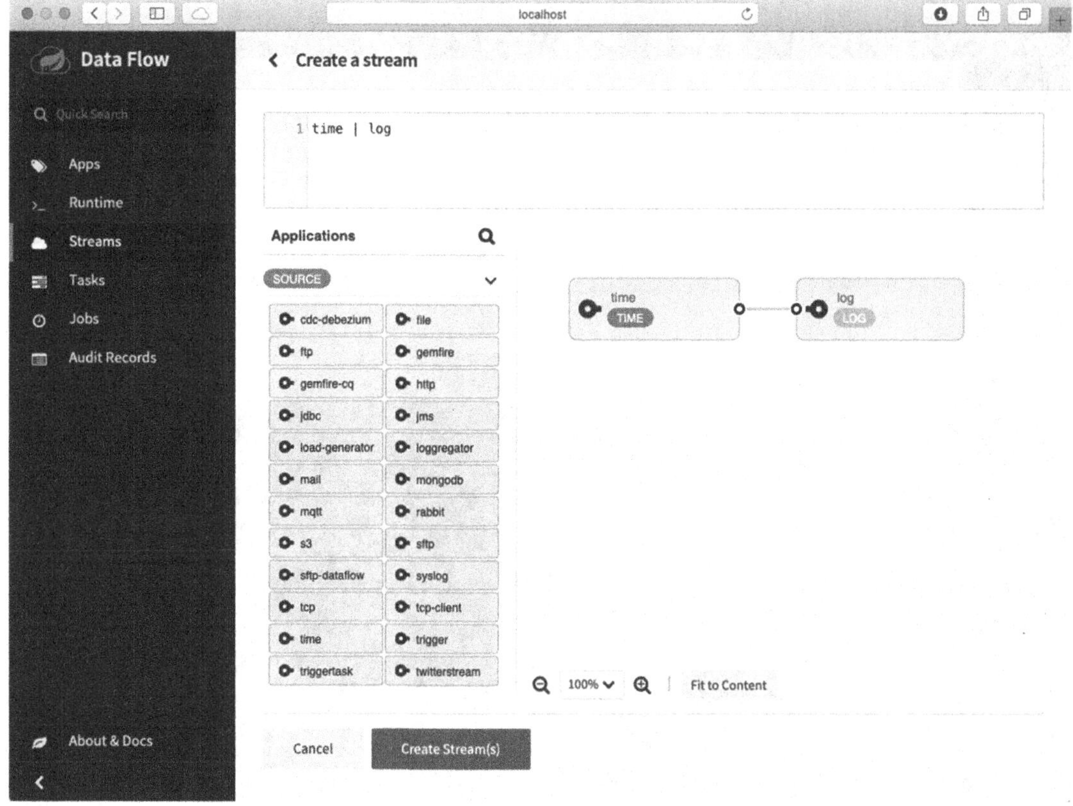

Figure 8-10. *Stream Definition: http://localhost:9393/dashboard/#/streams/create*

Next, click the Create Stream(s) button, which opens a pop-up dialog asking for the name and description. Enter **simple** in the Name field and **Just a Test** in the Description field (see Figure 8-11).

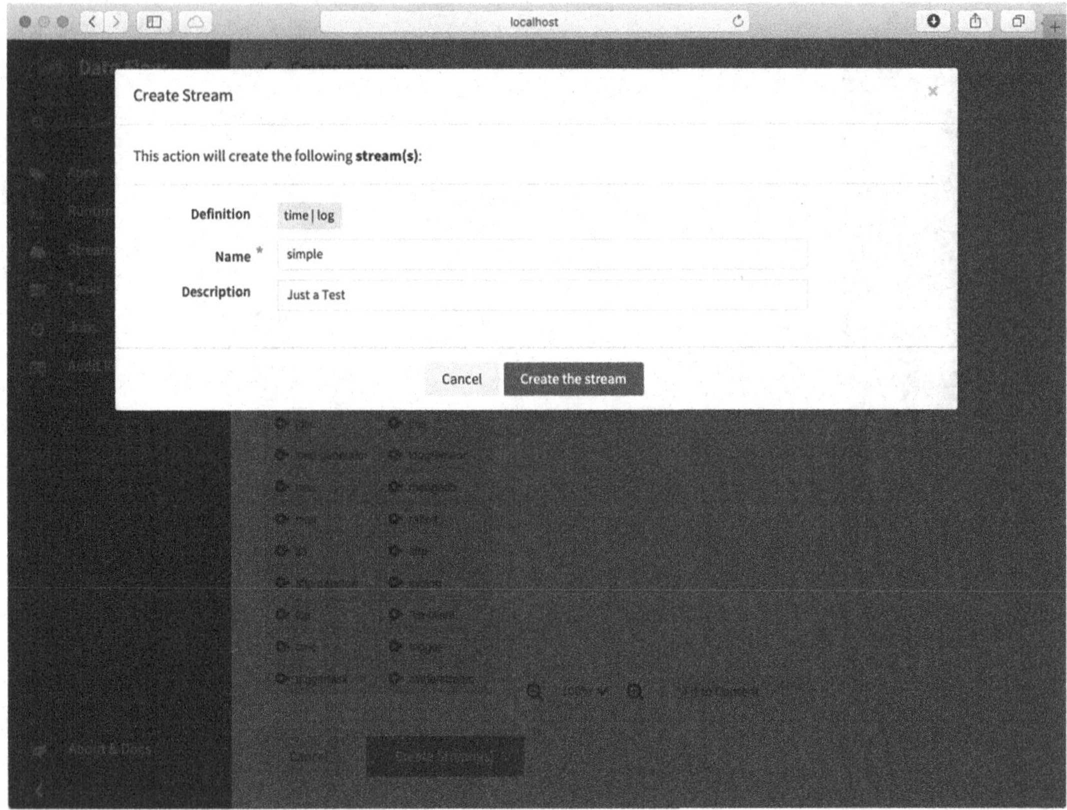

Figure 8-11. *Create stream*

Click the **Create the stream** button to create the stream and then return to the Streams section. There you see a list of stream definitions, and you see your "simple" stream (see Figure 8-12).

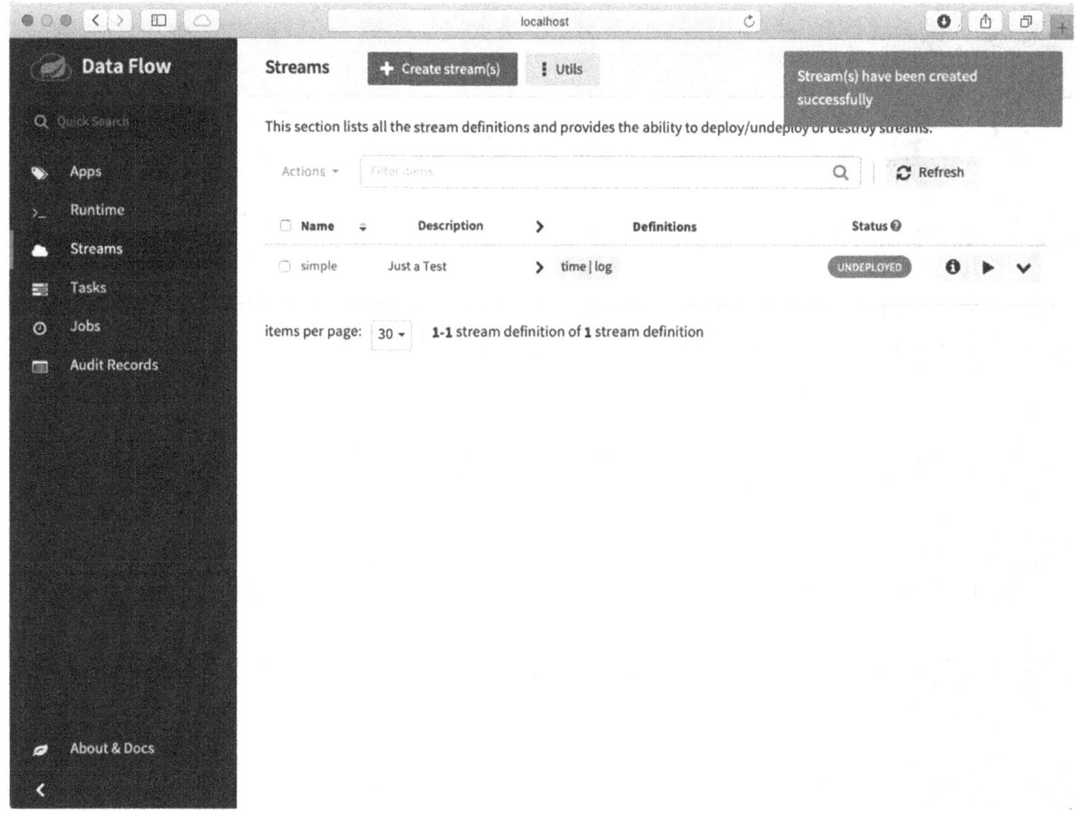

Figure 8-12. *Stream created*

Next, click the Play button at the end of the stream row. This takes you to the Deploy Stream Definition page, where you can add properties to every application and add CPU, memory, disk space, and the number of instances needed for your application. In this case, you see three columns, one for global, where you add common settings for both apps (remember, `time` and `log` are two different microservices apps and are part of the app starter) and a column for each microservice—one for the time and one for the log (see Figure 8-13).

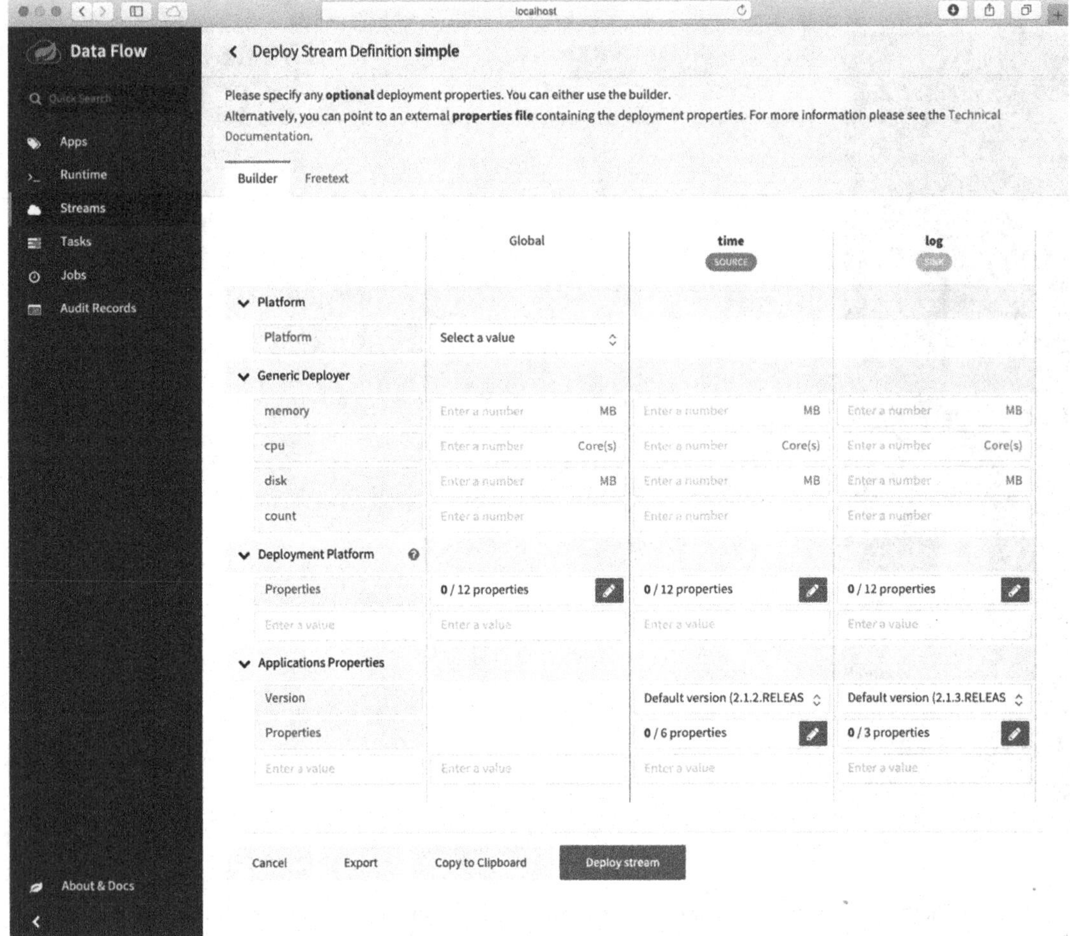

Figure 8-13. *Deploy Stream simple: http://localhost:9393/dashboard/#/streams/definitions/simple/deploy*

In this case, you are not setting any new properties, so click the **Deploy stream** button. This sends the instruction to deploy the two applications, and it returns you to the Streams page. Look at your simple stream. You see the DEPLOYING status. If you click the Refresh button at the top of the list, you see that your app has already DEPLOYED (see Figures 8-14 and 8-15).

Status

DEPLOYING

Figure 8-14. *Status: DEPLOYING*

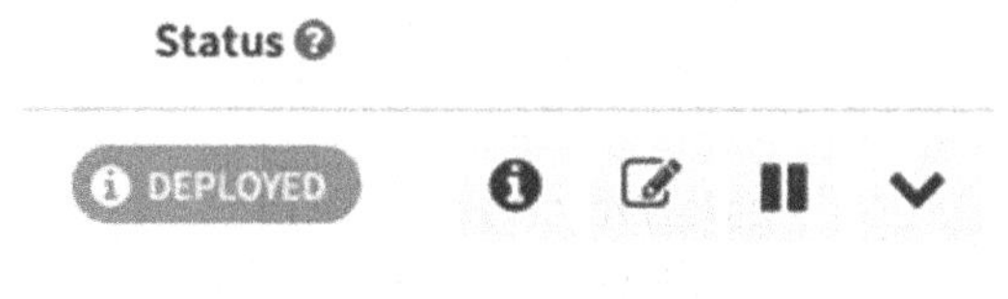

Figure 8-15. *Status: DEPLOYED*

So, how do you know if this stream is working? Based on the DSL, "`time | log`" means that you are using a `time` source (with a RabbitMQ binder, `time-source-rabbit`) and a log-sink (with a RabbitMQ binder, `log-sink-rabbit`). The `time` source is sending every second, and the log-sink logs it into the console. If you click the "i" (Show details) button next to the status, it takes you to the stream's details and the current logs for both apps (see Figure 8-16).

localhost
Data Flow
Apps
Runtime
Streams
Tasks
Jobs
Audit Records
About & Docs

Stream simple DEPLOYED
Undeploy stream | Update stream | Destroy stream
Summary | Graph | History

Description: Just a Test
Definition: time --spring.rabbitmq.host=rabbitmq | log --spring.rabbitmq.host=rabbitmq
Status: DEPLOYED
Applications:

Name	Type
time	SOURCE
log	SINK

Deployment Info:

log

resource	maven://org.springframework.cloud.stream.app:log-sink-rabbit:jar
spring.cloud.deployer.group	simple
version	2.1.3.RELEASE

time

resource	maven://org.springframework.cloud.stream.app:time-source-rabbit:jar
spring.cloud.deployer.group	simple
version	2.1.2.RELEASE

Runtimes:

App Id	# of Instances
simple.log-v1	1 instance
simple.time-v1	1 instance

Logs: simple.log-v1 Refresh

```
2020-05-01 02:05:43.219  INFO 109 --- [           main] trationDelegate$BeanPostProcessorChecker : Bean 'org.springframework.cloud.autoconfigure.ConfigurationPropertiesRebinderAutoConfiguration' of type [org.springframework.cloud.autoconfigure.ConfigurationPropertiesRebinderAutoConfiguration$$EnhancerBySpringCGLIB$$f47aa6f2] is not eligible for getting processed by all BeanPostProcessors (for example: not eligible for auto-proxying)
```

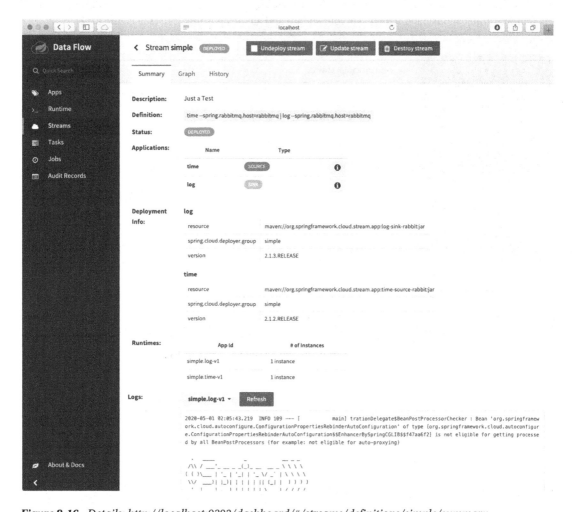

Figure 8-16. *Details: http://localhost:9393/dashboard/#/streams/definitions/simple/summary*

If you scroll, you see the Logs section. Select `simple.log-v1`. You see the logs and the time currently received by the log-sink. You should see something like the following.

```
...
INFO [e.time.simple-1] log-sink  : 05/01/20 02:20:59
INFO [e.time.simple-1] log-sink  : 05/01/20 02:21:00
INFO [e.time.simple-1] log-sink  : 05/01/20 02:21:01
INFO [e.time.simple-1] log-sink  : 05/01/20 02:21:02
INFO [e.time.simple-1] log-sink  : 05/01/20 02:21:03
INFO [e.time.simple-1] log-sink  : 05/01/20 02:21:04
INFO [e.time.simple-1] log-sink  : 05/01/20 02:21:05
...
```

Note that the apps were named using this pattern: `<stream-name>.<app>-<version>`. In this case, you have "`simple.time-v1`" and "`simple.log-v1`". Skipper did this. It keeps track of the version. If you undeploy and redeploy (stop and restart) the stream, you should see the version increment to `v2`.

Are you wondering if you can see live log? If you click the Runtime section (in the left pane), you go to the Runtime applications page, which lists your stream and all the apps involved (see Figure 8-17).

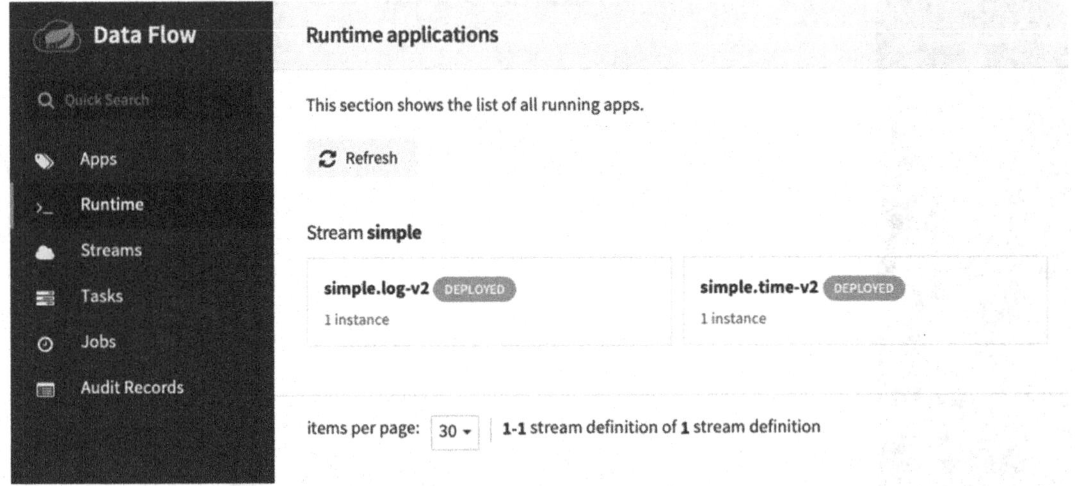

Figure 8-17. *Runtime: http://localhost:9393/dashboard/#/runtime/apps*

If you click `simple.log-v1/v2`, you see more information (see Figure 8-18).

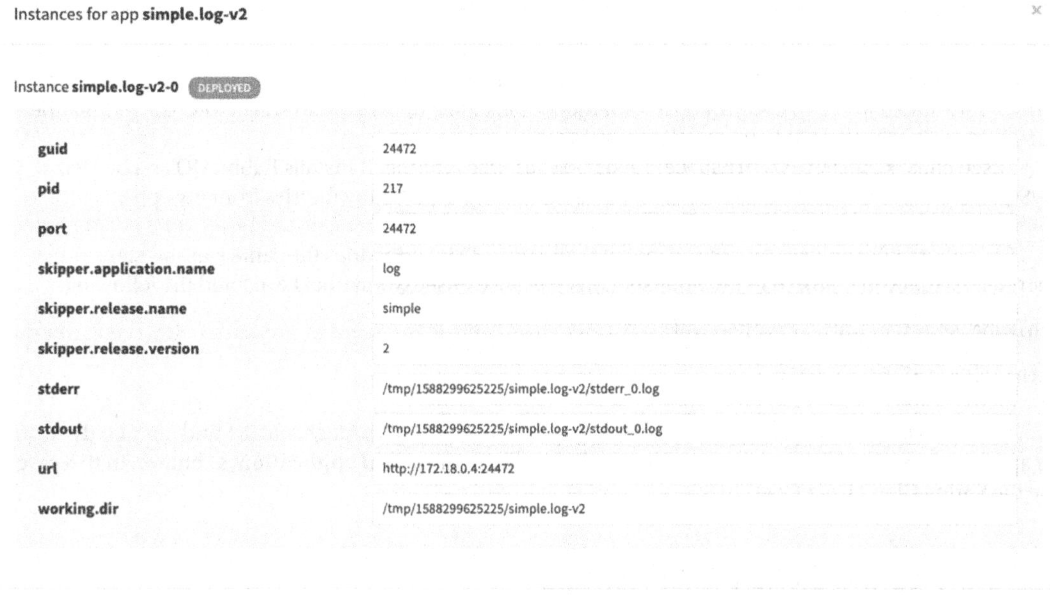

Figure 8-18. *Runtime details*

Figure 8-18 shows the details of the app's `simple.log-v1/v2`. Note the path in the `stdout` field. In this case, it is `/tmp/1588299625225/simple.log-v2/stdout_0.log`.

Open a terminal and execute the following command.

```
docker exec skipper tail -f /tmp/1588299625225/simple.log-v2/stdout_0.log
... log-sink : 05/01/20 02:33:21
... log-sink : 05/01/20 02:33:22
... log-sink : 05/01/20 02:33:23
... log-sink : 05/01/20 02:33:24
... log-sink : 05/01/20 02:33:25
... log-sink : 05/01/20 02:33:26
... log-sink : 05/01/20 02:33:27
... log-sink : 05/01/20 02:33:28
... log-sink : 05/01/20 02:33:29
... log-sink : 05/01/20 02:33:30
... log-sink : 05/01/20 02:33:31
... log-sink : 05/01/20 02:33:32
```

You see every second the time is printed. Return to the Stream pane and destroy the stream.

Congratulations! You have just created your first stream `time | log` with Docker Compose. Now, you can shut down your infrastructure with the following.

```
docker-compose -f docker-compose-rabbitmq.yml down
```

Next, let's deploy Spring Cloud Data Flow in Kubernetes.

Using Kubernetes

In this section, you deploy the same "`time | log`" stream using Kubernetes. Instead of using the dashboard, you use the Spring Cloud Data Flow shell. If you have the source code, the `install.sh` and `uninstall.sh` scripts were added to set up everything in Kubernetes. I installed Spring Cloud Data Flow using Minikube, but you can use any other Kubernetes cluster instance.

I used `ch08/kubernetes/workspace-rabbit-mysql-monitoring`. It installs RabbitMQ as a binder, MySQL for persistence, and Grafana and Prometheus to keep track of any metrics from my apps.

Go to that folder and execute the `./install.sh` script. This script does the same step-by-step instructions that you followed in previous sections. Because I used Minikube, I executed the following.

```
minikube service scdf-server --url
```

```
http://192.168.64.6:30724
```

If I open a browser, I need to point to `http://192.168.64.6:30724/dashboard`. I find out that there are no apps and I need to do the same procedure as before. Click the **+ Add application(s)** button. In this case, I use the Spring Cloud Data Flow shell.

Using the Spring Cloud Data Flow Shell

I haven't shown you this particular tool yet. You get a sneak peek of Spring Cloud Data Flow shell in this section. You are registering the applications and creating the same simple "`time | log`" stream.

In the stand-alone section, `download.sh` contains the shell, but if you don't remember it, create a `workspace-shell` folder and execute the following command in that folder.

```
wget https://repo.spring.io/release/org/springframework/cloud/spring-cloud-dataflow-
shell/2.4.2.RELEASE/spring-cloud-dataflow-shell-2.4.2.RELEASE.jar
```

Then, execute the following.

```
java -jar spring-cloud-dataflow-shell-2.4.2.RELEASE.jar
...
...
server-unknown:>
```

A prompt says, "`server-unknown`". One of the best commands is `help`. If you type `help` and press Enter, you see all the available commands. And if you type `help dataflow config server`, you see all the parameters that enable the connection to the Data Flow server.

Next, execute the following in the shell.

```
server-unknown:>dataflow config server --uri http://192.168.64.6:30724
Successfully targeted http://192.168.64.6:30724
dataflow:>
```

Now you see the `dataflow` prompt. If you type `app list`, you see the following.

```
dataflow:>app list
No registered apps.
You can register new apps with the 'app register' and 'app import' commands.
dataflow:>
```

This means that you need to register your apps. Earlier, I listed the URLs that contain all the descriptions of the app starters. For this, you use `https://dataflow.spring.io/rabbitmq-docker-latest`.

Next, type `app import` and pass the `uri` parameter with the URL.

```
dataflow:>app import --uri https://dataflow.spring.io/rabbitmq-docker-latest
Successfully registered 66 applications from ...
dataflow:>
```

If you execute the app list, you see the source, processor, and sink applications listed.

■ **Note** The Data Flow shell supports Tab completion if you need or forget any parameter.

Next, let's create the stream by executing the following.

```
dataflow:>stream create --name simple --definition "time | log"
Created new stream 'simple'
dataflow:>
```

The preceding command creates the `simple` stream with `"time | log"` as the definition. If you execute `stream list`, you see the list of streams created and their status.

```
dataflow:>stream list
...
simple    |    | time | log  |The app or group is known to the system, but is not currently
deployed.
...
dataflow>
```

Next, let's deploy it with the following.

```
dataflow:>stream deploy --name simple
Deployment request has been sent for stream 'simple'
dataflow:>
```

You can see the status with

```
dataflow:>stream info --name simple
...
```

or with

```
dataflow:>stream list
```

It should say "deployed".

How do you view the logs? The cool thing about doing this in Kubernetes is that it creates pods with the time and log apps, so you can open a new terminal and execute the following.

```
$ kubectl get pods
NAME                                  READY   STATUS    RESTARTS   AGE
grafana-5b89747547-h5x7l              1/1     Running   0          29m
mysql-5c59b756db-rggjw                1/1     Running   0          29m
```

```
prometheus-67896dcc8-s4qls            1/1     Running   0          29m
prometheus-proxy-86f5fd556b-6m9jn     1/1     Running   0          29m
rabbitmq-5bf579759d-c5rtj             1/1     Running   0          29m
scdf-server-5888868f84-qmwt2          1/1     Running   0          28m
simple-log-v1-5f88b7d546-g7cmb        1/1     Running   0          2m8s
simple-time-v1-5d7d4bc86f-gwq7w       1/1     Running   0          2m8s
skipper-66c685ff74-vc7b5              1/1     Running   0          29m
```

Note that Skipper created `simple-log` and `simple-time`; its naming convention is `<stream-name>-<app-name>-<version>-<pod-id>`. Now you can view the logs with the following.

```
$ kubectl logs -f pod/simple-log-v1-5f88b7d546-g7cmb
... log-sink  : 05/01/20 03:20:13
... log-sink  : 05/01/20 03:20:14
... log-sink  : 05/01/20 03:20:15
... log-sink  : 05/01/20 03:20:16
```

Congratulations! You created your stream using the Data Flow shell. Before you destroy the stream, let's look at Grafana. Go to your browser and open `http://192.168.64.6:30724/dashboard`. You see all the registered apps. Go to the Streams pane. At the top, you see the Grafana dashboard button. Click it to go to the Grafana landing page. The username is `admin`, and the password is `password`. Note that you have applications, streams, and task dashboards already configured. Look around—you see some data (see Figures 8-19 and 8-20).

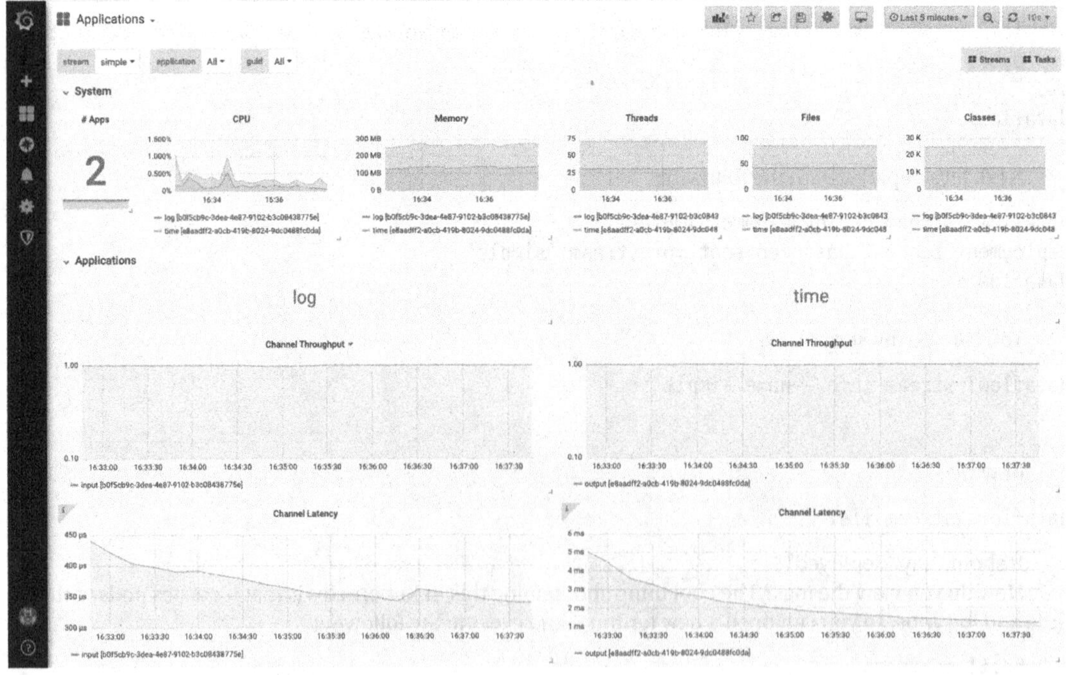

Figure 8-19. *Grafana applications: http://192.168.64.6:30018/d/scdf-applications/applications?orgId=1&refresh=10s#/apps*

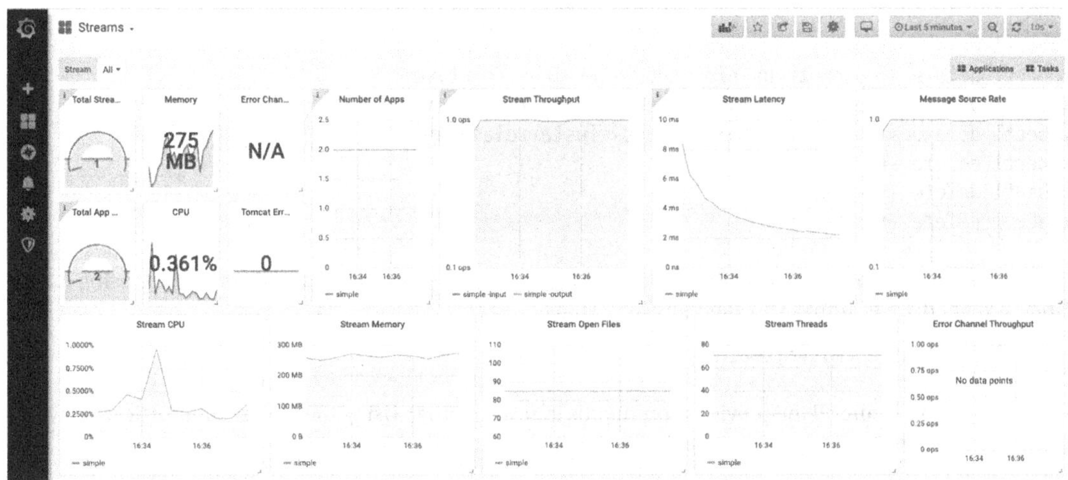

Figure 8-20. *Grafana Streams: http://192.168.64.6:30018/d/scdf-streams/streams?orgId=1&refresh=10s*

Now you can monitor your stream and apps closely.

It is time to shut down everything. To delete the stream, execute the following in the Data Flow shell.

```
dataflow:>stream destroy --name simple
Destroyed stream 'simple'
dataflow:>
```

If you execute `kubectl get pods` once more in your terminal, the simple pod is gone. You can quit the Data Flow shell with the `exit` command.

```
dataflow:>exit
```

Congratulations! You used the Spring Cloud Data Flow shell to register apps and create and destroy your stream. More actions are coming, so don't forget that you are still using the Data Flow shell.

Cleaning Up

If you want to clean up quickly, undo what you did to install and replace `create` with `delete` in the reverse order they were created.

```
kubectl delete -f server/server-deployment.yaml
kubectl delete -f server/server-svc.yaml
kubectl delete -f server/server-config.yaml
kubectl delete -f skipper/skipper-svc.yaml
kubectl delete -f skipper/skipper-deployment.yaml
kubectl delete -f skipper/skipper-config-rabbit.yaml
kubectl delete -f server/service-account.yaml
kubectl delete -f server/server-rolebinding.yaml
kubectl delete -f server/server-roles.yaml
kubectl delete -f grafana/
kubectl delete -f prometheus/prometheus-service.yaml
kubectl delete -f prometheus/prometheus-deployment.yaml
```

```
kubectl delete -f prometheus/prometheus-configmap.yaml
kubectl delete -f prometheus-proxy/
kubectl delete -f prometheus/prometheus-serviceaccount.yaml
kubectl delete -f prometheus/prometheus-clusterrolebinding.yaml
kubectl delete -f prometheus/prometheus-clusterroles.yaml
kubectl delete -f mysql/
kubectl delete -f kafka/
kubectl delete -f rabbitmq/
```

Of course, there are more methods to remove the services, deployments, and pods, such as using the labels provided; for example, you can remove Grafana.

```
kubectl delete all,cm,svc,secrets -l app=grafana
```

Or you can execute all the previous commands in reverse order. Using the file declaration (YAML) will do the trick and remove the services, but in the end, it depends on what you like.

Summary

This chapter explained the importance of Spring Cloud Data Flow and showed you how to create your first stream. We get into more detail in the next chapter, where I show you the internals of Spring Cloud Data Flow and how you can get more out of it. I also show you different ways to set up Spring Cloud Data Flow. There are several supported platforms, but Kubernetes is the de facto technology for cloud infrastructure and container orchestration.

PART II

Spring Cloud Data Flow: Internals

CHAPTER 9

Spring Cloud Data Flow Internals

In Chapter 8, you briefly looked at Spring Cloud Data Flow. This chapter provides an in-depth discussion of what this technology can do. I review what you can do with stream and batch processing and show you how Spring Cloud Task creates finite workloads using Spring Batch.

Let's start digging into Spring Cloud Data Flow.

Spring Cloud Data Flow Architecture

Spring Cloud Data Flow orchestrates and choreographs Stream apps and batch jobs. It relies on a cloud platform to manage our app's scalability and high availability and the resiliency and fault tolerance of the underlying infrastructure (VMs, physical machines). You need to take care of the business logic.

Spring Cloud Data Flow has several components for orchestrating and choreographing Stream apps and batch jobs. It identifies an application type and deploys it based on its DSL (domain-specific language), similar to a Unix-like syntax when executing a shell command. The app types are source, processor, sink, and task. I introduce Spring Cloud Task later in the chapter.

On the server-side, Spring Cloud Data Flow has two main components.

- *Data Flow server*. This server exposes a REST API, the main entry point for the dashboard and the shell. The Data Flow server can run on several cloud platforms, such as Kubernetes, Cloud Foundry, Mesos, and Yarn and your local machine (running stand-alone or using Docker or Docker Compose). The Data Flow server keeps track of streams and their state using a relational database (MySQL, PostgreSQL, Oracle, DB2, MS SQL Server, H2, or HSQLDB). You only need to declare in the `spring.datasource.*` properties the right driver. If there is no `datasource` property defined, by default, use the H2 embedded DB to keep everything in memory. The Data Flow server is responsible for the following.
    - Registers artifacts such as JARs (stand-alone, HTTP, or in Maven coordinates) and Docker images
    - Parses the stream or batch job definitions based on the DSL (This is the Unix-like shell command (e.g., `time | filter | transform | log`). You learn more about DSL in the remaining chapters.)
    - Validates and persists Stream and Task apps and batch job definitions using a relational database
    - Deploys batch job definitions to one or more cloud platforms
    - Queries task and batch job execution history

F. Gutierrez, *Spring Cloud Data Flow*, https://doi.org/10.1007/978-1-4842-1239-4_9

- Delegates Stream deployment to Skipper
- Delegates job scheduling to a cloud platform
- Adds extra information to streams when deploying to the cloud platform, including additional properties such as configuration for the apps (ports, channel names, expressions using SpEL, app property specific), input and output, binder properties, instances to run, memory and CPU allocations, and partitioning groups
- Adds security for authentication and authorizations (OAuth 2.0, SSO, LDAP, or add your own security provider), access through SSL, and secures your dashboard
- Tries to connect to the Spring Cloud Config server at port 8888, but you can use your own configuration by overriding the properties
- Configures Maven repositories and Docker registries for easy access to your Stream and Task apps
- Provides an extensive RESTful API and a web dashboard using port 9393 by default; it can be overridden by using properties

It can be used without Skipper, but you remove the capacity to upgrade or make rollbacks (the ability to do blue/green deployments), deployment history, and some other features.

- *Skipper server*. The Skipper server is responsible for deploying the stream to one or more platforms. It can do upgrades and rollbacks by keeping track of the version of the stream published. It uses state machine algorithms to do blue-green deployments. You can also add security for authentication and authorization (OAuth 2.0, SSO, or add your own security provider) and use SSL for secured communication.

  The Skipper server keeps track of any stream and its state, and versions of the streams using a relational database (MySQL, PostgreSQL, Oracle, DB2, MS SQL Server, H2, and HSQLDB can be used). You only need to declare in the `spring.datasource.*` properties the right driver. If there is no `datasource` property defined, by default, use the H2 embedded DB to keep everything in memory.

  It has a default connection to the Spring Cloud config server at port 8888, but you can easily override this and add your own.

On the client-side, Spring Cloud Data Flow has several components.

- *Dashboard*. The dashboard is part of the Data Flow server, and its server the port 9393. It does REST calls to the Data Flow server. It is a GUI that visualizes streams (it uses the Spring Flo project, `https://spring.io/projects/spring-flo`). You can take advantage of the following on the dashboard with Flo.
  - Create, manage, and monitor your stream pipelines using the DSL or a canvas
  - Register your apps, single or in a bulk
  - Stop, start, and destroy Stream and Task apps
  - Monitor your streams and individually your applications using Grafana and Prometheus (if configured)
  - View of analytics for your stream and use the right graphs to represent your data streams and logic

    - Stop and resume jobs (the dashboard and Flo are the next iterations of the Spring Batch GUI version to manages task and batch jobs)
    - Use the content assist and autocomplete features
    - Adjust the grid layout for a more efficient way to see and configure your pipelines
    - See a visual representation of your distributed deployment
    - Add metadata for the deployer, such as CPU, instances, and memory

  You can get the source code of the Data Flow dashboard at `https://github.com/spring-cloud/spring-cloud-dataflow-ui`.

- *Shell.* This is another component that communicates with the Data Flow server through REST API calls. It uses the Spring Shell project. The following are some of its features.
    - Tab completion, colorization, and script execution
    - Integration with bean validation API, so you can execute your logic through objects
    - Dynamic enablement of commands based on domain-specific criteria
    - The same functionality as the dashboard but using a command-line-like interface
    - Easily extends to use programming models for creating custom commands
- *Java client.* You can use the `spring-cloud-dataflow-rest-client` module to create your streams programmatically. It provides `StreamBuilder`, `StreamDefinition`, `Stream`, `StreamApplication`, and `DataFlowTemplate` DSL classes that offer a fluent API for easy development (see Figure 9-1).

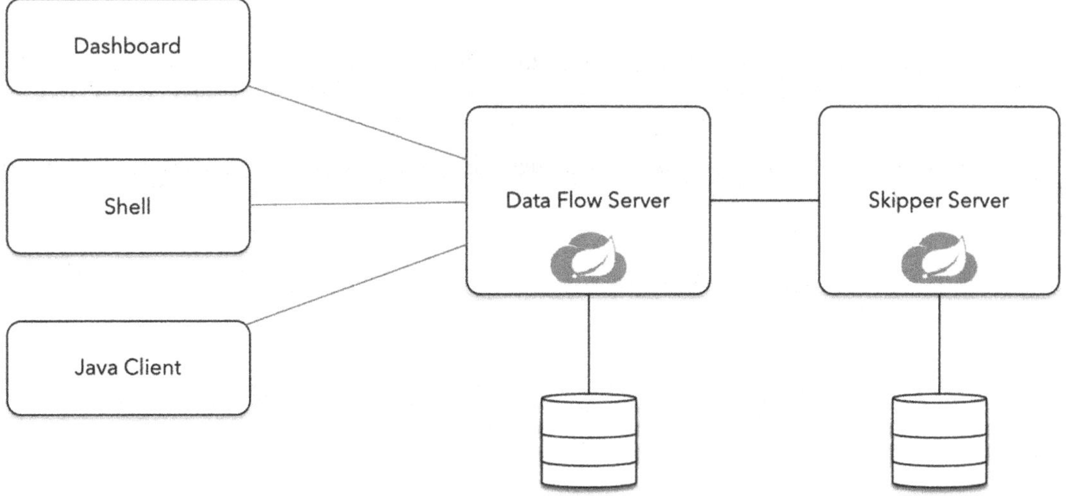

Figure 9-1. *Spring Cloud Data Flow components*

Before going into each component, let's talk about the application types. You already know that the apps that conform to the stream are Spring Cloud Stream and Spring Cloud Task apps, but each has an important difference.

- *Long-lived* applications have input and output and need a broker to communicate. Some apps have multiple inputs and outputs, and in other cases, they don't need a broker to communicate. Most of the time, you find that the long-lived apps are created using Spring Cloud Stream modules.
- *Short-lived* applications have a finite duration. They start, process, and finish. These apps are tasks that run and can save their status in the Data Flow database. Normally Spring Cloud Task is used. An extension of these apps uses Spring Batch. It saves the status, restarts from where a failure left off, and much more.

You don't need to use Spring to create either long-lived or short-lived apps. You can practically use any programming language. When creating these apps, you can package them as a Spring Boot Uber-JAR that can be accessed using Maven (hosted in a Maven repository) as a file or HTTP, or as a Docker image hosted in a Docker registry.

Client Tools: cURL Command, Data Flow Shell, Java Client, Dashboard

In this section, I cover all the available ways to connect to the Spring Data Flow server by creating simple examples, and in the next chapters, you can use any tools for complex solutions. Let's start by having our infrastructure for Spring Cloud Data Flow (Data Flow server, Skipper server, MySQL, RabbitMQ, or Kafka) up and running; you can use either Docker Compose or Kubernetes. Also, let's define our pipeline DSL.

Before using the client tools, make sure you have this extra set of tools to help you.

- `jq` (`https://stedolan.github.io/jq/`) processes JSON objects.
- `yq` (`https://mikefarah.gitbook.io/yq/`) processes YAML objects.
- `httpie` (`https://httpie.org/`). HTTP client. This tool depends on Python 3.6 or greater.

  If any of these tools do not help you, have the `cURL` command installed. If you are using Windows OS, you can download it from `https://curl.haxx.se/windows/`. You can also use Postman (`www.postman.com/downloads/`).

Next, let's define the DSL that you work with through the chapter. Refer to it as the *movie stream pipeline DSL* or the *stream pipeline* (see Figure 9-2).

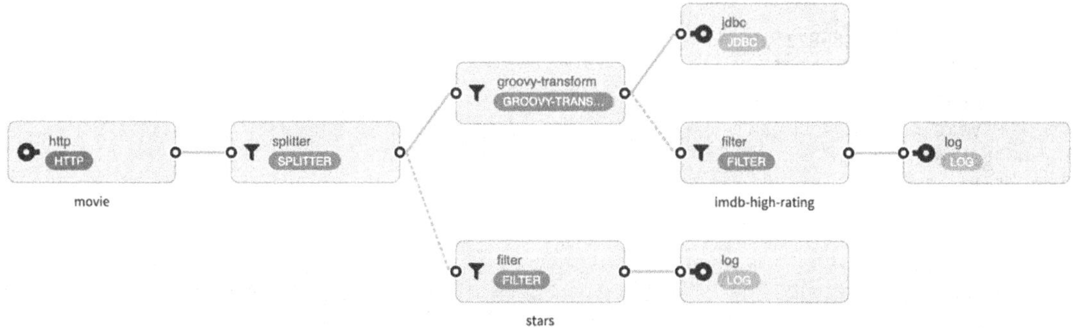

Figure 9-2. *Movie stream DSL*

Figure 9-2 shows the stream pipeline as a graph. Remember that each block is a Spring Cloud Stream app that is independent of the others. They are communicating through any *binder broker* you select (RabbitMQ, Kafka, NATS, etc.). When deployed, there can be one or more instances of each app. Because the Spring Cloud Data Flow server runs in a cloud environment/cloud platform (Docker Compose—local or Kubernetes, Cloud Foundry, Mesos, Yarn), it has scalability, high availability, fault tolerance, and visibility (monitoring) for any microservice architecture. Let's review what you already know about Spring Cloud Stream apps.

- `http`. First, you create an `http` app that listens for any incoming request. This is a source. The sample data you send is listed in Listing 9-1).

Listing 9-1. Sample data

```
{
  "movies": [
    {
        "id": "tt0133093",
      "title": "The Matrix",
      "actor": "Keanu Reeves",
       "year": 1999,
      "genre": "fiction",
      "stars": 5
    },
    {
        "id": "tt0209144",
      "title": "Memento",
      "actor": "Guy Pearce",
       "year": 2000,
      "genre": "drama",
      "stars": 4
    },
    {
       "id": "tt0482571",
      "title": "The Prestige",
      "actor": "Christian Bale",
       "year": 2006,
      "genre": "drama",
      "stars": 3
    },
```

```
    {
        "id": "tt0486822",
      "title": "Disturbia",
      "actor": "Shia LaBeouf",
       "year": 2007,
      "genre": "drama",
      "stars": 3
    }
  ]
}
```

Analyze the data (you are sending an `id`, and an array of movies, instead of one).

- `splitter`. The `splitter` is a messaging pattern. Based on the expression given, a message can be split into several pieces, and in this case, you split the message one movie at a time. In this case, the `splitter` app produces four messages. The `splitter` is a *processor*.
- `groovy-transform`. You used this in previous chapters. This time, the `groovy-transform` app goes to an external system to get the "real ratings." You use the RapidAPI (`https://rapidapi.com`) site that offers several APIs, including the IMDB (Internet Movie Database, `www.imdb.com`), and sends the ID to get the movie's worldwide ratings. Once it returns with the IMDB rating, it enhances our movie message by adding the `rating` and `ratingCount` properties. The `groovy-transform` app is another processor.
- `filter`. There are two `filter` apps: one that comes from the `splitter` app, meaning that it receives the same message as the `groovy-transform` app, and it uses the `star` property to let pass only movies with more than three stars. The other `filter` app lets pass only movies with a high rating (> 8.0). The `filter` apps are *processor* apps.
- `jdbc`. A `jdbc` app saves the movie message in a database. This message includes the original message and the new properties collected by the `groovy-transform` app. It is a very simple thing to do. The `jdbc` app is a *sink*.
- `log`. The `log` apps log what is let go from the `filter` apps. Note that you can use a different sink (Rabbit, HDFS, Mongo, FTP, S3, etc.). A `log` app is a *sink*.

How do you create the stream pipeline for this example? Spring Cloud Data Flow provides a simple way to expose your apps and connect them using a Unix-like DSL syntax. The Spring Cloud Stream apps (you can see them as Unix commands) can communicate to other apps by using the | symbol (Unix | pipe) and redirect using the > symbol. Our example should be very simple to implement in a stream pipeline DSL (see Listing 9-2).

Listing 9-2. Movie Stream Pipeline DSL Simple Form

```
movie = http | splitter | groovy-transform | jdbc
stars = :movie.splitter > filter | log
imdb-high-rating = :movie.groovy-transform > filter | log
```

Listing 9-2 shows the movie stream pipeline. Let's analyze it.

- `http | splitter | groovy-transform | jdbc`. Imagine this is a Unix command (like `cat myfile | grep "hello" | awk '{print $2}' ...`). Do you see some similarities? What you are saying is, use the `http` app send the message to the `splitter` app, then the `splitter` app send multiple messages (one at a time) to the `groovy-transform` app that collect some info, and it sends the message to the `jdbc` app that saves the record into a database. The | symbol is used as the connector or the information channel to the next app (Unix pipelines).

  The `movie =` declaration can be treated as a name of the DSL and its definition (like a variable named movie that has a value of `http | splitter | groovy-transform | jdbc`, such as Unix).

- `splitter > filter | log`. This is saying that from the `splitter` get a copy of the message and send it to the `filter` app and then to the `log` app. The > symbol is a redirection. Don't worry too much. You learn more when you use the > and the : symbols.

  The `stars = :move.splitter` declaration means that you are creating a tap (named `stars`). You are reaching to the first definition `movie =` (or making reference to the variable `movie`, if you think of Unix shell terms) and accessing the `splitter` app with the declaration `:movie.splitter`; this means that you are creating a *wire tap* (a message pattern, a copy of the message) and sending it to the `filter` app with the > symbol.

- `groovy-transform > filter | log`. This part says get a copy of the message from `groovy-transform` (once it finishes processing the message), send it to the `filter` app, and then send it to the `log` app.

  The `imdb-high-rating = :movie.groovy-transform` declaration means that you are creating a tap (named `imdb-high-rating`), and you are reaching to the first definition `movie =` and accessing the `groovy-transform`; this means that you are creating a wire tap that gets a copy of the message once `groovy-transform` returns and sending it to the `filter` app with the > symbol.

The = and : symbols (there are more) have meanings that I describe later when I discuss labels, taps, and destinations; for now, think of them as ways to name a portion of the stream and a way to reach an app and apply other symbols, Unix shell-like.

Each app can have multiple properties (or parameters/arguments if you think in terms of Unix shell). Either declare them in the DSL or have an external property file (either a local or remote cloud config server). You use them for now in the same DSL.

Now that you know the DSL, it is time to test it and see it running. Let's begin with the command line.

Using cURL, Httpie, and jq

The Spring Cloud Data Flow server exposes a REST API and can be accessed programmatically through any REST client or any command-line utility, such as `cURL`, `wget`, or `Httpie`. In this section, I'll show you how to create the pipeline DSL using command-line utilities. Let's do this step by step.

1. Make sure you have one of the command utilities. I'll show you the commands using `cURL` and `Httpie`. Because the Spring Cloud Data Flow server exposes its data in JSON format, it's worth installing the jq utility.

2. Make sure you already have Spring Cloud Data Flow and Spring Cloud Data Flow Skipper server running. You can use any method—the local setup using Docker Compose or a Kubernetes cluster. Ensure you can reach by exposing the Spring Cloud Data Flow server using a `LoadBalancer` type. By default, it uses port 9393 to expose the REST API and the path `/dashboard` for the GUI; but you must look at the services and the port (e.g., `kubectl get svc -o wide`). (I'm using Docker Compose, using RabbitMQ and MySQL for persistence. I'm testing against `localhost`).

   ```
   $ curl -s http://localhost:9393 | jq .
   ```

   Use Httpie if you don't need to use the jq tool to format the output.

   ```
   $ http :9393
   ```

   If you are using a local infrastructure (like Docker Compose), you don't need to use the server name; it goes to localhost by default. With the preceding commands, you can see all the exposed API, so now you know what to do.

3. See if there are already apps registered by using

   ```
   $ curl -s http://localhost:9393/apps | jq .
   ```

   or

   ```
   $ http :9393/apps
   ```

   If you don't have any apps, you can go to the next step; you can skip it if you do.

4. Register the apps. Depending on which type of broker and infrastructure you used, choose one of the following.

   - Using Maven
     - `https://dataflow.spring.io/kafka-maven-latest`
     - `https://dataflow.spring.io/rabbitmq-maven-latest`
     - `https://dataflow.spring.io/task-maven-latest`
   - Using Docker
     - `https://dataflow.spring.io/kafka-docker-latest`
     - `https://dataflow.spring.io/rabbitmq-docker-latest`
     - `https://dataflow.spring.io/task-docker-latest`

   You can execute the following command (I'm using Maven and RabbitMQ).

   ```
   $ curl -s -X POST \
    -d "uri=https://dataflow.spring.io/rabbitmq-maven-latest" \
    -d "force=true" \
    localhost:9393/apps | jq .
   ```

Or you can use this next one.

```
$ http -f POST \
 :9393/apps \
 uri=https://dataflow.spring.io/rabbitmq-maven-latest \
 force=true
```

Determine if the apps were registered by executing the command from the previous step.

5. There is a `jdbc` app, which means that all the movie objects are sent to this sink, and it needs to be ready to accept the incoming row. You need to set up the database. It is important to have access to the MySQL database. If you are using Kubernetes and an instance different from the one used by Data Flow or Skipper, you must add the right server name to the properties and make sure you have access to it. If you are using the Docker Compose (and the `docker-compose.yml` file from the book's source code), you can get access using the following.

   ```
   $ docker exec -it dataflow-mysql -uroot -prootpw
   ```

   You need to create the `reviews` databases and the `movies` table.

   ```
   mysql> create database reviews;
   mysql> use reviews
   mysql> create table movies(
           id varchar(10) primary key,
           title varchar(200),
           actor varchar(200),
           year int,
           genre varchar(25),
           stars int,
           rating decimal(2,1),
           ratingcount int);
   ```

6. One of the Stream apps is the `groovy-transform`. This app reaches out to an external REST API call. You use the RapidAPI (`https://rapidapi.com/`) site. Please, take a moment to open a new account (it's free); the service to use is `https://rapidapi.com/apidojo/api/imdb8`. You need to get the API key for this. The final URL you use is `https://imdb8.p.rapidapi.com/title/get-ratings?tconst=${movie.id}`, where you pass the movie's ID. Once you get your API key, write it down because you'll need it next.

7. The `groovy-transform` app needs a script to execute. This script is in your Git repository (you can use any Git server—GitHub, GitLab, BitBucket, etc.). It must be public to make things easier. Create a new repo and add the following Groovy script; name it `movie-transform.groovy` (see Listing 9-3).

Listing 9-3. movie-transform.groovy

```
import groovy.json.JsonSlurper
import groovy.json.JsonOutput

def jsonSlurper = new JsonSlurper()
def movie = jsonSlurper.parseText(new String(payload))

def connection = new URL( "https://imdb8.p.rapidapi.com/title/get-ratings?tconst=${movie.id}")
                .openConnection() as HttpURLConnection

connection.setRequestProperty( 'x-rapidapi-host', 'imdb8.p.rapidapi.com' )
connection.setRequestProperty( 'x-rapidapi-key', 'YOURKEY')
connection.setRequestProperty( 'Accept', 'application/json' )
connection.setRequestProperty( 'Content-Type', 'application/json')

if ( connection.responseCode == 200 ) {

    def imdb = connection.inputStream.withCloseable { inStream ->
        new JsonSlurper().parse( inStream as InputStream )
    }

    movie.imdb = [ "rating": imdb.rating, "ratingCount": imdb.ratingCount ]

} else {
    println connection.responseCode + ": " + connection.inputStream.text
}

JsonOutput.toJson(movie)
```

Before continuing, analyze the script. Note that it goes to the RapidAPI URL and gets information. It enhances the message by adding the `imdb` section that contains the `rating` and `ratingCount` properties. These properties are from the response to the external call. Also, note that you need to add your key in the `x-rapidapi-key` header and use the URL mentioned. It's important to access this script in a RAW format. For example, in GitHub, you can access at `https://raw.githubusercontent.com/<your-user-id>/<your-repo>/master/movie-transform.groovy`. Note this URL.

8. It is time to create the movie pipeline DSL. This is the final version you work with (see Listing 9-4).

Listing 9-4. Movie Pipeline DSL

```
movie=http --port=9001 | splitter --expression="#jsonPath(payload, '$.movies')" | groovy-transform --script="https://raw.githubusercontent.com/<user>/<repository>/master/movie-transform.groovy" | jdbc --columns="id:id,title:title,actor:actor,year:year,genre:genre,stars:stars,rating:imdb.rating,ratingcount:imdb.ratingCount" --table-name="movies" --password="rootpw" --driver-class-name="org.mariadb.jdbc.Driver" --username="root" --url="jdbc:mysql://mysql:3306/reviews?autoReconnect=true&useSSL=false"
```

```
stars=:movie.splitter > filter --expression="#jsonPath(payload,'$.stars') > 3" | log

imdb-high-rating=:movie.groovy-transform > filter --expression="#jsonPath(payload,'$.imdb.
rating') > 8.0" | log
```

This movie pipeline DSL is composed of three statements.

- `movie = http | splitter | groovy-transform | jdbc`. `movie` is the name of the stream, and it is useful in the next statements. Note that the definition uses properties like `--port` because it is looking for a local infrastructure. If you use the Kubernetes approach, you need to add a service to the `http` app with a `LoadBalancer` type to get an IP and access it. The `splitter` app splits the message into several `movie` objects based on the `movies` set. The JSON send contains a set of `movies`. The `groovy-transform` has the script property pointing to the RAW file in your Git Repository/server (Make sure it is a RAW file). Finally, it goes to the `jdbc` app that saves the enhanced movie object (JSON) from the `groovy-transform` to the `review` database and `movies` table. Look at the `--columns` property. It defines the table columns mapping the JSON result.
- `stars = :movie.splitter > filter | log`. `stars` is the name of the stream. You see this later because you call it a tap. The `:movie.splitter` is saying "create a tap in the `movie` stream and after the `splitter` app"—in other words, get a copy of the message once you do the split. You collect a copy of the `movie` object (JSON) from the set of `movies` (JSON); then, you pass that `movie` object (JSON) to the `filter` app. Note that you are using the > symbol instead of | because that's the syntax needed to tap a message. The tap is the wire tap message integration pattern implementation. The `filter` app uses a JSON expression to get the stars, and if greater than three, it passes it to the log app. The log app writes to the console.
- `imdb-high-rating = :movie.groovy-transform > filter | log`. `imdb-high-rating` is the name of the stream, and it gets a copy of the movie stream at the `groovy-transform` app, and it redirects to the `filter` that evaluates the `imdb.rating`, and it passes it to the `log` app if it's greater than 8.0. The `log` app writes to the console.

You execute three different commands, one per statement.

```
$ curl -s -X POST \
 --form 'name=movie' \
 --form 'definition=movie=http --port=9001 | splitter --expression="#jsonPath
 (payload,'\''$.movies'\'')" | groovy-transform --script=https://raw.githubuser
 content.com/<user>/<repo>/master/movie-transform.groovy | jdbc --columns=
 id:id,title:title,actor:actor,year:year,genre:genre,stars:stars,rating:imdb.
 rating,ratingcount:imdb.ratingCount --table-name=movies --password=rootpw --driver-
 class-name=org.mariadb.jdbc.Driver --username=root --url=jdbc:
 mysql://mysql:3306/reviews?autoReconnect=true&useSSL=false' \
 localhost:9393/streams/definitions | jq .

$ curl -s -X POST \
--form 'name=stars' \
--form 'definition=stars= :movie.splitter > filter --expression="#jsonPath
(payload,'\''$.stars'\'') > 3" | log' \
http://localhost:9393/streams/definitions | jq .
```

```
$ curl -s -X POST \
--form 'name=imdb-high-rating' \
--form 'definition=imdb-high-rating= :movie.groovy-transform > filter --expressio
n="#jsonPath(payload,'\''$.imdb.rating'\'') > 8.0" | log' \
http://localhost:9393/streams/definitions | jq .
```

In every command, you need the name and the `definition` parameters. Don't forget to use your own `user` and `repository` for your Git server. If you copy from this text, make sure to notice the difference between a single vs. double quote and the single quote scaped.

Remember that I am using a local Docker Compose. That's why the first DSL stream definition in the http app has the `--port=9001`, meaning that I post some a set of movies pointing to that port. If you are using Kubernetes, you don't need (you can remove that property), and then make sure you can reach the `http` app by adding a service to it with `LoadBalancer` type or forward the port.

■ **Note** In the `ch09/streams` folder in the book's companion source code, there is a file named `curl-movie-stream-pipeline` with the right characters. You can copy them or execute that file.

---

9. Verify that our definition exists by executing the following.

```
$ curl -s localhost:9393/streams/definitions | jq .
```

In this command, you see all the stream definitions: `movie`, `stars`, `imdb-high-rating`.

10. Deploy the streams. To do this, you need to execute the following commands.

```
$ curl -s -X POST \
http://localhost:9393/streams/deployments/movie | jq .

$ curl -s -X POST \
http://localhost:9393/streams/deployments/stars | jq .

$ curl -s -X POST \
http://localhost:9393/streams/deployments/imdb-high-rating | jq .
```

11. Now that the movie stream is deployed, it is time to send some data.

```
$ curl -s -X POST \
 -H "Content-Type: application/json" \
-d '{"movies":[{"id":"tt0133093","title":"The Matrix","actor":"Keanu Ree
ves","year":1999,"genre":"fiction","stars":5},{"id":"tt0209144","title":
"Memento","actor":"Guy Pearce","year":2000,"genre":"drama","stars":4},{"
id":"tt0482571","title": "The Prestige","actor":"Christian Bale","year":
2006,"genre":"drama","stars":3},{"id":"tt0486822","title":"Disturbia",
"actor":"Shia LaBeouf","year":2007,"genre":"drama","stars":3}]}' \
http://localhost:9001 | jq .
```

Note that you are sending a set of movies. If you are using Docker Compose (and docker-compose.yml from the source code), the Skipper server is where all the apps are running. To send the data, you need to enter the following in the skipper docker container.

```
$ docker exec -it skipper bash
$ curl -s -X POST ....
```

If you are using Kubernetes, you need to expose the http app or do a port forward and then do the POST.

12. Check out the logs. To see if everything worked, get the app's runtime information. Execute the following command.

```
$ curl -s localhost:9393/runtime/apps | jq .
```

This command gives you all the information about the logs (for the stars and the imdb-high-rating streams). You should find the name (deploymentId) as stars.log-v1 and imdb-high-rating.log-v1 and the stdout property. If you are using the Docker Compose (and docker-compose.yml from the book's source code), then you must go to the skipper-docker container and do a tail over the path from the stdout property.

```
$ docker exec skipper tail -n 500 -f /tmp/1590548505908/stars.log-v1/stdout_0.log
```

If you are using Kubernetes, you should see all the apps as pods, with the same naming convention; to see the logs for start-logs-v1, you should execute the following.

```
$ kubectl get pods
$ kubectl logs -f pod/star-logs-v1-xxxx
```

The xxxx is the ID added to the pod.
If you have access to the MySQL database, you should see something similar to the following.

```
mysql> select * from movies \G
*************************** 1. row ***************************
         id: tt0133093
      title: The Matrix
      actor: Keanu Reeves
       year: 1999
      genre: fiction
      stars: 5
     rating: 8.7
ratingcount: 1609934
*************************** 2. row ***************************
         id: tt0209144
      title: Memento
      actor: Guy Pearce
       year: 2000
      genre: drama
      stars: 4
     rating: 8.4
ratingcount: 1084378
```

```
*************************** 3. row ***************************
         id: tt0482571
      title: The Prestige
      actor: Christian Bale
       year: 2006
      genre: drama
      stars: 3
     rating: 8.5
ratingcount: 1136643
*************************** 4. row ***************************
         id: tt0486822
      title: Disturbia
      actor: Shia LaBeouf
       year: 2007
      genre: drama
      stars: 3
     rating: 6.8
ratingcount: 214786
```

Congratulations! You created a movie stream pipeline DSL using the REST API.

If you want to undeploy your stream, you can do it one by one using the following.

```
$ curl -s -X DELETE \
http://localhost:9393/streams/deployments/movie | jq .

$ curl -s -X DELETE \
http://localhost:9393/streams/deployments/stars | jq .

$ curl -s -X DELETE \
http://localhost:9393/streams/deployments/imdb-high-rating | jq .
```

Or all at once with the following.

```
$ curl -s -X DELETE \
http://localhost:9393/streams/deployments | jq .
```

If you want to remove the streams, you can do one at a time as follows.

```
$ curl -s -X DELETE \
http://localhost:9393/streams/definitions/movie | jq .

$ curl -s -X DELETE \
http://localhost:9393/streams/definitions/stars | jq .

$ curl -s -X DELETE \
http://localhost:9393/streams/definitions/imdb-high-rating | jq .
```

Or all at once, as follows.

```
$ curl -s -X DELETE \
http://localhost:9393/streams/definitions | jq .
```

Next, use the Spring Cloud Data Flow shell interactively and more practically to create streams.

Using Spring Cloud Data Flow Shell

There are more options to create streams, and in this section, you see the Spring Cloud Data Flow shell in action. You can see this client as an interactive text-based/terminal tool where you can do testing. First, make sure you remove any stream DSL definitions and stop/restart your Spring Cloud Data Flow server because you need to register all the apps again.

There are two options for using the Spring Cloud Data Flow shell. If you are using a local deployment for your infrastructure, such as Docker Compose (`ch09/docker-compose`), you can reuse the Spring Cloud Data Flow server. After you start your infrastructure, you can use the Data Flow shell as follows.

```
$ docker exec -it dataflow-server java -jar shell.jar
```

Your screen should look something like Figure 9-3.

Figure 9-3. *Spring Cloud Data Flow shell*

The other option is to download the Uber-JAR from `https://repo.spring.io/release/org/springframework/cloud/spring-cloud-dataflow-shell/2.6.0/spring-cloud-dataflow-shell-2.6.0.jar`. Once you download it, execute the following command.

```
$ java -jar spring-cloud-dataflow-shell-2.6.0.jar --help
```

This command shows you all the parameters that you can override (see Figure 9-4).

```
> java -jar spring-cloud-dataflow-shell-2.6.0.jar --help
Data Flow Options:
  --dataflow.uri=<uri>                              Address of the Data Flow Server [default: http://localhost:9393].
  --dataflow.username=<USER>                        Username of the Data Flow Server [no default].
  --dataflow.password=<PASSWORD>                    Password of the Data Flow Server [no default].
  --dataflow.credentials-provider-command=<COMMAND> Executes an external command which must return an
                                                    OAuth Bearer Token (Access Token prefixed with 'Bearer '),
                                                    e.g. 'Bearer 12345'), [no default].
  --dataflow.skip-ssl-validation=<true|false>       Accept any SSL certificate (even self-signed) [default: no].
  --dataflow.proxy.uri=<PROXY-URI>                  Address of an optional proxy server to use [no default].
  --dataflow.proxy.username=<PROXY-USERNAME>        Username of the proxy server (if required by proxy server) [no default].
  --dataflow.proxy.password=<PROXY-PASSWORD>        Password of the proxy server (if required by proxy server) [no default].
  --spring.shell.historySize=<SIZE>                 Default size of the shell log file [default: 3000].
  --spring.shell.commandFile=<FILE>                 Data Flow Shell executes commands read from the file(s) and then exits.
  --help                                            This message.
```

***Figure 9-4.** Spring Cloud Data Flow shell with --help parameter*

Before continuing, check out all the parameters. The Data Flow shell (client) has defaults, such as the `uri` parameter that tries to connect to `localhost:9393`.

Now execute the command again but without the `--help` parameter.

```
$ java -jar spring-cloud-dataflow-shell-2.6.0.jar
```

If you are still using Docker Compose and exposed port 9393, you have a successful connection, but if your Data Flow server is running in Kubernetes, you must have either the IP or the domain assigned to that server. Because it fails to connect to `localhost:9393`, it shows you a `server-unknown` prompt. In this case, you can use the following command.

```
server-unknown:>dataflow config server https://my-scdf-server
```

It reaches out and connects to your Data Flow server (see Figure 9-5).

```
> java -jar spring-cloud-dataflow-shell-2.6.0.jar
  ____                              ____ _                __
 / ___| _ __  _ __(_)_ __   __ _   / ___| | ___  _   _  __| |
 \___ \| '_ \| '__| | '_ \ / _` | | |   | |/ _ \| | | |/ _` |
  ___) | |_) | |  | | | | | (_| | | |___| | (_) | |_| | (_| |
 |____/| .__/|_|  |_|_| |_|\__, |  \____|_|\___/ \__,_|\__,_|
  ____ |_|    _          __|___/                 __________
 |  _ \  __ _| |_ __ _  |  ___| | _____      __  \ \ \ \ \ \
 | | | |/ _` | __/ _` | | |_  | |/ _ \ \ /\ / /   \ \ \ \ \ \
 | |_| | (_| | || (_| | |  _| | | (_) \ V  V /    / / / / / /
 |____/ \__,_|\__\__,_| |_|   |_|\___/ \_/\_/    /_/_/_/_/_/

2.6.0

Welcome to the Spring Cloud Data Flow shell. For assistance hit TAB or type "help".
WARNING - Problem connecting to the Spring Cloud Data Flow Server:
"Unable to contact Data Flow Server at 'http://localhost:9393/': 'org.springframework.web.client.ResourceAccessException: I/O error
 on GET request for "http://localhost:9393/security/info": Connect to localhost:9393 [localhost/127.0.0.1, localhost/0:0:0:0:0:0:0:
1] failed: Connection refused (Connection refused); nested exception is org.apache.http.conn.HttpHostConnectException: Connect to l
ocalhost:9393 [localhost/127.0.0.1, localhost/0:0:0:0:0:0:0:1] failed: Connection refused (Connection refused)'."
Please double check your startup parameters and either restart the Data Flow Shell (with any missing configuration including securi
ty etc.) or target the Data Flow Server using the 'dataflow config server' command.

server-unknown:>dataflow config server https://my-scdf-server
```

***Figure 9-5.** Spring Cloud Data Flow shell: server Unknown*

If you use Docker Compose, I recommend the following command to start the Data Flow shell because it is easier to send data to our `http` app.

```
$ docker exec -it dataflow-server java -jar shell.jar
```

Using the Uber-JAR requires exposing Skipper server port 9001, meaning that you need to add the `ports` property in the `docker-compose.yml` file.

The Data Flow shell exposes more than 60 commands with tab completion that allow you to view, list, create, delete, destroy, and much Uri more with streams and tasks. Spring Cloud Data Flow shell is a REST API client but with more capacity than a simple `cURL` or `Httpie` command-line utilities.

Let's start by reviewing some of the commands that you can execute from the Data Flow shell. I think one of your best friends in the Data Flow shell is the `help` command. Type **help** and hit return, and you see the 60+ commands you can execute (see Figure 9-6).

```
dataflow:>help
```

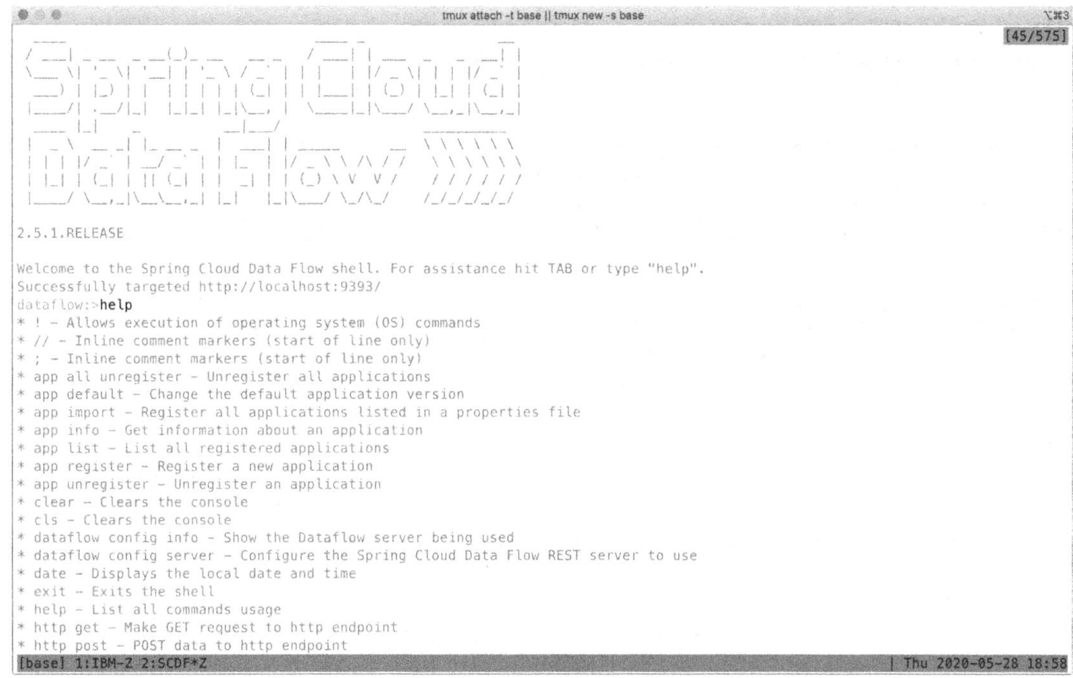

***Figure 9-6.** Spring Cloud Data Flow shell: using the help command*

You can also use the `help [command [options]]` syntax. For example, you use the `stream` command so you can do type.

```
dataflow:>help stream
```

the preceding command shows you the list of available options for the `stream` command, and you can execute:

```
dataflow:>help stream create
```

Analyze the output and note that it comes with a description of what you need to create a stream. The Data Flow shell comes with TAB completion, so you can execute, for example, the stream command and hit twice the TAB key to get the available options such as all, info, create, list, deploy, undeploy, and so forth.

When you start creating streams, you see that every command has options and these options have parameters that need to start with a double dash. For example,

```
dataflow:>stream deploy --name=movie
```

and sometimes you need to pass values in enclosed single quotes (') or double quotes (") you need to be very careful. Of course, you find that you need to scape some characters, but don't worry, get the time comes. I show you how to do it. Other rules are not covered here, but you can read about them at https://docs.spring.io/spring-cloud-dataflow/docs/current/reference/htmlsingle/#_shell_rules.

Another great benefit of the Spring Data Flow shell is the way it parses the DSL. You must choose one effective method to add your expressions and not combine them. For example, the filter app requires passing an expression parameter (as you saw earlier with the cURL/Httpie commands), and you must choose any of the following.

```
filter --expression=payload>5.0
filter --expression=#jsonPath(payload,'$.imdb.rating')>5.0
filter --expression='#jsonPath(payload,''$.imdb.rating'') > 5.0'
```

The preceding expressions use the #jsonPath that is a SpEL (Spring Expression Language) and general objects such as payload. Note the spaces and single quotes. There are no double quotes. You can still add double single quotes. Also, you can scape characters with the backslash \. You can get more sense of it here, https://docs.spring.io/spring-cloud-dataflow/docs/current/reference/htmlsingle/#_dsl_parsing_rules and here https://docs.spring.io/spring-cloud-dataflow/docs/current/reference/htmlsingle/#_spel_syntax_and_spel_literals.

Talking about properties, you can pass all the parameters using an external properties file. Normally the file can be where the JAR was executed. The parameters should not be with any single or double quote. The syntax for these properties is app.<app-name>.<parameter>=<value>. For example,

```
app.filter.expression=#jsonPath(payload, '$imdb.rating') > 5.0
```

To understand better some of these features, let's start by creating the same movie stream pipeline DSL.

13. Register the apps. In the prompt execute the following command.

    ```
    dataflow:>app import --uri https://dataflow.spring.io/rabbitmq-maven-
    latest
    ```

    Remember that you need the http, filter, jdbc, log, splitter, and groovy-transform apps. Also, you need to use one broker, in the preceding command I'm assuming you are using RabbitMQ. You can use Kafka as well. Once you import them, you can have them listed with

    ```
    dataflow:>app list
    ```

14. Create the movie streams. First, let's look at the streams with

    ```
    dataflow:>stream list
    ```

It should be empty. Next, let's add the first stream. Don't forget to change your Git server's user and repository.

```
dataflow:> stream create --name movie --definition "http --port=9001 |
splitter --expression=#jsonPath(payload,'$.movies')| groovy-
transform --script=https://raw.githubusercontent.com/<user>/<repo>/
master/movie-transform.groovy | jdbc --columns=id:id,title:title,actor:
actor,year:year,genre:genre,stars:stars,rating:imdb.rating,ratingcount:
imdb.ratingCount --table-name=movies --password=rootpw --driver-class-
name=org.mariadb.jdbc.Driver --username=root --url=jdbc:mysql://
mysql:3306/reviews?autoReconnect=true&useSSL=false"

dataflow:> stream create --name stars --definition ":movie.splitter >
filter --expression=\"#jsonPath(payload,'$.stars')>3\" | log"

dataflow:> stream create --name imdb-high-rating --definition ":movie.
groovy-transform > filter --expression=\"#jsonPath(payload,'$.imdb.
rating') > 8.0\" | log"
```

In the scaped characters, note the \". You can look at the definitions with the following.

```
dataflow:> stream list
```

There are no scaped characters in the information.

15. It's time to deploy. Execute the following commands.

```
dataflow:>stream deploy --name movie
dataflow:>stream deploy --name stars
dataflow:>stream deploy --name imdb-high-rating
```

You can look see the status using the following.

```
dataflow:> stream info --name movie
dataflow:> stream info --name stars
dataflow:> stream info --name imdb-high-rating
```

The status should be *deployed*.

16. It's time to send some data. The Spring Data Flow shell comes with a REST API client that you can use right there in the shell. The command is `http`. You can use `help http` to find out which parameters are important to send information. To send some data, you can execute the following command.

```
dataflow:> http post --target http://<change-me>:9001 --data
'{"movies":[{"id": "tt0133093","title": "The Matrix","actor":
"Keanu Reeves", "year": 1999,"genre":"fiction","stars": 5},{"id":
"tt0209144","title": "Memento","actor": "Guy Pearce","year":
2000,"genre": "drama","stars": 4},{"id": "tt0482571","title":
"The Prestige","actor": "Christian Bale","year": 2006,"genre":
"drama","stars": 3  },{"id": "tt0486822","title": "Disturbia","actor":
```

```
"Shia LaBeouf","year": 2007,"genre": "drama","stars": 3}]}'
--contentType "application/json"
```

If you look in the `http post` command, there is the `--target` parameter. This is where the `http` app is running; it cannot be `localhost`. If you are using Kubernetes, it is easy because you should expose the `http` app with a `LoadBalancer` type; but if you are using the Docker Compose (`docker-compose.yml`) from the book's source code (`ch09/docker-compose`), you need to make sure the `skipper` server is reachable; either you use the `ports` and expose `"9001:9001"` in `docker-compose.yml` (in the `skipper` service), or you can use the `docker shell.jar` that is in the `dataflow-server`. In other words, you need to know which IP was assigned to the `skipper` container.
To get the IP of the `skipper` container, you can run.

```
$ docker inspect -f '{{range .NetworkSettings.Networks}}{{.IPAddress}}
{{end}}' skipper
```

17. It's time to check the logs. To do that, you need to use the runtime apps command.

```
dataflow:>runtime apps
```

This command shows you the `name`, `status`, and some other properties such as `stdout` and `stderr`. You are interested in the `stdout` property that is showing the logs. If you are using Docker Compose, then you can execute the following command.

```
$ docker exec skipper tail -n 500 -f /tmp/1590548505908/stars.log-v1/
stdout_0.log
```

If you are using Kubernetes, it is easier; check out the pods and use the logs command.

```
$ kubectl get pods
$ kubectl logs start-log-v1-xxxx
```

18. Review the MySQL database and execute the SELECT statement.

Congratulations! You used the Spring Cloud Data Flow shell.

To remove and delete everything, you can use the same `stream` command.

```
dataflow:> stream destroy --name imdb-high-rating
dataflow:> stream destroy --name stars
dataflow:> stream destroy --name movie
```

Now, you can exit with the command exit. You can shut down your infrastructure if you want. Next, let's do this again using the dashboard.

Using the Dashboard

Even though you already know about the dashboard, now it's time to use it to deploy the movie stream pipeline DSL. For this section, it is good to start from scratch, so please stop/restart your infrastructure; either you use Docker Compose or a Kubernetes instance. If you are using Kubernetes, try to reconstruct the MySQL database so it's clean from having records of the apps and streams. Let's get started.

1. Make sure you have the Spring Cloud Data Flow and Skipper servers up and running. If you are using Kubernetes, make sure you expose the Spring Cloud Data Flow server using LoadBalancer type so you can have a physical IP address to reach out to. Also, don't forget about creating the `reviews` database and the `movies` table in the MySQL instance.

2. Open your browser and go to http://<your-ip-or-name-server>:[9393]/dashboard (see Figure 9-7).

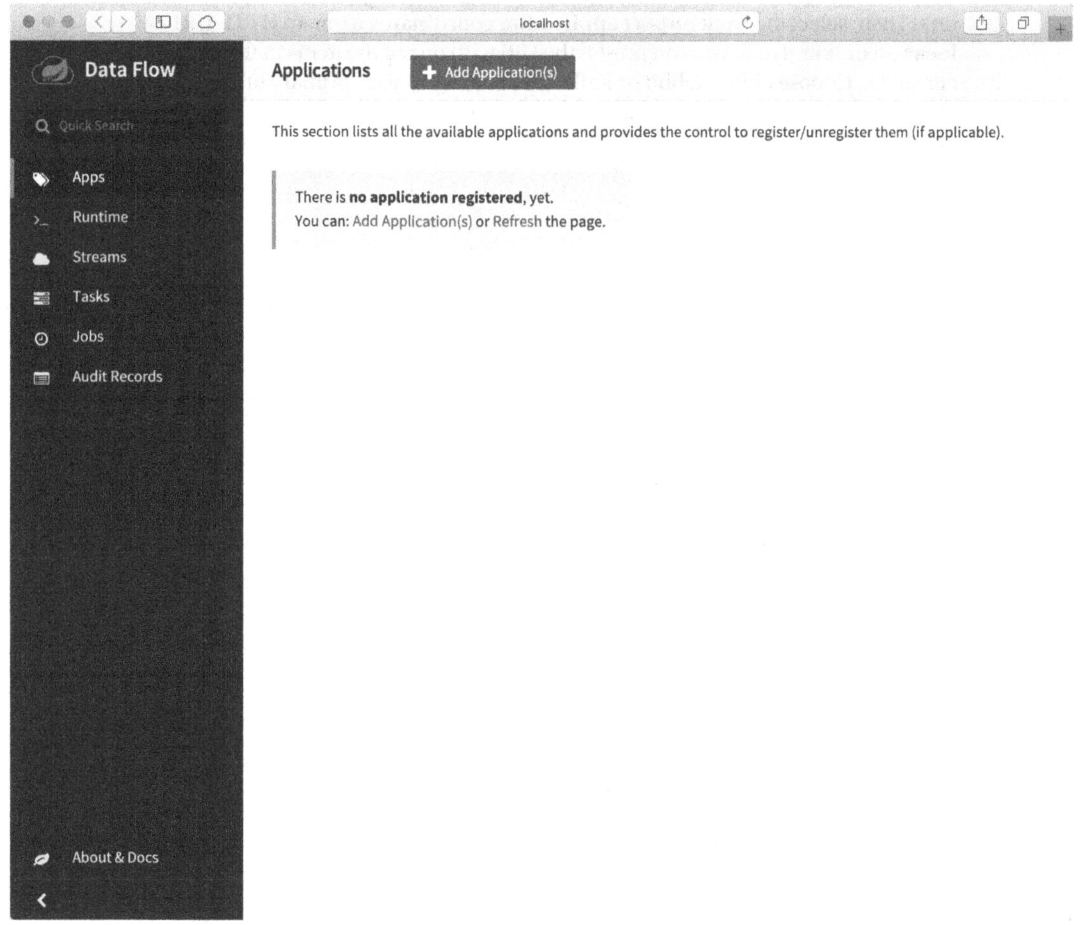

Figure 9-7. *Dashboard*

Figure 9-7 shows the dashboard. In the left pane, you find the following.

3. Apps. That's where you register all the available apps, including our own (you see this later). Remember that apps are based on the binder and either Maven or Docker coordinates.

    - Runtime (where you can see all the deployments)
    - Streams
    - Tasks
    - Jobs
    - Audit records

4. Let's register the apps. Remember that you can choose between Rabbit or Kafka and between Maven or Docker coordinates. Later on, you see how you can bring on our custom Stream apps and the NATs broker and play along with other apps.

    Click the Apps pane, and in the right pane, click the + Add Application(s) button/link. Then, select the **Bulk import application coordinates from an HTTP URI location** option. Then, you can pre-fill the URI with one of the items in the list by clicking it. Choose either Rabbit or Kafka (depending on your primary broker) and either Maven or Docker. Then you can click **Import application(s)**. This imports the apps, and it takes you to the main page. You should have something like Figure 9-8.

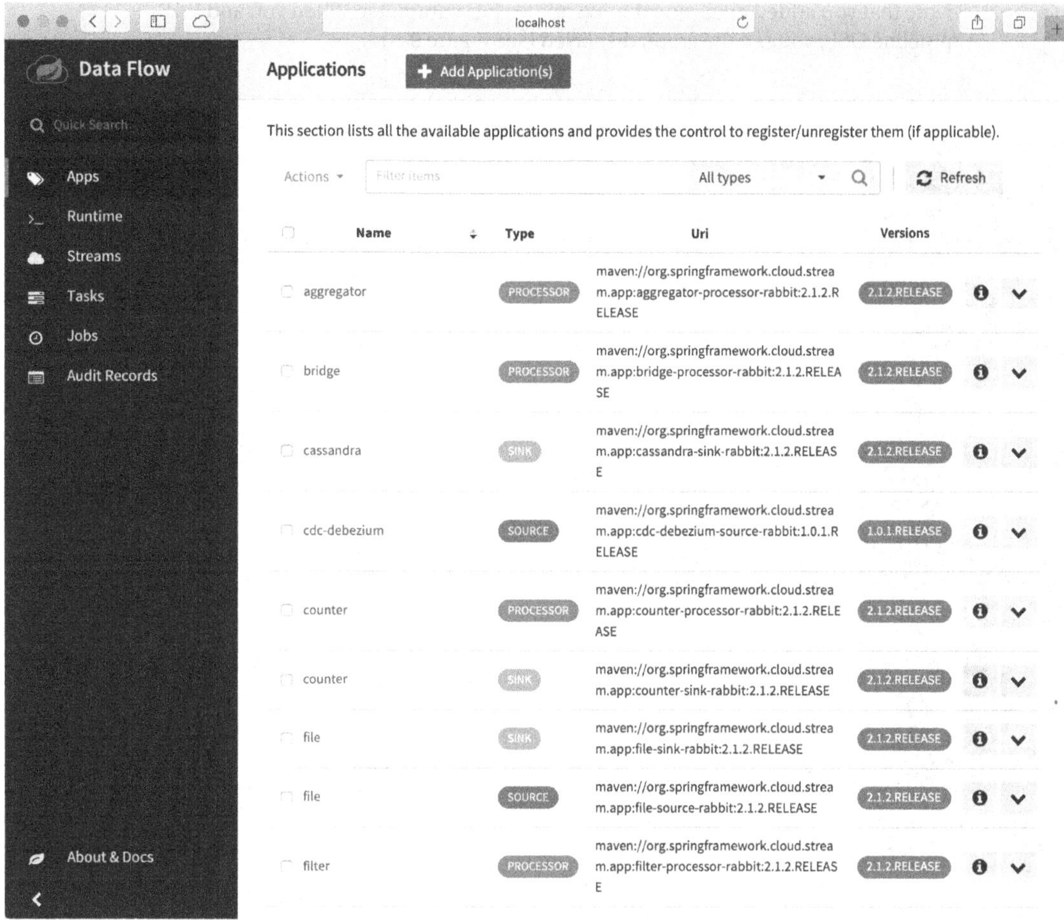

Figure 9-8. *Dashboard: Imported apps*

5. In the left pane, click the Streams option. Then in the right pane, click the + Create Stream(s) button/link . This take you to the GUI part where you can drag-n-drop apps into the canvas or you can write the DSL. To make things easier, you can add the following DSL.

```
movie=http --port=9001 | splitter --expression="#jsonPath(payload, '$.movies')"
| groovy-transform --script="https://raw.githubusercontent.com/felipeg48/scdf-
scripts/master/movie-transform.groovy" | jdbc --columns="id:id,title:title,
actor:actor,year:year,genre:genre,stars:stars,rating:imdb.rating,
ratingcount:imdb.ratingCount" --table-name="movies" --password="rootpw" --driver-
class-name="org.mariadb.jdbc.Driver" --username="root" --url="jdbc:mysql://
mysql:3306/reviews?autoReconnect=true&useSSL=false"
stars=:movie.splitter > filter --expression="#jsonPath(payload,'$.stars')
 > 3" | log
imdb-high-rating=:movie.groovy-transform > filter --expression="#jsonPa
th(payload,'$.imdb.rating') > 8.0" | log
```

Note that you added enclosing double quotes per parameter. When you add this pipeline DSL, you see the graph displayed (see Figure 9-9).

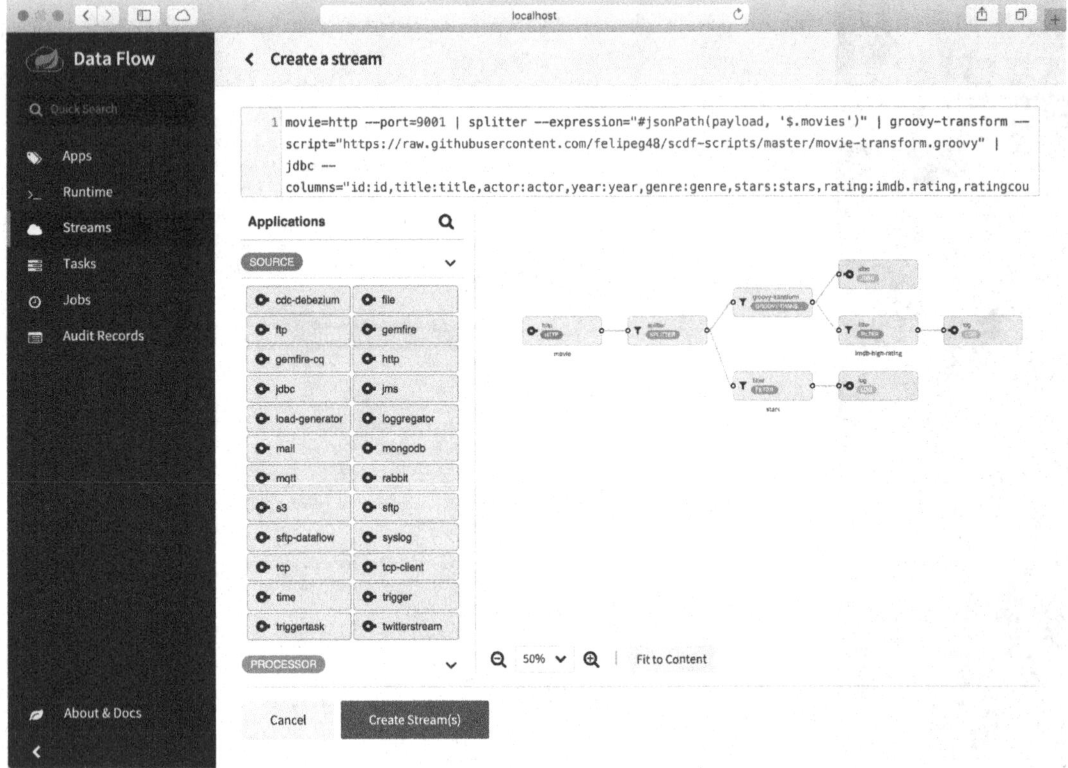

Figure 9-9. *Dashboard: Movie Pipeline DSL*

You can now play with it by removing some of the components, or in the DSL area, you can remove all the properties and have in plain sight what the DSL looks like without parameters (see Figure 9-10). movie= http | splitter | groovy-transform | jdbc

```
stars= :movie.splitter > filter | log
imdb-high-rating= :movie.groovy-transform > filter | log
```

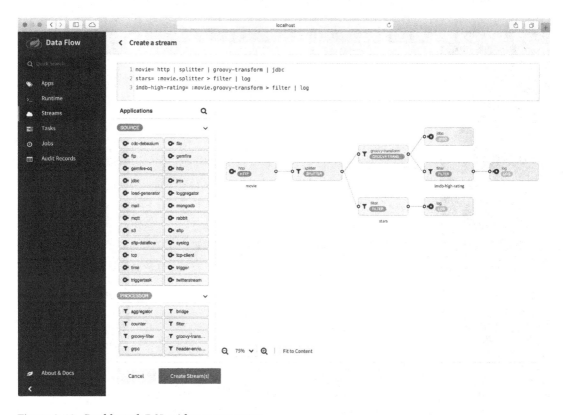

Figure 9-10. *Dashboard: DSL with no parameters*

If you want to add parameters without adding them to the DSL area because you want to avoid any double/single quote confusion, you can select any app from the graph, and it shows you the Options and Delete links. You can select Options. A pop-up window appears, where you can add the parameter value. In the case of the `http` app, you can add port value 9001 (see Figures 9-11 and 9-12).

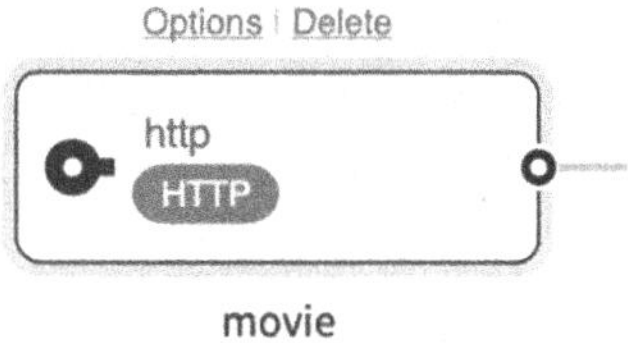

Figure 9-11. *Dashboard: http app selected*

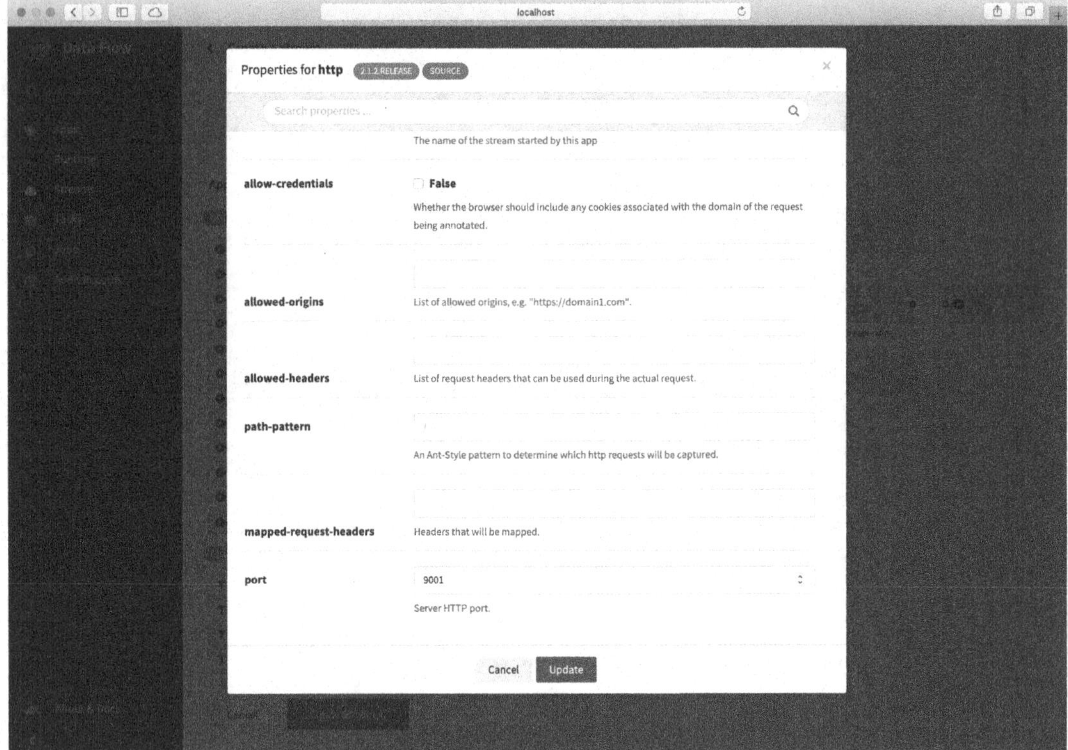

***Figure 9-12.** Dashboard: http app parameters*

If you click Update, it updates the DSL, and you see `--port=9001` in the DSL area.

6. Add the DSL where you have all the parameters set. Click the Create Stream(s) button, which opens a pop-up where you need to add any description (this is optional) and a name that by default is the one you added already into the DSL (see Figure 9-13).

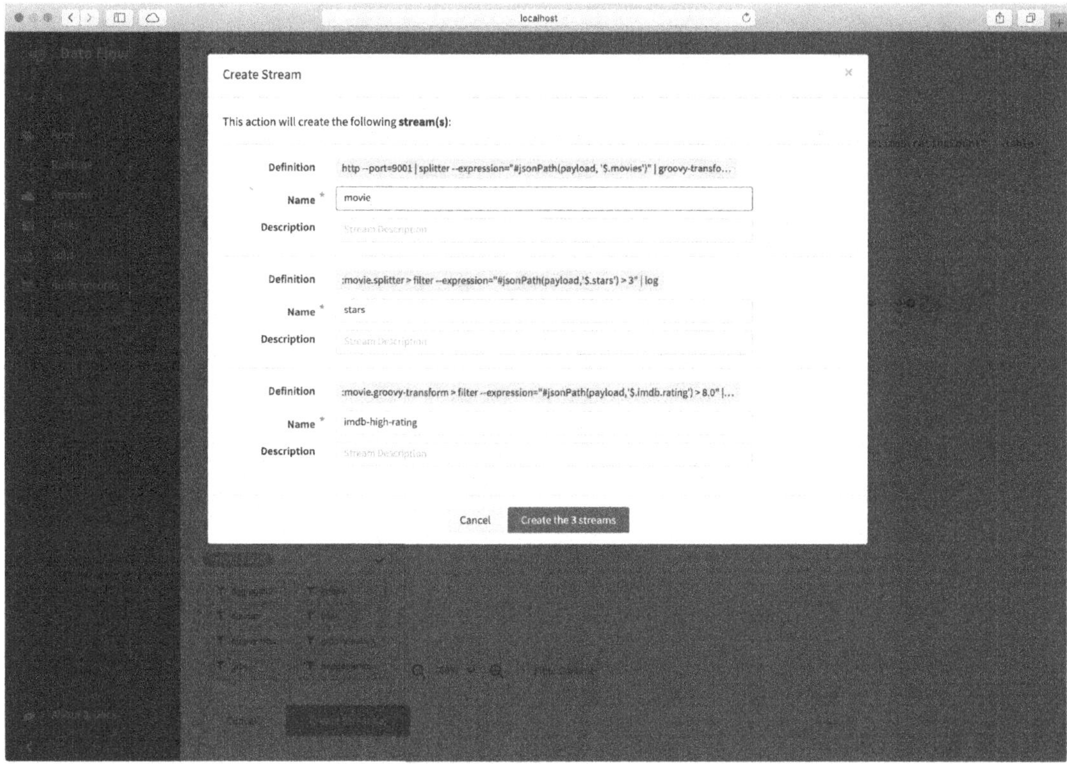

Figure 9-13. *Dashboard: Create streams*

You can click **Create the three streams**, which takes you back to where the streams are listed. In that list, you see the streams' definitions. At the end of every row are the status and three icons. The first icon shows the stream's details. The second icon (the Play icon) deploys the stream, and the last icon (a caret facing down) shows you options like Show details, Deploy, Undeploy, Destroy stream. If you click the > icon next to each stream's definition, you find a graph related to the stream (see Figures 9-14, 9-15, and 9-16).

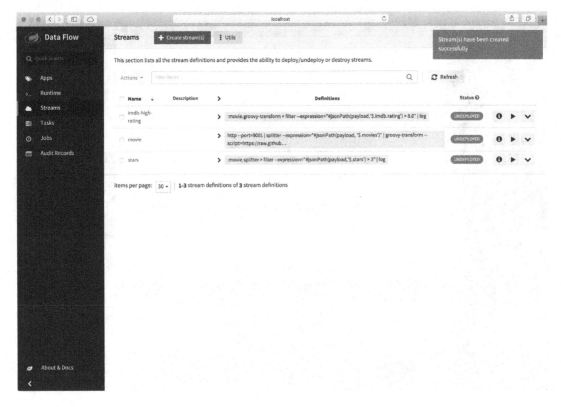

Figure 9-14. *Dashboard stream listing*

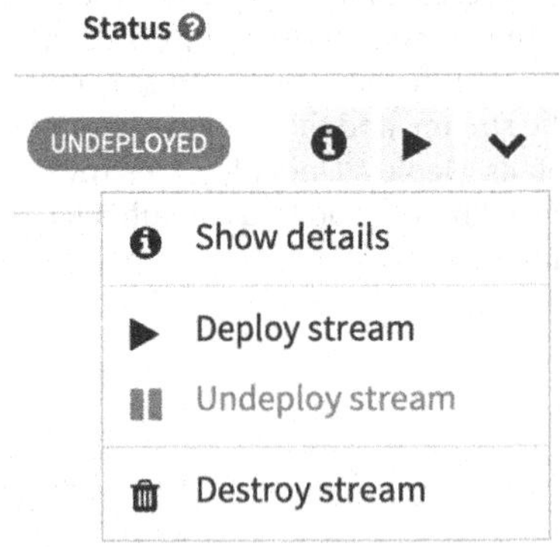

Figure 9-15. *Dashboard: Stream icons*

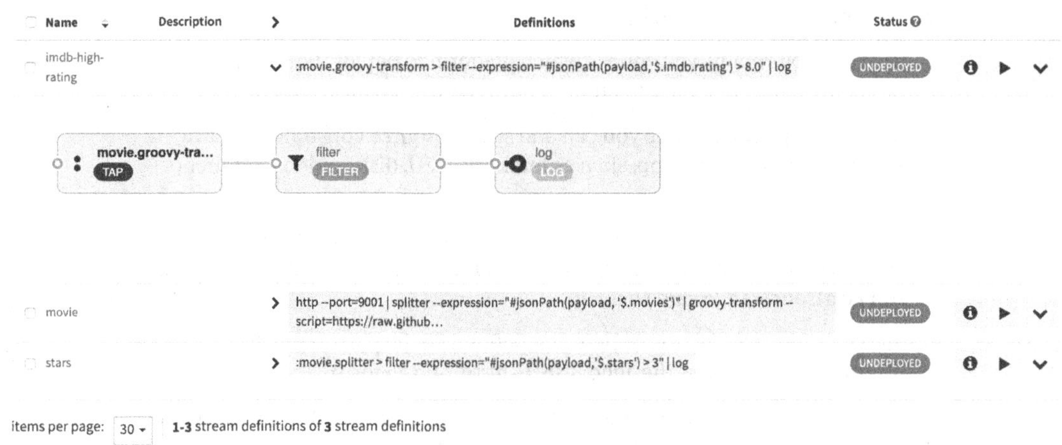

Figure 9-16. *Dashboard: Stream graph*

7. It's time to deploy one by one. You start first with the `movie` stream. Then you can select any of the other in any order. In the end, the `stars` and `imdb-high-rating` streams depend on the `movie` to start first. You can click the Play icon to deploy. When you do, another pop-up appears where there are extra settings that can help with the deployment, and there are more related to the platform where the streams are deployed. Also, you have another chance to change the existing parameters if you needed them to (see Figure 9-17).

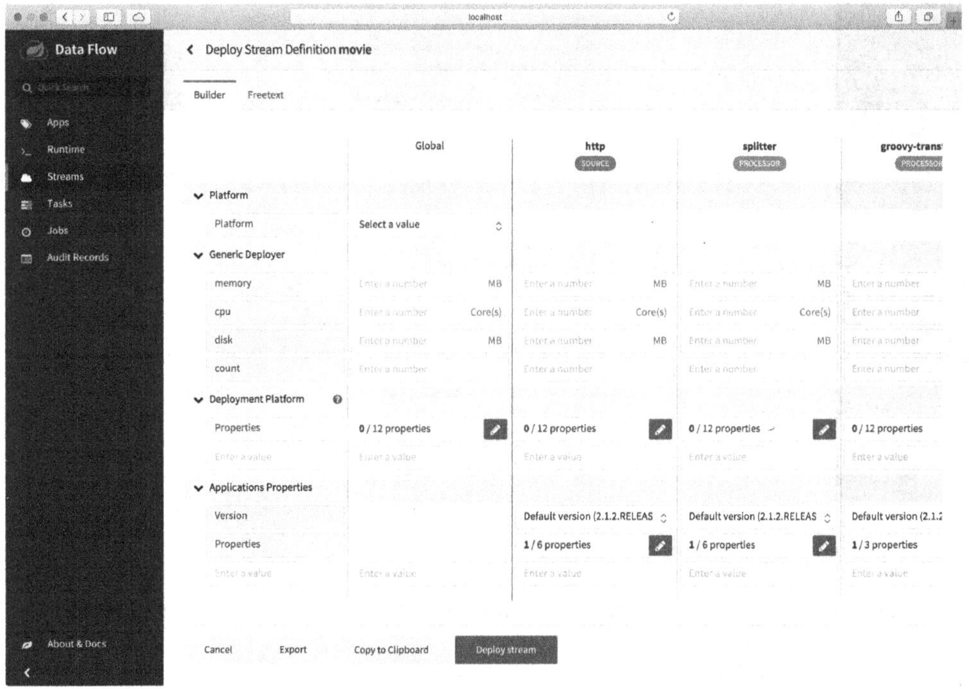

Figure 9-17. *Dashboard: Stream-deployment properties*

The parameters are separated by the following.

- `Platform`. Normally, you choose which platform to deploy, but this is a hybrid option to deploy to a Cloud Foundry, Kubernetes, or a local instance.
- `Generic deployer`. Where you can add some resource constraints to save resources for any other app, such as memory, CPU, disk, and the number of instances.
- `Deployment platform`. It is related to a Spring Cloud and the Java VM properties, such as java-opts, debug-port, java-command (a command with special flags to run java), port range, and so forth.
- `Application properties`. Where you defined all the parameters for the apps, like the `http port`, like the `jdbc table-name`, and so forth.

Note that you have the same properties for each app defined in the `movie stream`. And if you are okay with everything, click the Deploy Stream button. This takes you to the main stream list. The Status column shows that your stream is being deployed (see Figure 9-18).

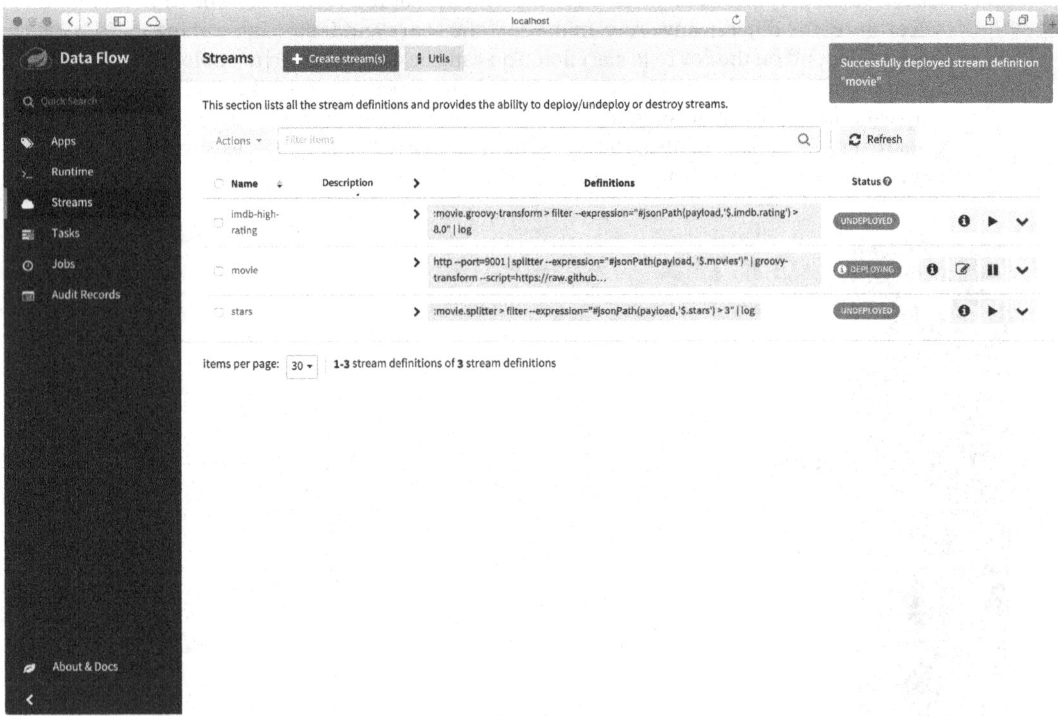

Figure 9-18. *Dashboard: Stream List-Status: Deploying*

You can repeat the same for the `stars` and `imdb-high-rating` streams (see Figure 9-19).

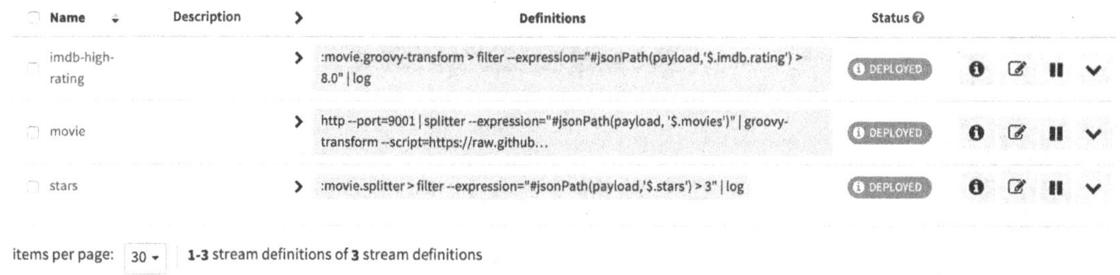

Figure 9-19. *Dashboard: Stream list*

8. Once all the streams have a Deployed status, there are several ways to see information about your app. Click `movie stream`. The information icon (i) shows the details (see Figure 9-20).

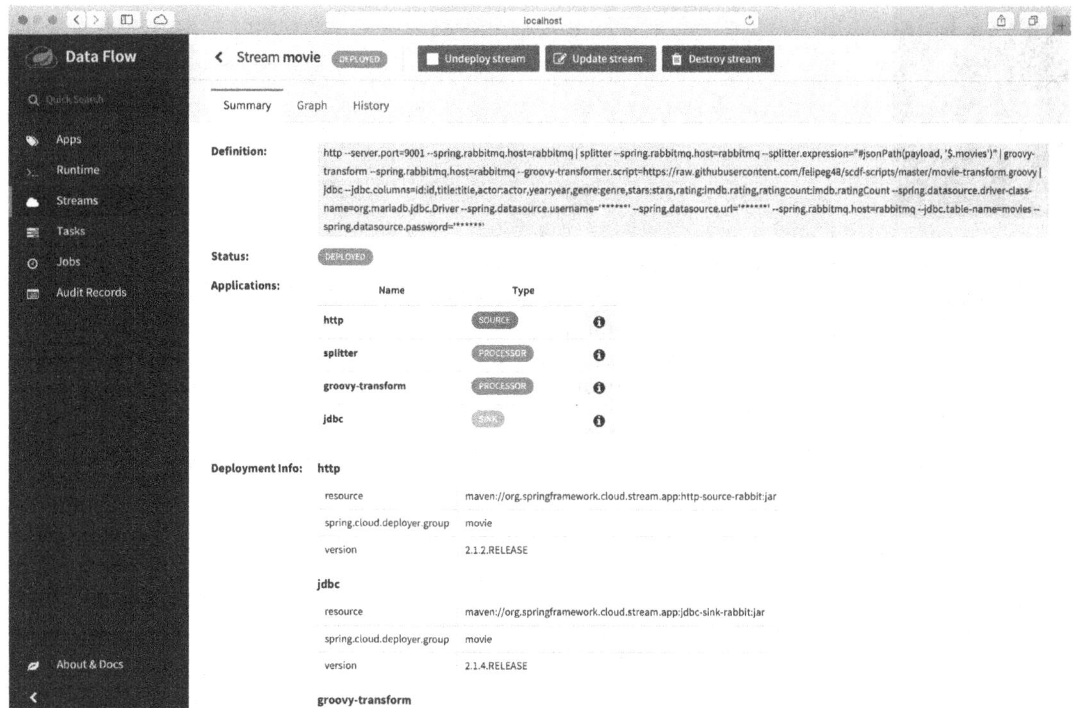

Figure 9-20. *Dashboard: Show Details-Summary-Movie Stream*

If you scroll down, you get more information about every app defined in the movie stream, and if you keep going scrolling down, you can see the logs. You have a dropdown list and choose the logs you want to see. At the top of this page, you see the Summary, Graph, and History tabs. You can check them out. The graph has the entire DSL definition, including the taps (see Figure 9-21).

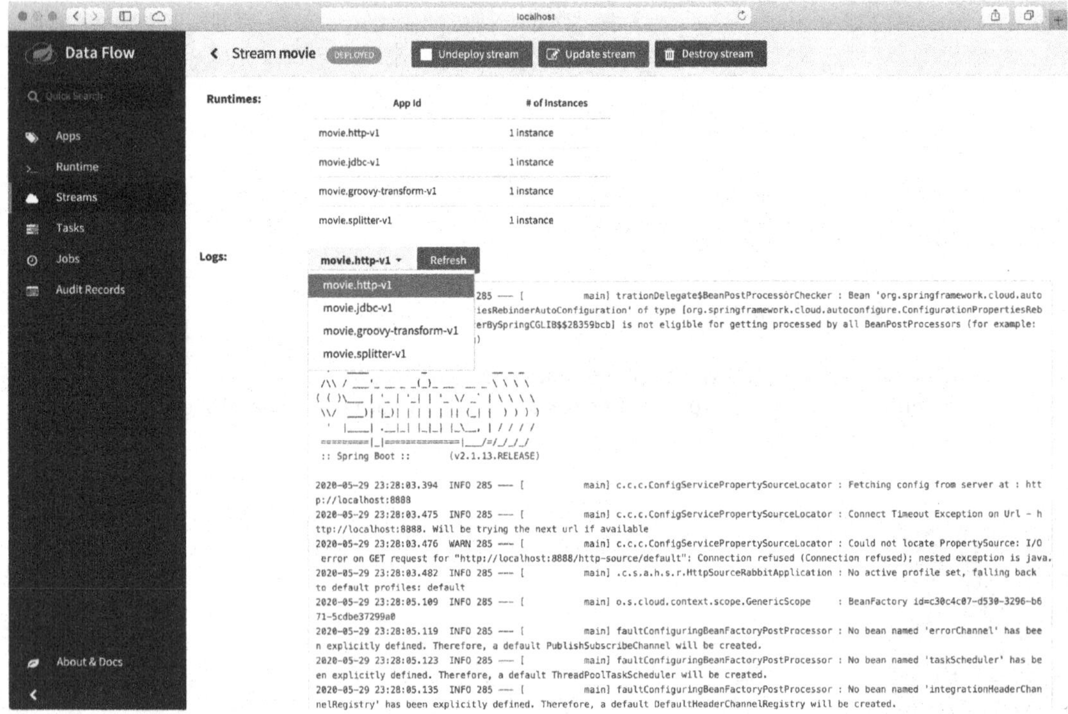

Figure 9-21. *Dashboard: Show Details-Summary-Movie Stream-Logs*

9. Another way to see more information is to get into the runtime. Click Runtime in the left pane. It shows you everything about your apps, such as process ID, port, instance name, version, and logs for `stdout` and `stderr`. You can click any of the boxes (see Figures 9-22 and 9-23).

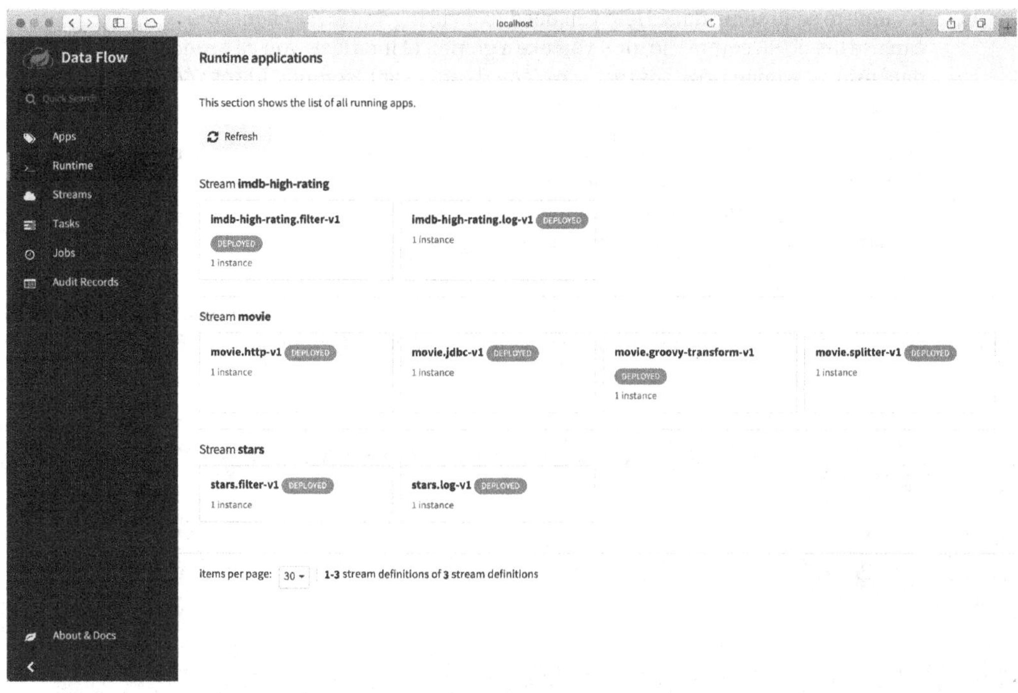

Figure 9-22. *Dashboard: Runtime-Stream apps with naming convention-<stream-name>-<app>-<version>*

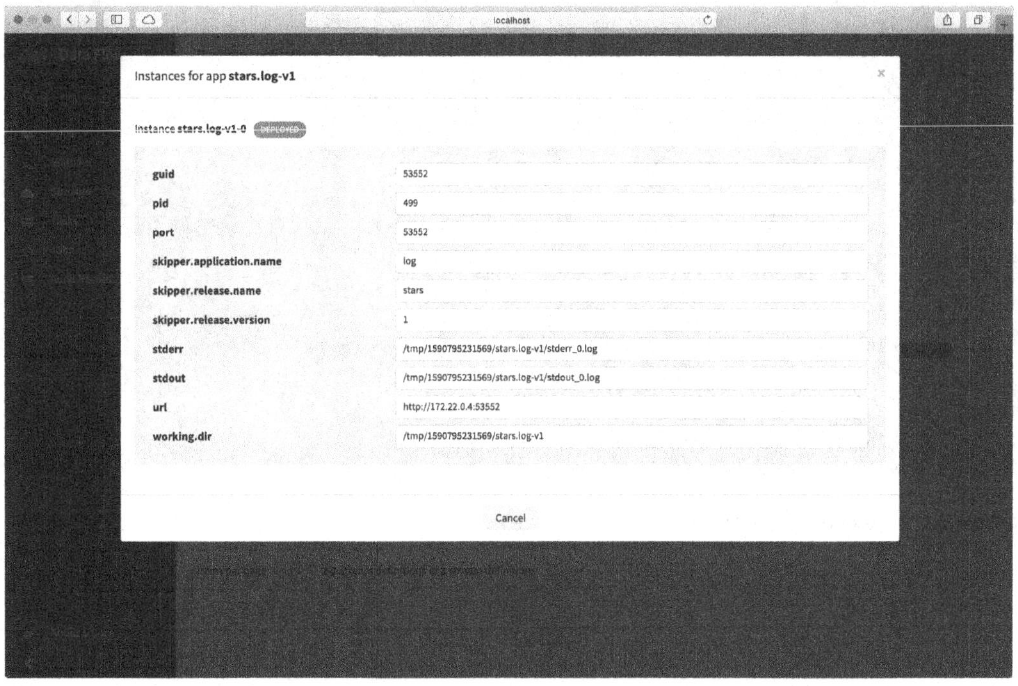

Figure 9-23. *Dashboard: Runtime-Stream App*

10. It's time to send some data. Here you need to do using any REST client. You can use the cURL command, or if you like a graphical interface, you can send data using Postman (`www.postman.com/downloads/`) or Insomnia (`https://insomnia.rest/`). You need to send the JSON data from earlier (see Listing 9-1).

11. You can go back to the stream list and click the `star` stream's details, for example. In the summary, scroll down to the logs and choose the `stars.log-v1,` and at the bottom, you should see some results about the data you just sent. You can also inspect the MySQL database to see if the records are there.

Congratulations! You have deployed the movie Stream DSL using the dashboard.

To delete the streams, go to the stream list, select the stream, click the upside-down caret, and select Destroy Stream. After prompting, if you are sure, click Destroy Streams Definitions (see Figure 9-24).

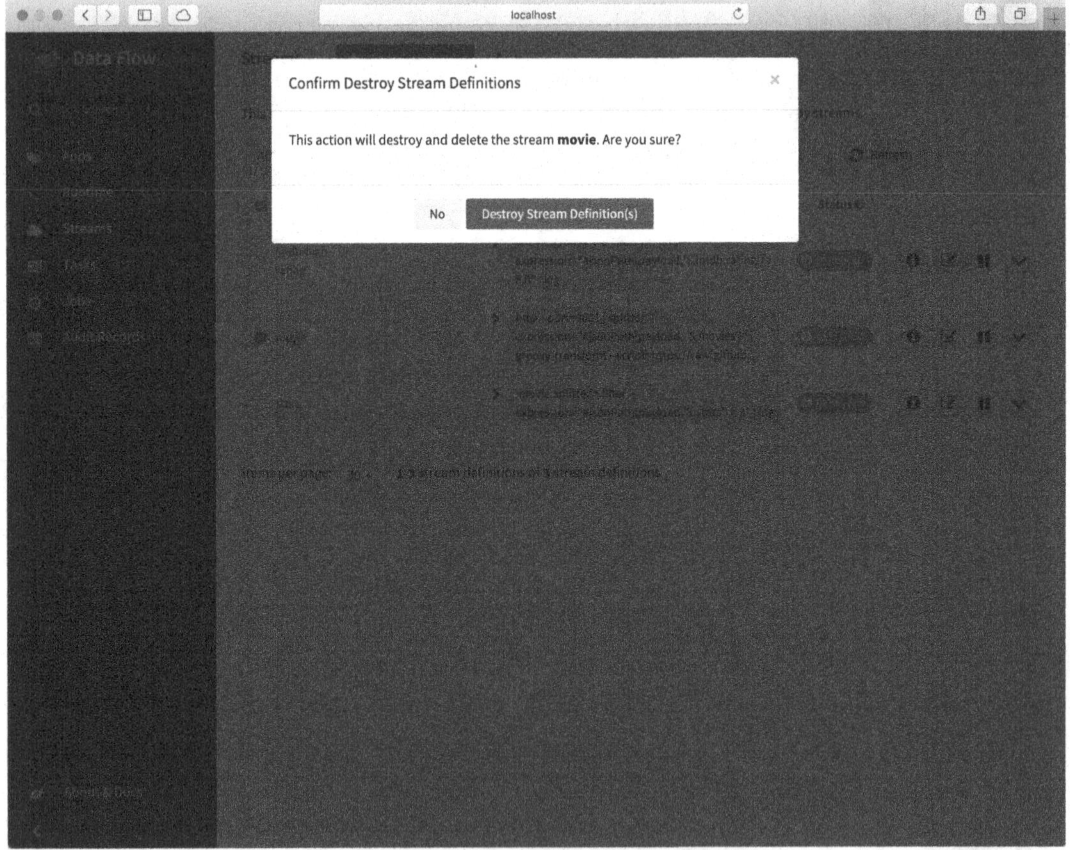

Figure 9-24. *Dashboard: Destroy Stream*

There are more features in the dashboard, which I discuss later with the tasks, jobs, and monitoring.

Creating the Stream Programmatically

An alternative to creating and deploying a stream is through Java DSL APIs exposed by Spring Cloud Data Flow modules. With this approach, you can create a dynamic way to integrate the streams' life cycle, depending on your business needs. This section shows you how to use this API and its key classes.

The Spring Cloud Data Flow API exposes two styles of Java DSL APIs.

- *Definition style.* This style allows you to use the DSL definitions that you have already deployed in previous sections. For example,

```
Stream.builder(dataFlowOperations)
  .name("simple-stream")
  .definition("http | log")
  .create();
```

- *Fluent style.* This style offers a way to create your Stream application using a fluent chain of methods, like `source.processor.sink`, to develop a more dynamic solution. For example,

```
Stream.builder(dataFlowOperations)
  .name("simple-stream")
  .source(httpSource)
  .sink(logSink)
  .create();
```

Java DSL API: Definition Style

Let's create the movie stream pipeline DSL using the Spring Cloud Data Flow Java DSL API, starting with the definition style.

12. Open your browser and point to `https://start.spring.io`. Complete the metadata with the following information.

    - Group: `com.apress.cloud.stream`
    - Artifact: `movie-dsl`
    - Package name: `com.apress.cloud.stream.movie`
    - Dependencies: Cloud Stream, Lombok

    Click the Generate button to download a ZIP. You can uncompress and import it in the IDE of your choice (see Figure 9-25).

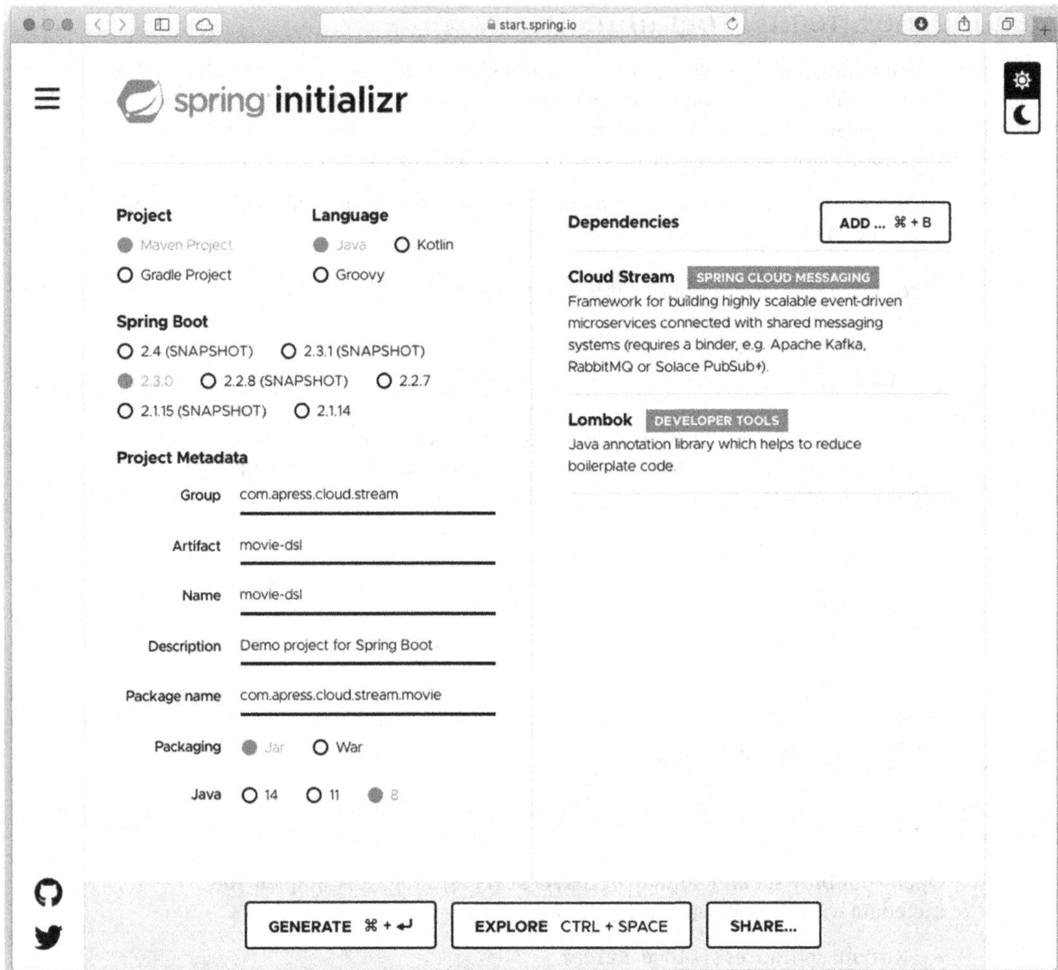

Figure 9-25. *Spring Initializr movie-dsl project*

13. Open the `pom.xml` file and add the following and required dependency.

```
<dependency>
        <groupId>org.springframework.cloud</groupId>
        <artifactId>spring-cloud-dataflow-rest-client</artifactId>
        <version>2.6.0</version>
</dependency>
```

    At the time of this book writing, the version was `2.6.0` of the `spring-cloud-rest-client` dependency. This module provides new classes, which I discuss soon.

14. Create a `MovieDslStream` enum. It holds information about the definitions and their names (see Listing 9-5).

Listing 9-5. src/main/java/com/apress/cloud/stream/movie/MovieDslStream.java

```
package com.apress.cloud.stream.movie;

public enum MovieDslStream {
    MOVIE("movie",
            "http --port=9001 | splitter --expression=\"#jsonPath(payload, '$.movies')\" | " +
            "groovy-transform --script=\"https://raw.githubusercontent.com/felipeg48/scdf-
            scripts/master/movie-transform.groovy\" | " +
            "jdbc --columns=\"id:id,title:title,actor:actor,year:year,genre:genre,stars:star
            s,rating:imdb.rating,ratingcount:imdb.ratingCount\" " +
            "--table-name=\"movies\" --password=\"rootpw\" --driver-class-name=\"org.
            mariadb.jdbc.Driver\" --username=\"root\" " +
            "--url=\"jdbc:mysql://mysql:3306/reviews?autoReconnect=true&useSSL=false\""),
    STARS("stars",":movie.splitter > filter --expression=\"#jsonPath(payload,'$.stars') >
    3\" | log"),
    IMDB("imdb-high-rating",":movie.groovy-transform > filter --expression=\"#jsonPath(paylo
    ad,'$.imdb.rating') > 8.0\" | log");

    private String name;
    private String definition;

    MovieDslStream(String name, String definition){
        this.name = name;
        this.definition = definition;
    }

    public String getName(){
        return this.name;
    }
    public String getDefinition() {
        return this.definition;
    }
}
```

Listing 9-5 shows the `MOVIE`, `STARS`, `IMDB` enum types and their two values: the name (`getName()` method) and the `definition` (`getDefinition()` method).

15. Create the `MovieDslProperties` that holds one field (see Listing 9-6).

Listing 9-6. src/main/java/com/apress/cloud/stream/movie/MovieDslProperties.java

```
package com.apress.cloud.stream.movie;

import lombok.Data;
import org.springframework.boot.context.properties.ConfigurationProperties;

@Data
@ConfigurationProperties(prefix = "movie")
public class MovieDslProperties {
    private String action = "create"; // create | deploy | destroy
}
```

This class holds an action that can be `create`, `deploy`, or `destroy`. It calls the right method to execute and create, deploy, or destroy the stream. Even though it is only one property, you can add more behavior to react to some values.

16. Create the `MovieDslService` (see Listing 9-7).

Listing 9-7. src/main/java/com/apress/cloud/stream/movie/MovieDslService.java

```
package com.apress.cloud.stream.movie;

import lombok.AllArgsConstructor;
import org.springframework.cloud.dataflow.rest.client.DataFlowOperations;
import org.springframework.cloud.dataflow.rest.client.dsl.DeploymentPropertiesBuilder;
import org.springframework.cloud.dataflow.rest.client.dsl.Stream;

@AllArgsConstructor
public class MovieDslService {

    private DataFlowOperations dataFlowOperations;

    public void create(){
        java.util.stream.Stream.of(MovieDslStream.values()).forEach( c -> {
            createStream(c.getName(),c.getDefinition());
        });
    }

    public void deploy(){
        java.util.stream.Stream.of(MovieDslStream.values()).forEach( c -> {
            deployStream(c.getName());
        });
    }

    public void destroy(){
        java.util.stream.Stream.of(MovieDslStream.values()).forEach( c -> {
            destroyStream(c.getName());
        });
    }

    private void createStream(String name, String definition){
        Stream.builder(dataFlowOperations)
                .name(name)
                .definition(definition)
                .create();
    }

    private void deployStream(String name){
        dataFlowOperations.streamOperations().deploy(name,
                new DeploymentPropertiesBuilder().build());
    }
```

```
    private void destroyStream(String name){
        dataFlowOperations.streamOperations().destroy(name);
    }
}
```

Listing 9-7 shows the definition style. The `createStream` method uses the `Stream` class with a fluent API, and in this case, you are using the definition method to create, deploy, or destroy. In this case, you are creating the DSL by using a definition. Note that you have a `DataFlowOperations` interface. The `DataFlowTemplate` class implements this interface. The `DataFlowTemplate` class is based on the template pattern and interacts with the Spring Cloud Data Flow server REST API. Look at the other methods, and you see that this is very simple and straightforward. Note that the `create`, `deploy` and `destroy` methods are iterating the `MovieDslStream` enum and using the `getName()` and `getDefinition()` to get the values.

17. Create the `MovieDslConfiguration` class that wires up all the necessary Spring beans (see Listing 9-8).

Listing 9-8. src/main/java/com/apress/cloud/stream/movie/MovieDslConfiguration.java

```
package com.apress.cloud.stream.movie;

import org.springframework.boot.CommandLineRunner;
import org.springframework.boot.context.properties.EnableConfigurationProperties;
import org.springframework.cloud.dataflow.rest.client.DataFlowOperations;
import org.springframework.cloud.dataflow.rest.client.DataFlowTemplate;
import org.springframework.context.annotation.Bean;
import org.springframework.context.annotation.Configuration;

import java.lang.reflect.Method;
import java.net.URI;

@EnableConfigurationProperties(MovieDslProperties.class)
@Configuration
public class MovieDslConfiguration {

    @Bean
    public DataFlowOperations dataFlowOperations(){

        URI dataFlowUri = URI.create("http://localhost:9393");
        DataFlowOperations dataFlowOperations = new DataFlowTemplate(dataFlowUri);
        dataFlowOperations.appRegistryOperations().importFromResource(
                "https://dataflow.spring.io/rabbitmq-maven-latest", true);

        return dataFlowOperations;
    }

    @Bean
    public CommandLineRunner actions(MovieDslService movieDslService, MovieDslProperties
    movieDslProperties){
        return args -> {
            Method method = movieDslService.getClass()
```

```
                .getMethod(movieDslProperties.getAction(),null);

            assert method != null;
            method.invoke(movieDslService,null);
        };
    }

    @Bean
    public MovieDslService movieDslService(DataFlowOperations dataFlowOperations){
        return new MovieDslService(dataFlowOperations);
    }

}
```

Listing 9-8 shows the configuration that you use. Let's analyze it.

- `dataflowOperations`. This method creates an instance of the `DataFlowOperations` interface, in this base using the `DataFlowTemplate` class; this class points to the Data Flow server REST API (http://localhost:9393 in this case). Also it's importing the apps using the `rabbitmq-maven-latest` URI.
- `movieDslService`. This declaration creates the Spring Bean `movieDslService` passing the `DataFlowOperations` interface.
- `actions`. This method is executed when the Spring Application Container is ready to execute the program. This method has the `movieDSL` and `movieDslProperties` parameters. Note that you are using the Java Reflection API to execute the MovieDslService methods, a small implementation of a Command pattern based on the properties given: create, deploy, or destroy.

18. Add the following content to the `application.properties` file.

```
## Movie properties
# action = create, deploy, destroy
movie.action=create
```

You can use create, deploy, or destroy when you run the program.

19. Before running this project, you need to make sure you have your infrastructure running using either Docker Compose or Kubernetes. Also make sure you re-create the database where the movies are saved.

20. Run your project. When it is finished, you can look at the `/dashboard` path in your browser and see that the apps are registered, and the three movie DSL streams are created (if you go to the Stream section in your browser).

21. Change the `movie.action` property to deploy and run the App. Your pipeline DSL has been deployed. And you can send a movie set with the following.

```
curl -s -X POST \
-H "Content-Type: application/json" \
-d '{"movies":[{"id":"tt0133093","title":"The Matrix","actor":"Keanu
Reeves","year":1999,"genre":"fiction","stars":5},{"id":"tt0209144",
"title":"Memento","actor":"Guy Pearce","year":2000,"genre":"drama",
```

```
"stars":4},{"id":"tt0482571","title": "The Prestige","actor":
"Christian Bale","year":2006,"genre":"drama","stars":3},{"id":
"tt0486822","title":"Disturbia","actor":"Shia LaBeouf","year":2007,
"genre":"drama","stars":3}]}' \
http://localhost:9001
```

Change the address according to your deployment (Docker Compose or Kubernetes). Next, look at the logs and database (refer to the previous sections).

22. After the run, deploy, and review the logs and database. You can change the `movie.action` property to `destroy`, run the project, and see your DSL being removed in the dashboard.

Congratulations! You have programmatically created, deployed, and destroyed a movie stream pipeline DSL using the Java DSL definition style.

Java DSL API: Fluent Style

This section covers the Java DSL fluent style.

23. You can create another project using the following metadata.
    - Group: `com.apress.cloud.stream`
    - Artifact: `movie-dsl-fluent`
    - Package name: `com.apress.cloud.stream.movie`
    - Dependencies: Cloud Stream, Lombok
24. Click the Generate button to download a ZIP file. Uncompress and import it into your favorite IDE.
25. You can copy the `MovieDslStream` enum and the `MovieDslProerties` classes, and the `application.properties` file, you reuse them.
26. Create the `MovieDslService` class (see Listing 9-9).

Listing 9-9. src/main/java/com/apress/cloud/stream/movie/MovieDslService.java

```java
package com.apress.cloud.stream.movie;

import lombok.AllArgsConstructor;
import org.springframework.cloud.dataflow.rest.client.DataFlowOperations;
import org.springframework.cloud.dataflow.rest.client.dsl.DeploymentPropertiesBuilder;
import org.springframework.cloud.dataflow.rest.client.dsl.Stream;
import org.springframework.cloud.dataflow.rest.client.dsl.StreamApplication;
import org.springframework.cloud.dataflow.rest.client.dsl.StreamBuilder;

@AllArgsConstructor
public class MovieDslService {

    private DataFlowOperations dataFlowOperations;
    private StreamApplication httpSource;
    private StreamApplication splitterProcessor;
    private StreamApplication groovyTransformProcessor;
```

```
    private StreamApplication jdbcSink;

    public void create(){
        createFluentStream(MovieDslStream.MOVIE.getName());
        java.util.stream.Stream.of(MovieDslStream.values()).filter(c -> !c.getName().
        equals(MovieDslStream.MOVIE.getName())).forEach( c -> {
            createStream(c.getName(),c.getDefinition());
        });
    }

    public void deploy(){
        java.util.stream.Stream.of(MovieDslStream.values()).forEach( c -> {
            deployStream(c.getName());
        });
    }

    public void destroy(){
        java.util.stream.Stream.of(MovieDslStream.values()).forEach( c -> {
            destroyStream(c.getName());
        });
    }

    private void createFluentStream(String name){
        Stream.builder(dataFlowOperations)
                .name(name)
                .source(httpSource)
                .processor(splitterProcessor)
                .processor(groovyTransformProcessor)
                .sink(jdbcSink)
                .create();
    }

    private void createStream(String name, String definition){
        Stream.builder(dataFlowOperations)
                .name(name)
                .definition(definition)
                .create();
    }

    private void deployStream(String name){
        dataFlowOperations.streamOperations().deploy(name,new DeploymentPropertiesBuilder().
        build());
    }

    private void destroyStream(String name){
        dataFlowOperations.streamOperations().destroy(name);
    }
}
```

Listing 9-9 shows the `MovieDslService` class. The important part here is the `createFluentStream` method; note that you are not using the definition. You can use the source, processor, or sink method.

27. Create the `MovieDslConfiguration` class (see Listing 9-10).

Listing 9-10. src/main/java/com/apress/cloud/stream/movie/MovieDslConfiguration.java

```
package com.apress.cloud.stream.movie;

import org.springframework.boot.CommandLineRunner;
import org.springframework.boot.context.properties.EnableConfigurationProperties;
import org.springframework.cloud.dataflow.core.ApplicationType;
import org.springframework.cloud.dataflow.rest.client.DataFlowOperations;
import org.springframework.cloud.dataflow.rest.client.DataFlowTemplate;
import org.springframework.cloud.dataflow.rest.client.dsl.StreamApplication;
import org.springframework.context.annotation.Bean;
import org.springframework.context.annotation.Configuration;

import java.lang.reflect.Method;
import java.net.URI;

@EnableConfigurationProperties(MovieDslProperties.class)
@Configuration
public class MovieDslConfiguration {

    @Bean
    public CommandLineRunner actions(MovieDslService movieDslService, MovieDslProperties
    movieDslProperties){
        return args -> {
            Method method = movieDslService.getClass()
                    .getMethod(movieDslProperties.getAction(),null);

            assert method != null;
            method.invoke(movieDslService,null);
        };
    }

    @Bean
    public MovieDslService movieDslService(DataFlowOperations dataFlowOperations,
                                           StreamApplication httpSource,StreamApplication
                                           splitterProcessor,StreamApplication
                                           groovyTransformProcessor,
                                           StreamApplication jdbcSink, StreamApplication
                                           logSink){
        return new MovieDslService(dataFlowOperations,httpSource,splitterProcessor,groovyTra
        nsformProcessor,jdbcSink);
    }
```

```
@Bean
public DataFlowOperations dataFlowOperations(){

    URI dataFlowUri = URI.create("http://localhost:9393");
    DataFlowOperations dataFlowOperations = new DataFlowTemplate(dataFlowUri);

    dataFlowOperations.appRegistryOperations().register("http", ApplicationType.source,
            "maven://org.springframework.cloud.stream.app:http-source-
            rabbit:2.1.4.RELEASE",
            "maven://org.springframework.cloud.stream.app:http-source-rabbit:jar:metada
            ta:2.1.4.RELEASE",
            true);
    dataFlowOperations.appRegistryOperations().register("splitter", ApplicationType.
    processor,
            "maven://org.springframework.cloud.stream.app:splitter-processor-
            rabbit:2.1.3.RELEASE",
            "maven://org.springframework.cloud.stream.app:splitter-processor-rabbit:jar:
            metadata:2.1.3.RELEASE",
            true);
    dataFlowOperations.appRegistryOperations().register("groovy-transform",
    ApplicationType.processor,
            "maven://org.springframework.cloud.stream.app:groovy-transform-processor-
            rabbit:2.1.3.RELEASE",
            "maven://org.springframework.cloud.stream.app:groovy-transform-processor-rab
            bit:jar:metadata:2.1.3.RELEASE",
            true);
    dataFlowOperations.appRegistryOperations().register("filter", ApplicationType.
    processor,
            "maven://org.springframework.cloud.stream.app:filter-processor-
            rabbit:2.1.3.RELEASE",
            "maven://org.springframework.cloud.stream.app:filter-processor-rabbit:jar:me
            tadata:2.1.3.RELEASE",
            true);
    dataFlowOperations.appRegistryOperations().register("jdbc", ApplicationType.sink,
            "maven://org.springframework.cloud.stream.app:jdbc-sink-
            rabbit:2.1.6.RELEASE",
            "maven://org.springframework.cloud.stream.app:jdbc-sink-rabbit:jar:metadata
            :2.1.6.RELEASE",
            true);
    dataFlowOperations.appRegistryOperations().register("log", ApplicationType.sink,
            "maven://org.springframework.cloud.stream.app:log-sink-
            rabbit:2.1.4.RELEASE",
            "maven://org.springframework.cloud.stream.app:log-sink-rabbit:jar:metadata:
            2.1.4.RELEASE",
            true);

    return dataFlowOperations;
}
```

```
    @Bean
    public StreamApplication httpSource(){
        return new StreamApplication("http")
                .addProperty("port",9001);
    }

    @Bean
    public StreamApplication splitterProcessor(){
        return new StreamApplication("splitter")
                .addProperty("expression","\"#jsonPath(payload,'$.movies')\"");
    }

    @Bean
    public StreamApplication groovyTransformProcessor(){
        return new StreamApplication("groovy-transform")
                .addProperty("script","\"https://raw.githubusercontent.com/felipeg48/scdf-
                 scripts/master/movie-transform.groovy\"");
    }

    @Bean
    public StreamApplication jdbcSink(){
        return new StreamApplication("jdbc")
                .addProperty("columns","\"id:id,title:title,actor:actor,year:year,genre:
                genre,stars:stars,rating:imdb.rating,ratingcount:imdb.ratingCount\"")
                .addProperty("table-name","\"movies\"")
                .addProperty("username","\"root\"")
                .addProperty("password","\"rootpw\"")
                .addProperty("driver-class-name","\"org.mariadb.jdbc.Driver\"")
                .addProperty("url","\"jdbc:mysql://mysql:3306/reviews?autoReconnect=true&
                useSSL=false\"");
    }
}
```

Listing 9-10 shows the MovieDslConfiguration class. Take a moment to analyze it and see what the difference is. Note that in this class, I used older versions. You can fix this and use the latest. You should be fine.

In this class, you find that the `DataFlowOperations` register only the applications you use; this is another alternative instead of the whole. Note that you are using in the registration the `name`, `ApplicationType`, and the `maven` coordinates. Also, check out the `StreamApplication` beans that create the source, processor, and sink, and the usage of the `addProperty` method that defines the parameters passed to the application.

28. You can run the project and send some data.

I know that this project could be in only one, but I wanted to have this separated it from the other, so you have a clear picture of what style to choose.

Congratulations! You created a movie stream pipeline DSL using a fluent style.

■ **Note** Remember that all the code is on the Apress web site in the `ch09` folder.

Summary

This chapter covered Spring Cloud Data Flow components and explained how to deploy streams. I showed you the different ways you can create streams, from command-line utilities to creating a dynamic stream using the Java DSL.

The next chapter discusses stream processing, and you add your own NATs broker. You see Spring Cloud Task and learn how it creates batch processing. You can consider the next chapter a continuation of this one.

CHAPTER 10

Custom Stream Apps with Spring Cloud Data Flow

In the previous chapter, I showed you the Spring Cloud Data Flow components and how they work together to create a stream solution for processing data. I showed you how to create streams using simple cURL commands by pointing to the Spring Cloud Data Flow server that exposes a REST API. I showed you how a Data Flow shell works by creating, deploying, and destroying streams. I discussed how to programmatically create dynamic solutions by using Java DSL for creating stream definitions. And, I said that you could run the same streams in any cloud platform, such as Kubernetes, and take advantage of high availability and load balancing, among other features.

This chapter uses custom Stream apps and explains how to plug them into Stream definitions. You are using a custom NATs binder. First, let's review some concepts.

Custom Stream Apps: A Quick Review

A stream is defined as processing data without interaction or interruption, which is useful for near real-time use-cases, such as predictive analysis, credit card fraud detection, spam, business intelligence, and if you plug into these streams with machine learning processes, then you have a very robust solution.

Spring Cloud Stream offers a solution of using streams as separated applications that are normally event-driven and can be connected through any messaging middleware. By connecting these apps, you can create a runtime environment that consists of a streaming data pipeline, which can be either linear or non-linear, depending on your business logic. With Spring Cloud Stream, you can use any middleware that suits your infrastructure; you don't need to learn a specific API to send or receive messages from one app to another. You can use any binder from the community or the ones supported by the Spring Cloud Stream team, like RabbitMQ and Kafka. In this chapter, you use a custom broker from past chapters. Spring Cloud Data Flow and its components act as an orchestrator that creates, deploys, updates, and destroys complex streams using any cloud platform infrastructure.

In this chapter, you create a custom stream and use a custom binder, so you need to remember some of the key points of creating custom Spring Cloud Stream apps.

- You need to choose the type of stream you are creating: a source, processor, sink, or task. (Task apps are discussed in the next chapter.)
- You need to choose the `spring-cloud-stream` dependency. If you are using a broker supported by the Spring Cloud Stream team, you add `spring-cloud-stream-binder-rabbit` (for RabbitMQ) or `spring-cloud-stream-binder-kafka-streams` (for Kafka dependencies).

F. Gutierrez, *Spring Cloud Data Flow*, https://doi.org/10.1007/978-1-4842-1239-4_10

- You can choose from different programming styles. You can use `@EnableBinding` (<Stream type class: `Source`, `Processor`, `Sink`), `@StreamListener` (for receiving messages), `@SendTo` (for reply/response, normally a `Processor` make use of this), or you can do functional programming and use the `Supplier`, `Function`, or `Consumer` interfaces from the `java.util.function` Java package and Project Reactor with `Mono` or `Flux` interfaces.
- You need to configure all the Stream app *input* and *output*, also known as *destinations*; and any other properties that you need.

Remember that the Spring Cloud Stream team created stand-alone and out-of-the-box Stream apps that you can use for creating stream data pipelines solutions.

Now that you have recalled all of this, it's time to create custom Stream applications, use a custom NATs binder, and use the Spring Cloud Data Flow dashboard or Data Flow shell to orchestrate a pipeline DSL.

Custom Stream Apps in Spring Cloud Data Flow

Everything in this section uses Docker Compose technology for a local environment, but if you already have the Spring Cloud Data Flow components running in your own Kubernetes cluster, by all means, you can use it to create, update, and deploy your stream data pipeline.

Let's define the final pipeline (see Figure 10-1).

Figure 10-1 illustrates what we are going to do. When expressed in a DSL, it looks like the following.

```
movie-web | splitter | movie-imdb | movie-log
```

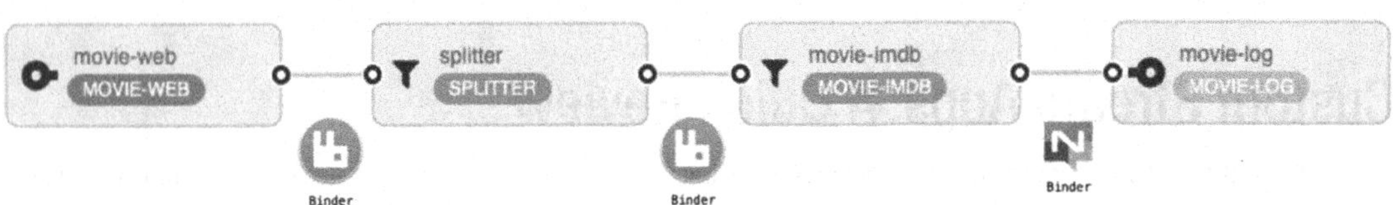

Figure 10-1. *Custom stream pipeline*

Even though it is a simple stream pipeline, I want to show you how to use customs apps with GUI or the Data Flow shell and how to use a custom binder. If you take a closer look at the DSL, the *splitter* app starter is combined with three custom Stream apps.

Movie Web App: movie-source

This application exposes a REST API in which you send a collection of movies. Let's start by opening a browser and going to Spring Initializr (`https://start.spring.io`) website. Use the following data.

- Group: `com.apress.cloud.stream`
- Artifact: `movie-source`
- Package name: `com.apress.cloud.stream.movie`
- Dependencies: Cloud Stream, Spring Web, Lombok

Press the Generate button to download a ZIP file. Uncompress it and import the project into your favorite IDE (see Figure 10-2).

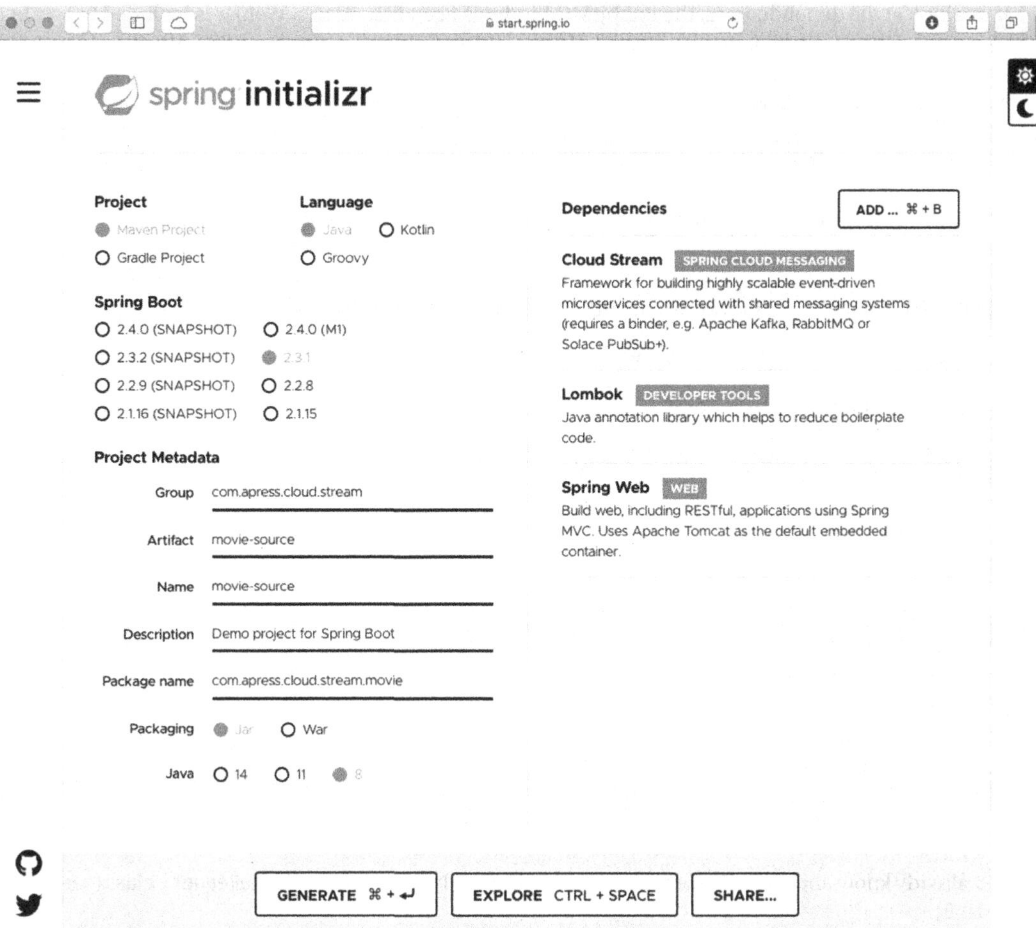

Figure 10-2. *Spring Initializr movie-source*

Next, open `pom.xml` and add the following dependencies.

```
<dependency>
        <groupId>org.springframework.cloud</groupId>
        <artifactId>spring-cloud-stream-binder-rabbit</artifactId>
</dependency>
<!-- WebJars -->
<dependency>
        <groupId>org.webjars</groupId>
        <artifactId>bootstrap</artifactId>
        <version>4.5.0</version>
</dependency>
<dependency>
        <groupId>org.webjars</groupId>
        <artifactId>jquery</artifactId>
        <version>3.5.1</version>
</dependency>
```

If you look at the dependencies, the RabbitMQ binder is used first. Also, a WebJar is included to create an `index.html` page to send the movies instead of any cURL command or another REST API client. I want you to see solutions other than the command line.

Next, modify the version and remove the snapshot work, so it is as follows.

```
<version>0.0.1</version>
```

This is important for deployment (I'll explain later). Next, let's create the model. Create the `Movie` class (see Listing 10-1).

Listing 10-1. src/main/java/com/apress/cloud/stream/movie/Movie.java

```
package com.apress.cloud.stream.movie;

import lombok.AllArgsConstructor;
import lombok.Data;
import lombok.NoArgsConstructor;

@AllArgsConstructor
@NoArgsConstructor
@Data
public class Movie {
    private String id;
    private String title;
    private String actor;
    private int year;
    private String genre;
    private int stars;
}
```

You already know about the `Movie` class, so let's continue by creating the `MovieRequest` class (see Listing 10-2).

Listing 10-2. src/main/java/com/apress/cloud/stream/movie/MovieRequest.java

```
package com.apress.cloud.stream.movie;

import lombok.AllArgsConstructor;
import lombok.Data;
import lombok.NoArgsConstructor;

import java.time.LocalDateTime;

@NoArgsConstructor
@AllArgsConstructor
@Data
public class MovieRequest {
    String action;
    Iterable<Movie> movies;
    LocalDateTime created;
}
```

Listing 10-2 shows the `MovieRequest` class. As you can see, it's very simple. Normally when you want to expose an API, you should wrap your data as a best practice. This helps to see when the request happens, who did it, and so forth when using auditing tools. Next, you need a `MovieResponse` class (see Listing 10-3).

Listing 10-3. src/main/java/com/apress/cloud/stream/movie/MovieResponse.java

```
package com.apress.cloud.stream.movie;

import lombok.AllArgsConstructor;
import lombok.Data;
import lombok.NoArgsConstructor;

import java.time.LocalDateTime;

@NoArgsConstructor
@AllArgsConstructor
@Data
public class MovieResponse {

    Integer code;
    String message;
    LocalDateTime responseTime;

}
```

Listing 10-3 shows the `MovieResponse` class. Even though this class is simple, you can use it to report special codes that make sense to your business logic and to send a message that exposes any issues. Next, let's create the `MovieController` class (see Listing 10-4).

Listing 10-4. src/main/java/com/apress/cloud/stream/movie/MovieController.java

```
package com.apress.cloud.stream.movie;

import lombok.AllArgsConstructor;
import lombok.extern.log4j.Log4j2;
import org.springframework.cloud.stream.function.StreamBridge;
import org.springframework.http.HttpStatus;
import org.springframework.http.ResponseEntity;
import org.springframework.web.bind.annotation.*;

import java.time.LocalDateTime;
import java.util.Collection;

@Log4j2
@AllArgsConstructor
@RequestMapping("/v1/api")
@RestController
public class MovieController {

    private StreamBridge streamBridge;

    @PostMapping("/movies")
```

```
    @ResponseStatus(HttpStatus.ACCEPTED)
    public ResponseEntity<MovieResponse> toMovieBinding(@RequestBody MovieRequest
    movieRequest) {
        assert  movieRequest != null;
        movieRequest.setCreated(LocalDateTime.now());

        log.debug("Sending: {} ", movieRequest);
        assert streamBridge != null;
        streamBridge.send("movie-out-0", movieRequest);

        return ResponseEntity
                .accepted()
                .body(new MovieResponse(HttpStatus.OK.value(),"Movies processed: " +
                ((Collection)movieRequest.getMovies()).size(), LocalDateTime.now()) );
    }
}
```

Listing 10-4 shows the `MovieController` class. The important part is the usage of the `StreamBridge` class that sends data to an *output binding*. The send method is using the `movie-out-0` binding. The main API endpoint is `/v1/api` and the `MovieRequest` endpoint is `/v1/api/movies`.

Next, let's create `index.html` and the JavaScript for creating a homepage that posts to the `/v1/api/movies` endpoint (see Listings 10-5 and 10-6).

Listing 10-5. src/main/resources/static/index.html

```
<!DOCTYPE html>
<html lang="en">
<head>
    <meta charset="UTF-8">
    <script src="/webjars/jquery/3.5.1/jquery.min.js"></script>
    <script src="/webjars/bootstrap/4.5.0/js/bootstrap.min.js"></script>
        <link rel="stylesheet"
          href="/webjars/bootstrap/4.5.0/css/bootstrap.min.css" />
    <title>Title</title>
</head>
<body>
<div class="jumbotron jumbotron-fluid">
    <div class="container">
        <h1 class="display-4">Movie API</h1>
        <p class="lead">This is a Movie API Stream App.</p>
    </div>
</div>
<div class="container">
    <!-- Example row of columns -->
    <div class="row">
        <div class="col-md-6">
            <h2>Movies</h2>
            <p>You can send this JSON movie request, or modify it accordingly.</p>
            <div class="form-group">
                <textarea class="form-control" id="movieRequest" rows="15"></textarea>
            </div>
```

```
            <p><a class="btn btn-primary btn-lg" href="#" role="button"
            id="sendRequest">Send</a></p>
        </div>

    </div>
    <hr>

</div>
<script src="js/main.js"></script>
</body>
</html>
```

Listing 10-6. src/main/resources/static/js/main.js

```
function getMovieRequest(){
    return `{
  "MovieRequest": {
    "action": "create",
    "movies": [
      {
        "id": "tt0133093",
        "title": "The Matrix",
        "actor": "Keanu Reeves",
        "year": 1999,
        "genre": "fiction",
        "stars": 5
      },
      {
        "id": "tt0209144",
        "title": "Memento",
        "actor": "Guy Pearce",
        "year": 2000,
        "genre": "drama",
        "stars": 4
      }
    ]
  }
}
    `;
}

$(function(){
    $('#movieRequest').val(getMovieRequest());
    $('#sendRequest').click(function (){

        $.ajax
        ({
            type: "POST",
            url: '/v1/api/movies',
            dataType: 'json',
            async: false,
```

```
            contentType: 'application/json',
            data: $('#movieRequest').val(),
            success: function (data) {
                alert(data.MovieResponse.message);
            }
        })
    });


});
```

As you can see from previous files, these are very simple—nothing complicated, just a POST using `$.ajax` (from jQuery). Note that you already are populating the text area with the movies JSON payload. This could be an SPA (single-page application), for example.

Next, let's open the `application.properties` file. Add the content from Listing 10-7.

Listing 10-7. src/main/resource/application.properties

```
# Server
server.port=8080

# Jackson Root Properties
spring.jackson.serialization.wrap-root-value=true
spring.jackson.deserialization.unwrap-root-value=true

# Spring Cloud Stream
spring.cloud.stream.source=movie
spring.cloud.stream.bindings.movie-out-0.destination=movie

# Logging
logging.level.com.apress.cloud.stream.movie=DEBUG
```

Listing 10-7 shows the `application.properties` file. Note that you are adding the `spring.jackson.*` properties to wrap the `MovieRequest` and `MovieResponse` objects into a JSON object. Also, to use the `StreamBridge` class, you need to define the name of the source, in this case, `movie`. Also, it is necessary to create the bindings that are based on the naming convention, which is `movie-out-0` (you saw this in previous chapters).

You can test this Stream app by connecting it to `log-app-starter` or `splitter-app-starter` to see how it works.

■ **Note** In the source code, the `ch10/app-starters` folder contains a `setup.sh` script that downloads the splitter and log app-starters and sets up the `application.properties` file to test the `movie-source` project. You need RabbitMQ to test it.

Movie IMDB App: movie-processor

This app receives movies in JSON format. It uses a movie's ID to go to a third-party API service (`https://rapidapi.com`). Remember that you need to sign in (RapidAPI is free) and use the IMDB Service. You are using the free service (`https://imdb8.p.rapidapi.com`) and the `/title/get-ratings` endpoint to get the ratings. This Stream app is very similar to the `groovy-transform` script you created in the previous chapter. This Stream app uses the NATs server and the RabbitMQ binders.

Open your browser and go to the Spring Initializr (`https://start.spring.io`) web site. Use the following data.

- Group: `com.apress.cloud.stream`
- Artifact: `movie-processor`
- Package name: `com.apress.cloud.stream.movie`
- Dependencies: Cloud Stream, Lombok

Press the Generate button to download a ZIP file. Uncompress it and import the project into your favorite IDE (see Figure 10-3).

***Figure 10-3.** Spring Initializr movie-processor*

Next, open pom.xml and add the following dependencies.

```
<dependency>
        <groupId>org.springframework.cloud</groupId>
        <artifactId>spring-cloud-stream-binder-rabbit</artifactId>
</dependency>

                <!-- NATs Server -->
<dependency>
        <groupId>com.apress.nats</groupId>
        <artifactId>nats-messaging-binder</artifactId>
        <version>0.0.1-SNAPSHOT</version>
</dependency>

<!-- Apache Commons -->
<dependency>
        <groupId>org.apache.httpcomponents</groupId>
        <artifactId>httpclient</artifactId>
        <version>4.5.12</version>
</dependency>

<dependency>
        <groupId>org.springframework.boot</groupId>
        <artifactId>spring-boot-configuration-processor</artifactId>
        <optional>true</optional>
</dependency>
```

You are adding the NATs binder dependency and httpclient that does the request. (You can use the RestClient provided by Spring Web, but I wanted to use an alternative). Also, you are adding configuration-processor to your own properties.

In the same pom.xml file's build/plugins section, add the following plugin.

```
<plugin>
        <groupId>org.springframework.cloud</groupId>
        <artifactId>spring-cloud-app-starter-metadata-maven-plugin</artifactId>
        <version>2.0.0.RELEASE</version>
        <executions>
                <execution>
                        <id>aggregate-metadata</id>
                        <phase>compile</phase>
                        <goals>
                                <goal>aggregate-metadata</goal>
                        </goals>
                </execution>
        </executions>
</plugin>
```

This creates the metadata JAR that contains all the information about the properties you need to setup the stream. Next, modify the version and remove the snapshot work, so that it is

```
<version>0.0.1</version>
```

This is important for deployment.

Next, you need to create the models that hold the new information. You are enhancing the `Movie` object. Create the `Movie` and `MovieImdb` classes (see Listings 10-8 and 10-9).

Listing 10-8. src/main/java/com/apress/cloud/stream/movie/Movie.java

```
package com.apress.cloud.stream.movie;

import lombok.AllArgsConstructor;
import lombok.Data;
import lombok.NoArgsConstructor;

@AllArgsConstructor
@NoArgsConstructor
@Data
public class Movie {
    private String id;
    private String title;
    private String actor;
    private int year;
    private String genre;
    private int stars;
    private MovieImdb imdb;
}
```

Listing 10-9. src/main/java/com/apress/cloud/stream/movie/MovieImdb.java

```
package com.apress.cloud.stream.movie;

import lombok.AllArgsConstructor;
import lombok.Data;
import lombok.NoArgsConstructor;

@NoArgsConstructor
@AllArgsConstructor
@Data
public class MovieImdb {
    Float rating;
    Integer ratingCount;
}
```

Listing 10-9 shows the `MovieImdb` class. This class holds the information taken from the IMDB service. Next, let's create the `MovieProperties` class, which holds the information about the IMDB service, such as the host and some headers required for the call (see Listing 10-10).

Listing 10-10. src/main/java/com/apress/cloud/stream/movie/MovieProperties.java

```
package com.apress.cloud.stream.movie;

import lombok.Data;
import org.springframework.boot.context.properties.ConfigurationProperties;

@Data
@ConfigurationProperties(prefix = "movie")
public class MovieProperties {
    String apiServer;
    String headerHost;
    String headerKey;
}
```

Next, let's create the MovieStream class (see Listing 10-11).

Listing 10-11. src/main/java/com/apress/cloud/stream/movie/MovieStream.java

```
package com.apress.cloud.stream.movie;

import com.fasterxml.jackson.databind.DeserializationFeature;
import com.fasterxml.jackson.databind.ObjectMapper;
import lombok.extern.log4j.Log4j2;
import org.apache.http.HttpEntity;
import org.apache.http.client.methods.HttpGet;
import org.apache.http.impl.client.CloseableHttpClient;
import org.apache.http.impl.client.HttpClients;
import org.apache.http.util.EntityUtils;
import org.springframework.boot.context.properties.EnableConfigurationProperties;
import org.springframework.context.annotation.Bean;
import org.springframework.context.annotation.Configuration;
import reactor.core.publisher.Flux;

import java.io.IOException;
import java.net.URI;
import java.net.URISyntaxException;
import java.nio.charset.StandardCharsets;
import java.util.function.Function;

@Log4j2
@EnableConfigurationProperties(MovieProperties.class)
@Configuration
public class MovieStream {

    private MovieProperties movieProperties;
    private final CloseableHttpClient httpclient = HttpClients.createDefault();
    private final HttpGet getRequest = new HttpGet();
```

```
    public MovieStream(MovieProperties movieProperties) {
        this.movieProperties = movieProperties;
        getRequest.addHeader("Accept", "application/json");
        getRequest.addHeader("x-rapidapi-host", movieProperties.getHeaderHost());
        getRequest.addHeader("x-rapidapi-key", movieProperties.getHeaderKey());
        getRequest.addHeader("Content-Type", "application/json");
    }

    @Bean
    public Function<Flux<Movie>, Flux<Movie>> movieProcessor(ObjectMapper objectMapper) {
        return movieFlux -> movieFlux.map(
                movie -> {
                    try {

                        getRequest.setURI(new URI(movieProperties.getApiServer().
                        replace("ID", movie.getId())));
                        HttpEntity entity = httpclient.execute(getRequest).getEntity();
                        movie.setImdb(objectMapper.readValue(EntityUtils.toString(entity,
                        StandardCharsets.UTF_8), MovieImdb.class));

                    } catch (IOException | URISyntaxException e) {
                        e.printStackTrace();
                    }

                    log.debug("About ot send: {}", movie);
                    return movie;
                });
    }

    @Bean
    public ObjectMapper objectMapper(){
        ObjectMapper objectMapper = new ObjectMapper();
        objectMapper.configure(DeserializationFeature.FAIL_ON_UNKNOWN_PROPERTIES,false);
        return objectMapper;
    }

}
```

Listing 10-11 shows the `MovieStream` class. Let's analyze this class. Note that you are using `Flux<Movie>` in the `movieProcessor` method. Because it is declared as a Spring bean, it recognizes the main method for processing the incoming streaming and sends the data to the right bindings. You are using the `httpclient` instance to call the service with the right data, the movie ID, and headers like the host and the key. Look at the `entity` instance. You are executing the request and getting an entity to map back to the `MovieImdb` class. The mapper ignores the missing properties from the response to map the class.

Next, let's create an `src/main/resources/META-INF` folder, which contains the `spring-configuration-metadata.json` file. This file has useful information about each property, which helps other developers reuse and configure this stream (see Listing 10-12).

Listing 10-12. src/main/resource/META-INF/spring-configuration-metadata.json

```
{
  "groups": [
    {
      "name": "movie",
      "type": "com.apress.cloud.stream.movie.MovieProperties",
      "sourceType": "com.apress.cloud.stream.movie.MovieProperties"
    },
    {
      "name": "spring.nats",
      "type": "com.apress.nats.NatsProperties",
      "sourceType": "com.apress.nats.NatsProperties"
    }
  ],
  "properties": [
    {
      "name": "spring.nats.host",
      "type": "java.lang.String",
      "description": "This NATs Server host. Default to localhost.",
      "sourceType": "com.apress.nats.NatsProperties",
      "defaultValue": "localhost"
    },
    {
      "name": "spring.nats.port",
      "type": "java.lang.Integer",
      "description": "This NATs Server port. Default to 4222.",
      "sourceType": "com.apress.nats.NatsProperties",
      "defaultValue": 4222
    },
    {
      "name": "movie.api-server",
      "type": "java.lang.String",
      "description": "Default to: https://imdb8.p.rapidapi.com/title/get-
      ratings?tconst=ID. The ID will be replaced, so it's necessary",
      "sourceType": "com.apress.cloud.stream.movie.MovieProperties",
      "defaultValue": "https://imdb8.p.rapidapi.com/title/get-ratings?tconst=ID"
    },
    {
      "name": "movie.header-host",
      "type": "java.lang.String",
      "description": "Default to: imdb8.p.rapidapi.com.",
      "sourceType": "com.apress.cloud.stream.movie.MovieProperties",
      "defaultValue": "imdb8.p.rapidapi.com"
    },
    {
      "name": "movie.header-key",
      "type": "java.lang.String",
      "description": "This header-key can be obtain in your https://rapidapi.com/ profile.",
      "sourceType": "com.apress.cloud.stream.movie.MovieProperties"
```

```
    }
  ],
  "hints": []
}
```

Next, in the same `META-INF/` folder, add the `spring-configuration-metadata-whitelist.properties` file that has classes marked with the `@ConfigurationProperties` annotation. This generates the metadata to get information about the Stream app (see Listing 10-13).

Listing 10-13. src/main/resource/META-INF/spring-configuration-metadata-whitelist.json

```
configuration-properties.classes=\
  com.apress.nats.NatsProperties,\
  com.apress.cloud.stream.movie.MovieProperties
configuration-properties.names=movie.api-server,movie.header-host,movie.header-key,spring.
nats.host,spring.nats.port
```

See that you are adding our NatsProperties, because those properties are necessary to tell where is the NATs broker. Also you are whitelisting the properties you are using. This is necessary if you need something like `server.port`. For this example, you don't need them, with the classes is enough, but to illustrate that, you can include some other properties that are already included as part of the whole stream app.

Next, open the `application.properties` file and add the content in Listing 10-14.

Listing 10-14. src/main/resource/META-INF/application.properties

```
# Server
server.port=8082

# IMDB API
movie.api-server=https://imdb8.p.rapidapi.com/title/get-ratings?tconst=ID
movie.header-host=imdb8.p.rapidapi.com
movie.header-key=YOUR-KEY

# Binders
spring.cloud.stream.bindings.movieProcessor-in-0.binder=rabbit
spring.cloud.stream.bindings.movieProcessor-out-0.binder=nats

# Bindings - Nats - RabbitMQ
spring.cloud.stream.bindings.movieProcessor-in-0.destination=imdb
spring.cloud.stream.bindings.movieProcessor-out-0.destination=log

# Logging
logging.level.com.apress.cloud.stream.movie=DEBUG
```

Listing 10-14 shows the `application.properties`. Note that this file has the `movie.*` properties. Some of them are default. Also look at the binders (which are used for incoming streams; the broker uses them for streaming) and note how you need to enter the input and the output destinations. Remember the naming convention that takes the name of the method (`movieProcessor`) and adds the `-in-0` and `-out-0` terminations.

Movie Log App: movie-sink

This Stream app logs the enhanced `Movie` object with the IMDB ratings. A very easy app. Open your browser and go to the Spring Initializr web site (`https://start.spring.io`). Use the following data.

- Group: `com.apress.cloud.stream`
- Artifact: `movie-sink`
- Package name: `com.apress.cloud.stream.movie`
- Dependencies: Cloud Stream, Lombok

Press the Generate button to download a ZIP file. Uncompress it and import the project in your favorite IDE (see Figure 10-4).

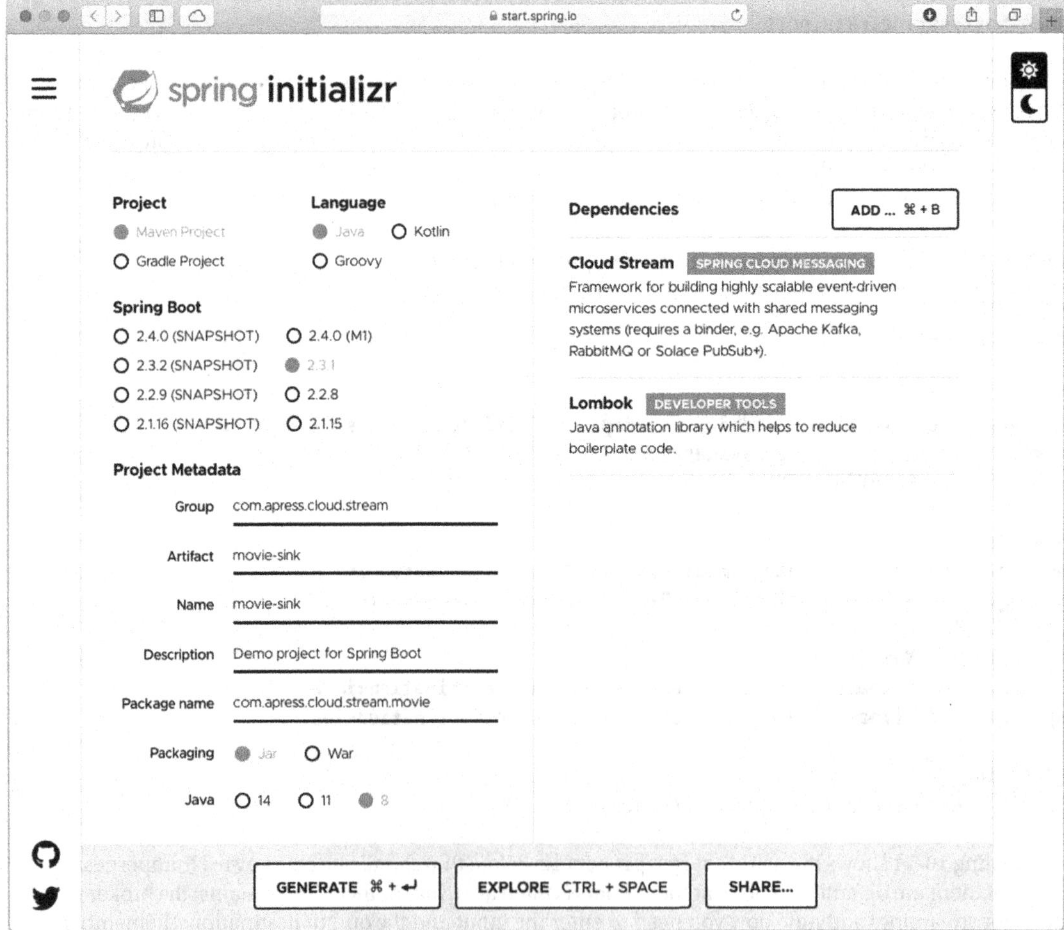

Figure 10-4. Spring Initializr movie-sink

Open pom.xml and add the following dependencies.

```
<!-- NATs Server -->
<dependency>
        <groupId>com.apress.nats</groupId>
        <artifactId>nats-messaging-binder</artifactId>
        <version>0.0.1-SNAPSHOT</version>
</dependency>
```

This Stream app uses the NATs binder, so that's the only dependency you need. Next, modify the version and remove the snapshot work, so that it is

```
<version>0.0.1</version>
```

Next, copy/paste the previous Movie and MovieImdb classes (see Listings 10-8 and 10-9).

Next, create the MovieStream class (see Listing 10-15).

Listing 10-15. src/main/java/com/apress/cloud/stream/movie/MovieStream.java

```
package com.apress.cloud.stream.movie;

import lombok.extern.log4j.Log4j2;
import org.springframework.context.annotation.Bean;
import org.springframework.context.annotation.Configuration;
import reactor.core.publisher.Flux;

import java.util.function.Consumer;

@Log4j2
@Configuration
public class MovieStream {
    @Bean
    public Consumer<Flux<Movie>> log() {
        return movie -> movie.subscribe(actual -> log.info(actual));
    }
}
```

Listing 10-15 shows the MovieStream class. As you can see, it is very simple; you are simply subscribing and receiving the Movie object.

Next, open the application.properties file and add the content in Listing 10-16.

Listing 10-16. src/main/resources/application.properties

```
# Server
server.port=8083

# Bindings
spring.cloud.stream.bindings.log-in-0.destination=log
```

Packaging and Deploy Stream Apps

Now, you are ready to use Spring Cloud Data Flow to create a stream pipeline, but first, you need to decide how to package every Stream app. In the end, you can have Uber-JARs and run them stand-alone. But you need something that orchestrates the pipeline without doing everything manually. And for all of this, you need to choose how you want the Spring Cloud Data Flow server to use your Stream apps. The Spring Cloud Data Flow server can use the Stream apps by providing either Maven or Docker coordinates and the local JAR (but this should be only for development).

You are using Maven coordinates here, and for that, you need to package and deploy your Stream apps. If you are an experienced developer and already know how to package and deploy Maven artifacts to a Maven repository, you can skip this section.

To package your apps, go into each project's root and execute the following.

```
./mvnw clean -DskipTests package
```

This command generates the files you need in the `target/` folder. If you look at the `movie-processor` project's `target/` folder, you find `movie-processor-0.0.1-metadata.jar` with `spring-configuration-metadata.*` files that are useful when you request information about the app.

Next, it's necessary to deploy these artifacts to a Maven repository. Let me tell you that there are a lot of solutions for creating a Maven repo, such as using Docker images or Apache Archiva, Nexus, or JFrog. You can also use your Git server as a Maven repo. In this case, I used a open source Maven repo called Bintray (`https://bintray.com`). You can sign up for free (see Figure 10-5).

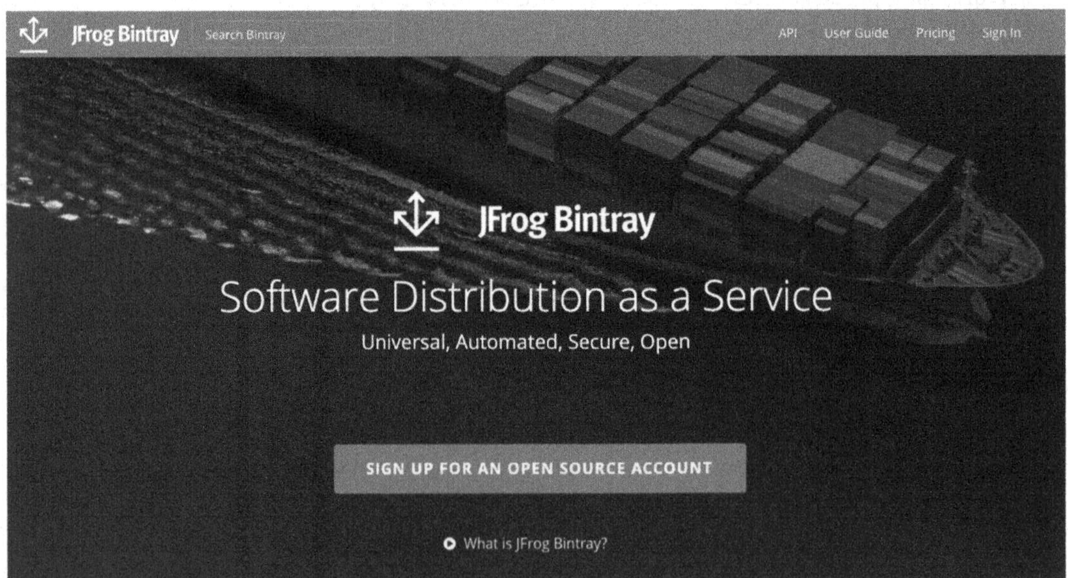

Figure 10-5. *Bintray*

Once you set up your account, you need to create a repository and a package that holds your Stream apps. I created the `scdf` repository and the package name is `movie-streams`. My final Maven repo URL is `https://bintray.com/felipeg48/scdf` (see Figure 10-6).

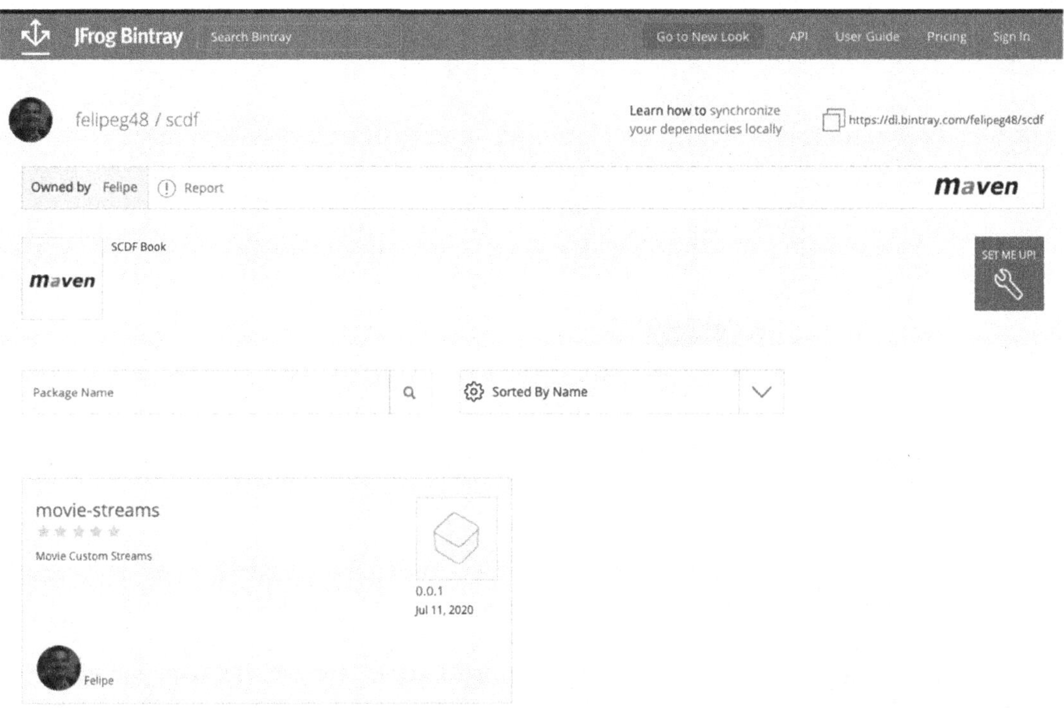

Figure 10-6. *`https://bintray.com/felipeg48/scdf`*

Once you have finished setting up your Maven repo and package name, you need to add some credentials and dependencies to the `pom.xml` file so you can do the deployment. First, go to your profile at `https://bintray.com/profile/edit`. Select the API key from the menu on the left. Copy it to a safe place because you are using it later (see Figure 10-7).

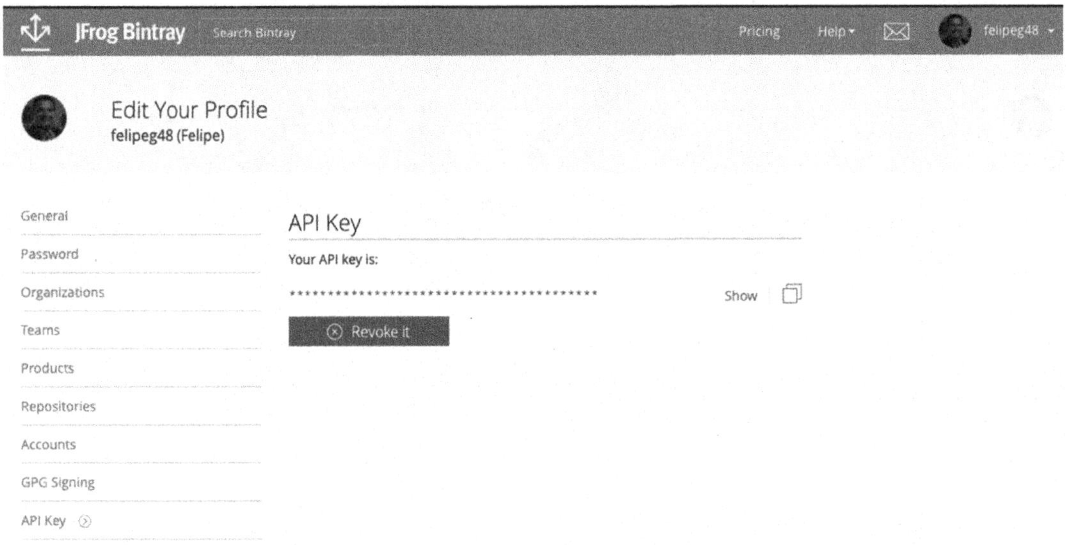

Figure 10-7. *https://bintray.com/profile/edit*

In your Home directory look for the (`~/.m2`) folder. Open or create `~/.m2/settings.xml` and add the following content.

```
<?xml version='1.0' encoding='UTF-8'?>
<settings xsi:schemaLocation='http://maven.apache.org/SETTINGS/1.0.0 http://maven.apache.
org/xsd/settings-1.0.0.xsd'
          xmlns='http://maven.apache.org/SETTINGS/1.0.0' xmlns:xsi='http://www.w3.org/2001/
          XMLSchema-instance'>
    <servers>
        <server>
            <id>bintray-USERNAME-scdf</id>
            <username>YOUR_USERNAME</username>
            <password>YOUR_KEY</password>
        </server>
    </servers>
</settings>
```

The `<id>` tag should be the same as the following configuration. Next, open the `pom.xml` file for every project and add the following content (this is my personal information).

```
<distributionManagement>
        <repository>
                <id>bintray-felipeg48-scdf</id>
                <name>felipeg48-scdf</name>
                <url>https://api.bintray.com/maven/felipeg48/scdf/movie-streams/;publish=1
                </url>
        </repository>
</distributionManagement>
```

The `<id>` *must* be the same as the one you set in `settings.xml`; `<name>` can be anything you want. It is important to know that the URL is the API in this format.
`https://api.bintray.com/maven/<username>/<repository>/<package-name>/;publish=1`

Also, it *must* contain the username, repository, and the package name at the end. In my case, it is as follows.

```
https://api.bintray.com/maven/felipeg48/scdf/movie-streams/;publish=1
```

If you have any issues with setting this up, the Bintray webpage has a SET ME UP! button (see Figure 10-6). Click it to find more information on setting up Maven for uploading.

Now you can upload the apps by executing the following in every project's root.

```
./mvnw -DskipTests deploy
```

This command uploads all the files. You can verify this by going to your repo/package (see Figure 10-8).

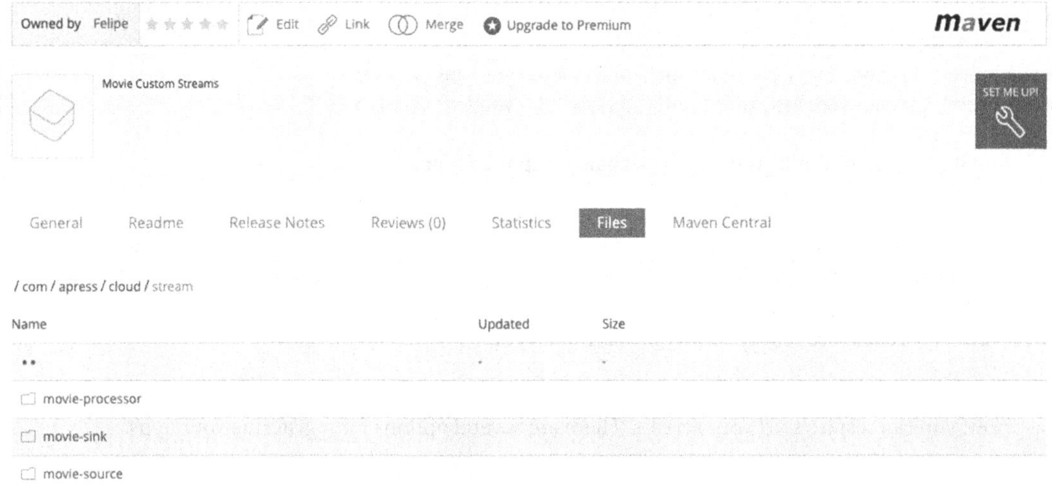

Figure 10-8. *`https://bintray.com/<username>/scdf/movie-streams#files/com/apress/cloud/stream`*

You can inspect every folder and see that your apps are there. In the `movie-processor` app, you see the metadata JARs. Now, you are ready to use them in Spring Cloud Data Flow. It's important to know that this repository is personal and is not available to the community, so you need to tell Spring Cloud Data Flow server how to find it. You see this in the next section.

Registering Stream Apps

Now that you have everything ready, it is time to use your apps in the Spring Cloud Data Flow server. You must add your Maven repo to tell the Spring Cloud Data Flow server where to find your apps. Use the following property to point to your Maven repository.

```
maven.remote-repositories.repo1.url=https://dl.bintray.com/felipeg48/scdf
```

This property must be set before the Spring Cloud Data Flow server starts. If you are using Kubernetes, you can add that property to the YAML file's env section where the container is set.

```
...
env:
  - name: maven.remote-repositories.repo1.url
  - value: https://dl.bintray.com/felipeg48/scdf
  ...
```

I copied this URL from the top-right corner of the Bintray main page (see Figure 10-6). If you are using Docker Compose, you can add the same environment variable in the environment section.

```
...
environment:
  - maven.remote-repositories.repo1.url=https://dl.bintray.com/felipeg48/scdf
...
```

If your company uses a private Maven repo and requires a username and password, add the following properties.

```
maven.remote-repositories.repo1.auth.username=<your-username>
maven.remote-repositories.repo1.auth.password=<your-password>
```

And if you have multiple Maven repos, change `repo1` to `repo2`.. `repoN`.

```
...
maven.remote-repositories.repo1.url=...
maven.remote-repositories.repo2.url=..
maven.remote-repositories.repo3.url=..
maven.remote-repositories.repo2.auth.username=...
...
```

Now, you can restart/start your servers. There are several options for registering your apps.

- You can use the cURL command to register as you did in previous chapters.
- You can use the Spring Cloud Data Flow shell to register them.
- You can use the Spring Cloud Data Flow dashboard.
- You can programmatically register the apps.

I'll show you how to do this using either the Spring Data Flow shell or the dashboard. First, make sure your Spring Cloud Data Flow components are up and running. Remember that the Spring Data Flow server must start with the Maven repo environment variable pointing to your Maven repo. When registering the apps, it is important to know the type—source, processor, or sink, the name you gave to the app as recognized by the Spring Data Flow server, and the Maven coordinates in the following form.

```
maven://<groupId>:<artifactId>:<version>
```

If you created `spring-configuration-metadata.json` properties, you need to register your metadata artifact in the following form.

```
maven://<group>:artifactId>:jar:metadata:<version>
```

Using the Spring Cloud Data Flow Shell to Register Custom Apps

If you want to use the Spring Cloud Data Flow shell, make sure your servers are running and then start your shell. You can connect in several ways. If you have an Uber-JAR, you can point to the Spring Data Flow server, and that's it.

```
java -jar spring-cloud-dataflow-shell-VERSION.RELEASE.jar  \
  --dataflow.uri=http://my-server:9393  \
  --dataflow.username=my_username  \
  --dataflow.password=my_password   \
  --skip-ssl-validation=true
```

If you are already in and you see "`server-unknown`", you can connect with the `dataflow` keyword.

```
server-unknown:>dataflow config server --uri  http://my-server:9393 --username=my_username
```

Next, register the apps with the following shell command.

```
dataflow:>app register --name movie-imdb --type source --uri maven://com.apress.cloud.
stream:movie-source:0.0.1

dataflow:>app register --name movie-imdb --type processor --uri maven://com.apress.
cloud.stream:movie-processor:0.0.1 --metadata-uri maven://com.apress.cloud.stream:movie-
processor:jar:metadata:0.0.1

dataflow:>app register --name movie-log --type sink --uri maven://com.apress.cloud.
stream:movie-sink:0.0.1
```

After executing this shell command, list the apps as follows.

```
dataflow:>app list
```

You should see your custom stream listed. You need the splitter app for the pipeline DSL that you are creating, so you can register as follows.

```
dataflow:>app register --name splitter --type processor --uri maven://org.springframework.
cloud.stream.app:splitter-processor-rabbit:2.1.2.RELEASE --metadata-uri maven://org.
springframework.cloud.stream.app:splitter-processor-rabbit:jar:metadata:2.1.2.RELEASE
```

Perhaps you are wondering if there is a better way to register—without having to add your apps one by one. In the previous chapter, you saw that you can use the bulk option by using the `https://dataflow.spring.io/rabbitmq-maven-latest` URI. If you download that file, you see the coordinates in the following format.

```
<type>.<name>[.metadata]=maven://<groupId>:<artifactId>[:jar:metadata]:<version>
```

■ **Note** Remember that you can use Docker coordinates. In such a case, you need to create an image from your custom Stream app and push it to a registry, either a public one like `hub.docker.com` or your private registry. The coordinate is something like `docker://<your-docker-id>/<your-image>:<version>`.

If you want information about your app, you can execute the following command.

```
dataflow:>app info --name movie-imdb --type processor
```

With this command, you should see all the movie.* and the spring.nats.* properties and their definitions.

Using the Dashboard to Register Custom Apps

In this section, I show you how to use the dashboard with a simple procedure. Open your dashboard at http://<your-server>[:9393]/dashboard. Go to the Apps tab and click + **Add Applications(s)** button. Select the third option, **Bulk import application**. In the Apps as Properties field, copy and paste the following content.

```
source.movie-web=maven://com.apress.cloud.stream:movie-source:0.0.1
processor.movie-imdb=maven://com.apress.cloud.stream:movie-processor:0.0.1
processor.movie-imdb.metadata=maven://com.apress.cloud.stream:movie-
processor:jar:metadata:0.0.1
processor.splitter=maven://org.springframework.cloud.stream.app:splitter-processor-
rabbit:2.1.2.RELEASE
processor.splitter.metadata=maven://org.springframework.cloud.stream.app:splitter-processor-
rabbit:jar:metadata:2.1.2.RELEASE
sink.movie-log=maven://com.apress.cloud.stream:movie-sink:0.0.1
```

Note that the splitter app is already included. Analyze the naming convention. You can have an external file and import it as well (see Figure 10-9).

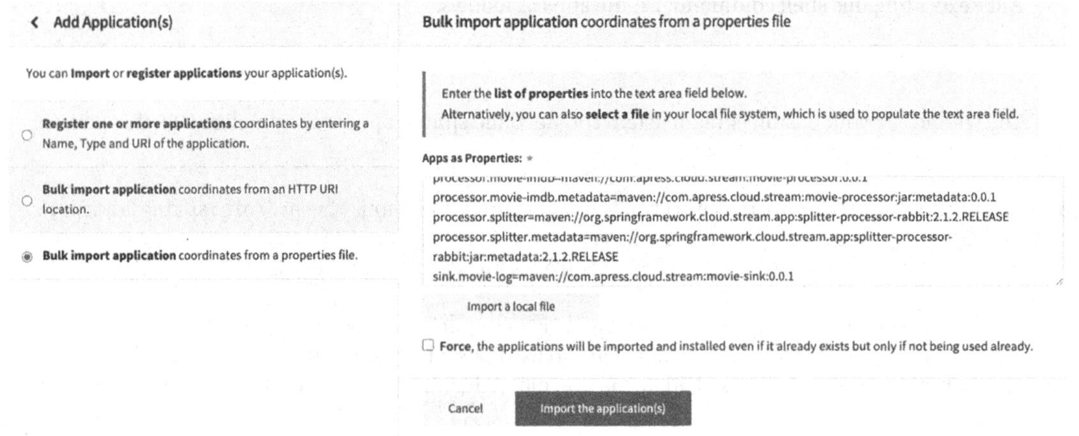

***Figure 10-9.** Bulk import application*

Click the **Import the application** button. You should see the apps listed (see Figure 10-10).

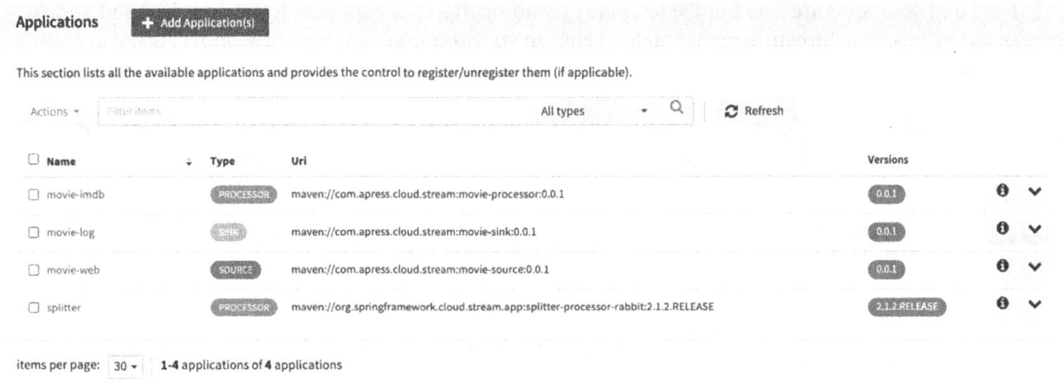

Figure 10-10. *Applications*

Now you are ready to create and deploy your stream pipeline.

Create and Deploy Custom Streams

You are creating a pipeline DSL using the dashboard here, but you are welcome to do the same in the Data Flow shell. Go to your dashboard and click Stream (in the left pane) and then click the **+ Create stream(s)** button. Add the DSL in the text area (see Figure 10-11).

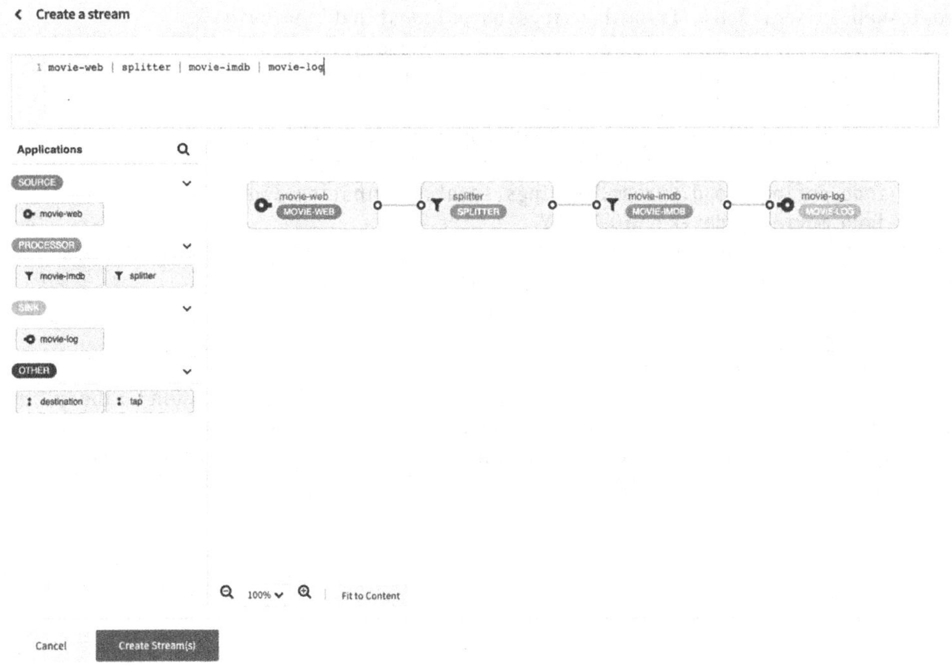

Figure 10-11. *Create a stream*

Note that your apps are listed in the left pane, meaning that they can be dragged and dropped and connected to any other Stream app that makes sense in your solution. You may be wondering if you are using some properties. Yes, you are, but you are using a different method, so as to not clutter the stream pipeline.

Next, click the Create Stream(s) button. Name it `movie-stream` and click **Create the stream** button. This takes you to the Streams list page (see Figure 10-12).

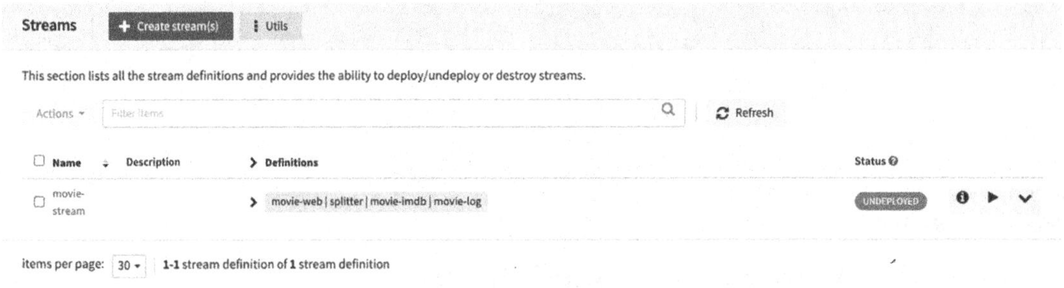

Figure 10-12. *Streams*

Next, click the Play button (>), which opens a Deployment and Properties page, where you can set the properties for every app to function. At the top of this page, click the Freetext tab and copy the following content.

```
app.movie-web.server.port=8081
app.movie-web.spring.cloud.stream.bindings.output.destination=movie
app.splitter.expression=#jsonPath(payload,'$.MovieRequest.movies')
app.splitter.spring.cloud.stream.bindings.input.destination=movie
app.splitter.spring.cloud.stream.bindings.output.destination=imdb
app.movie-imdb.spring.cloud.stream.bindings.input.binder=rabbit
app.movie-imdb.spring.cloud.stream.bindings.output.binder=nats
app.movie-imdb.spring.cloud.stream.bindings.input.destination=imdb
app.movie-imdb.movie.header-key=YOUR-KEY
app.movie-imdb.spring.nats.host=nats
app.movie-imdb.spring.cloud.stream.bindings.output.destination=log
app.movie-log.spring.cloud.stream.bindings.input.destination=log
app.movie-log.spring.nats.host=nats
```

Before continuing, analyze the properties. Note that you are adding the expression for the splitter app. You are setting the host for the NATs server and naming the destination property for each app. Spend time here until it makes sense to you. Note that you need at least the key for the IMDB Service API. You can change this accordingly (see Figure 10-13).

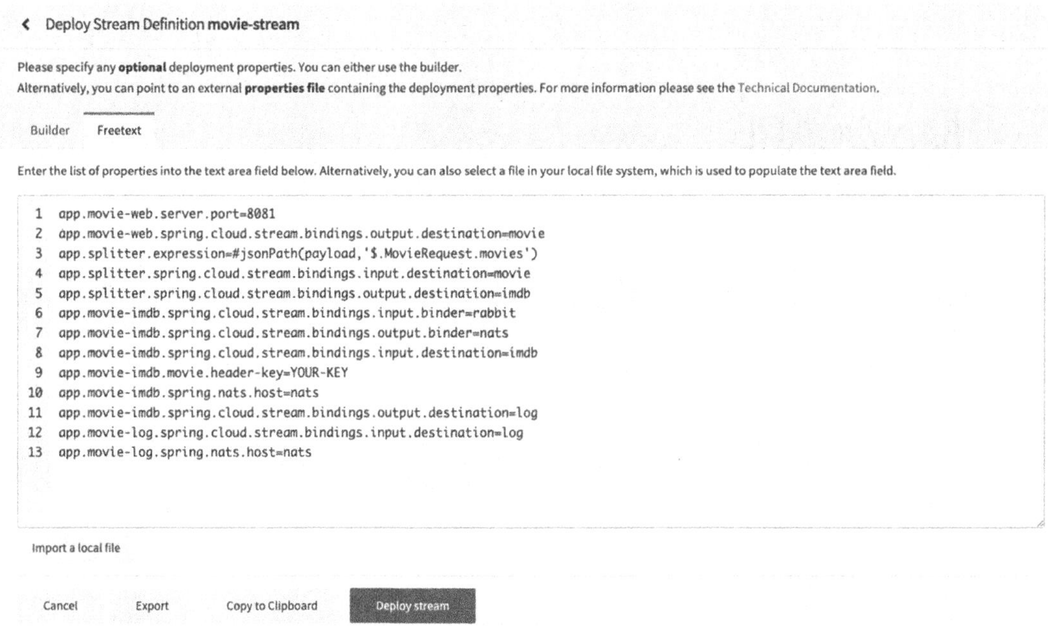

Figure 10-13. *App properties*

Next, you can click the **Deploy stream** button. If everything goes well, all of your apps should have deployed. You can open your browser and go to your movie-web app. If you deployed it using Kubernetes, you can expose the `movie-web-xxx` pod as `LoadBalancer` and access it (see Figure 10-14).

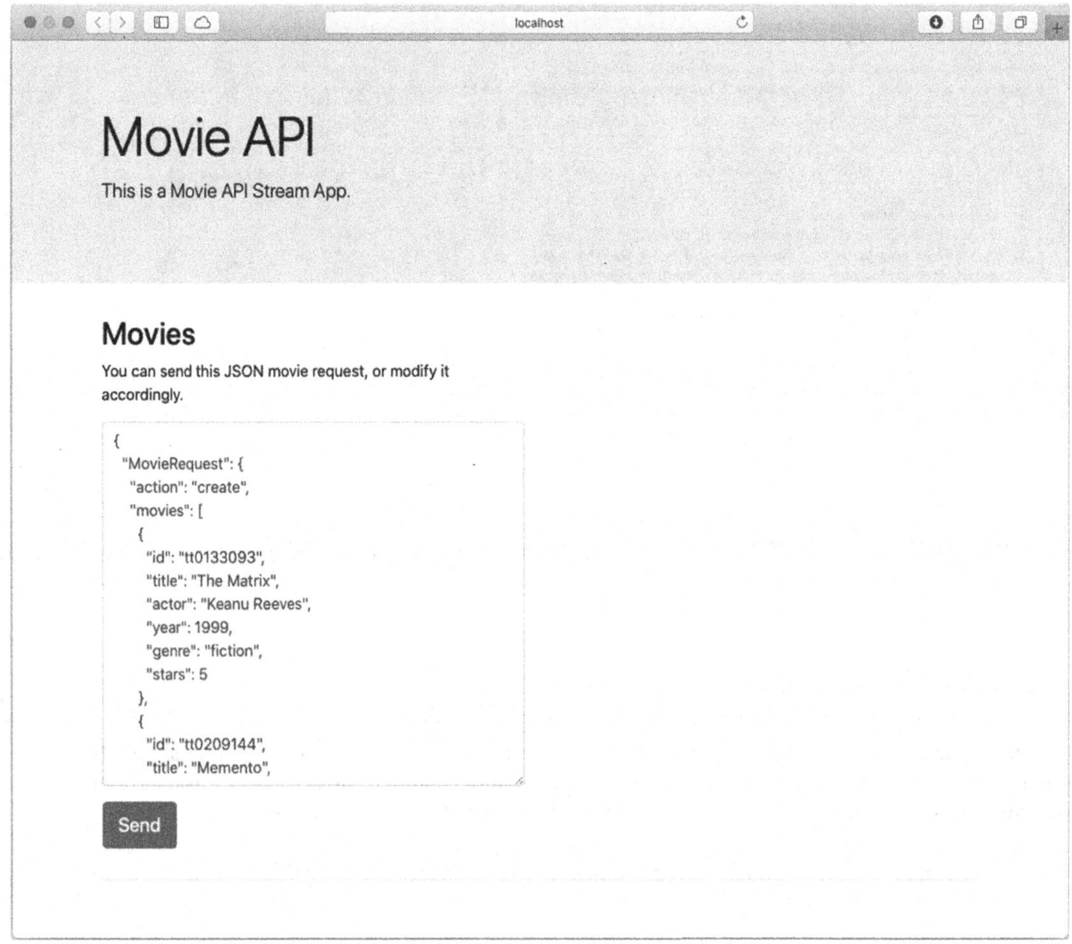

Figure 10-14. *Movie web app*

Now you are ready to send the `MovieRequest` JSON object. Press the Send button, and you should get a message stating that two movies were processed. If you look at the movie-log app stream logs, you should see the enhanced `Movie` object with ratings.

```
Movie(id=tt0133093, title=The Matrix, actor=Keanu Reeves, year=1999, genre=fiction, stars=5,
imdb=MovieImdb(rating=8.7, ratingCount=1620794))
Movie(id=tt0209144, title=Memento, actor=Guy Pearce, year=2000, genre=drama, stars=4,
imdb=MovieImdb(rating=8.4, ratingCount=1090922))
```

Congratulations, you have just created custom Stream apps and deployed a stream pipeline using RabbitMQ and your custom NATs binder.

■ **Note** All the source code is in the `ch10` folder. Most of the subfolders have README files and scripts for easy setup.

Summary

In this chapter, I showed you how to use custom Stream apps and a custom binder to create a stream data pipeline. I showed you how to use Maven coordinates for easy access within the Spring Cloud Data Flow server. Also, you saw how to use the Data Flow shell and the dashboard.

Once you are familiar with these scenarios, you find Spring Cloud Data Flow easy to use. Remember that you can use either a local development with Docker Compose or a more robust solution such a cloud infrastructure like Kubernetes, which can take care of high availability and other cool cloud features.

The next chapter covers Spring Cloud Task and using Spring Batch to process and transform large amounts of data triggered by streams.

CHAPTER 11

Task and Batch Apps with Spring Cloud Data Flow

In the previous chapter, I showed you how to create and deploy custom streams using multiple binders in Spring Cloud Data Flow. This chapter continues with more features by creating stream DSL apps, running and/or triggering tasks and batch processes, and more. In previous chapters, you saw how companies need to run overnight processes—finite jobs that process data and modify it by enhancing its contents or doing a transformation, and applying some filtering.

Spring Cloud Task Primer

Spring Cloud Task is a technology that allows you to create finite microservices, keeping track of when something starts, when it fails, and when it ends; in other words, Spring Cloud Task keeps track of any event happening during the execution of the app.

Why is a task is necessary in a cloud environment in which you always have processes running? Today, there are millions of requests per second, and we want our services to be reliable and fault-tolerant. But sometimes we need to do heavy loads that should not impact the performance of our apps. That's why batch apps allow us to create fine-grained applications that can run in the cloud and take care of the heavy lifting by loading and processing data.

Spring Cloud Task is the first of its kind to do this and has the advantage of tracking what is happening. The following are some of Spring Cloud Task's features.

- It uses an in-memory database to keep track of the job execution, but you can use any other database engine, including DB2, Oracle, MySQL, Postgres, SQL Server, HSQLDB, and H2. When an application starts, by default, a task repository is created to keep track of tasks by creating schemas and inserting the events that are occurring in execution time, either using an embedded database such as H2, HSQL or Derby, or any SQL driver by configuring the `spring.datasource.*` properties. This provides a record of the successful or unsuccessful job executions. Spring Cloud Task models this information using the `TaskExecution` class with the following properties.
    - `taskName` is the name of the task.
    - `startTime` is the time when the task started and is issued by the `SmartLifecyle` call.
    - `endTime` is the time when the task completed, issued by the `ApplicationReadyEvent`.

F. Gutierrez, *Spring Cloud Data Flow*, https://doi.org/10.1007/978-1-4842-1239-4_11

    - executionId is a unique ID for the task's run.
    - exitCode is a code generated by the ExitCodeExceptionMapper implementation. It is issued with ApplicationFailedEvent with a value of 1 if it fails; otherwise 0.
    - exitMessage is any information available at the time of the exit. It is set in TaskExecutionListener.
    - errorMessage is the exception caused at the end of the task (issued from the ApplicationFailedEvent with value 1).
    - arguments are the arguments passed into the executable app.
- It is based on Spring Boot and is an opinionated technology with defaults that can be overridden using the DefaultTaskConfigurer or SimpleTaskConfiguration classes. Spring Cloud Task uses a datasource for storing all the task executions/events, and it uses some schema defaults and naming conventions that can be overridden if necessary. The tables it generates are prefixed with TASK_, TASK_EXECUTION and TASK_EXECUTION_PARAMS, which can be easily overridden by using the spring.cloud.task.table-prefix property. If you don't want to initialize any tables, you can override it by setting the spring.cloud.task.initialize-enabled property to false.
- It contains TaskExecutionListener, which registers listeners for specific events in the task life cycle. You only need to implement the TaskExecutionListener interface; your implementation is notified of the following events.
    - onTaskStartup happens before saving any information about TaskExecution.
    - onTaskEnd happens before updating the TaskExecution entry.
    - onTaskFailed happens before onTaskEnd is invoked.

  Or you can use the specialized @BeforeTask, @AfterTask, and @FailedTask annotations on any method you want to process that calls by accepting TaskExecution as the parameter to get information.

Simple Task Demo

To see Spring Cloud Task in action, let's create a simple task. Open your browser and point to the Spring Initializr at https://start.spring.io. Use the following metadata.

- Group: com.apress.cloud.task
- Artifact: task-demo
- Package name: com.apress.cloud.task
- Dependencies: Task, Lombok, H2, and MySQL

Press the Generate button to download a ZIP file. You can unzip and import it into your favorite IDE (see Figure 11-1).

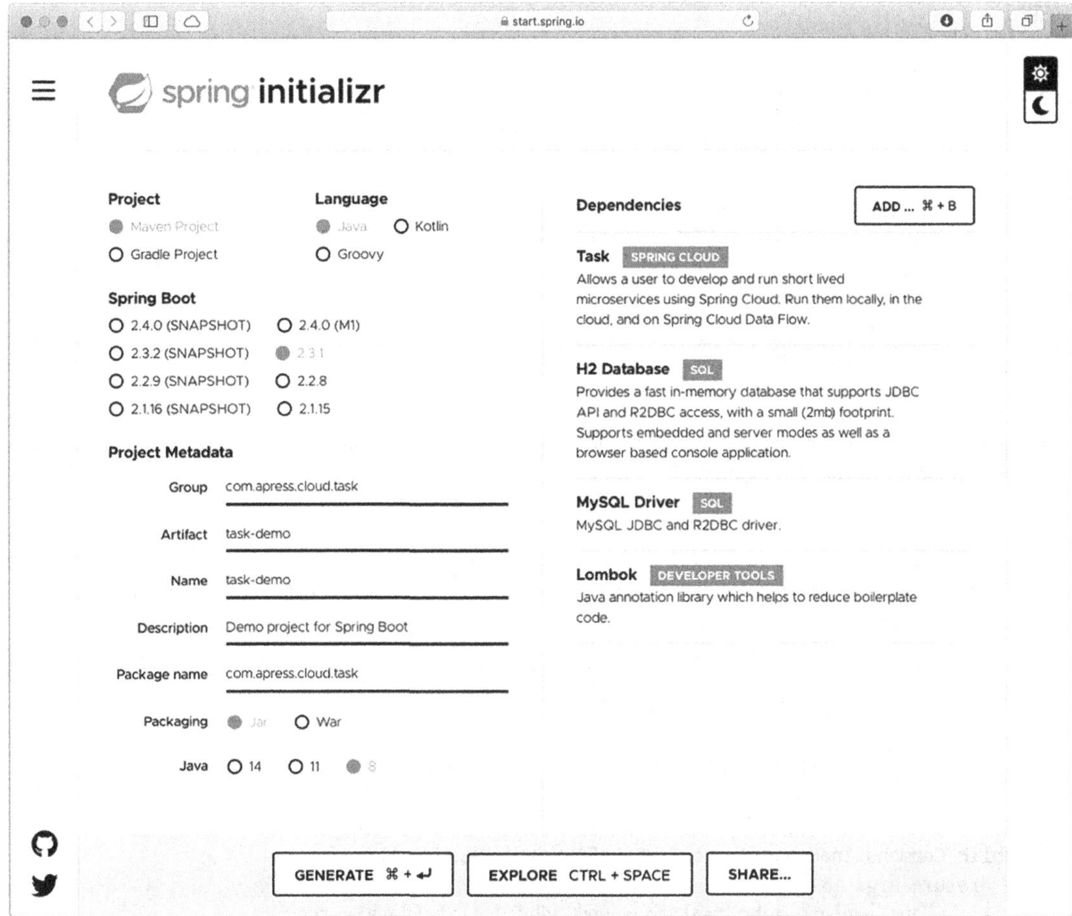

Figure 11-1. *Spring Initializr task-demo*

The `spring-cloud-starter-task` dependency is in the `pom.xml` file. Spring Task Cloud depends on the database. That's why you use the H2 or MySQL dependencies.

Next, create the `TaskDemoConfiguration` class (see Listing 11-1).

Listing 11-1. src/main/java/com/apress/cloud/task/TaskDemoConfiguration.java

```
package com.apress.cloud.task;

import lombok.extern.log4j.Log4j2;
import org.springframework.boot.CommandLineRunner;
import org.springframework.cloud.task.configuration.EnableTask;
import org.springframework.context.annotation.Bean;
import org.springframework.context.annotation.Configuration;
import org.springframework.jdbc.core.JdbcTemplate;

import javax.sql.DataSource;
```

```
@Log4j2
@EnableTask
@Configuration
public class TaskDemoConfiguration {

    private final String MOVIES_TABLE_SQL = "CREATE TABLE IF NOT EXISTS movies(" +
            " id varchar(10) primary key," +
            " title varchar(200)," +
            " actor varchar(200)," +
            " year int," +
            " genre varchar(25)," +
            " stars int," +
            " rating decimal(2,1)," +
            " ratingcount int);";

    private final String MOVIES_INSERT_SQL_1 = "insert into movies (id,title,actor,year,
    genre,stars,rating,ratingcount) " +
            "values ('tt0133093','The Matrix','Keanu Reeves',1999,'fiction',
            5,8.7,1605968);";

    private final String MOVIES_INSERT_SQL_2 = "insert into movies (id,title,actor,year,
    genre,stars,rating,ratingcount) " +
            "values ('tt0209144','Memento','Guy Pearce',2000,'drama',4,8.4,1090922);";

    private final String MOVIES_INSERT_SQL_ERROR = "insert into movies (year,genre,stars,
    rating,ratingcount) " +
            "values ('tt0209144','Memento','Guy Pearce',2000,'drama',4,8.4,1090922);";

    @Bean
    public CommandLineRunner process(DataSource dataSource){
        return args -> {
            JdbcTemplate jdbcTemplate = new JdbcTemplate(dataSource);
            jdbcTemplate.execute(MOVIES_TABLE_SQL);
            jdbcTemplate.execute(MOVIES_INSERT_SQL_1);
            jdbcTemplate.execute(MOVIES_INSERT_SQL_2);
            //jdbcTemplate.execute(MOVIES_INSERT_SQL_ERROR);
        };
    }

    @Bean
    public TaskDemoListener taskDemoListener(){
        return new TaskDemoListener();
    }
}
```

Listing 11-1 shows the `TaskDemoConfiguration` class. If you take a closer look, the only new keyword you are using is the `@EnableTask` annotation. This annotation triggers all the task life cycles. It is a simple SQL CREATE and INSERT. I commented out the last line of `jdbcTemplate` because I introduced a SQL syntax error that you are reviewing for the events. The end of the class declares a `taskDemoListener` bean.

Next, create the `TaskDemoListener` class (see Listing 11-2).

Listing 11-2. src/main/java/com/apress/cloud/task/TaskDemoListener.java

```
package com.apress.cloud.task;

import lombok.extern.log4j.Log4j2;
import org.springframework.cloud.task.listener.annotation.AfterTask;
import org.springframework.cloud.task.listener.annotation.BeforeTask;
import org.springframework.cloud.task.listener.annotation.FailedTask;
import org.springframework.cloud.task.repository.TaskExecution;

@Log4j2
public class TaskDemoListener {

    @BeforeTask
    public void beforeTask(TaskExecution taskExecution) {
        log.debug("[@BeforeTask] - {}", taskExecution);
    }

    @AfterTask
    public void afterTask(TaskExecution taskExecution) {
        log.debug("[@AfterTask] - {}", taskExecution);
    }

    @FailedTask
    public void failedTask(TaskExecution taskExecution, Throwable throwable) {
        log.debug("[@FailedTask] - {}", taskExecution);
        log.error("[@FailedTask] - {}", throwable);
    }
}
```

Listing 11-2 shows the TaskDemoListener class. It uses the @BeforeTask, @AfterTask, and @FailedTask annotations. The only thing to do is declare it and make this class a Spring bean, and the rest is done thanks to Spring Cloud Task. Now you are attached to the events.

■ **Note** You can find the source code in the ch11/tasks folder. I also added the TaskDemoListener class to implement TaskExecutionListener, which is an alternative for listening Spring Cloud Task events.

Next, open your application.properties and add the content in Listing 11-3.

Listing 11-3. src/main/resources/application.properties

```
# Application Name
spring.application.name=task-demo

# Logging Level
logging.level.org.springframework.cloud.task=DEBUG
logging.level.com.apress.cloud.task=DEBUG
```

It's important to know that you need to declare the logging level and add the `spring.application.name` property, so you can get information when running the program. Next, if you run it, you should see the following output.

```
...

 DEBUG - [main] ... : Initializing task schema for h2 database

 DEBUG - [main] ... : Creating: TaskExecution{executionId=0, parentExecutionId=null,
                      exitCode=null, taskName='task-demo', startTime=Mon Jul 13 20:05:02 EDT
                      2020, endTime=null, exitMessage='null', externalExecutionId='null',
                      errorMessage='null', arguments=[]}
DEBUG - [main] ... :  [@BeforeTask] - TaskExecution{executionId=1, parentExecutionId=null,
                      exitCode=null, taskName='task-demo' ...
  INFO - [main] ... : Started TaskDemoApplication in 1.095 seconds (JVM running for 1.686)
DEBUG - [main] ... :  [@AfterTask] - TaskExecution{executionId=1, parentExecutionId=null,
                      exitCode=0, taskName='task-demo', ...
 DEBUG - [main] ... : Updating: TaskExecution with executionId=1 with the following
                      {exitCode=0, endTime=Mon Jul 13 20:05:02 EDT 2020, exitMessage='null',
                      errorMessage='null'}

...
```

This shows the timestamp for when started, how long it took to complete, and the events that are being listened to, such as before task and after task executions. It follows the cloud task life cycle. You can un-comment the SQL error. You should also see the task event that failed to be executed.

As you can see, Spring Cloud Task is very easy to apply to any microservice that can execute anything from a simple job to an extensive workload. Next, let's look at how to integrate Spring Cloud Task with Spring Cloud Stream.

Spring Cloud Stream Integration

There are different ways to integrate Spring Cloud Task's functionalities within Spring Cloud Stream. You can use a sink that listens for any task event (as with the TaskDemo project) such as before-task, after-task, and failed-task events; or you can create a stream pipeline DSL and launch a task. Launching a task requires either using a custom sink that uses `@EnableTaskLauncher` to run sink task starters such as `task-launcher-local` and `task-launcher-dataflow`. So, let's review some of these options.

Task Events Within Spring Cloud Stream

Spring Cloud Task emits events during task processing, and it can also send events to a stream by using the predefined channel/destination named `task-events`. The only thing you need to do is add the binder, and Spring Cloud Task does the rest (see Figure 11-2).

***Figure 11-2.** Task events*

The following steps demonstrate this.

1. Get RabbitMQ up and running. You use it as a binder and can run it with Docker.

```
docker run -d --rm --name rabbit -p 5672:5672 -p 15672:15672
rabbitmq:3.8.3-management-alpine
```

2. Download the `log-sink-rabbit` app-starter JAR from `https://repo.spring.io/libs-release/org/springframework/cloud/stream/app/log-sink-rabbit/`.

3. Create an `application.properties` file with the following content.

```
# Server
server.port=8083

# Spring Cloud Stream
spring.cloud.stream.bindings.input.destination=task-events
```

4. Run it with

```
java -jar log-sink-rabbit-2.1.3.RELEASE.jar
```

5. Reopen your TaskDemo project and add the following dependency.

```
<dependency>
        <groupId>org.springframework.cloud</groupId>
        <artifactId>spring-cloud-starter-stream-rabbit</artifactId>
        <scope>compile</scope>
</dependency>
```

6. Run your TaskDemo project and note the logs in the log-sink app starter.

```
-- log-sink : {"executionId":1,"parentExecutionId":null,"exitCode":null,
"taskName":"task-demo","startTime":"2020-07-15T00:40:19.168+00:00",
"endTime":null,"exitMessage":null,"externalExecutionId":null,"errorMessage":
null,"arguments":[]}
-- log-sink : {"executionId":1,"parentExecutionId":null,"exitCode":0,
"taskName":"task-demo","startTime":"2020-07-15T00:40:19.168+00:00",
"endTime":"2020-07-15T00:40:19.289+00:00","exitMessage":null,"external
ExecutionId":null,"errorMessage":null,"arguments":[]}
```

By adding the binder (`spring-cloud-starter-stream-rabbit`) dependency to the pom.xml file in your TaskDemo project, Spring Cloud Task creates the `task-events` destination and sends all the events through that channel/destination.

Launching Tasks in Spring Cloud Data Flow

There are a few options where you can launch a task by registering your Task app in Spring Cloud Data Flow or by having a sink that has the task launcher (a custom sink or a task launcher Data Flow sink app starter). In this section, you learn how to register a task and to launch it through the dashboard.

Image to Dropbox Task

Let's create a simple task and assume we need to connect to a database where we already have a movie-art URL. You need to download an image and send it to a Dropbox folder. Because you are using the Dropbox API, go to `www.dropbox.com/developers/`. If you don't have an account, you can get one for free. You need to create an application (I named mine movie-art). You can have a folder or a full-access permission type. There is a section where you need to click **Generate access token**. This is the token that you uploads the images into the folder you want. Of course, you can create a folder where the movies art will be placed. I created an `IMDB/` folder.

Let's start by opening a browser and going to Spring Initializr. Use the following data.

- Group: `com.apress.cloud.task`
- Artifact: `image-to-dropbox`
- Package name: `com.apress.cloud.task`
- Dependencies: MySQL Driver, JDBC API, Lombok, Task

Press the Generate button to download a ZIP file. You can unzip and import it into your favorite IDE (see Figure 11-3).

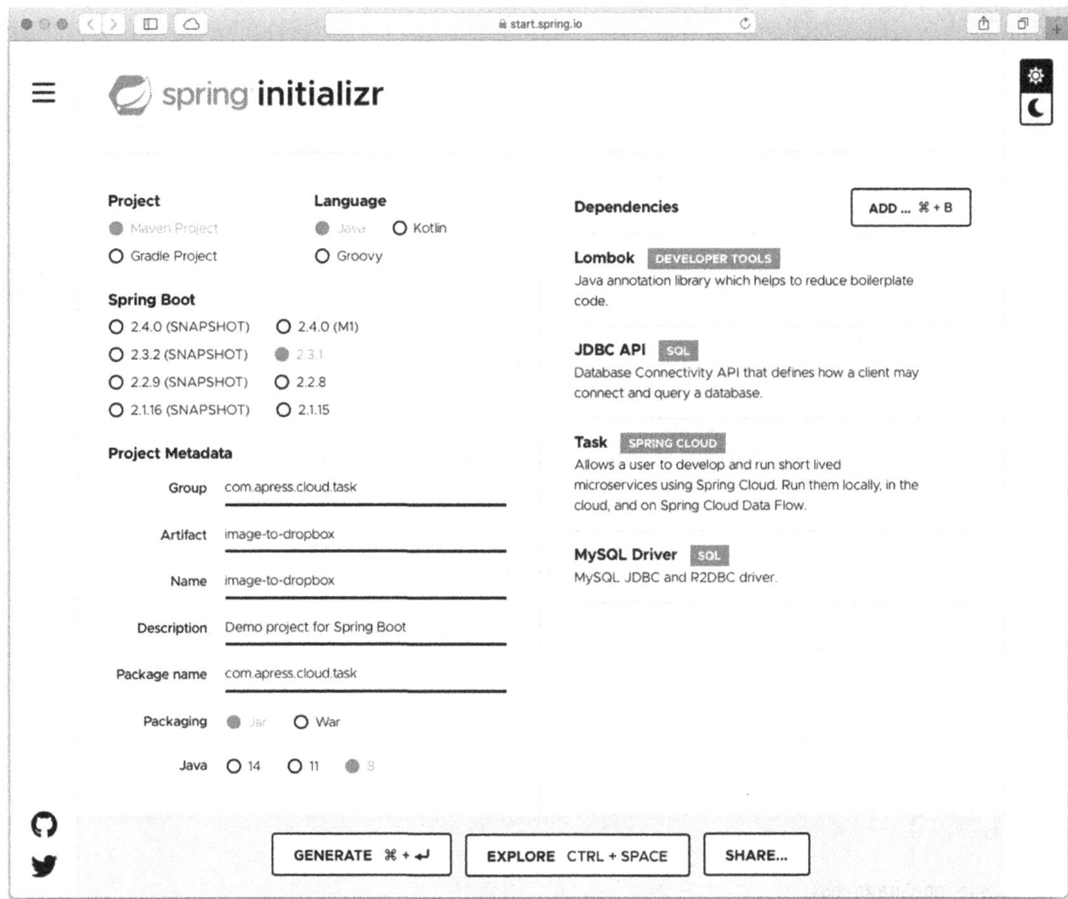

Figure 11-3. *Spring Initializr image-to-dropbox*

This project needs to be deployed to a Maven repository, so you are doing the same as in the previous chapter. I used the JFrog Bintray (`https://bintray.com`) open source solution. Open the `pom.xml` file and add the following dependencies.

```
...
<!-- DropBox -->
<dependency>
        <groupId>com.dropbox.core</groupId>
        <artifactId>dropbox-core-sdk</artifactId>
        <version>3.1.4</version>
</dependency>

<!-- Apache Commons IO -->
<dependency>
        <groupId>commons-io</groupId>
        <artifactId>commons-io</artifactId>
        <version>2.7</version>
</dependency>
```

```
<dependency>
          <groupId>org.mariadb.jdbc</groupId>
          <artifactId>mariadb-java-client</artifactId>
        <scope>runtime</scope>
</dependency>
...

<build>
        <plugins>

                ...
                <plugin>
                        <groupId>org.springframework.cloud</groupId>
                        <artifactId>spring-cloud-app-starter-metadata-maven-plugin
                        </artifactId>
                        <version>2.0.0.RELEASE</version>
                        <executions>
                                <execution>
                                        <id>aggregate-metadata</id>
                                        <phase>compile</phase>
                                        <goals>
                                                <goal>aggregate-metadata</goal>
                                        </goals>
                                </execution>
                        </executions>
                </plugin>
                ...
        </plugins>
</build>

<distributionManagement>
        <repository>
                <id>bintray-felipeg48-scdf</id>
                <name>felipeg48-scdf</name>
                <url>https://api.bintray.com/maven/felipeg48/scdf/movie-tasks/;publish=1
                 </url>
        </repository>
</distributionManagement>
...
```

Replace the `mysql` dependency with MariaDB because you are reusing the one from the Data Flow server. Remember to switch to your own account for the distribution management tag and to use version 0.0.1 and remove the snapshot text.

```
<version>0.0.1</version>
```

This is useful for deploying a project into a Maven repository.

Next, create the `ImageToDropboxProperties` class, which holds the key/token API from Dropbox (see Listing 11-4). (The one just generated for your Dropbox app description).

Listing 11-4 src/main/java/com/apress/cloud/task/ImageToDropboxProperties.java

```
package com.apress.cloud.task;

import lombok.Data;
import org.springframework.boot.context.properties.ConfigurationProperties;

@Data
@ConfigurationProperties(prefix = "dropbox")
public class ImageToDropboxProperties {

    private String apiKey = null;
    private String path = "/IMDB/";
    private String localTmpFolder = "/tmp/";

}
```

Listing 11-4 shows the properties used for Dropbox, including the path where you are uploading the images, `localTempFolder`, where you download the image and then upload it to Dropbox. Token is the value for `apiKey`.

Next, create the `ImageToDropbox` class (see Listing 11-5).

Listing 11-5. src/main/java/com/apress/cloud/task/ImageToDropboxUtils.java

```
package com.apress.cloud.task;

import com.dropbox.core.DbxException;
import com.dropbox.core.DbxRequestConfig;
import com.dropbox.core.v2.DbxClientV2;
import com.dropbox.core.v2.files.FileMetadata;
import lombok.extern.log4j.Log4j2;
import org.apache.commons.io.FileUtils;

import java.io.File;
import java.io.FileInputStream;
import java.io.IOException;
import java.io.InputStream;
import java.net.URL;

@Log4j2
public class ImageToDropboxUtils {

    private ImageToDropboxProperties imageToDropboxProperties;
    private DbxClientV2 client;

    public ImageToDropboxUtils(ImageToDropboxProperties imageToDropboxProperties){
        this.imageToDropboxProperties = imageToDropboxProperties;
        DbxRequestConfig config = DbxRequestConfig.newBuilder("dropbox/scdf-imdb").build();
        this. client = new DbxClientV2(config, this.imageToDropboxProperties.getApiKey());
    }
```

```
    public void fromUrlToDropBox(String fromUrl, String filename) throws DbxException,
    IOException {
        log.debug("Attempting to download: " + fromUrl);
        FileUtils.copyURLToFile(new URL(fromUrl), new File(this.imageToDropboxProperties.
        getLocalTmpFolder() + filename), 10000, 10000);

        InputStream in = new FileInputStream(this.imageToDropboxProperties.
        getLocalTmpFolder() + filename);
        log.debug("Attempting to Save to Dropbox in: {}", this.imageToDropboxProperties.
        getPath() + filename);
        client.files()
              .uploadBuilder(this.imageToDropboxProperties.getPath() + filename)
              .uploadAndFinish(in);
        log.debug("Uploaded to Dropbox");

        log.debug("Removing temporal file: {}", this.imageToDropboxProperties.
        getLocalTmpFolder() + filename);
        FileUtils.deleteQuietly(new File(this.imageToDropboxProperties.getLocalTmpFolder() +
        filename));

    }
}
```

Listing 11-5 shows the utils class. Analyze it, and note that the Apache Commons library is used to download the image from a URL. The Dropbox path is used to upload the image. A temp folder is used to place it with a name. You are using the movie's ID as the name of the file.

Next, create the ImageToDropboxConfiguration class (see Listing 11-6).

Listing 11-6. src/main/java/com/apress/cloud/task/ImageToDropboxConfiguration.java

```
package com.apress.cloud.task;

import lombok.extern.log4j.Log4j2;
import org.springframework.boot.CommandLineRunner;
import org.springframework.boot.context.properties.EnableConfigurationProperties;
import org.springframework.cloud.task.configuration.EnableTask;
import org.springframework.context.annotation.Bean;
import org.springframework.context.annotation.Configuration;
import org.springframework.jdbc.core.JdbcTemplate;

import javax.sql.DataSource;

@Log4j2
@EnableTask
@Configuration
@EnableConfigurationProperties({ImageToDropboxProperties.class})
public class ImageToDropboxConfiguration {

    @Bean
    public ImageToDropboxUtils imageToDropBoxUtils(ImageToDropboxProperties
    imageToDropboxProperties){
        return new ImageToDropboxUtils(imageToDropboxProperties);
    }
```

```
    private final String MOVIES_TABLE_SQL = "CREATE TABLE IF NOT EXISTS art(" +
            " id varchar(10) primary key," +
            " url varchar(500));";

    private final String MOVIES_INSERT_SQL_1 = "insert into art (id,url) " +
            "values ('tt0133093','https://m.media-amazon.com/images/M/
            MV5BNzQzOTk3OTAtNDQ0Zi00ZTVkLWI0MTEtMDllZjNkYzNjNTc4L2ltYW
            dlXkEyXkFqcGdeQXVyNjU0OTQ0OTY@._V1_.jpg');";
    private final String MOVIES_INSERT_SQL_2 = "insert into art (id,url) " +
            "values ('tt0209144','https://m.media-amazon.com/images/M/
            MV5BZTcyNjk1MjgtOWI3Mi00YzQwLWI5MTktMzY4ZmI2NDAyNzYzXk
            EyXkFqcGdeQXVyNjU0OTQ0OTY@._V1_.jpg');";

    private final String MOVIES_QUERY_SQL = "select url from art where id=?;";

    private final String MATRIX_ART_ID = "tt0133093";
    private final String MEMENTO_ART_ID = "tt0209144";

    @Bean
    public CommandLineRunner process(DataSource dataSource, ImageToDropboxUtils
    imageToDropBoxUtils){
        return args -> {
            log.debug("Connecting to: {} ", dataSource.getConnection().getMetaData().
            getURL());

            JdbcTemplate jdbcTemplate = new JdbcTemplate(dataSource);
            jdbcTemplate.execute(MOVIES_TABLE_SQL);
            jdbcTemplate.execute(MOVIES_INSERT_SQL_1);
            jdbcTemplate.execute(MOVIES_INSERT_SQL_2);

            String url = null;

            url = jdbcTemplate.queryForObject(
                    MOVIES_QUERY_SQL, new Object[]{MATRIX_ART_ID}, String.class);
            log.debug("URL: {}", url);
            imageToDropBoxUtils.fromUrlToDropBox(url,MATRIX_ART_ID + ".jpg");

            url = jdbcTemplate.queryForObject(
                    MOVIES_QUERY_SQL, new Object[]{MEMENTO_ART_ID}, String.class);
            log.debug("URL: {}", url);
            imageToDropBoxUtils.fromUrlToDropBox(url,MEMENTO_ART_ID + ".jpg");
        };
    };

}
```

Listing 11-6 shows the task configuration. `@EnableTask` is used. This is cheating because we are creating a table and inserting a hard-coded URL to mimic using a database to get the URL for the movie's art.

Next, open your `application.properties` file and add the content in Listing 11-7.

Listing 11-7. src/main/resources/application.properties

```
# Application Name
spring.application.name=image-to-dropbox

# DropBox
dropbox.api-key=YOUR-KEY
dropbox.path=/IMDB/

# Logging Level
logging.level.org.springframework.cloud.task=DEBUG
logging.level.com.apress.cloud.task=DEBUG

# DataSource
spring.datasource.url=jdbc:mysql://localhost:3306/movies?useSSL=false&requireSSL=false
spring.datasource.driverClassName=org.mariadb.jdbc.Driver
spring.datasource.username=root
spring.datasource.password=rootpw
```

Here you are using the MySQL database engine, so you need to set up the datasource. Also add your Dropbox token and the path where the images are uploaded. The logging level sees everything about the task and your code.

You can run it to test this locally, but make sure you have the MySQL engine up and running. You can use Docker with the following command.

```
docker run -d --rm --name mysql \
 -e MYSQL_DATABASE=movies \
 -e MYSQL_USER=root \
 -e MYSQL_ROOT_PASSWORD=rootpw \
 -p 3306:3306 \
 mysql:5.7.25
```

You are creating a `movies` database, passing the username and password for the connection, and exposing port 3306. Now, you can run the app, which should show the following output.

```
...
-- : Initializing task schema for mysql database
-- : Creating: TaskExecution{executionId=0, parentExecutionId=null, exitCode=null,
     taskName='image-to-dropbox', startTime=Sun Jul 19 21:27:44 EDT 2020, endTime=null,
     exitMessage='null', externalExecutionId='null', errorMessage='null', arguments=[]}
-- : Started ImageToDropboxApplication in 1.062 seconds (JVM running for 1.475)
-- : Connecting to: jdbc:mysql://localhost:3306/movies?useSSL=false&requireSSL=false
-- : URL: https://m.media-amazon.com/images/M/MV5BNzQzOTk3OTAtNDQ0ZiooZTV
     kLWIOMTEtMDllZjNkYzNjNTc4L2ltYWdlXkEyXkFqcGdeQXVyNjUOOTQ0OTY@._V1_.jpg
-- : Attempting to download: https://m.media-amazon.com/images/M/MV5BNzQzOTk3OTAtNDQ0ZiooZTV
     kLWIOMTEtMDllZjNkYzNjNTc4L2ltYWdlXkEyXkFqcGdeQXVyNjUOOTQ0OTY@._V1_.jpg
-- : Attempting to Save to Dropbox in: /IMDB/tt0133093.jpg
-- : Uploaded to Dropbox
-- : Removing temporal file: /tmp/tt0133093.jpg
-- : URL: https://m.media-amazon.com/images/M/MV5BZTcyNjk1MjgtOWI3MiOOYzQwLWI5MTktMz
     Y4ZmI2NDAyNzYzXkEyXkFqcGdeQXVyNjUOOTQ0OTY@._V1_.jpg
```

```
-- : Attempting to download: https://m.media-amazon.com/images/M/MV5BZTcyNjk1MjgtOWI3MiOOYzQw
     LWI5MTktMzY4ZmI2NDAyNzYzXkEyXkFqcGdeQXVyNjUOOTQOOTY@._V1_.jpg
-- : Attempting to Save to Dropbox in: /IMDB/tt0209144.jpg
-- : Uploaded to Dropbox
-- : Removing temporal file: /tmp/tt0209144.jpg
-- : Updating: TaskExecution with executionId=1 with the following {exitCode=0, endTime=Sun
     Jul 19 21:27:53 EDT 2020, exitMessage='null', errorMessage='null'}
...
```

If you check your Dropbox folder, you can see two movie's images. After you test it, you need to package and deploy it to the Maven/Bintray repository with the following commands.

```
./mvnw -DskipTests clean package
./mvnw -DskipTests deploy
```

Using the Dashboard

After you deploy the `image-to-dropbox` artifacts, you need to have the Spring Cloud Data Flow server up and running. You can use either the local Docker Compose or your Kubernetes installation. You need to create the `movies` database in the MySQL instance you are using for the Spring Cloud Data Flow server. Also, you need to remember that one of the main environment properties is the Maven repo.

```
maven.remote-repositories.repo1.url=https://dl.bintray.com/felipeg48/scdf
```

As a best practice, I recommend using environment variables to add your Dropbox token. If you are using Kubernetes, you can add ConfigMap as an environment variable when running your pods. You also need to add the key.

```
dropbox.api-key=YOUR-TOKEN
```

Once you are ready, go to your dashboard and register the task like you register an application. You are registering an application of type `task`. Choose the bulk import application and add the following coordinates in the Apps as Properties text area (see Figure 11-4).

```
task.image-to-dropbox=maven://com.apress.cloud.task:image-to-dropbox:0.0.1
task.image-to-dropbox.metadata=maven://com.apress.cloud.task:image-to-
dropbox:jar:metadata:0.0.1
```

Note that you are using the following format.

```
task:<app-name>[.<metadata>]=maven://<group>:<artifact>[:jar:metadata]:version
```

The type is the task.

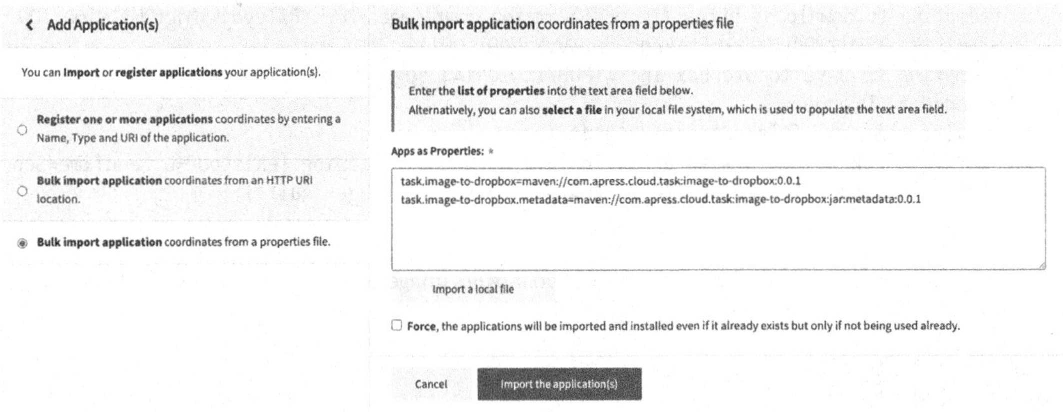

Figure 11-4. *App/add/import from properties*

Click the **Import the application(s)** button. You should see your task listed now (see Figure 11-5).

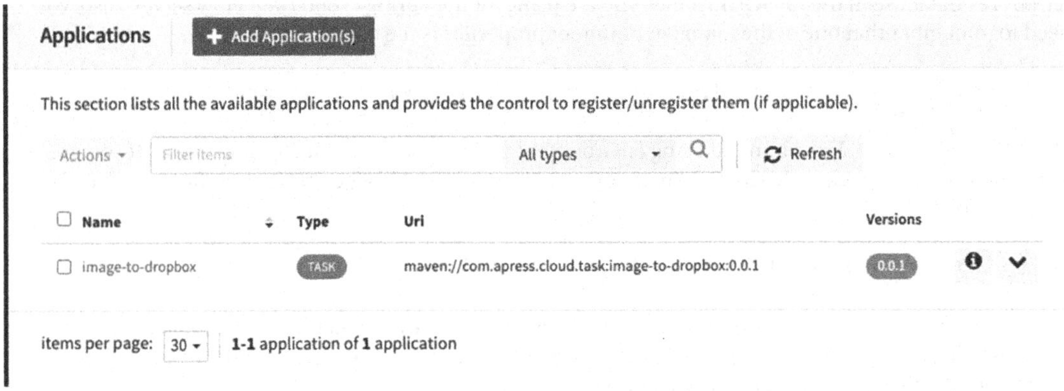

Figure 11-5. *Apps*

Next, in the left pane, click the Task tab. This takes you to the Task page. Click the **+ Create task(s)** button, which takes you to the familiar Flow UI that you know from the Streams. You should see the "image-to-dropbox" task listed in the left pane. You can drag and drop it, or you can enter the name of the task app, image-to-dropbox, in the text area. If you drag and drop, you need to connect the task to the start and end icons (see Figure 11-6).

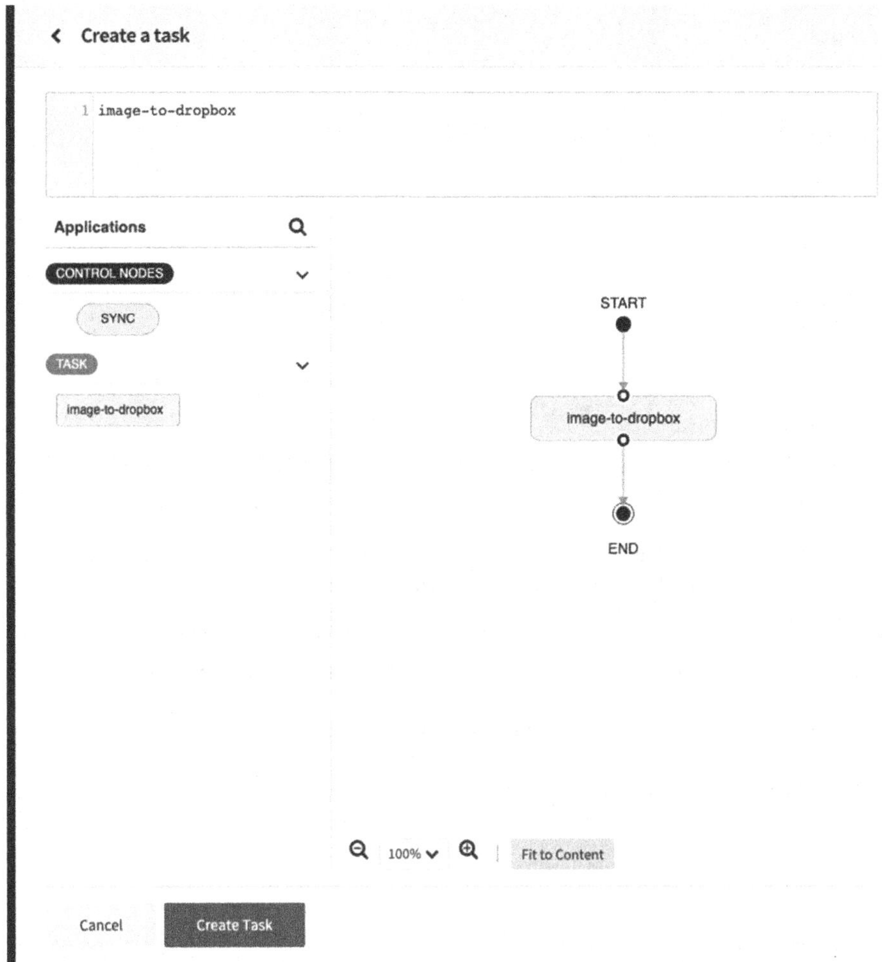

Figure 11-6. *Create a task*

Next, click the Create Task button, which opens a dialog where you name the task. Please set it to `movie-task`. Then click the **Create the task** button (see Figure 11-7).

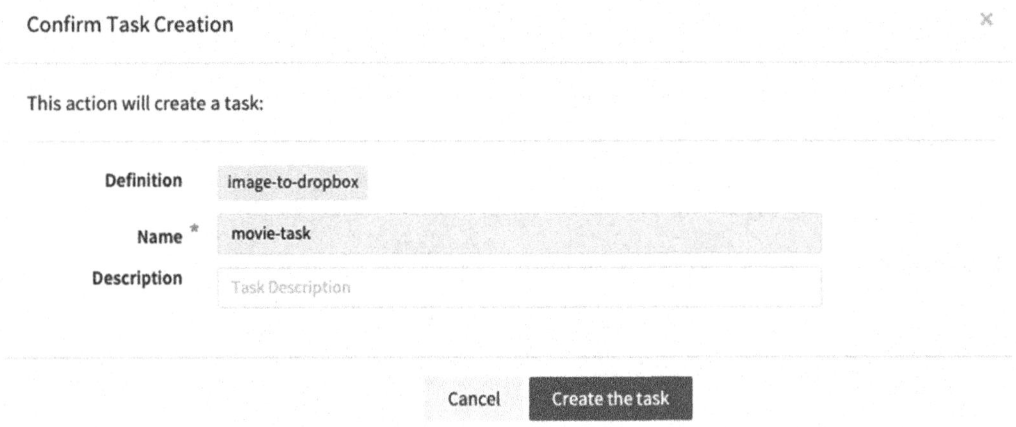

Confirm Task Creation

This action will create a task:

Definition image-to-dropbox

Name * movie-task

Description Task Description

Cancel Create the task

Figure 11-7. *Confirm Task Creation*

After you create `movie-task`, the list of available tasks needs to be launched. To launch a task, click the Play button (>). You are shown any additional properties that you need. In this case, you must add the following properties as arguments.

```
--movie.datasource.url=jdbc:mysql://mysql:3306/movies?useSSL=false&requireSSL=false
```

If you forgot to add the Dropbox token, you can add it here as well (see Figure 11-8).

```
--dropbox.api-key=YOUR-TOKEN
```

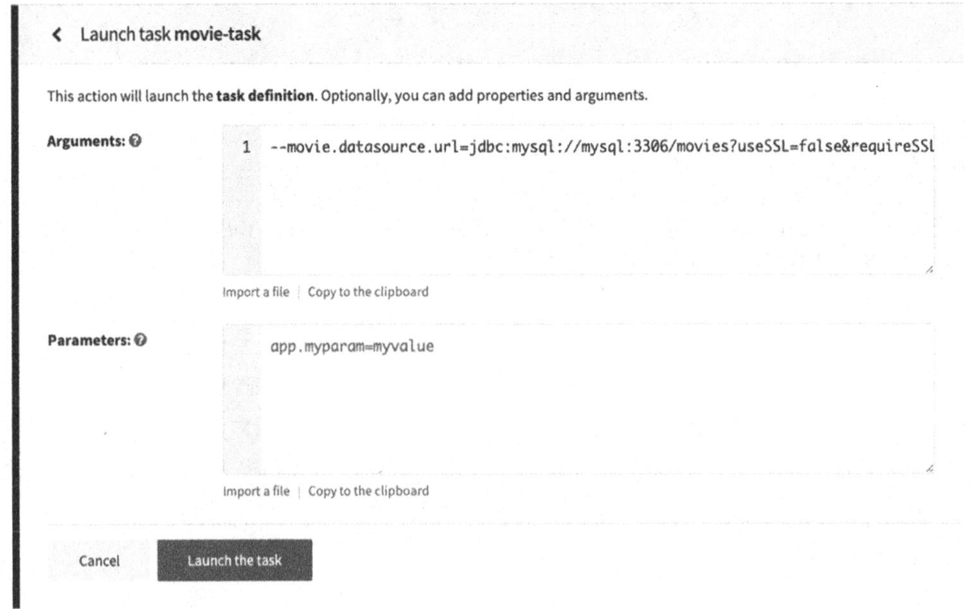

Figure 11-8. *Launch task movie-task*

Then click **Launch the task**. After that, return to the list of tasks to see if it was completed. You can refresh the page (see Figure 11-9).

Tasks
+ Create task(s)
Utils
Task
Executions
Actions
Filter items
Refresh

Name	Description	Definitions	Status
movie-task		image-to-dropbox	COMPLETE

items per page: 30
1-1 task definition of 1 task definition

Figure 11-9. *Task completed*

Click the Executions tab to see the status, and click Task Execution Id to see more information, including the task logs. If you are using Kubernetes, a pod was launched, executed, and terminated (see Figures 11-10 and 11-11).

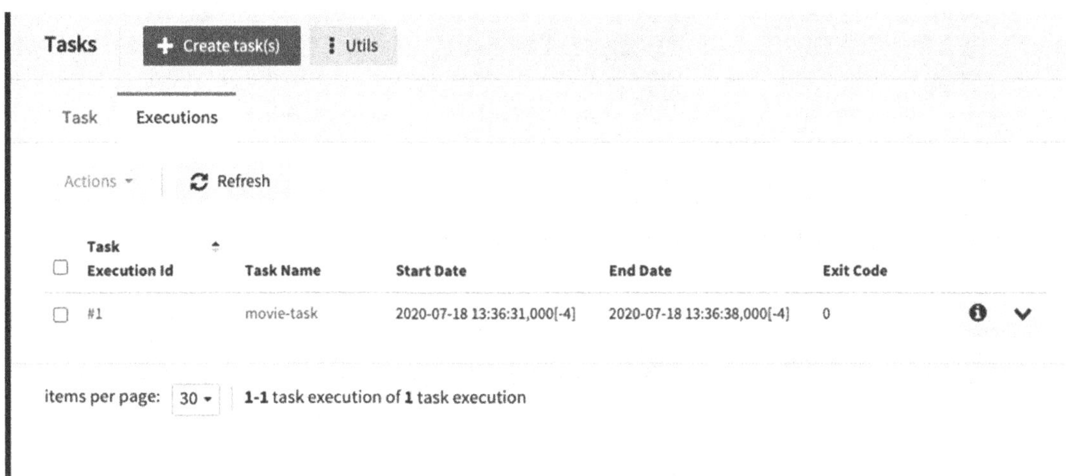

Figure 11-10. *Executions list*

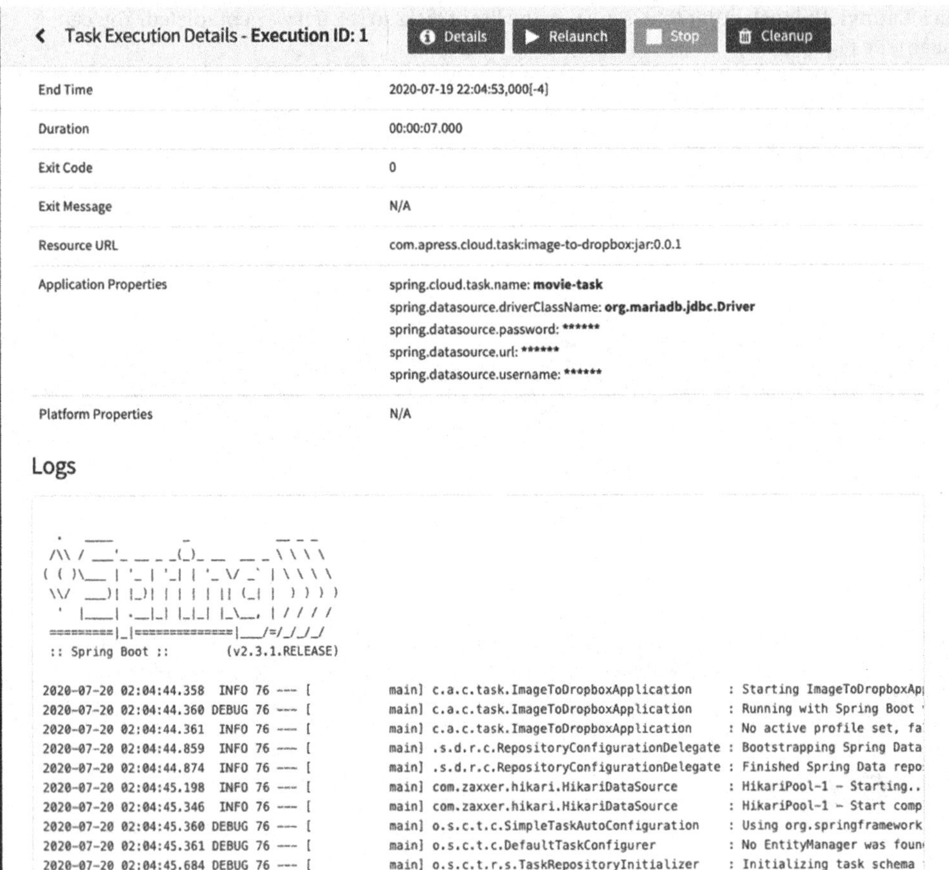

Figure 11-11. *Task execution details Execution ID: 1*

Check your Dropbox folder. The images should be there (see Figure 11-12).

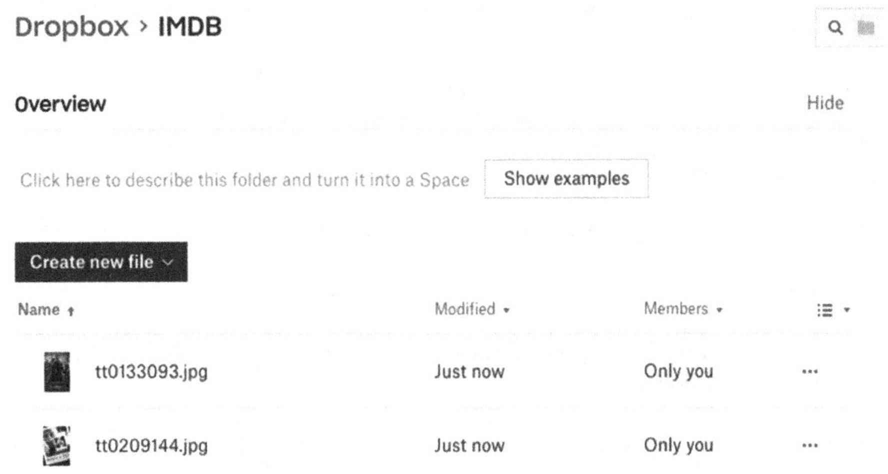

Figure 11-12. *Dropbox IMDB*

Congratulations. You have launched your task in Data Flow! Another way to execute tasks is by using streams. You can create custom streams that can launch a task. Select either a source or processor using the `app-starters-task-launch-request-common` dependency, and send a JSON payload in the following format.

```
{
  "name":"<task-name>",
  "deploymentProps": {"key1":"val1","key2":"val2"},
  "args":["--debug", "--foo", "bar"]
}
```

At a minimum, you can just use the name.

```
{"name":"foo"}
```

The name is related to the task that is already registered as an application. You need to send this payload to a sink that has the `@EnableTaskLauncher` annotation, and that's it. You don't need to do anything else. This automatically gets the JSON payload and launches the task by the name. An alternative way is to use the `TaskLaunchRequest` class in the source or processor to wrap the payload, making it even easier to send the payload to the sink.

And yes, there is an App Starter sink that launches the task: Task Launcher Data Flow Sink App Starter. Also, you can listen to all the task events by subscribing to the `task-events` destination.

Launching a Task Using Data Flow Shell

To launch a task in a Data Flow shell, you must first register your task as you did with the apps.

```
dataflow:> app register --name image-to-dropbox --type task --uri maven://com.apress.
cloud.task:image-to-dropbox:0.0.1 --metadata-uri maven://com.apress.cloud.task:image-to-
dropbox:jar:metadata:0.0.1
```

```
dataflow:> task create movie-task --definition "image-to-dropbox"
dataflow:> task list
```

After you register and create the task, you can launch it with the following.

```
dataflow:> task launch movie-task --arguments "--movie.datasource.url=jdbc:mysql://
mysql:3306/movies?useSSL=false&requireSSL=false"
```

You can review the task execution using the following.

```
dataflow:> task execution list
```

Look at the other commands that you can apply to the tasks. As you can see, they are very simple. If you want to destroy the task, execute the following.

```
dataflow:> task destroy --name movie-task
```

■ **Note** In this task, you needed to create the `movies` database. Remember that Spring Cloud Task initializes the tables with information about the task execution. If you already have this information but want to use the tables, you can disable the initialization by setting the following property: `spring.cloud.task.initialize-enabled=false`

Batch Processing

Let's talk about batch processing. If you take a closer look at Spring Cloud Task, you realize that you can only execute the task and received events. If a task fails during its execution, there is no way to start from where it left off; you need to fix the problem and then launch the task again. This is probably okay for easier tasks, but if you have a heavy load of millions of records, you don't want to start from the beginning. For this reason, you can combine the power of Spring Cloud Task with Spring Batch. Spring Cloud Task can be a wrapper for Spring Batch processing within a cloud environment. You get more control over the jobs and steps and executing your business logic.

Movie Batch

Let's create a movie batch very similar to the previous task. In this case, it will be a more dynamic app because you download movie-art and then upload it to the Dropbox account; this means that you need to pass the Dropbox information along with the URL and the movie-art ID.

Let's start by opening the browser and going to Spring Initializr. Use the following information.

- Group: `com.apress.cloud.batch`
- Artifact: `movie-batch`
- Package name: `com.apress.cloud.batch`
- Dependencies: Spring Batch, Task, Lombok, JDBC API, MySQL

Press the Generate button to download a ZIP file. You can unzip and import it into your favorite IDE (see Figure 11-13).

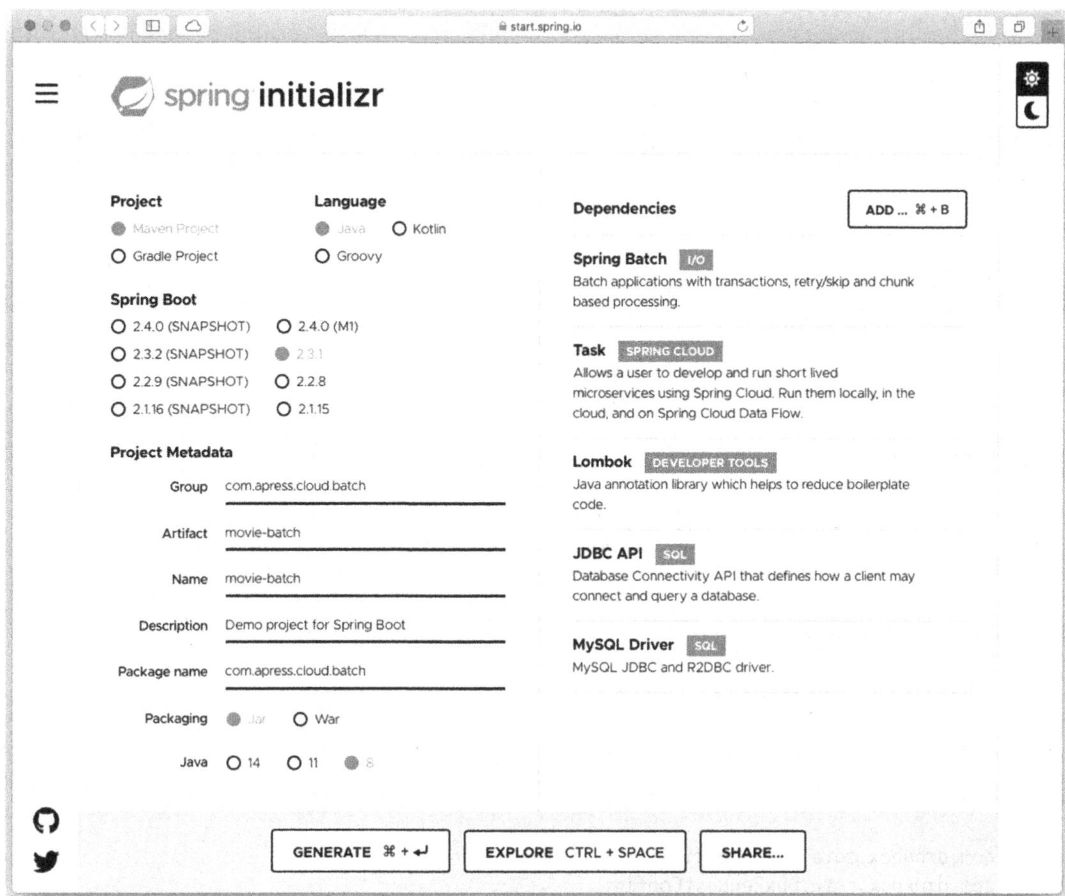

Figure 11-13. *Spring Initializr movie-batch*

Next, open `pom.xml` and add the following dependencies and sections.

```
...

<!-- DropBox -->
<dependency>
        <groupId>com.dropbox.core</groupId>
        <artifactId>dropbox-core-sdk</artifactId>
        <version>3.1.4</version>
</dependency>

<!-- Apache Commons IO -->
<dependency>
        <groupId>commons-io</groupId>
        <artifactId>commons-io</artifactId>
        <version>2.7</version>
</dependency>
```

```
<dependency>
        <groupId>org.mariadb.jdbc</groupId>
        <artifactId>mariadb-java-client</artifactId>
        <scope>runtime</scope>
</dependency>

...
...

<distributionManagement>
        <repository>
                <id>bintray-felipeg48-scdf</id>
                <name>felipeg48-scdf</name>
                <url>https://api.bintray.com/maven/felipeg48/scdf/movie-tasks/;publish=1</url>
        </repository>
</distributionManagement>
```

See that you are replacing the MySQL with the Maria DB connector. And you are adding a plugin to generate the metadata jar files and the distribution tag for the deployment to the Bintray Maven repository. Remember to change it to your own repo. Don't forget to remove the snapshot and use version 0.0.1.

```
<version>0.0.1</version>
```

Next, let's create the `DropboxUtils` class (see Listing 11-8).

Listing 11-8. src/main/java/com/apress/cloud/batch/dropbox/DropboxUtils.java

```
package com.apress.cloud.batch.dropbox;

import com.dropbox.core.DbxException;
import com.dropbox.core.DbxRequestConfig;
import com.dropbox.core.v2.DbxClientV2;
import lombok.extern.log4j.Log4j2;
import org.apache.commons.io.FileUtils;
import org.springframework.stereotype.Component;

import java.io.File;
import java.io.FileInputStream;
import java.io.IOException;
import java.io.InputStream;
import java.net.URL;

@Log4j2
@Component
public class DropboxUtils {

    private DbxClientV2 client = null;
    private DbxRequestConfig config = DbxRequestConfig.newBuilder("dropbox/scdf-imdb").
    build();
```

```
    public void fromUrlToDropBox(String fromUrl, String filename, String dropboxToken,
    String dropboxPath, String tmpFolder) throws DbxException, IOException {
        log.debug("Attempting to download: {}" , fromUrl);
        this. client = new DbxClientV2(config, dropboxToken);
        FileUtils.copyURLToFile(new URL(fromUrl), new File(tmpFolder + filename), 10000,
        10000);

        InputStream in = new FileInputStream(tmpFolder + filename);
        log.debug("Attempting to Save to Dropbox in: {}", dropboxPath + filename);
        client.files()
                .uploadBuilder(dropboxPath + filename)
                .uploadAndFinish(in);
        log.debug("Uploaded to Dropbox");

        log.debug("Removing temporal file: {}", tmpFolder + filename);
        FileUtils.deleteQuietly(new File(tmpFolder + filename));

    }
}
```

Listing 11-8 shows the DropboxUtils class, which is very similar to the previous task, but this time, you are excepting more parameters: the Dropbox's token, the path, and the tmp folder where you download the Movie's art. It became more dynamic.

Next, let's create the MovieBatchConfiguration class for the batch processing (see Listing 11-9).

Listing 11-9. src/main/java/com/apress/cloud/batch/MovieBatchConfiguration.java

```
package com.apress.cloud.batch;

import com.apress.cloud.batch.dropbox.DropboxUtils;
import lombok.AllArgsConstructor;
import lombok.extern.log4j.Log4j2;
import org.springframework.batch.core.Job;
import org.springframework.batch.core.Step;
import org.springframework.batch.core.configuration.annotation.EnableBatchProcessing;
import org.springframework.batch.core.configuration.annotation.JobBuilderFactory;
import org.springframework.batch.core.configuration.annotation.StepBuilderFactory;
import org.springframework.batch.core.configuration.annotation.StepScope;
import org.springframework.batch.core.step.tasklet.Tasklet;
import org.springframework.batch.repeat.RepeatStatus;
import org.springframework.beans.factory.annotation.Value;
import org.springframework.boot.context.properties.EnableConfigurationProperties;
import org.springframework.cloud.task.configuration.EnableTask;
import org.springframework.context.annotation.Bean;
import org.springframework.context.annotation.Configuration;

@Log4j2
@AllArgsConstructor
@EnableTask
@EnableBatchProcessing
@Configuration
```

```
public class MovieBatchConfiguration {

    private JobBuilderFactory jobBuilderFactory;
    private StepBuilderFactory stepBuilderFactory;
    private DropboxUtils dropboxUtils;

    @Bean
    @StepScope
    public Tasklet movieTasklet(
            @Value("#{jobParameters['url']}") String url,
            @Value("#{jobParameters['imdbId']}") String imdbId,
            @Value("#{jobParameters['dropbox.token']}") String token,
            @Value("#{jobParameters['dropbox.path']}") String path,
            @Value("#{jobParameters['dropbox.local-tmp-folder']}") String tmp) {
        return (stepContribution, chunkContext) -> {

            log.debug("Using Image ID: {} and URL: {}", imdbId, url);
            assert url!=null && imdbId!=null;

            dropboxUtils.fromUrlToDropBox(
                    url,
                    imdbId + ".jpg",
                    token,
                    path,
                    tmp);

            return RepeatStatus.FINISHED;
        };
    }

    @Bean
    public Step step1() {
        return stepBuilderFactory.get("step1")
                .tasklet(movieTasklet(null, null, null,null,null))
                .build();
    }

    @Bean
    public Job jobParametersJob() {
        return jobBuilderFactory.get("jobParametersJob")
                .start(step1())
                .build();
    }
}
```

Listing 11-9 shows the batch processing. Let's analyze the class.

- `jobParametersJob`. This method defines the job, which contains just one step. This method creates the `JobExecution`.
- `step1`. This method defines the step for the job and creates a tasklet. In this case, it is calling the `movieTasklet` method with null parameters. This is not wrong, you need to pass the parameters, but the definition is a holder that has a relation to the tasklet.

- `movieTasklet`. This method defines the tasklet. It uses the `@StepScope` annotation. This annotation is like a lazy instantiation, meaning that until the tasklet is called, it creates a Spring bean. That's why you can pass the `@Value` and evaluate the job parameter as a key. This is the `JobParameters` class, and in this context, the `jobParamters` instance is available as a map, so it's easy to access the keys. Of course, you can see this method with many parameters; so, you can pass just the `JobParameters` class as a parameter and use the `getParameters()` method to access all the keys.
- `@EnableTask`, `@EnableBatchProcessing`. Both annotations are used: one for the batch and the other to run in the cloud as a task.

Next, open `application.properties` and add the content in Listing 11-10.

Listing 11-10. src/main/resource/application.properties

```
# Application Name
spring.application.name=movie-batch

# Logging Level
logging.level.org.springframework.cloud.task=DEBUG
logging.level.com.apress.cloud.batch=DEBUG

# DataSource
spring.datasource.url=jdbc:mysql://localhost:3306/movies?useSSL=false&requireSSL=false
spring.datasource.driverClassName=org.mariadb.jdbc.Driver
spring.datasource.username=root
spring.datasource.password=rootpw

# Batch
spring.batch.initialize-schema=ALWAYS
```

You are using a MySQL database, and for now, it is pointing to a local database. To run this example, you need to have the MySQL engine up and running. You can do it using the Docker command.

```
docker run -d --rm --name mysql \
 -e MYSQL_DATABASE=movies \
 -e MYSQL_USER=root \
 -e MYSQL_ROOT_PASSWORD=rootpw \
 -p 3306:3306 \
 mysql:5.7.25
```

Next, run the app using your IDE, but remember that you need to pass some parameters. Another way to run it is by using the command line (a single line).

```
./mvnw spring-boot:run -Dspring-boot.run.arguments="url=https://bit.ly/2ZM57Kq imdbId=spring
dropbox.path=/IMDB/ dropbox.local-tmp-folder=/tmp/ dropbox.token=YOUR-TOKKEN"
```

Add your Dropbox token. It is just a single line, and there are spaces between the parameters. You should have the `spring.jpg` image in your Dropbox folder. If you run it again with the same parameters, you get an error, which is okay because the job parameters are associated with the job execution to prevent re-running a job by mistake. If you want to test it again, you can change the `url` and `imbdId` parameters.

An alternative is to run it by creating an executable JAR.

```
./mvnw -DskipTests clean package

java -jar target/movie-batch-0.0.1.jar \
 url=https://bit.ly/2ZM57Kq \
 imdbId=spring \
 dropbox.path=/IMDB/ \
 dropbox.local-tmp-folder=/tmp/ \
 dropbox.token=YOUR-TOKEN
```

This can be in multiple lines (remember that this is for a Unix OS; for Windows, it must be on one line).

After testing the `movie-batch` app, you need to deploy it to the Maven repository. Also, Bintray is being used for this example. Go to your command line and execute the following.

```
./mvnw -DskipTests clean package
./mvnw -DskipTests deploy
```

Now, you are ready for the next step.

Launching a Task/Batch with a Stream in Data Flow

In Spring Cloud Data Flow, there are many ways to launch a task. You saw that you can use the dashboard to launch, but what happens if you have a stream and want to trigger or launch a task/batch process? Spring Cloud Stream and Spring Cloud Task offer a way to launch a task/batch process in a stream. The only thing you need to do is use a source or processor and a simple payload that contains the name of the registeredtask app, or you can use the `TaskLaunchRequest` class to accomplish the same. The launcher must be a sink, which can be the `task-launcher-dataflow` app starter, or you can create a custom sink that uses `@EnableTaskLauncher`. This annotation takes care of the rest by consuming the payload message and launching the task.

Movie Batch Streams

Let's create a stream pipeline DSL that launches the `movie-batch` app in Spring Cloud Data Flow. Let's review what we are using (see Figure 11-14).

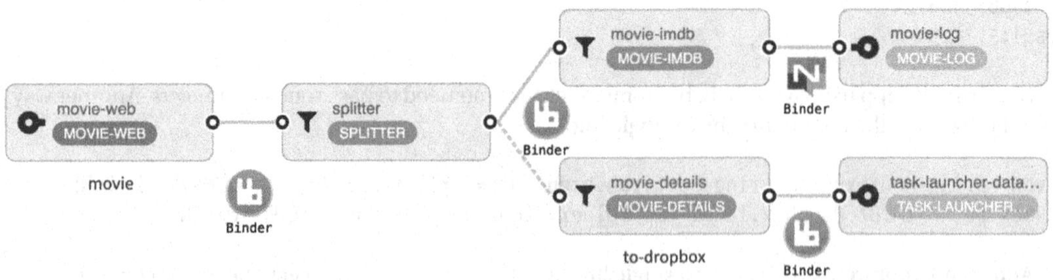

Figure 11-14. *Stream pipeline DSL*

Figure 11-14 shows the stream DSL you are building. As you can see, it is the same as in the previous chapter, and because you already have some of the apps in the Maven repository, you can reuse them. Note that the only new parts are the `movie-details` and the `task-launcher-dataflow` apps. So, you need to create a Movie Details project.

Movie Details

Let's start by opening the browser and going to Spring Initializr. Use the following information.

- Group: `com.apress.cloud.stream`
- Artifact: `movie-details`
- Package name: `com.apress.cloud.stream.movie`
- Dependencies: Spring Batch, Task, Lombok, JDBC API, MySQL

Press the Generate button to download a ZIP file. You can unzip and import it into your favorite IDE (see Figure 11-15).

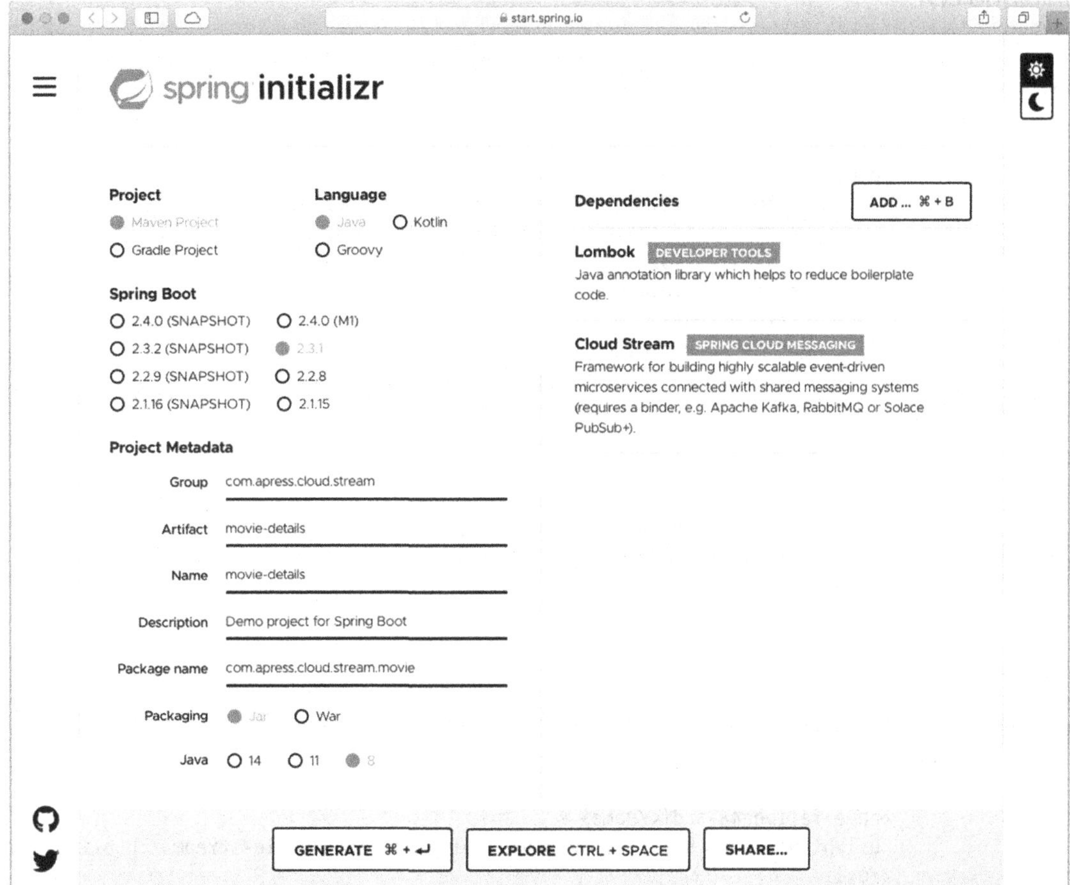

Figure 11-15. *Spring Initializr movie-details stream processor*

Next, open the `pom.xml` file, and add the following dependencies and sections.

```
..s.

<dependency>
        <groupId>org.springframework.cloud</groupId>
        <artifactId>spring-cloud-stream-binder-rabbit</artifactId>
</dependency>

<!-- Apache Commons -->
<dependency>
        <groupId>org.apache.httpcomponents</groupId>
        <artifactId>httpclient</artifactId>
        <version>4.5.12</version>
</dependency>

<dependency>
        <groupId>com.jayway.jsonpath</groupId>
        <artifactId>json-path</artifactId>
</dependency>
....
....
<build>
        <plugins>
                ...
                <plugin>
                        <groupId>org.springframework.cloud</groupId>
                        <artifactId>spring-cloud-app-starter-metadata-maven-plugin
                        </artifactId>
                        <version>2.0.0.RELEASE</version>
                        <executions>
                                <execution>
                                        <id>aggregate-metadata</id>
                                        <phase>compile</phase>
                                        <goals>
                                                <goal>aggregate-metadata</goal>
                                        </goals>
                                </execution>
                        </executions>
                </plugin>
                ...
        </plugins>
</build>

<distributionManagement>
        <repository>
                <id>bintray-felipeg48-scdf</id>
                <name>felipeg48-scdf</name>
                <url>https://api.bintray.com/maven/felipeg48/scdf/movie-streams/;publish=1
                </url>
        </repository>
</distributionManagement>
```

Don't forget to remove the snapshot and use version 0.0.1.

```
<version>0.0.1</version>
```

Next, let's create the `DropboxProperties` and `MovieProperties` classes. Remember that you need to pass along some of these properties to launch the `movie-batch` app successfully (see Listings 11-11 and 11-12).

Listing 11-11. src/main/java/com/apress/cloud/stream/movie/DropboxProperties.java

```
package com.apress.cloud.stream.movie;

import lombok.Data;
import org.springframework.boot.context.properties.ConfigurationProperties;

@Data
@ConfigurationProperties(prefix = "dropbox")
public class DropboxProperties {

    private String token = null;
    private String path = "/IMDB/";
    private String localTmpFolder = "/tmp/";
}
```

Listing 11-12. src/main/java/com/apress/cloud/stream/movie/MovieProperties.java

```
package com.apress.cloud.stream.movie;

import lombok.Data;
import org.springframework.boot.context.properties.ConfigurationProperties;

@Data
@ConfigurationProperties(prefix = "movie")
public class MovieProperties {
    String apiServer = "https://imdb8.p.rapidapi.com/title/get-details?tconst=ID";
    String headerHost = "imdb8.p.rapidapi.com";
    String headerKey = null;
    String taskName = "movie-dropbox-batch";
    DropboxProperties dropbox = new DropboxProperties();
}
```

As you can see, it is nearly the same as before, but the URL has changed. You are accessing the `/title/get-details` endpoint that brings the movie's images URL. Also a new field, `taskName,` was added to hold the name of the task you want to launch. Next, create the `Movie` and the `MoviePayload` classes (see Listings 11-13 and 11-14).

Listing 11-13. src/main/java/com/apress/cloud/stream/movie/Movie.java

```
package com.apress.cloud.stream.movie;

import lombok.AllArgsConstructor;
import lombok.Data;
import lombok.NoArgsConstructor;

@AllArgsConstructor
@NoArgsConstructor
@Data
public class Movie {
    private String id;
    private String title;
    private String actor;
    private int year;
    private String genre;
    private int stars;
}
```

Listing 11-14. src/main/java/com/apress/cloud/stream/movie/MoviePayload.java

```
package com.apress.cloud.stream.movie;

import lombok.AllArgsConstructor;
import lombok.Data;

@AllArgsConstructor
@Data
public class MoviePayload {
    String name;
    String[] args;
}
```

Listing 11-14 shows the payload sent to the `task-launcher-dataflow` app, so it can launch the `movie-batch` task with the right job parameters in the `args` field. The name is the task being created.

Next, create the `MovieStream` class (see Listing 11-15).

Listing 11-15. src/main/java/com/apress/cloud/stream/movie/MovieStream.java

```
package com.apress.cloud.stream.movie;

import com.fasterxml.jackson.databind.ObjectMapper;
import com.jayway.jsonpath.JsonPath;
import lombok.extern.log4j.Log4j2;
import org.apache.http.HttpEntity;
import org.apache.http.client.methods.HttpGet;
import org.apache.http.impl.client.CloseableHttpClient;
import org.apache.http.impl.client.HttpClients;
import org.apache.http.util.EntityUtils;
import org.springframework.boot.context.properties.EnableConfigurationProperties;
import org.springframework.cloud.stream.annotation.EnableBinding;
```

```
import org.springframework.cloud.stream.messaging.Processor;
import org.springframework.integration.annotation.Transformer;
import org.springframework.messaging.support.GenericMessage;

import java.io.IOException;
import java.net.URI;
import java.net.URISyntaxException;
import java.nio.charset.StandardCharsets;

@Log4j2
@EnableConfigurationProperties({MovieProperties.class, DropboxProperties.class})
@EnableBinding(Processor.class)
public class MovieStream {

    private MovieProperties movieProperties;
    private final CloseableHttpClient httpclient = HttpClients.createDefault();
    private final HttpGet getRequest = new HttpGet();

    public MovieStream(MovieProperties movieProperties) {
        this.movieProperties = movieProperties;
        getRequest.addHeader("Accept", "application/json");
        getRequest.addHeader("x-rapidapi-host", movieProperties.getHeaderHost());
        getRequest.addHeader("x-rapidapi-key", movieProperties.getHeaderKey());
        getRequest.addHeader("Content-Type", "application/json");
    }

    @Transformer(inputChannel = Processor.INPUT, outputChannel = Processor.OUTPUT)
    public Object process(Movie movie){
        try {
            getRequest.setURI(new URI(movieProperties.getApiServer().replace("ID", movie.
            getId())));
            HttpEntity entity = httpclient.execute(getRequest).getEntity();
            String url = JsonPath.parse(EntityUtils.toString(entity, StandardCharsets.
            UTF_8)).read("$.image.url",String.class).toString();
            log.debug("Movie's URL: {}", url);

            ObjectMapper mapper = new ObjectMapper();
            String payload = mapper.writeValueAsString(new MoviePayload(movieProperties.
            getTaskName(),
                    new String[] {
                            "url=" + url,
                            "imdbId=" + movie.getId(),
                            "dropbox.token=" + movieProperties.getDropbox().getToken(),
                            "dropbox.path=" + movieProperties.getDropbox().getPath(),
                            "dropbox.local-tmp-folder=" + movieProperties.getDropbox().
                            getLocalTmpFolder()
                    }));

            return new GenericMessage<>(payload);
        } catch (IOException | URISyntaxException e) {
            e.printStackTrace();
```

```
        }
        throw new RuntimeException("Can't process the Movie.");

    }
}
```

Listing 11-15 shows the MovieStream class. You already know about this stream style, where you are declaring @EnableBinding and configuring the stream as a processor. The @Transformer annotation uses input and output channels. Apache Commons requests the /title/details to get the Movie's Art URL and passing to the MoviePayload instance, and you are sending to the sink just a GenericMessage with this simple payload. The name of the task you want to launch and its job parameters.

Next, open the application.properties file and add the content in Listing 11-16.

Listing 11-16. src/main/resources/application.properties

```
# Server
server.port=8085

# IMDB API
movie.api-server=https://imdb8.p.rapidapi.com/title/get-details?tconst=ID
movie.header-host=imdb8.p.rapidapi.com
movie.header-key=YOUR-KEY
movie.task-name=movie-dropbox-batch
movie.dropbox.token=YOUR-TOKEN

# Bindings - RabbitMQ
spring.cloud.stream.bindings.input.destination=imdb
spring.cloud.stream.bindings.output.destination=task

# Logging
logging.level.com.apress.cloud.stream.movie=DEBUG
```

Of course, some of these properties must be set and not be part of the final JAR, such as the keys and the name of the task. Now you can compile, package, and deploy to your Maven repository.

```
./mvnw -DskipTests clean package
./mvnw -DskipTests deploy
```

Using the Dashboard

Now it's time to use the dashboard to create the stream pipeline DSL. Make sure your Spring Cloud Data Flow server and its component are up and running. You also need to have the NATs server running. Open your dashboard and go to App Registration. Select **Bulk import application**. Use the following properties in the Apps as Properties text area.

```
source.http=maven://org.springframework.cloud.stream.app:http-source-rabbit:2.1.2.RELEASE
source.http.metadata=maven://org.springframework.cloud.stream.app:http-source-rabbit:jar:me
tadata:2.1.2.RELEASE
source.movie-web=maven://com.apress.cloud.stream:movie-source:0.0.1
processor.movie-imdb=maven://com.apress.cloud.stream:movie-processor:0.0.1
```

```
processor.movie-imdb.metadata=maven://com.apress.cloud.stream:movie-
processor:jar:metadata:0.0.1
processor.movie-details=maven://com.apress.cloud.stream:movie-details:0.0.1
processor.movie-details.metadata=maven://com.apress.cloud.stream:movie-
details:jar:metadata:0.0.1
processor.splitter=maven://org.springframework.cloud.stream.app:splitter-processor-
rabbit:2.1.2.RELEASE
processor.splitter.metadata=maven://org.springframework.cloud.stream.app:splitter-processor-
rabbit:jar:metadata:2.1.2.RELEASE
sink.movie-log=maven://com.apress.cloud.stream:movie-sink:0.0.1
sink.task-launcher-dataflow=maven://org.springframework.cloud.stream.app:task-launcher-
dataflow-sink-rabbit:1.1.0.RELEASE
sink.task-launcher-dataflow.metadata=maven://org.springframework.cloud.stream.app:task-
launcher-dataflow-sink-rabbit:jar:metadata:1.1.0.RELEASE
sink.log=maven://org.springframework.cloud.stream.app:log-sink-rabbit:2.1.3.RELEASE
sink.log.metadata=maven://org.springframework.cloud.stream.app:log-sink-rabbit:jar:metadata
:2.1.3.RELEASE
task.movie-batch=maven://com.apress.cloud.batch:movie-batch:0.0.1
task.movie-batch.metadata=maven://com.apress.cloud.batch:movie-batch:jar:metadata:0.0.1
```

Once you submit these properties, several apps should be listed. Note the newly registered apps (and their types). You are including the `task-launcher-dataflow` sink app that expects a payload with a name and some arguments (the job parameters) (see Figure 11-16).

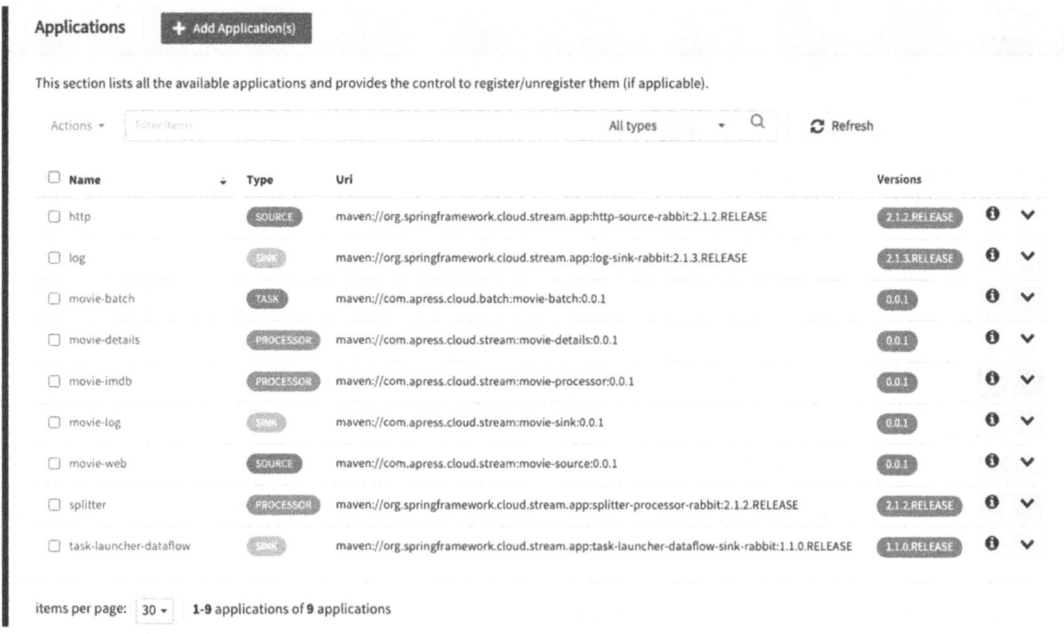

Figure 11-16. *Applications*

Next, go to the Streams pane and create the stream DSL (see Figure 11-17).

```
movie= movie-web | splitter | movie-imdb | movie-log
to-dropbox= :movie.splitter > movie-details | task-launcher-dataflow
```

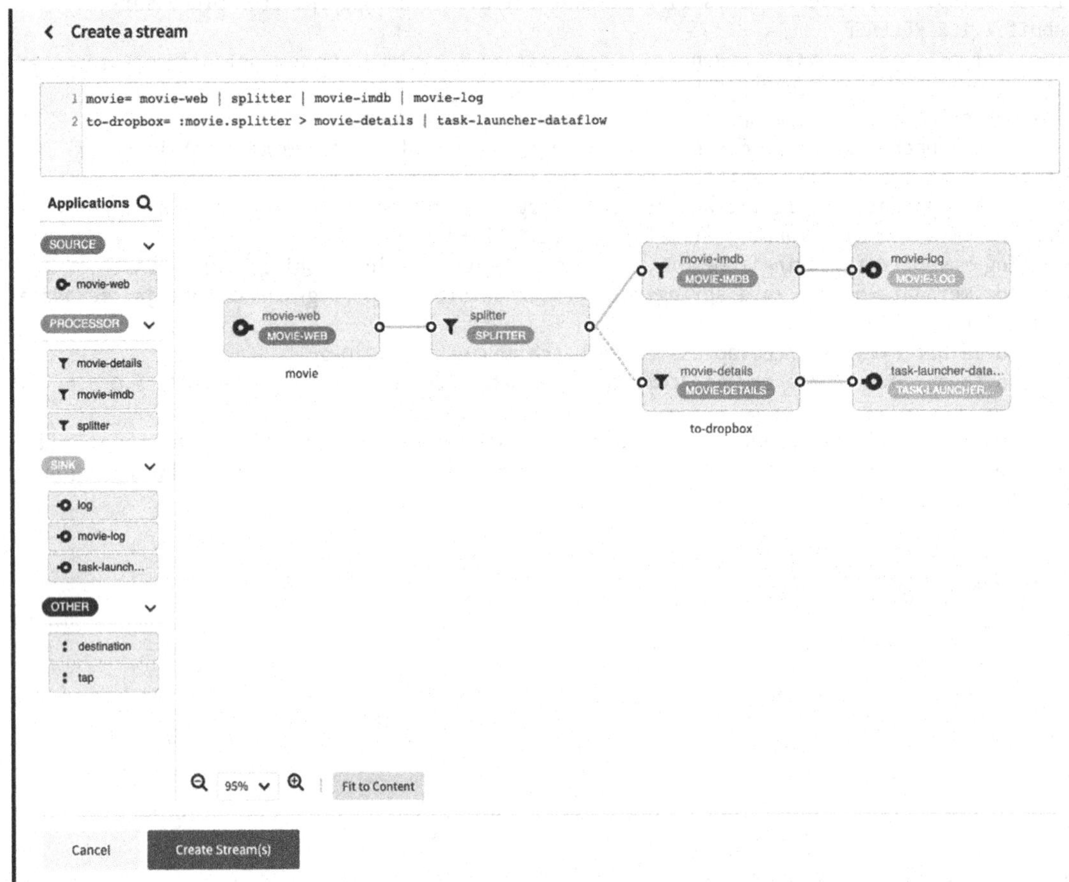

Figure 11-17. *Create streams*

You can create the stream by clicking the Create Stream(s) button. Leave the default names (`movie` and `to-dropbox`) (see Figures 11-18 and 11-19).

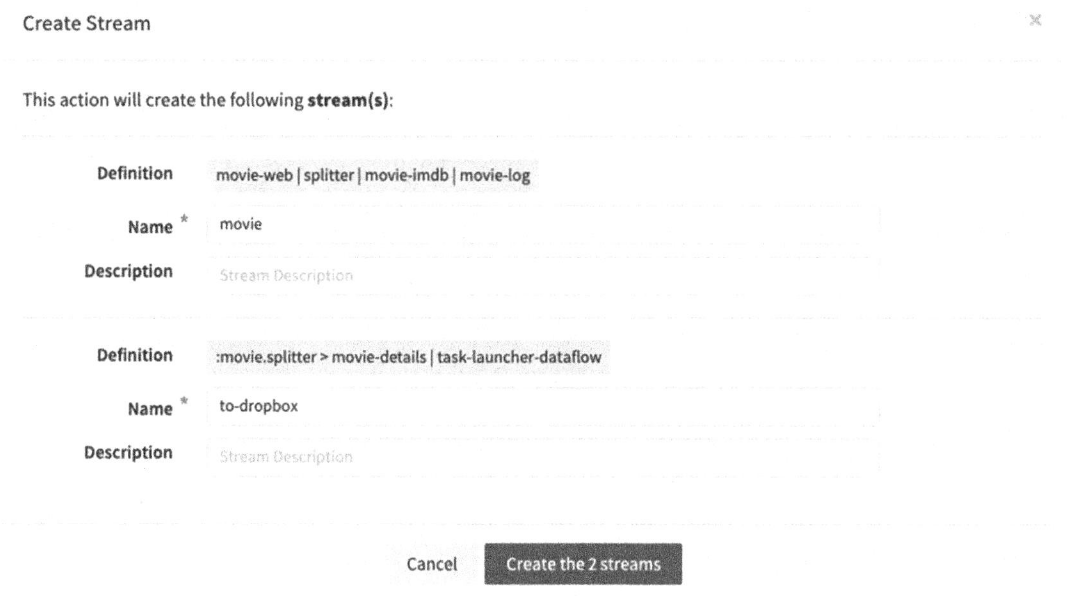

Create Stream

This action will create the following **stream(s)**:

Definition movie-web | splitter | movie-imdb | movie-log

Name * movie

Description Stream Description

Definition :movie.splitter > movie-details | task-launcher-dataflow

Name * to-dropbox

Description Stream Description

Cancel Create the 2 streams

Figure 11-18. *Create streams*

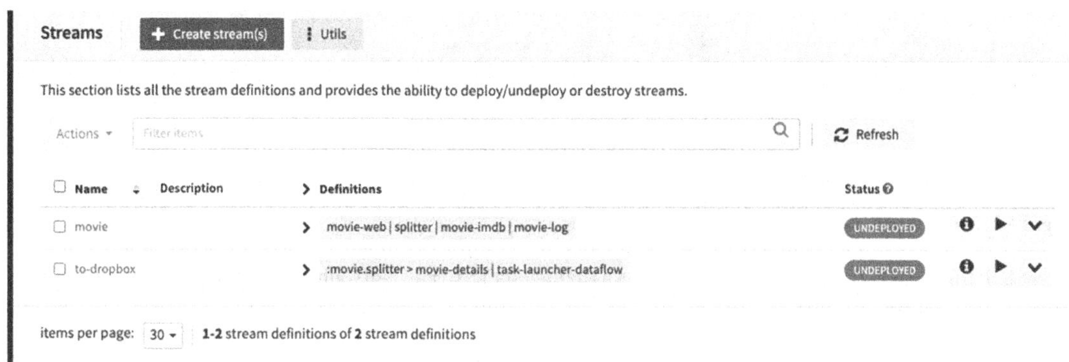

Figure 11-19. *Streams*

Next, go to the Tasks pane and create a task. The `movie-batch` app should be listed (see Figure 11-20).

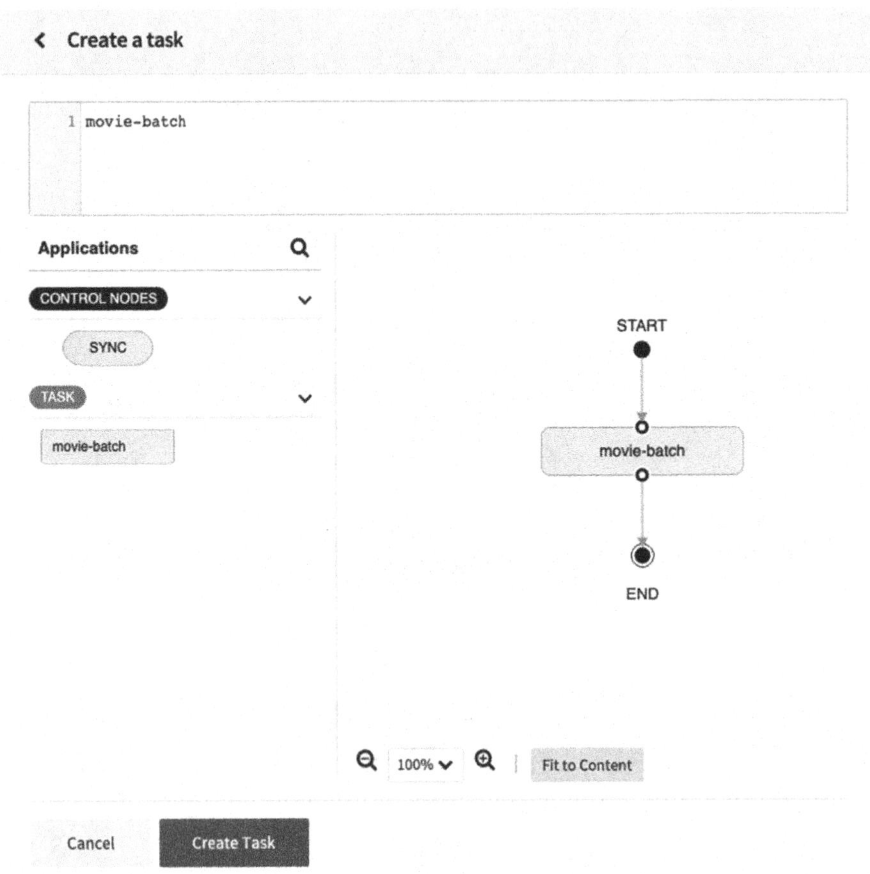

Figure 11-20. *Create tasks*

Click the Create Task button, which opens a dialog. Set it to `movie-dropbox-batch` (see Figure 11-21).

Confirm Task Creation

This action will create a task:

Definition movie-batch

Name * movie-dropbox-batch

Description Task Description

Cancel Create the task

Figure 11-21. *Task creation*

Click the **Create the task** button. Now you are set to run the stream DSL. Go to the Streams pane. Click the movie stream Play button (>). In the Freetext pane, use the following properties.

```
app.movie-web.server.port=8081
app.movie-web.spring.cloud.stream.bindings.output.destination=movie
app.splitter.expression=#jsonPath(payload,'$.MovieRequest.movies')
app.splitter.spring.cloud.stream.bindings.input.destination=movie
app.splitter.spring.cloud.stream.bindings.output.destination=imdb
app.movie-imdb.spring.cloud.stream.bindings.input.binder=rabbit
app.movie-imdb.spring.cloud.stream.bindings.output.binder=nats
app.movie-imdb.spring.cloud.stream.bindings.input.destination=imdb
app.movie-imdb.movie.header-key=YOUR-KEY
app.movie-imdb.spring.nats.host=nats
app.movie-imdb.spring.cloud.stream.bindings.output.destination=log
app.movie-log.spring.cloud.stream.bindings.input.destination=log
app.movie-log.spring.nats.host=nats
```

Before continuing, let's look at these properties. YOUR-KEY needs to be added to the Movie IMDB Rest service. Note that in this example, movie-web runs in port 8081 because I used Docker Compose. But you can omit this property if you are running in Kubernetes because the movie-web app should be exposed with a LoadBalancer type (see Figure 11-22).

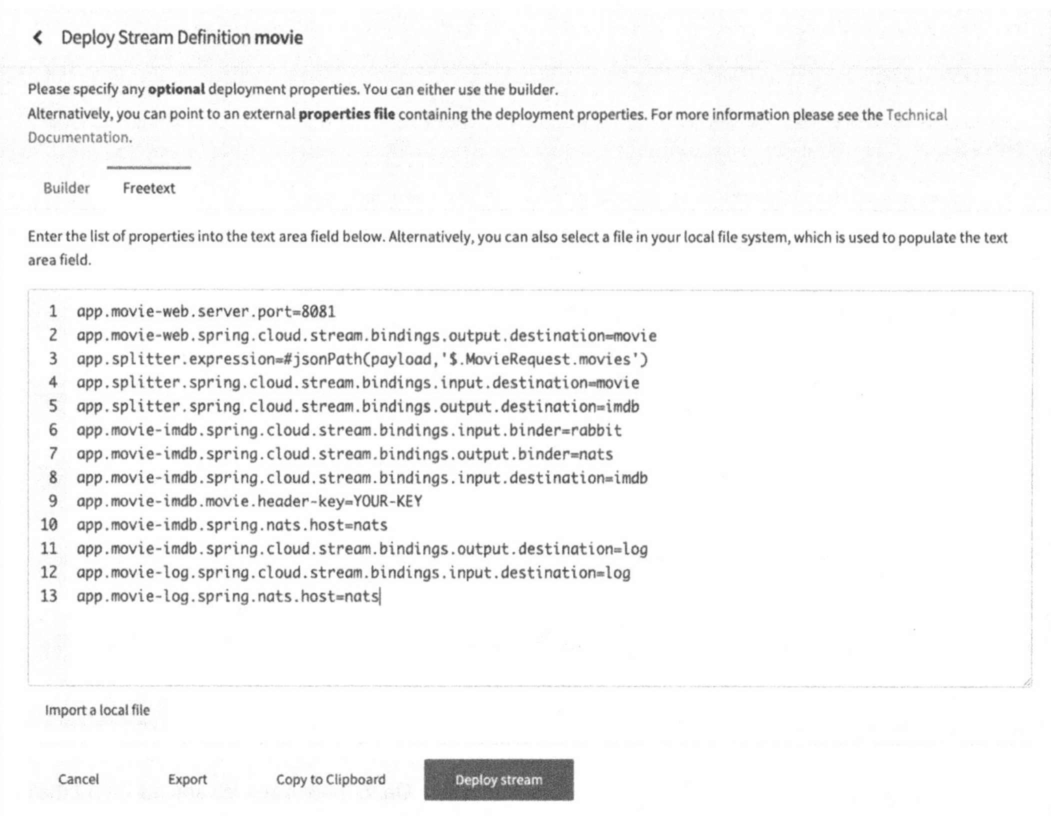
Deploy Stream Definition movie
Please specify any optional deployment properties. You can either use the builder.
Alternatively, you can point to an external properties file containing the deployment properties. For more information please see the Technical Documentation.
Builder
Freetext
Enter the list of properties into the text area field below. Alternatively, you can also select a file in your local file system, which is used to populate the text area field.
1 app.movie-web.server.port=8081
2 app.movie-web.spring.cloud.stream.bindings.output.destination=movie
3 app.splitter.expression=#jsonPath(payload,'$.MovieRequest.movies')
4 app.splitter.spring.cloud.stream.bindings.input.destination=movie
5 app.splitter.spring.cloud.stream.bindings.output.destination=imdb
6 app.movie-imdb.spring.cloud.stream.bindings.input.binder=rabbit
7 app.movie-imdb.spring.cloud.stream.bindings.output.binder=nats
8 app.movie-imdb.spring.cloud.stream.bindings.input.destination=imdb
9 app.movie-imdb.movie.header-key=YOUR-KEY
10 app.movie-imdb.spring.nats.host=nats
11 app.movie-imdb.spring.cloud.stream.bindings.output.destination=log
12 app.movie-log.spring.cloud.stream.bindings.input.destination=log
13 app.movie-log.spring.nats.host=nats
Import a local file
Cancel
Export
Copy to Clipboard
Deploy stream

Figure 11-22. *Freetext properties*

You can now click the Deploy Stream button. Next, click the Play button over the `to-dropbox` stream, and in the Freetext pane, use the following properties.

```
app.movie-details.movie.batch-uri=maven://com.apress.cloud.batch:movie-batch:0.0.1
app.movie-details.movie.header-key=YOUR-KEY
app.movie-details.movie.task-name=movie-dropbox-batch
app.movie-details.movie.dropbox.token=YOUR-TOKEN
app.movie-details.movie.dropbox.path=/IMDB/
app.movie-details.movie.dropbox.local-tmp-folder=/tmp/
app.movie-details.spring.cloud.stream.bindings.input.destination=imdb
app.movie-details.spring.cloud.stream.bindings.output.destination=task
app.task-launcher-dataflow.spring.cloud.stream.bindings.input.destination=task
app.task-launcher-dataflow.spring.cloud.dataflow.client.server-uri=http://dataflow-
server:9393
```

Before continuing, let's analyze these properties. You need your IMDB key and the Dropbox token. Also note that the `task-launcher-dataflow` app needs to know where the Data Flow server is located because you can launch tasks in different platforms and servers. You configure the destinations (see Figure 11-23).

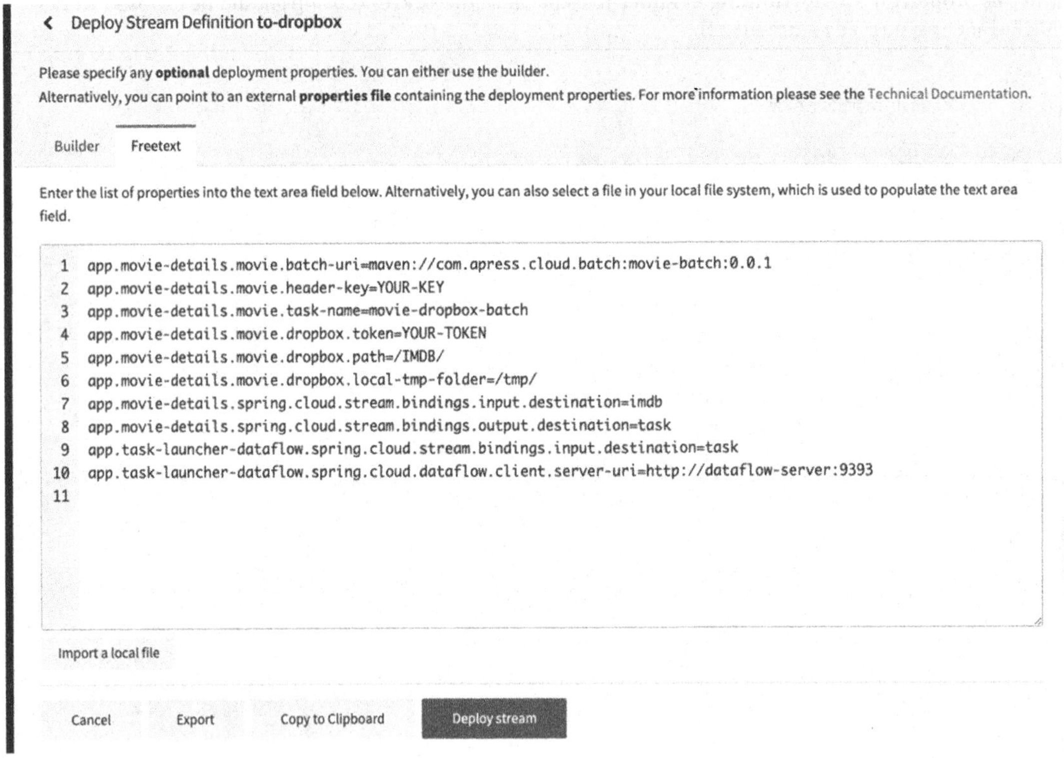

< Deploy Stream Definition **to-dropbox**

Please specify any **optional** deployment properties. You can either use the builder.
Alternatively, you can point to an external **properties file** containing the deployment properties. For more information please see the Technical Documentation.

Builder Freetext

Enter the list of properties into the text area field below. Alternatively, you can also select a file in your local file system, which is used to populate the text area field.

```
app.movie-details.movie.batch-uri=maven://com.apress.cloud.batch:movie-batch:0.0.1
app.movie-details.movie.header-key=YOUR-KEY
app.movie-details.movie.task-name=movie-dropbox-batch
app.movie-details.movie.dropbox.token=YOUR-TOKEN
app.movie-details.movie.dropbox.path=/IMDB/
app.movie-details.movie.dropbox.local-tmp-folder=/tmp/
app.movie-details.spring.cloud.stream.bindings.input.destination=imdb
app.movie-details.spring.cloud.stream.bindings.output.destination=task
app.task-launcher-dataflow.spring.cloud.stream.bindings.input.destination=task
app.task-launcher-dataflow.spring.cloud.dataflow.client.server-uri=http://dataflow-server:9393
```

Import a local file

Cancel Export Copy to Clipboard Deploy stream

Figure 11-23. *Freetext properties*

Click the **Deploy stream** button. Now you are ready to test it. Open the `movie-web` app and send the movies. If everything goes correctly in the Task pane, the execution list should show the time `movie-batch` was launched (see Figure 11-24).

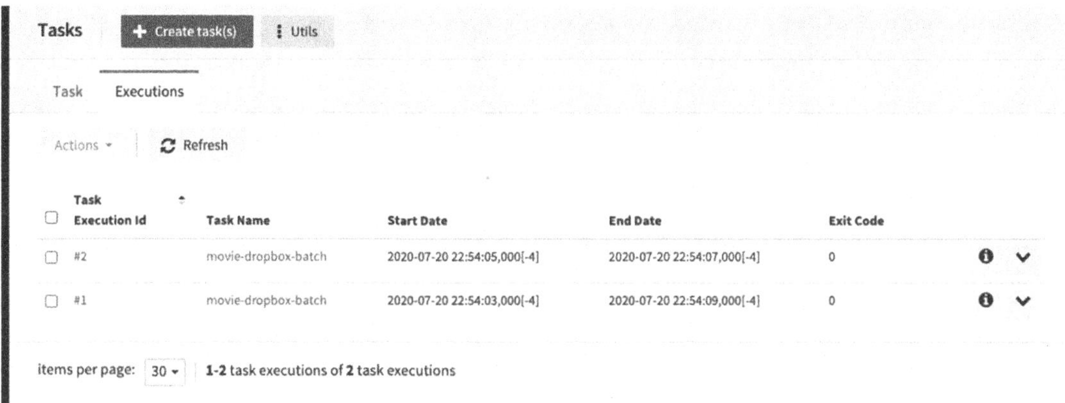

Figure 11-24. *Task executions*

Click the executing ID to see the logs and parameters that were used to launch the task.

Congratulations!! You have created a complete stream and launched a Spring Cloud Task/Batch application.

■ **Note** All the source code, scripts, properties, and READMEs are in the `ch11/` folder.

Summary

In this chapter, you learned about Spring Cloud Task and its benefits, which include creating ETL (extract, transform, load) using Spring Batch. You saw how to use streams to launch a task and had a quick review on how to create Spring Batch apps and run them as a Spring Cloud Task in Data Flow.

If you want to know more about Spring Cloud Task, visit `https://spring.io/projects/spring-cloud-task`.

CHAPTER 12

Monitoring

In the previous chapter, I showed you how to create Task apps and trigger them using streams. In this chapter, you take a step forward and learn about visibility in your apps and infrastructure. Recall that Chapter 1 discussed all the tools that allow you to react to any problems with the infrastructure, apps, or business logic. That's why monitoring is an important piece of delivering the right apps and solutions.

Spring Cloud Data Flow exposes metrics architecture based on Micrometer. Spring Boot is the primary technology for all Spring Cloud projects, including Spring Cloud Data Flow. Because Micrometer is a vendor-neutral metric, it supports a variety of monitoring systems. Spring Cloud Data Flow uses the most popular monitoring systems, including Prometheus, Wavefront, and InfluxDB. The good thing is that you can choose the one you want to use by adding a property.

This chapter covers the most popular metrics system in the cloud infrastructure community: Prometheus and Grafana. In the next sections, I show you what you need to do to expose metrics in streams and tasks, and you see how to access them from within the dashboard.

Micrometer

Micrometer is a "first-class citizen" for Spring Boot 2.x applications with metrics, a health checker, and other non-functional requirements. You only need to add the `spring-boot-starter-actuator` dependency and the `micrometer-registry-<name-of-the-metrics-collector>` dependency for any other metrics technology, which means that Spring Cloud Data Flow was created with metrics in mind.

Micrometer is a *dimensional-first* metrics collection facade that allows you to register time, counters, and gauge solutions for your code with a vendor-neutral API. With this, your application can register time series related to throughput, total time, maximum latency, pre-computed percentiles, percentiles, histograms, SAL boundary counts, and more. Micrometer uses dimensional metrics and hierarchical names for older systems, like JMX and Ganglia. Among the new dimensional monitoring systems available, Micrometer works well with Prometheus, CloudWatch, Ganglia, Graphite, InfluxDB, Netflix Atlas, New Relic, StatsD, Datadog, Wavefront, SignalFx, JMX, AppOptics, Azure Application Insights, Dynatrace, ElasticbSearch, and StackDriver.

By default, Spring Boot 2 autoconfigures several metrics, including the following.

- JVM, report utilization of
    - Various memory and buffer pools
    - Statistics related to garbage collection
    - Thread utilization
    - Number of classes loaded/unloaded

F. Gutierrez, *Spring Cloud Data Flow*, https://doi.org/10.1007/978-1-4842-1239-4_12

- CPU usage
- Spring MVC and WebFlux request latencies
- RestTemplate latencies
- Cache utilization
- Datasource utilization, including HikariCP pool metrics
- RabbitMQ connection factories
- File descriptor usage
- Logback: records the number of events logged to log back at each level
- Uptime: uptime gauge and a fixed gauge representing the application's absolute start time
- Tomcat usage

Spring Boot 2 configures a `io.micrometer.core.instrument.MeterRegistry` composite so that you can add registry implementations, allowing you to ship your metrics to more than one monitoring system. Through `MeterRegistryCustomizer`, you can customize a whole set of registries at once or individual implementations.

Spring Boot allows you to override and configure some of the defaults, so you can create your own metrics distribution and disable the JVM report utilization, for example.

```
management.metrics.enable.jvm=false
management.metrics.distribution.percentiles-histogram.http.server.requests=true
management.metrics.distribution.sla.http.server.requests=1ms,5ms
```

To use Micrometer, you must add the following dependencies.

```
<dependency>
    <groupId>org.springframework.boot</groupId>
    <artifactId>spring-boot-starter-actuator</artifactId>
</dependency>
<dependency>
  <groupId>io.micrometer</groupId>
  <artifactId>micrometer-registry-YOUR-METRICS-TECH</artifactId>
</dependency>
```

Add the following to your configuration.

```
@Bean
MeterRegistryCustomizer<MeterRegistry> metricsCommonTags(@Value("${spring.application.
name}") String appName) {
  return registry -> registry.config().commonTags("application", appName);
}
```

It is important to note that in your `application.properties`, you need to add the name of your app.

```
spring.application.name=movie-web
```

You can consider this a best practice.

Health Checks and Monitoring Stream Apps

Spring Cloud Stream not only provides out-of-the-box metrics for your Stream apps, but also *health indicators* for the binders. Remember that the communication that is happening between Stream apps is thanks to the binders you select, either a single binder like RabbitMQ or Kafka, or you can choose multiple binders for the same Stream app. When you need this type of visibility (metrics and health indicators) and more insight on what is going on with the binders, you must tell you app that you are using a health indicator for your binding by doing the following.

1. First, add the following dependencies to your `pom.xml`.

```
<dependency>
     <groupId>org.springframework.boot</groupId>
     <artifactId>spring-boot-starter-web</artifactId>
</dependency>
<dependency>
    <groupId>org.springframework.boot</groupId>
    <artifactId>spring-boot-starter-actuator</artifactId>
</dependency>
<dependency>
    <groupId>org.springframework.cloud.stream.app</groupId>
    <artifactId>app-starters-micrometer-common</artifactId>
    <version>2.1.5.RELEASE</version>
</dependency>
```

   If you are using WebFlux, replace the `spring-boot-starter-web` with `spring-boot-starter-webflux`.

2. Next, you need to set up the following properties.

```
management.health.binders.enabled=true
management.endpoints.web.exposure.include=bindings
```

With these settings, you can visualize the current bindings with the `/actuator/bindings` endpoint. If you want to know about a single binder, visit `/actuator/bindings/<binding-name>`.

You can stop, start, pause, and resume a binding by executing a POST.

```
curl -d '{"state":"STOPPED"}' -H "Content-Type: application/json" -X POST
http://<host>:<port>/actuator/bindings/<binding-name>
curl -d '{"state":"STARTED"}' -H "Content-Type: application/json" -X POST
http://<host>:<port>/actuator/bindings/<binding-name>
curl -d '{"state":"PAUSED"}' -H "Content-Type: application/json" -X POST
http://<host>:<port>/actuator/bindings/<binding-name>
curl -d '{"state":"RESUMED"}' -H "Content-Type: application/json" -X POST
http://<host>:<port>/actuator/bindings/<binding-name>
```

Suppose that you create a DSL Stream like the following.

```
http --server.port=9095 | filter --expression=#jsonPath(payload,'$.msg').contains('Hello') | log
```

Assuming that you have the Data Flow server running with Prometheus and Grafana, you are running it locally, and you named this stream `simple`, you can access the `http` app in port 9095. You can get the bindings with `http://localhost:9095/actuator/bindings` and `http://localhost:9095/actuator/bindings/simple.http` (see Figure 12-1).

```
[
  {
    "name": "simple.http",
    "group": null,
    "pausable": false,
    "state": "running",
    "input": false,
    "extendedInfo": {
      "bindingDestination": "simple.http",
      "ExtendedProducerProperties": {
        "autoStartup": true,
        "partitionCount": 1,
        "requiredGroups": [
          "simple"
        ],
        "extension": {
          "exchangeType": "topic",
          "declareExchange": true,
          "exchangeDurable": true,
          "exchangeAutoDelete": false,
          "delayedExchange": false,
          "queueNameGroupOnly": false,
          "bindQueue": true,
          "bindingRoutingKey": null,
          "ttl": null,
          "expires": null,
          "maxLength": null,
          "maxLengthBytes": null,
          "maxPriority": null,
          "deadLetterQueueName": null,
          "deadLetterExchange": null,
          "deadLetterExchangeType": "direct",
          "declareDlx": true,
          "deadLetterRoutingKey": null,
          "dlqTtl": null,
          "dlqExpires": null,
          "dlqMaxLength": null,
          "dlqMaxLengthBytes": null,
          "dlqMaxPriority": null,
          "dlqDeadLetterExchange": null,
          "dlqDeadLetterRoutingKey": null,
          "autoBindDlq": false,
          "prefix": "",
          "lazy": false,
          "dlqLazy": false,
          "overflowBehavior": null,
          "dlqOverflowBehavior": null,
          "compress": false,
          "batchingEnabled": false,
          "batchSize": 100,
          "batchBufferLimit": 10000,
          "batchTimeout": 5000,
          "transacted": false,
          "deliveryMode": "PERSISTENT",
          "headerPatterns": [
```


Figure 12-1. *Actuator/bindings http://localhost:9095/actuator/bindings*

This means that out-of-the-box app starters have the `web` and `actuator` dependencies integrated and preconfigured to use Micrometer technology.

■ **Note** In `ch12/docker-compose` there is a `README file` and the files to run Prometheus and Grafana with the Spring Cloud Data Flow server. Review Chapter 8 to learn how to run this in Kubernetes (a better solution for your apps).

To use or add *metrics* in Stream apps, you need to add the dependencies I mentioned earlier. By default, when Spring Cloud streams discover that you have added actuator and metrics technologies, it autoconfigures the metrics. You must include the following properties if using *Prometheus* as a metrics technology.

```
management.metrics.export.prometheus.enabled=true
management.endpoints.web.exposure.include=prometheus
spring.cloud.streamapp.security.enabled=false
```

You also see metrics in visualization tools like Grafana, for example. Then, you can add any business logic for registering metrics. If you want to learn more about metrics, visit the Micrometer web site at `https://micrometer.io`.

Monitoring Task Apps

To enable task/batch metrics, you need to have the following dependencies.

```
<dependencies>
  <dependency>
      <groupId>org.springframework.boot</groupId>
      <artifactId>spring-boot-starter-actuator</artifactId>
  </dependency>
</dependencies>

<dependencyManagement>
    <dependencies>
        <dependency>
                <groupId>org.springframework.cloud</groupId>
                <artifactId>spring-cloud-dependencies</artifactId>
                <version>Hoxton.SR7</version>
                <type>pom</type>
                <scope>import</scope>
        </dependency>
    </dependencies>
</dependencyManagement>
```

Because Spring Cloud Task/Batch apps are short-lived applications, they require a service-discovery component to configure the endpoint for any metrics the apps expose. So, you need the following.

```
<dependency>
        <groupId>io.micrometer.prometheus</groupId>
        <artifactId>prometheus-rsocket-spring</artifactId>
        <version>1.0.0</version>
</dependency>
<dependency>
        <groupId>io.micrometer.prometheus</groupId>
        <artifactId>prometheus-rsocket-client</artifactId>
        <version>1.0.0</version>
</dependency>
```

With Prometheus, if you want to use Wavefront, use the following.

```
<dependency>
    <groupId>io.micrometer</groupId>
    <artifactId>micrometer-registry-wavefront</artifactId>
</dependency>
<dependency>
    <groupId>com.wavefront</groupId>
    <artifactId>wavefront-sdk-java</artifactId>
    <version>2.6.0</version>
</dependency>
```

If you want to use InfluxDB, use the following.

```
<dependency>
    <groupId>io.micrometer</groupId>
    <artifactId>micrometer-registry-influx</artifactId>
</dependency>
```

Now, that you know how to add metrics and health checks to your streams, let's use the stream pipeline DSL from previous chapters with these features to monitor Stream apps.

Movie Stream Pipeline DSL: Putting It All Together

Make sure to have your Spring Cloud Data Flow up and running and with Prometheus and Grafana enabled. In the source code, I created the `ch12/docker-compose` folder with all the necessary YAML files if you want to run this locally.

This is the final pipeline DSL deploy (see Figure 12-2).

```
movie=movie-web | splitter | groovy-transform | jdbc
imdb-high-rating=:movie.groovy-transform > filter | log
stars=:movie.splitter > movie-imdb | movie-log
to-dropbox= :movie.splitter > movie-details | task-launcher-dataflow
```

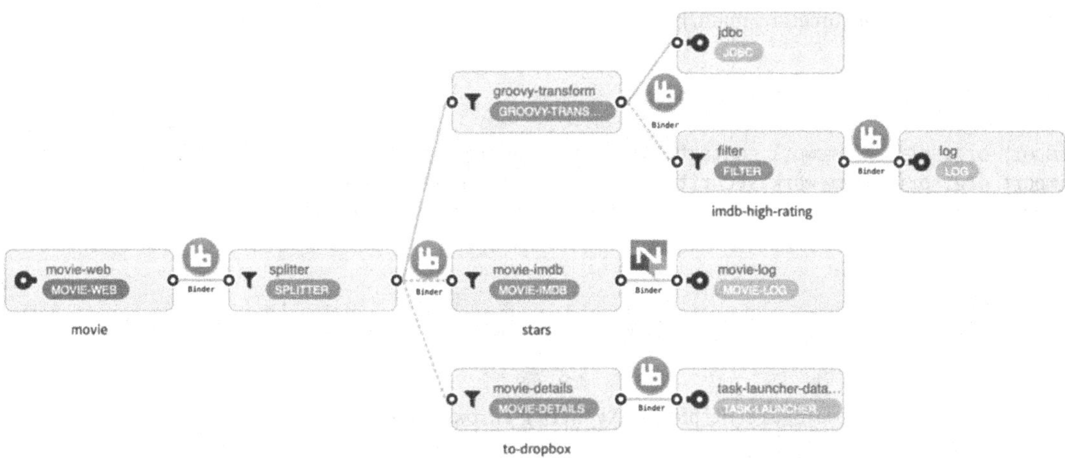

Figure 12-2. *Movie pipeline DSL*

I added all the Stream apps in the `ch12/streams` folder, if you want to import them and see the results. If you want to follow along, you need to add on each Stream app: `spring-boot-starter-web`, `spring-boot-starter-actuator`, `micrometer-registry-prometheus`, `app-starters-micrometer-common`, and `prometheus-rsocket-spring` for the Batch app.

```
<dependency>
        <groupId>org.springframework.boot</groupId>
        <artifactId>spring-boot-starter-actuator</artifactId>
</dependency>
<dependency>
        <groupId>io.micrometer</groupId>
        <artifactId>micrometer-registry-prometheus</artifactId>
</dependency>
<dependency>
        <groupId>io.micrometer.prometheus</groupId>
        <artifactId>prometheus-rsocket-spring</artifactId>
              <version>1.0.0</version>
</dependency>
<dependency>
        <groupId>org.springframework.cloud.stream.app</groupId>
        <artifactId>app-starters-micrometer-common</artifactId>
        <version>2.1.5.RELEASE</version>
</dependency>
```

For each app, you must increase the version—in this case, up to 0.0.2.

■ **Note** The `app-starters-micrometer-common` dependency provides security to your apps, so it is necessary to configure security in the `movie-source` app (see Listing 12-1).

Listing 12-1. movie-source: src/main/java/com/apress/cloud/stream/movie/MovieSecurityConfiguration.java

```
package com.apress.cloud.stream.movie;

import org.springframework.context.annotation.Configuration;
import org.springframework.security.config.annotation.web.builders.HttpSecurity;
import org.springframework.security.config.annotation.web.configuration.
WebSecurityConfigurerAdapter;

@Configuration
public class MovieSecurityConfiguration extends WebSecurityConfigurerAdapter {

    @Override
    protected void configure(HttpSecurity http) throws Exception {
        http.csrf().disable()
            .authorizeRequests()
            .antMatchers("/**","/v1/api/movies").permitAll();
    }

}
```

This is only for testing purposes. In the end, you must add security.

You need to add the following dependencies to the pom.xml file for the movie-batch app.

```
<dependency>
        <groupId>io.micrometer.prometheus</groupId>
        <artifactId>prometheus-rsocket-spring</artifactId>
        <version>1.0.0</version>
</dependency>
<dependency>
        <groupId>io.micrometer.prometheus</groupId>
        <artifactId>prometheus-rsocket-client</artifactId>
        <version>1.0.0</version>
</dependency>
```

Everything should be configured for deploying the JARs to a Maven repository. You can compile and deploy each Stream and Batch app. I created a script to package and deploy the JARs; of course, you can also add this as a CI/CD pipeline, even to deploy a stream pipeline DSL.

Now, you can compile, package, and deploy your Stream and Batch apps.

Make sure you have all your infrastructure running. Next, you need to create the Movies database in the MySQL database that the Spring Cloud Data Flow server is using. It is useful for the jdbc app and the movie-batch app.

```
mysql -uroot -prootpw -e "create database movies"
```

If you are running Kubernetes, make sure you have access to the MySQL database by using a port-forward command, or if your database engine is a service, you can access it through LoadBalancer.

Next, open a browser and go to your Spring Cloud Data Flow dashboard. In the Apps pane, click the **+ Add application** button and select the third option, **Bulk import application**. Add the following apps in the text area.

```
source.movie-web=maven://com.apress.cloud.stream:movie-source:0.0.2
processor.filter=maven://org.springframework.cloud.stream.app:filter-processor-
rabbit:2.1.3.RELEASE
processor.filter.metadata=maven://org.springframework.cloud.stream.app:filter-processor-rabb
it:jar:metadata:2.1.3.RELEASE
processor.movie-imdb=maven://com.apress.cloud.stream:movie-processor:0.0.2
processor.movie-details=maven://com.apress.cloud.stream:movie-details:0.0.2
processor.splitter=maven://org.springframework.cloud.stream.app:splitter-processor-
rabbit:2.1.2.RELEASE
processor.splitter.metadata=maven://org.springframework.cloud.stream.app:splitter-processor-
rabbit:jar:metadata:2.1.2.RELEASE
processor.groovy-transform=maven://org.springframework.cloud.stream.app:groovy-transform-
processor-rabbit:2.1.3.RELEASE
processor.groovy-transform.metadata=maven://org.springframework.cloud.stream.app:groovy-
transform-processor-rabbit:jar:metadata:2.1.3.RELEASE
sink.movie-log=maven://com.apress.cloud.stream:movie-sink:0.0.2
sink.task-launcher-dataflow=maven://org.springframework.cloud.stream.app:task-launcher-
dataflow-sink-rabbit:1.1.0.RELEASE
sink.task-launcher-dataflow.metadata=maven://org.springframework.cloud.stream.app:task-
launcher-dataflow-sink-rabbit:jar:metadata:1.1.0.RELEASE
sink.log=maven://org.springframework.cloud.stream.app:log-sink-rabbit:2.1.3.RELEASE
sink.log.metadata=maven://org.springframework.cloud.stream.app:log-sink-rabbit:jar:metadata
:2.1.3.RELEASE
sink.jdbc=maven://org.springframework.cloud.stream.app:jdbc-sink-rabbit:2.1.5.RELEASE
sink.jdbc.metadata=maven://org.springframework.cloud.stream.app:jdbc-sink-rabbit:jar:metada
ta:2.1.5.RELEASE
task.movie-batch=maven://com.apress.cloud.batch:movie-batch:0.0.2
```

Take a moment to analyze the apps. Note that you are using out-of-the-box app starters: `splitter`, `filter`, `jdbc`, `groovy-transform`, and `task-launcher-dataflow`.

Stream Pipeline DSL

Next, click the Streams pane and then click the **+ Create stream(s)** button (see Figure 12-3). Add the following DSL in the text area.

```
movie=movie-web | splitter | groovy-transform | jdbc
imdb-high-rating=:movie.groovy-transform > filter | log
stars=:movie.splitter > movie-imdb | movie-log
to-dropbox= :movie.splitter > movie-details | task-launcher-dataflow
```

Streams | Create stream(s) | Grafana Dashboard | Utils

This section lists all the stream definitions and provides the ability to deploy/undeploy or destroy streams.

Actions | Filter items | Refresh

Name	Description	Definitions	Status
imdb-high-rating		:movie.groovy-transform > filter | log	UNDEPLOYED
movie		movie-web | splitter | groovy-transform | jdbc	UNDEPLOYED
stars		:movie.splitter > movie-imdb | movie-log	UNDEPLOYED
to-dropbox		:movie.splitter > movie-details | task-launcher-dataflow	UNDEPLOYED

items per page: 30 **1-4** stream definitions of **4** stream definitions

***Figure 12-4.** Streams*

Next, click the Create Stream(s) button. Then click the four streams (see Figure 12-4).

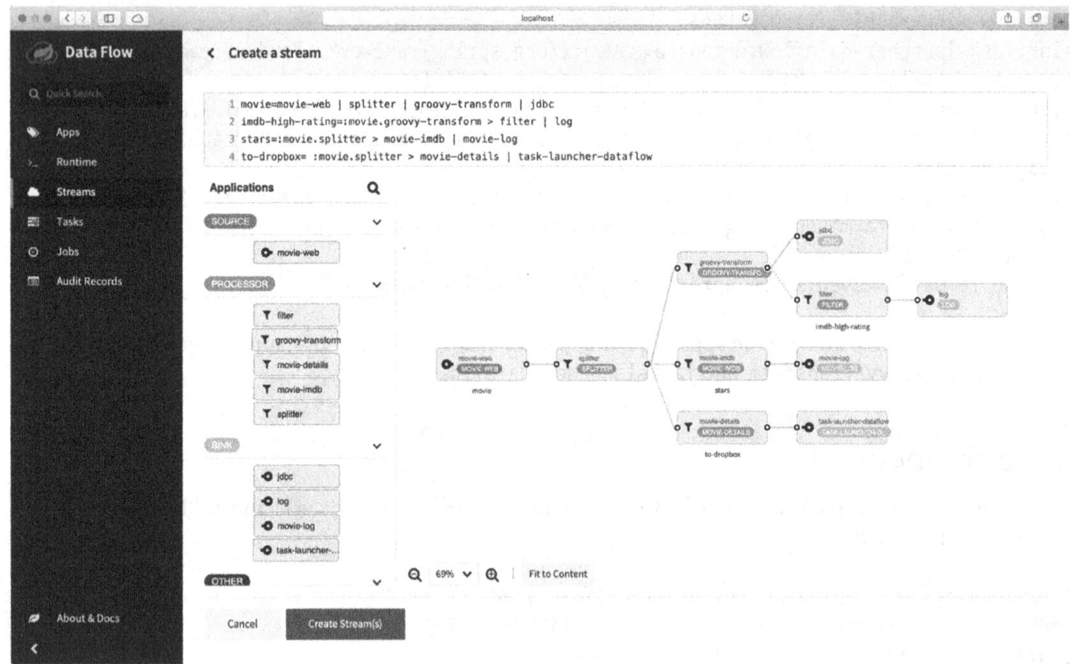

***Figure 12-3.** Stream DSL*

The Grafana dashboard appears. You can use it after you deploy the streams and tasks.

Task Creating

Click the Task pane, + Create task(s), and then add `movie-batch` (see Figure 12-5).

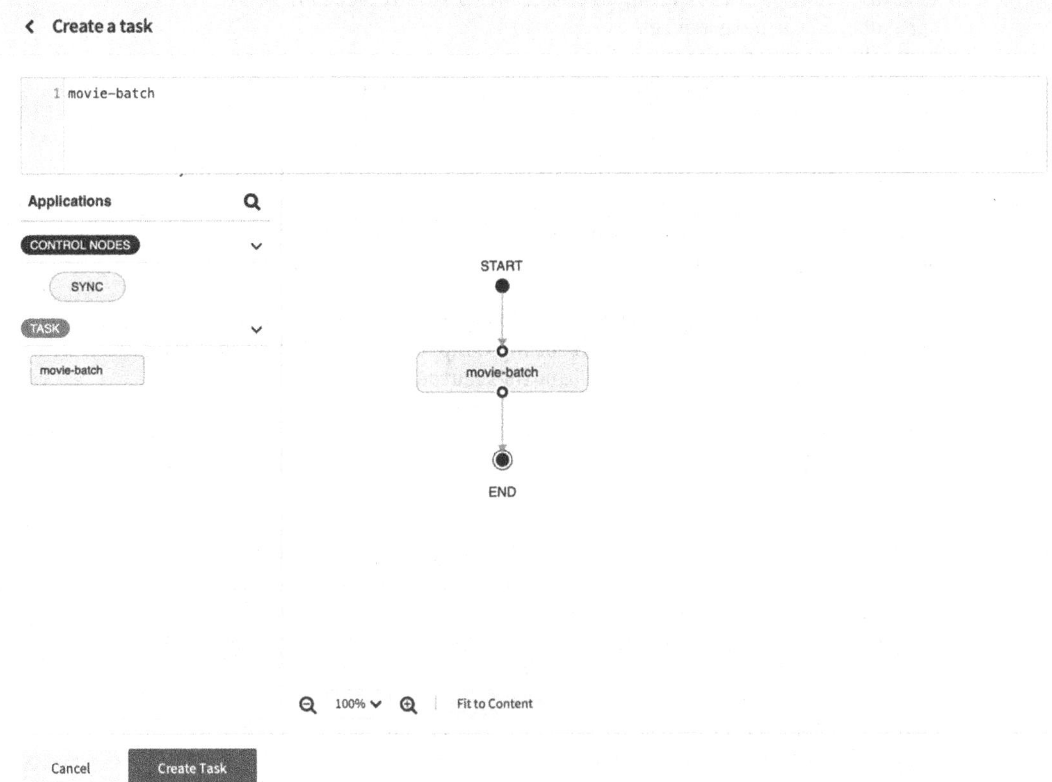

Figure 12-5. *movie-batch task*

Click the Create Task button. Set the Name field to `movie-dropbox-batch`. Click the **Create the task** button, and you are set here.

Stream Deployment

Next, let's deploy our streams. Click the Play button (>) on each stream and add the following properties.

- `movie`. Use the following properties by selecting the Freetext pane, and add the following in the text area.

```
app.movie-web.server.port=9095
app.movie-web.spring.cloud.stream.bindings.output.destination=movie
app.splitter.expression=#jsonPath(payload,'$.MovieRequest.movies')
app.splitter.spring.cloud.stream.bindings.input.destination=movie
app.splitter.spring.cloud.stream.bindings.output.destination=imdb
app.groovy-transform.script=https://raw.githubusercontent.com/felipeg48/
scdf-scripts/master/movie-transform.groovy
```

```
app.groovy-transform.spring.cloud.stream.bindings.input.destination=imdb
app.groovy-transform.spring.cloud.stream.bindings.output.
destination=transform
app.jdbc.columns=id:id,title:title,actor:actor,year:year,genre:genre,sta
rs:stars,rating:imdb.rating,ratingcount:imdb.ratingCount
app.jdbc.table-name=movies
app.jdbc.password=rootpw
app.jdbc.driver-class-name=org.mariadb.jdbc.Driver
app.jdbc.username=root
app.jdbc.url=jdbc:mysql://mysql:3306/reviews?autoReconnect=true&useSSL=false
app.jdbc.spring.cloud.stream.bindings.input.destination=transform
```

- `imdb-high-rating`. Use the following properties by selecting the Freetext pane and add the following in the text area.

```
app.filter.expression="#jsonPath(payload,'$.stars') > 3"
app.filter.spring.cloud.stream.bindings.input.destination=transform
app.filter.spring.cloud.stream.bindings.output.destination=log
app.log.spring.cloud.stream.bindings.input.destination=log
```

- `stars`. Use the following properties by selecting the Freetext pane. In the text-area, add the following.

```
app.movie-imdb.spring.cloud.stream.bindings.input.binder=rabbit
app.movie-imdb.spring.cloud.stream.bindings.output.binder=nats
app.movie-imdb.spring.cloud.stream.bindings.input.destination=imdb
app.movie-imdb.spring.cloud.stream.bindings.output.destination=movie-log
app.movie-imdb.movie.header-key=YOUR-KEY
app.movie-imdb.spring.nats.host=nats
app.movie-log.spring.cloud.stream.bindings.input.destination=movie-log
app.movie-log.spring.nats.host=nats
```

- Note that you need to add your key for the IMDB External service.

```
to-dropbox. Use the following properties by selecting the Freetext pane
and adding the following in the text-area.app.movie-details.movie.batch-
uri=maven://com.apress.cloud.batch:movie-batch:0.0.2
app.movie-details.movie.header-key=YOUR-KEY
app.movie-details.movie.task-name=movie-dropbox-batch
app.movie-details.movie.dropbox.token=YOUR-TOKEN
app.movie-details.movie.dropbox.path=/IMDB/
app.movie-details.movie.dropbox.local-tmp-folder=/tmp/
app.movie-details.spring.cloud.stream.bindings.input.destination=imdb
app.movie-details.spring.cloud.stream.bindings.output.destination=task
app.task-launcher-dataflow.spring.cloud.stream.bindings.input.
destination=task
app.task-launcher-dataflow.spring.cloud.dataflow.client.server-
uri=http://dataflow-server:9393
```

Here you need to add your IMDB key and the Dropbox token.

Open the Movie Web app. If you are using Docker Compose, it should be running in port 9095. If you are using Kubernetes, you can use the `port-forward` command or make sure that it is available in the load balancer (see Figures 12-6 and 12-7).

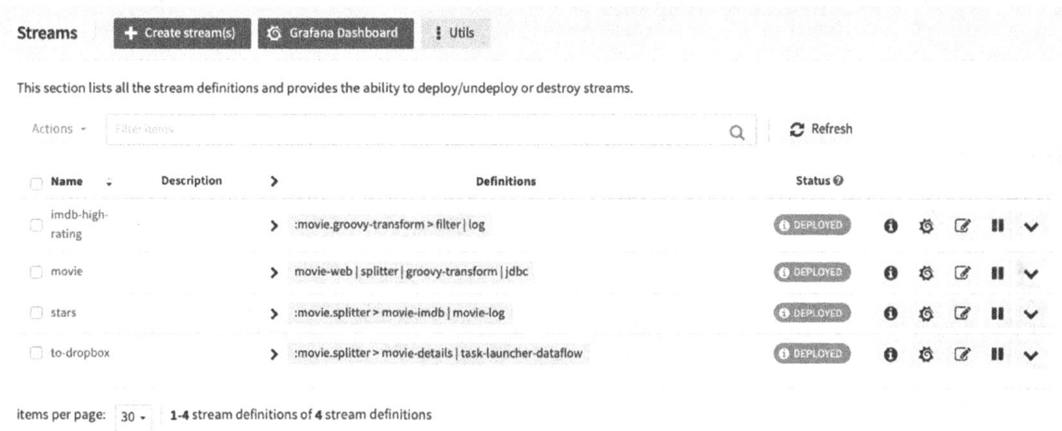

Figure 12-6. *Stream deployed*

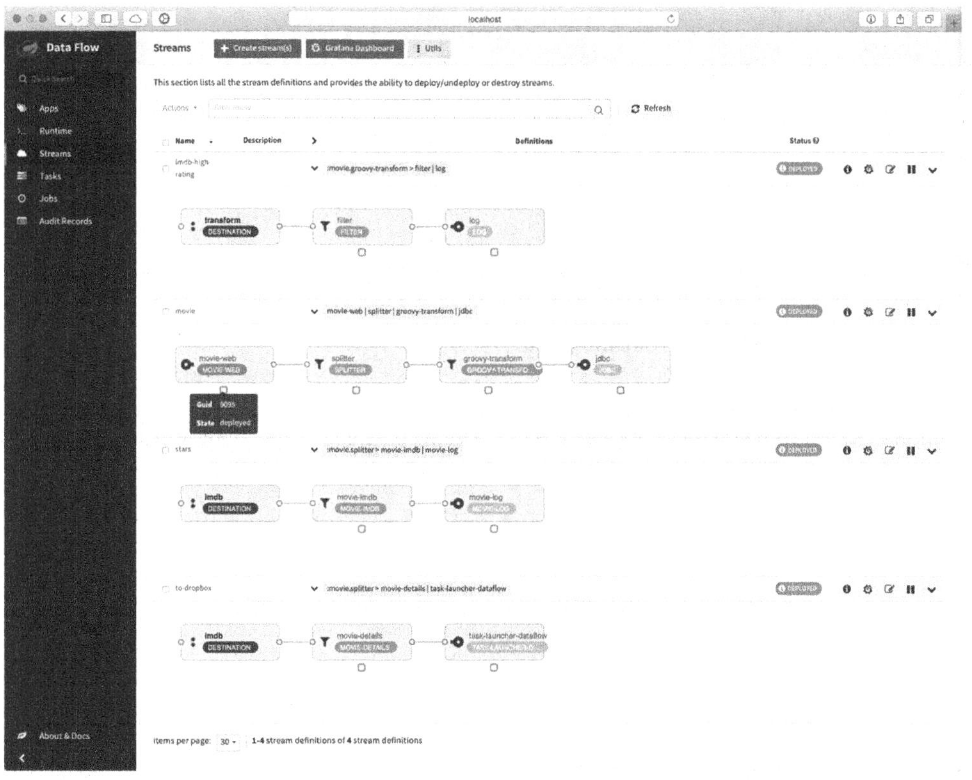

Figure 12-7. *Expand deployed*

If you expand the deployed streams, you see a little green square with GUID and the state, which is useful for being recognized within Prometheus and Grafana.

Next, you click the Grafana Dashboard button. On the Grafana webpage, log in with **admin/admin**. Click the Skip button, if you want; if not, you need a new password for the admin user. You can navigate to see the Stream `movie`. An example is shown in Figure 12-8.

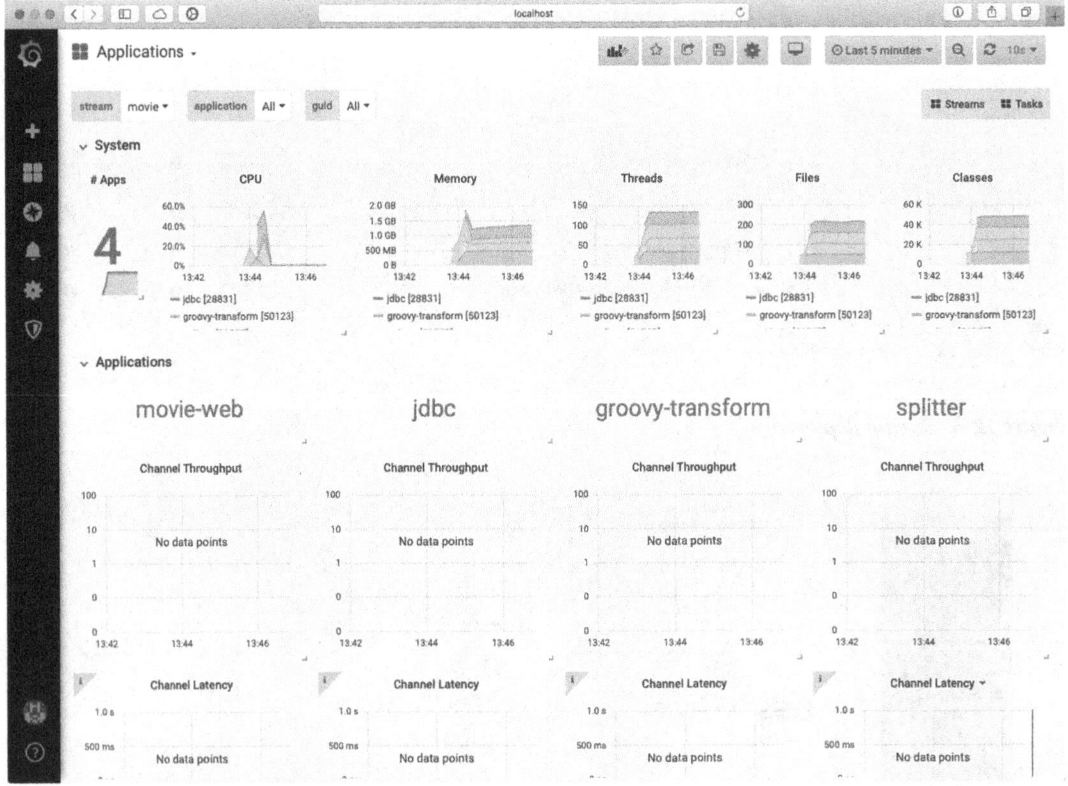

Figure 12-8. *Grafana/Applications/Stream/movie*

Next, open your Web app. If you are using the local environment, you can reach it in port 9095. Click the Send button to see all your streams work. Look at the Grafana dashboard and identify every Stream and Task application (see Figure 12-9).

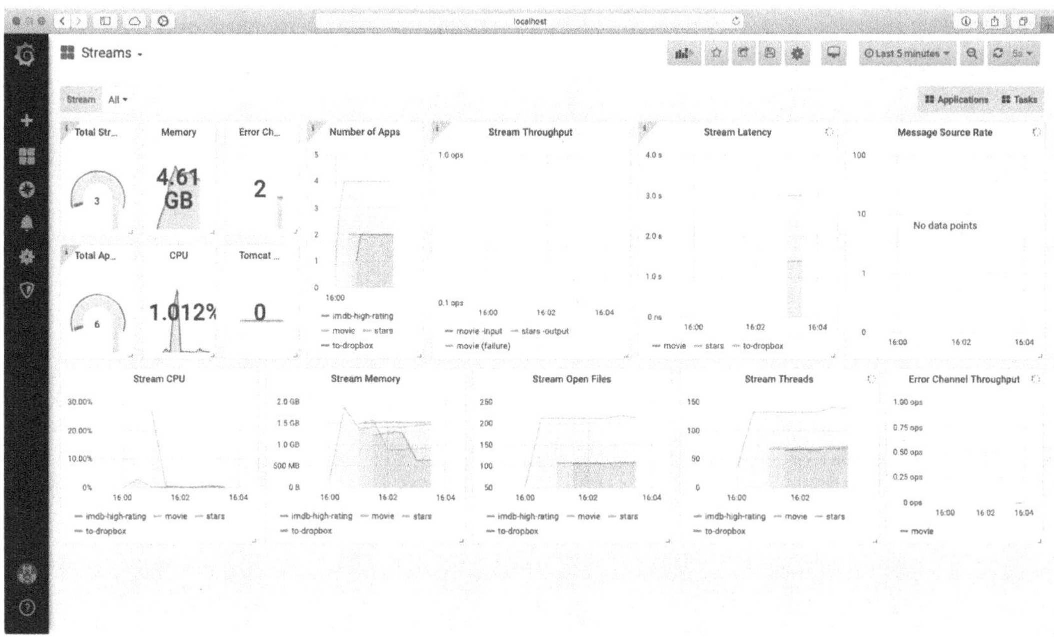

Figure 12-9. *Grafana dashboard*

Congratulations! Now you can visualize what is happening in your environment by exporting the metrics for your Stream and Task/Batch applications and react to what is happening in your streams.

■ **Note** All the source code, scripts, properties, and READMEs are in the `ch12/` folder.

Summary

In this chapter, I showed you how to monitor your Stream and Batch applications. You can add any new custom metric and expose it by integrating Spring Boot Micrometer. It offers the visibility required to react to any event in your stream, including business logic and tracing to locate bottlenecks. Remember that you can create more instances in the deployment properties, so you never lose processing control.

Index

A, B

C

F. Gutierrez, *Spring Cloud Data Flow*, https://doi.org/10.1007/978-1-4842-1239-4

T, U, V, W, X, Y, Z

Printed in the United States
By Bookmasters